Misogyny, Misandry, and Misanthropy

Edited and with a New Introduction by
R. Howard Bloch and Frances Ferguson

University of California Press

BERKELEY   LOS ANGELES   LONDON

University of California Press
Berkeley and Los Angeles, California

University of California Press, Ltd.
London, England

© 1989 by
The Regents of the University of California

Originally published as *Representations*, no. 20, Fall 1987

Library of Congress Cataloging-in-Publication Data

Misogyny, misandry, and misanthropy / edited and with a new
   introduction by R. Howard Bloch and Frances Ferguson.
     p. cm.
     "Originally published as Representations, no. 20, Fall 1987"—T.p.
  verso.
     Includes index.
     ISBN 0-520-06544-1 (alk. paper). — ISBN 0-520-06546-8 (pbk.)
     1. Misogyny in literature. 2. Misandry in literature.
  3. Misanthropy in literature. 4. Women in literature. 5. Sexism in
  literature. 6. Misogyny in art. 7. Misandry in art.
  8. Misanthropy in art. I. Bloch, R. Howard. II. Ferguson,
  Frances.
  PN56.M538M58   1989
  809′.93353—dc19   89-30553
                                              CIP

Printed in the United States of America
1   2   3   4   5   6   7   8   9

CONTENTS

INTRODUCTION

OUR CHOICE OF MISOGYNY (along with misandry and misanthropy) as the organizing topic for this collection, which originally appeared as a special issue of *Representations*, calls for some explanation. Certainly we did not imagine that the essays collected herein would discover misogyny. The past twenty-five years of feminist research and criticism have already provided ample evidence of the existence—and persistence—of misogyny and attempts to escape from it. Assuming, then, its existence, we were attracted to misogyny as a question that makes visible certain perhaps intractable antagonisms between texts and their readers, as well as between texts and the persons who become the objects of their representations. That is, misogyny seemed to us to emblematize the problem that representation poses when it creates oppositions between what we perceive and what we endorse. And in that sense, misogyny provides the occasion for a discussion of the limits of idealism, or of a conflict between authors and readers comparable to the conflict between misogynists and the women who are misrepresented by its pervasive, but often unrecognized, images.

Some recent feminist writing has imagined that this disjunction could be healed by a science fiction, a utopian vision that would realign our desires with our views about the world; but, while accepting the spirit of that vision, the essays in this volume largely concern themselves with the difficulties of enacting an easy fit between representation and what one might think of as a political will. More precisely, they explore the relation between gender, eroticism, and violence through close analysis of the never simple—in fact, always complicated—modes by which sexual and social difference are mediated by symbolic practice. Within a perspective that embraces so-called high and popular culture, the essays treat a wide variety of genres and forms, ranging from theological tracts and polemical satires, to lyric and epic poetry, to novels, novellas, popular pamphlets, magazines, aesthetic treatises, and advice manuals. On the visual arts, material extends from seventeenth-century painting, to a series of turn-of-the-century monotypes, to the contemporary slasher film. The intent is not, however, to arrive at anything like a general theory based on the accumulation of examples. For, despite the numerous and important points of convergence between essays covering such widely divergent types, each essay is rooted in a specific historical context. Their unity lies less in a common approach or method than in a historically rooted relation between particularity of context and the persistence of certain strikingly obsessive themes and rhetorical strategies in the staging of sexual difference through disparate cultural modes and moments across almost two millennia.

R. Howard Bloch begins from the premise that in the early centuries of Christianity something fundamental changed in the articulation of sexual difference, which was not to be found in exactly the same form in Platonic, Stoic, Jewish, Gnostic, or late Roman tradition. This enduring break has to do with a linking of the feminine with the aesthetic—the decorative, the ornamental, and the materially contingent—which, as one of the deep-seated mental structures of the West, also evident in the misogyny of Schopenhauer, Proudhon, and Nietzsche, for example, has served historically to define woman as being outside of history and thus to naturalize the notion of the female as secondary, less essential. Bloch carries this association to its logical conclusion by identifying the medieval reproach against woman as verbal abuse—garrulous, contradictory, argumentative; a liar, deceiver, and seducer with words—with the reproach against rhetoric characteristic of the philosophy of language of the Middle Ages. His focus on the relation between the notion of the feminine and literary voice poses questions relevant not only to the Middle Ages but to succeeding centuries, and thereby to this volume as a whole.

Thus Bloch asks: "Is misogyny a matter of the portrayal of women or a more specific discourse? If a question of how women are portrayed, does one such portrayal suffice? Is it still misogyny if men are also so depicted? Is it misandry? Is there a masculine equivalent of misogyny? Are we still dealing with misogyny if good women are presented alongside of negative examples? Or, as some maintain, does such balance constitute merely another misogynistic ruse? Is an obsession with women, in other words, misogynistic? Is the designation of misogyny as a topic for academic discourse ultimately a misogynistic gesture?" (p. 7). Bloch's essay also poses several significant questions having to do with intention and interpretation where misogyny is concerned. If misogyny is a topos, a virtual element, found potentially in almost any work, how ascribable is it to something on the order of individual authorial intention? Finally, given the intention of most misogynistic literature to dissuade its audience from associating with women, and given the association between rhetoric and the feminine, how is it possible for any writer to seek to persuade his or her intended audience not to be seduced without himself or herself performing the very acts of verbal deceit and seduction s/he denounces?

In her essay "Making Up Representation: The Risks of Femininity," Jacqueline Lichtenstein shows how the link between the ornamental and the feminine remains in force in the seventeenth century.[1] She situates the aesthetic debate between the colorists and the partisans of line within the classical quarrel over good versus bad rhetoric, which becomes translated, where gender is concerned, into the terms of the pro- and antifeminists of the neoclassical period. Thus decorative aesthetic principle, associated with ornate rhetoric (not necessarily with all rhetoric, as in Bloch's argument), is equated morally with prostitution, as color assumes the delinquent burdens of illicit pleasure. Cosmetic illusion, aesthetic adultery, is, in the century's own terms, the equivalent of libertinage—profligate feminine sexuality in particular—which, as in the discourse of the early church fathers, is to be condemned because of the instantaneous, ephemeral effects of all bodily sensation.

Joel Fineman, resuming in "Shakespeare's *Will*: The Temporality of Rape" the assumptions of his recent book on Shakespeare, locates in the Renaissance the transformation of a preexisting poetic tradition based on praise into a poetics of literary subjectivity with a specific characterological profile.[2] According to Fineman, Shakespeare's internally divided, postidealist, resolutely male subject experiences "his own phenomenal substantiality as a materialized heterogeneity" and thus becomes "subject of an unprecedentedly heterosexual, and therefore misogynist, desire for an object that is not admired" (29). By its very nature the Shakespearean subject is complicated, such complication being most powerfully expressed in rhetorical tropes involving hopelessly imbricated contradiction. It is, in fact, the indeterminacy of such endless signifying figures, what Fineman defines as the "rhetorical structure of the cross-coupler" (38) that constitutes in spoken—poetic—language a resistance that is understood to motivate desire in general and rape in particular. In this explanation of the formation of Shakespearean character, which is synonymous with the subject of the early modern period, the erotic and the poetic are indissolubly bound to the formation of literary subjectivity and to the psychologistic self in which is inscribed, following Fineman's argument, an unavoidable provocation to sexual violence.

Frances Ferguson's essay "Rape and the Rise of the Novel" links what in contemporary discussions of rape is sensed as the impossible logic of the crime to the questions of consent and intent as they first were articulated in eighteenth-century rape law. In a remarkable parallel to Fineman's "chiastic cross-coupling," Ferguson demonstrates the extent to which the notion of statutory rape is determined at the outset by the legal attempt to substitute invariable juridical formulae for manipulable terms governing psychological states, as the incoherence of rape law to this day becomes accountable to an inaugural opposition between the formal criteria governing proof and the possibility of determining the will of the victim. "For the statutory definitions establish the possibility—and indeed the inevitability—that consent and intention will be self-contradictory, or impossible, notions. They thus create the categories of consent that is not consent (for some hypothetically consenting female who has not reached the age of consent) and intention that is not intention (for some hypothetically intending and physically competent male who has not reached the age of legal discretion and competence). And these categories, in the very process of functioning as solutions to potential interpretative dilemmas, replicate exactly the kinds of problems that appear in any jury's deliberations concerning a charge of rape" (95–96).

If mental states reduced to self-contradictory constructs eliminate subjectivity from individual situations, the very permanence of contradiction serves to guarantee subjectivity itself; and it is here—at the intersection between eighteenth-century skepticism and prose fiction—that Ferguson situates the rise of the novel, which recapitulates and sustains the contradiction built into the law of rape. With special reference to *Clarissa*, Ferguson shows that Richardson establishes for the psychological novel "a pattern of psychological complexity that does not at all directly express mental states but rather relies on the contradiction built into the formal stipulation of them. Psychological complexity, that is, pits the stipulated mental state against one's actual mental state, so that one is able to resist without resisting, can have a mental state even in unconsciousness, and is unable to consent even if one wants to" (101). The plight of Clarissa is that of an insuperable volitional infancy which not only characterizes the dangerous sophism of rape law but embodies the difference that the novel inscribes between epistemology and psychology.

Gillian Brown's contribution, "The Empire of Agoraphobia," demonstrates how the passivity to which rape reduces Clarissa becomes normalized in the nineteenth century by the entrenched cultural assimilation of immobility, invalidism, and domesticity to the feminine. Using "Bartleby the Scrivener" as her prime example, but also drawing on such popular sources as *Godey's Lady's Book*, Brown explores the ways in which Melville's novella of agoraphobia and melodramatic hysteria sustains the opposition between self and the world, private and public space, that seems to work as a strategy of feminine self-containment. Conspiring to keep women at home and out of the marketplace, the "agoraphobic model of self-integrity" thus appears to guarantee the stability of a safe, feminine domestic sphere and to confirm the antifeminist ideal of home protection—housework and reproduction as rest cure. And yet, as Brown demonstrates, the ideal of the wall-hugging homebody, if carried to an extreme, can work to undermine the dynamism of the market; and the enabling effects of agoraphobia become inverted when the self, as in the case of Bartleby, becomes too stable. Bartleby's immobility, his refusal to eat or leave the walls of his Wall Street room, comes to constitute a means of "resistance to nineteenth-century consumerist domestic ideology" (145–46), his anorexia a repudiation of the marketplace altogether.

The model of literature as resistance carries over into Naomi Schor's "The Portrait of a Gentleman: Representing Men in (French) Women's Writing," which begins with questions about the strategies women writers enlist to represent men. Are they different, Schor asks, from those at work in men's writings about women? Do they cut across national boundaries and constitute a specificity of women's fiction? Why does it seem easier for men to represent women in fiction than for women to represent men? Why does misogyny seem to be more prevalent than misandry?

In answering these and other questions Schor focuses on analysis of three French novels by women and, in particular, on the recurrent novelistic scene—a virtual female topos found in Mme. de Lafayette's *Princesse de Clèves*, Mme. de Staël's *Corinne*, and George Sand's *Indiana*—in which a male protagonist observes a woman looking at a portrait that turns out to be either his own or that of another masculine figure. Here again, as in Gillian Brown's essay, the outcome is not always easily predictable. For instead of supporting as anticipated the "male subject's fascination with the evidence of phallic power," these scenes, as Schor demonstrates, work on the contrary to provoke in the observer consciousness of a process of supplementarity akin to that of fetishism. Rather than reinforce male egotism, they undermine the man's secure relationship to his own image. By revealing the link between male narcissism and fetishism these scenes subvert "the very foundations of the representational system elaborated by patriarchal society" (126). Having thus deconstructed male representation, Schor proposes as an alternative a "female iconoclasm," which "seals the end of the reign of the specular" because it no longer participates in the specularity of idealization. To the question of why there are "no images of men in women's writing" Schor responds, "because that writing is marked from the outset by a profound suspicion of the image and its grounding phallicism" (130).

Charles Bernheimer takes up the questions of fetishism and images by evoking the Mallarmean paradox, reported by Paul Valéry, that "a danseuse is not a woman who dances, because she is not a woman, and she does not dance" (158). "Degas's Brothels: Voyeurism and Ideology," in many ways the most psychoanalytic and most Marxian of these essays, comes to grips with the relation between male castration anxiety and misogyny as a principle of economic domination. Using Degas's little-known monotype brothel drawings, Bernheimer zeroes in on the creation of the feminine as an "aesthetic fiction" of the male voyeuristic gaze—which explains the presence, within the margins of these smeary, smutty drawings, of well-dressed potential clients whose eyes are fixed on the nude bodies immobilized and contained by the walls of the brothel, just as Gillian Brown's agoraphobic housewives are constrained by home. The ideological message seems on the surface to be one in which the prostitute is transformed—metamorphosed even by the very amorphous portrayal of the female body—into a pure object of consumption. And yet Bernheimer, again like Brown, sounds the paradox of commodification made so obvious that, by becoming conscious, it ceases to function. Degas, according to Bernheimer, replaces the substitutability of the prostitute with that of the client, thus reversing the anticipated relation of power. As in the example of Schor's viewings of the portrait being viewed, the monotypes reflect back the "discomforting impersonality of [the viewer's] ideological position," thereby subverting a capitalist misogynistic ideology (174). The specific effects of the monotypes are more difficult to interpret than they seemed at first glance. Like Schor's women writers who refuse the image, Degas comes to be seen finally as antimisogynistic because of the antirepresentational, modernistic breakdown of form that the monotypes imply.

Carol Clover pushes the commodification of the female to its limit in her analysis of the slasher film, which, she maintains, holds the key to contemporary sexual attitudes. In "Her Body, Himself: Gender in the Slasher Film," Clover posits a relation of horror to pornography as that of gender to sex, developing both an external taxonomy and an internal structural paradigm for such contemporary classics as *Psycho*, *The Texas Chain Saw Massacre* (I and II), *Halloween* (I and II), *Hell Night*, *Dressed to Kill*, *The Eyes of Laura Mars*, *Friday the Thirteenth*, *Nightmare on Elm Street*, and *Slumber Party Massacre*, not to mention the parodic *Buckets of Blood* and *Motel Hell*. The basic components of the horror film include the killers, males locked in childhood and filled with infantile rage; the Terrible Place, which is most often a house or a tunnel; weapons, which are generally pretechnological, as opposed even to guns; victims, whose lingering images are invariably female even where men are also killed; the Final Girl, or the woman who, having undergone the ordeal of witnessing death and mutilation, herself survives as the image of abject terror; shock, or the cultivation of intentionally outrageous violent special effects.

Given the slasher film's self-conscious formulae, which border on camp, what explains their attraction? What is the audience's stake in this "particular nightmare" of assault and counterassault? How can we rationalize, much less justify, the pleasure of viewing the violence of chase, mutilation, and death?

The answer to these and other questions does not lie in any simple equation of sex and violence. For, as Clover notes, rape is practically nonexistent in slasher films, sex and violence being not concomitant but alternative principles. Instead, Clover proposes that behind the fluidity of perspective of the slasher film, which in the beginning encourages identification with the killer and later shifts sympathies toward the Final Girl, lies a deeper delight in cross-gendering. The slasher is a gender bender; the killer being more often than not a male in "gender distress," the victim a female whose femininity is compromised by masculine interests and, in particular, by an "'active investigating gaze' normally reserved for males and hideously punished in females when they assume it themselves" (210). In the end the Final Girl is always rendered masculine, phallicized, as the final terrible struggle, despite the gendering of terror itself as female, remains wholly masculine: "It may be through the female body that the body of the audience is sensationalized, but the sensation is an entirely male affair" (213). The guilty pleasure of the slasher film has to do ultimately with the gender-identity game, the "play of pronoun function," the crossing of bounds that allow either sex to play— within the space of the movie theater—at being the other.

Although we set no agenda in soliciting the essays in this volume, the recurrence of the issue of visibility suggests the importance of the subject of seeing and being seen in today's discussions of gender. Indeed, the constellation of issues that have been located by Irigaray, Mulvey, and others around the male gaze emerge as pivotal for all the contributors. It is a notion particularly powerful for applying the aesthetic terms of spectatorship to questions more commonly seen in political terms. Thus, for Irigaray, the demand for meaning implicit in the male gaze entails a coercive desire to fix women, and the indeterminacy of woman's meaning constitutes a challenge to "representation's scoptophiliac objective." Although the aesthetic tradition that has descended to us from Kant emphasizes the primacy of an aesthetic experience in which the reader or viewer can claim validity for his or her perception despite its open contradiction of statements of authorial intention or historical possibility, such a stance obviously conflicts with any political discussion that emphasizes self-determination.

The strength of Irigaray's position is that it pits a desire for knowledge against indeterminacy in such a way as to reverse the lines of force: to be defined is to be powerless; to show the limits of definition can provide access to power. The strength of one competing version of American feminism—that of Catherine MacKinnon and Andrea Dworkin—is to reverse (almost precisely) Irigaray's line of argument: to be misdefined is to be powerless; to know the power of definition is to gain power. Thus, whereas Irigaray's feminism emphasizes feminine subjectivity, MacKinnon's and Dworkin's emphasizes the formal representation of subjectivity: the one expands the space between the perceivers (at the risk of sacrificing the notion of perceptibility); the other contracts it (to ensure legibility at the risk of sacrificing the notion of individual mental states).

These crucial feminist positions indicate some of the difficulties that representation poses for subjects that can, justifiably, ask for justice. For if the aesthetic solution to interpretative problems is to accord the reception its own authority (in a version of *così è, se vi pare*), a subject like misogyny can only arise from a palpable sense of the discrepancy between perspectives. Thus the status of the specular repeatedly is at issue in these essays. For R. Howard Bloch, in the opening essay, literature and misogyny alike arise from a specular relationship to rhetoric as well as to women, whereby both are viewed not as a condition of perceptibility but as an appendage—the merely decorative, the accidental, the contingent. The gaze, as the mechanism of seduction, establishes a pattern of conflict between perception and intellection. "For," as Bloch writes, "if a look engenders desire, desire, in turn, forecloses all future possibility of seeing" (15); sight becomes the instrument of the senses, of self-contamination by means of an external object of desire. And, in a crucial paradox—one of the many incoherences that characterize the discourse of misogyny—"there can be no such thing as a male gaze or desire" (15) because perception itself is in the Middle Ages so identified with woman that anyone perceiving a woman's beauty becomes feminized by the very act of gazing.

Like Bloch, Jacqueline Lichtenstein emphasizes the reactions of the gazer in tracing the link between misogyny and the decorative in seventeenth-century

France. Noting that the majority of writers of the *Grand Siècle* "indefatigably celebrated the acuteness and discrimination of 'feminine reason'"(77), Lichtenstein focuses on the seventeenth-century revival of a tradition that associates "a critique of women with a condemnation of makeup" and "the problematic of ornament" (77) with that of femininity. Indeed, she demonstrates that the force of this pejorative association was so strong as to underwrite an intense debate within painting itself, an art that by definition constitutes an appeal to the eyes. The conflict between the so-called colorists and anticolorists pits color against drawing, with the anticolorists claiming that color, frequently personified as a courtesan, was "as evanescent in its material nature as in its effects" (81). And whereas Bloch identifies the medieval aesthetic as one that repudiates the very desiring gaze that is conceived to be overcome by its object, Lichtenstein charts a triumphal progress for color and, by implication, for women in the aesthetics of French neoclassicism. In contrasting the Latin opposition between healthy and virile rhetoric and the eunuchlike eloquence of an emasculated language (79) with seventeenth-century France's emblematic contrasts between feminine figures, she provides a concluding and conclusive image for her argument that Asiaticism, in the form of a defense of the pleasure of submitting to the speechlessness induced by makeup and color, becomes a genuine alternative to the sterner pleasures of Atticism in neoclassical aesthetics.

Charles Bernheimer takes a somewhat different tack in emphasizing not only the impact of the male gaze on the gazer but also on the woman being viewed. He identifies a tradition in Degas criticism that proceeds from Huysmans and his celebration of what he took to be the artist's identification of his own point of view with "an attentive cruelty, a patient hatred" (161). It is, Bernheimer argues, a critical perspective that casts the artist as sadistic male gazer and his subjects as masochistic collaborators that makes misogyny both genderless and boundless, as "woman in Huysmans's interpretation of Degas's images is not simply the object of male disdain; she has internalized that disdain to the point that she is the degraded object of her own virulent execration" (162–63). And by that internalization, she seems to provide "evidence of woman's enlightened awareness of her irredeemably debased sexuality" (163). The brothel monotypes that Bernheimer focuses on might similarly appear to "address the male viewer's social privilege, to construe him as a voyeur, and to cater to his misogyny"(175); but they might also, he suggests, de-privilege that perspective in which the viewer "recognizes himself as desiring psychological subject in the mirror of his capitalist activity" (178). Instead of leaving these two alternatives in infinite oscillation, however, Bernheimer proceeds to suggest that the very reification of the prostitute's body aligns her with the mutilated representational forms—"the thumb prints, smudges, blots, and other traces" of Degas's "gestural life"—that emblematize Degas's attack on the norms of representational practice.

Bernheimer's Degas thus presents the possibility of "granting Degas's brothel inmates strength by insisting on the aesthetic value of their objectification" (180). And in that sense he perhaps instantiates a parallel to the kind of aesthetic development that Naomi Schor recognizes in her account of "female iconoclasm," a "peculiarly feminine form of antirepresentationalism" (128). Schor explores one particularly resonant, gendered asymmetry: while the pictorial and novelistic traditions have assumed male authority to "take" women's portraits with some insight, the tradition of commentary has suggested that women novelists have difficulty reversing this process and depicting male character. By analyzing a recurrent scene, one that "stages the violation by the male gaze of the female protagonist's private space and the male protagonist's discovery therein of a portrait, his own and/or that of another masculine figure" (114), Schor of course raises the possibility of misandry as "a sort of women writers' revenge" (115) or a turning of the tables. And, in consonance with a modernist claim that "representation stands for the interests of power," Schor's analysis suggests an eluding of visibility that thereby precludes as well the inevitably patriarchal transfer of power between succeeding generations of men as part of the process of socializing fetishism, a process initiated, according to the Freudian fable, at the moment in every little boy's life when he sees the genitals of the opposite sex. Schor thus imagines a "female iconoclasm" whose disruptive function is equivalent to that which Bernheimer posits for the smudged and truncated images constituting Degas's assault not on the prostitutes whom he represents but on the traditions of representation itself. Indeed, in Schor's account, the lack of images of men in French women's writing is no lack at all, but rather a gendered inauguration of the problematized images associated with modernism. French women's writing thus contains a critique of male representation that is much less an attack on men than an aesthetic rendering of representation as being "from its very inception in crisis" (130).

If Schor and Bernheimer would locate a representational crisis in the consciousness of a visual fetishism that can only translate its narcissism into the illusion of possession, Joel Fineman locates a representational crisis in Shakespeare's *The Rape of Lucrece* in the poem's continual suggestion that "the very act of speaking, true or false, . . . spells an end to the ideality of vision" (59). In Fineman's account, a visionary aesthetics of transparent imitation, "of presentational representation" (57), enlists the "skillful painting" to "function as powerful eyewitness of Lucrece's plight" (56). And this visionary pictorial aesthetic, though it implies "an equally perennial and equally visionary semiotics, one whereby a signifier, conceived as something visually iconic, is so fixedly and unequivocally related to its signified that by itself it can present its meaning or its referent to the 'eye of mind'" (57), collides, according to Fineman, with a language in which characters discover "misogynist erotics" in the form of an "internal sense of present broken self and retrospective temporality" and "turn into textured subjects when they learn firsthand how 'by our ears our hearts oft tainted be'" (66).

Language, with its appeal to the ear, revolves around the contradiction that painting (in its ideal form, of course) would skirt; in its ostentatious cross-coupling of truth with falsehood and desire with its frustration, Shakespeare's poem presents a structure that identifies misogyny less as an attack on women than as a condition of subjectivity under the representation of language.

Frances Ferguson, in her account of *Clarissa* and the psychological novel, likewise explores the contradictions inherent in representation, including the legal tradition that would identify and punish crime, specifically the crime of rape. Although rape law itself represents an attempt to make the crime visible, the visibility and legibility of the law depends on its establishing categories and stipulating their meanings. Yet this gesture of stipulation, of resorting to categories, recreates its own version of a conflict between individual intention and consent and the representation of those mental states in categorical terms. The achievement of *Clarissa* and of the psychological novel in general is to identify subjectivity neither as the visibility of individual mental states nor as their dissolution in larger and more visible categorical terms but rather as the perceptible conflict between the two. Even Clarissa's physical appearance is marked by this conflict, as Ferguson reads her self-wasting as her enactment of the stipulated state of non-consent.

In her reading of "Bartleby the Scrivener" and women's domestic handbooks of nineteenth-century America, Gillian Brown argues that Bartleby, in embodying agoraphobia, hysteria, and other "female" nervous disorders, accepts invalidism in protest against the demand that he—like the women who manifested similar symptoms—become visible in the world of the marketplace. Agoraphobia, according to Brown, is not so much fear of open spaces as fear of being seen when that process seems to imply an inevitable misunderstanding, on the model of an exchange that is always taken to be unequal. The agoraphobic, the wall-hugging homebody, seeks to become self-contained, most importantly by being visible only to herself/himself and by needing so little as to be sustained only by herself/himself. However, in attempting to be visible only to himself, the agoraphobic Bartleby becomes invisible even to himself, since the outcome of his protest against the marketplace is his own death—a death that can never be a complete enough retraction of his existence, his availability to the world of other people.

Finally, in contrast to Brown's account of feminized repudiation of the very notion of being the object of others' sight, Carol Clover argues that the slasher film may begin in a sadistic male gaze but becomes feminist in spite of itself. Addressing the subject of the audience and its relation to the physical violation, Clover complicates the model of the oppressive male gaze operating on the passive female victim. She questions the traditional equation of camera point of view with identification (in part because preserving that equation sometimes establishes impossible identities, as with the "birds-eye perspective" of Hitchcock's camera in *The Birds*), arguing that the slasher film provides the model for a realigned specularity: the cross-dressed perspective of many of the slasher's protagonists finds a counterpart in the person of the Final Girl, the masculinized female survivor who dares to gaze back at her masculine attackers.

From Bloch's account of how the medieval rhetorical tradition finds gender where there is none to Clover's discussion of how modern popular images appropriate sex in terms of permeable gender categories, these essays explore not only the ways in which gender is represented but also the changes to which representations subject questions of sexual difference.

Notes

1. In her recent book, *Reading in Detail: Aesthetics and the Feminine* (New York, 1987), Naomi Schor demonstrates the persistence of this link in nineteenth- and twentieth-century aesthetic theory and practice.
2. *Shakespeare's Perjured Eye: The Invention of Poetic Subjectivity in the Sonnets* (Berkeley, 1986).

R. HOWARD BLOCH

Medieval Misogyny

Woman as Riot

IF THE ABOVE TITLE SEEMS redundant, it is because the topic of
misogyny, like the mace or chastity belt, participates in a vestigial horror practically synonymous with the term *medieval*, and because one of the assumptions
governing our perception of the Middle Ages is the viral presence of antifeminism. The ritual denunciation of women constitutes something on the order of
a cultural constant, reaching back to the Old Testament as well as to Ancient
Greece and extending through the fifteenth century. Found in Roman tradition,
it dominates ecclesiastical writing, letters, sermons, theological tracts, discussions
and compilations of canon law; scientific works, as part and parcel of biological,
gynecological, and medical knowledge; and philosophy.[1] The discourse of misogyny runs like a rich vein throughout the breadth of medieval literature. Like
allegory itself, to which (for reasons we do not have time to explore) it is peculiarly
attracted, antifeminism is both a genre and a topos, or, as Paul Zumthor might
suggest, a "register"—a discourse visible across a broad spectrum of poetic types.[2]
Excellent examples are to be found in Latin satires like John of Salisbury's *Poli-
craticus*, Walter Map's *De nugis curialium* (especially the Letter of Valerius to
Rufinum), Andreas Capellanus's *Art of Courtly Love* (book 3), as well as in the *.XV.
Joies de mariage* and what is perhaps the most virulent antimatrimonial satire in
the vernacular tongue, Jehan Le Fèvre's translation of the *Lamentations de Matheolus*. Misogyny is virtually synonymous with the works grouped under the rubric
of "les genres du réalisme bourgeois": the comic tale or fabliaux (including
Middle English and Italian versions); the animal fable (*Roman de Renart*); the
comic theater or farce; but also certain mixed or unclassifiable forms like the
chantefable *Aucassin et Nicolette* or Adam de la Halle's *Jeu de la feuillée*; and, of
course, Jean de Meun's portion of the *Roman de la rose*.

So persistent is the discourse of misogyny—from the earliest church fathers
to Chaucer—that the uniformity of its terms furnishes an important link between
the Middle Ages and the present and renders the topic compelling because such
terms still govern (consciously or not) the ways in which the question of woman
is conceived by women as well as by men. Misogyny is not so much a historical
subject as one whose very lack of history is so bound in its effects that any attempt
merely to trace the history of woman-hating is hopelessly doomed, despite all
moral imperative, to naturalize that which it would denounce (more on this later).
This is not to imply that there have been no changes in the ways misogyny has

through time been received, understood, assimilated by particular cultures, implemented, or pressed ideologically in the service of repressive social practice. Rather, it suggests that the very tenacity of the topoi of antifeminism is significant in and of itself and, in fact, provides one of the most powerful ways of thinking the phenomenon, since the extreme complexity of defining just what misogyny is remains indissociable from its seeming ubiquity or from the essentializing definitions of woman apparent in the writings of just about anyone who has touched the subject from Tertullian to Nietzsche.

The endurance of many of the earliest formulations of the question of woman means that the question of where to begin to understand the Western current of woman-hating must first respond to the question of why it is possible to begin just about anywhere—which I propose to do with a passage, selected almost at random, from among the many misogynistic tirades of Jean de Meun's *Roman de la rose*:

> Ha! se Theofrastes creüsse,
> Ja fame espousee n'eüsse.
> Il ne tient pas homme por sage
> Qui fame prent par mariage,
> Soit lede ou bele ou povre ou riche,
> Car il dit, et por voir affiche,
> En son noble livre *Aureole*,
> Qui est bonz a lire en escole,
> Qu'il y a vie trop grevainne,
> Plene de torment et de painne.

> [Ha! If I had only believed Theophrastus, I would never have taken a wife. He holds no man to be wise who takes a woman in marriage, whether ugly or beautiful, poor or rich. For he says, and you can take it for truth, in his noble book *Aureole*, which is good to read in school, that there is there a life too full of torment and strife.][3]

Though the Theofrastes referred to (identified alternately with the author of the *Characters* and with a pupil of Aristotle) and his "livre *Aureole*" are otherwise unknown, both are cited by almost every misogynist writer of the Middle Ages. Together they constitute an absent *locus classicus* of misogyny "read," as Jean maintains, "in schools." Further, the passage at hand is less a true example of misogyny, a denunciation of the essential evil nature of woman, than a subgeneric topos known as the *molestiae nuptiarum* or antimarriage literature: "Il ne tient pas homme por sage / Qui fame prent par mariage."

Of what, it may be asked, do the pains of marriage consist?:

> Qu'il y a vie trop grevainne,
> Plene de torment et de painne,
> Et de contenz et de riotes
> Par les orguelz des femes sotes,

> Et de dangiers et de reprouches
> Que font et dient par lor bouches,
> Et de requestes et de plaintes
> Que truevent par ochoisons maintes.
> Si ra grant pene en eus garder
> Par lor fos voloirs retarder.

[That there is there a life too full of torment and strife and arguments and riotousness because of the pride of foolish women—and dangers and reproaches which they do and say with their mouths, and requests and complaints which they invent on many occasions. It takes a great effort to keep them and to hold back their foolish wills; lines 8569–78.]

Women are contentious, prideful, demanding, complaining, and foolish; they are uncontrollable, unstable, and insatiable: "Si ra grant pene en eus garder / Por lor fos voloirs retarder." To push a little further, one cannot help but notice the extent to which the pains of marriage involve verbal transgression, that the reproach against women is a form of reproach against language itself—"that which is said by the mouth"—to be more precise, *contenz* (contention, garrulousness, bickering, and quarrels), *reprouches* (criticism, reproach), *requestes* (demands), *orguelz* (pride). Woman is depicted as a constant source of anxiety, of dissatisfaction, but of an anxiety expressed—or, as the text suggests, "composed"—within language itself: "Que *truevent* par ochoisons maintes." I say this because the reproach against women, addressed to "anyone who marries," is posited as universal and a priori, but also because there is no position of innocence possible. Woman is conceived as a perpetually overdetermined signifier with respect to which man is always at risk. To wit: if she is poor, one must nourish, clothe, and shoe her: "Et qui vuet povre fame prendre, / A norrir la convient entendre / Et a vestir et a chaucier" (lines 8579–81), but if she is rich, she is uncontrollable:

> Et se tant se cuide essaucier
> Qu'il la prengne riche forment,
> A soffrir la ra grant torment,
> Tant la trueve orguilleuse et fiere
> Outrecuidie et bobanciere.

[And if one thinks he can escape by taking a rich one, he will suffer great torment again—so arrogant and prideful will he find her, so outrageous and full of presumption; lines 8582–86.]

If a woman is beautiful, all desire her (lines 8587–96), and she will in the end be unfaithful; yet if she is ugly, she will need all the more to please and, again, will eventually betray: "Maintes neïs par eus se baillent, / Quant li requerreor defaillent" (Many will give themselves willingly when suitors lack; lines 8658–59). If she is reasonable, she is subject to seduction: "Penelope neïz prendroit / Qui bien au prendre entenderoit; / Si n'ot il meillor fame en Grece" (One could take Penelope herself, and there was no better woman in Greece; lines 8605–7); yet if she is irrational, she becomes the victim, as in the example of Lucretia, of madness and suicide (lines 8607–10). Nor is such a view restricted to the Romance vernacular. John of Salisbury is just as precise: "A beautiful woman is quick to inspire love; an ugly one's passions are easily stirred. What many love is hard to protect; what no one desires to have is a humility to possess."[4] Chaucer echoes virtually the same motif in the Wife of Bath's reproach of all such reproaches: "Thou seist to me it is a greet meschief / To wedde a povre womman, for costage; / And if that she be rich, of heigh parage / Thanne seistow that it is a tormentrie / To soffre hire pride and hire malencolie."[5] Woman by definition finds herself in a position of constant determination, movement. She is, as Jean contends, "contenz et riotes," and, as Jehan Le Fèvre adds, of "tençon rioteuse."[6]

Woman as riot is a topos in medieval literature and has a special sense in Old French. The word *riote* itself, meaning "chaos" or "upset," also refers to a kind of poetic discourse belonging to the rich tradition of nonsense poetry—the *fatras*, *fatrasie*, *dervie*, *sotie*, and *farce* as well as to the more specific type known as the *riote del monde*, of which one example is the prose *Dit de l'herberie* and another the fabliau entitled "La Rencontre du roi d'Angleterre et du jongleur d'Ely." After a series of nonsensical parries capped by the poet's reminder that "one often hears a fool speak sanely, and the wise man is the one who speaks wisely,"[7] the crafty jongleur—in anticipation of the fool of Renaissance drama—seeks to teach the king a lesson about language in general:

> Et tot vus mostroi par ensample
> Qu'est si large et si aunple
> Et si pleyn de resoun,
> Que um ne dira si bien noun.
> Si vus estez simple et sage houm,
> Vus estes tenuz un feloun. . . .
> Et si vus les femmes amez,
> Et ou eux sovent parlez
> Et lowés ou honorez . . .
> Donques dirra ascun pautener:
> "Veiez cesti mavois holer,
> Come il siet son mestier
> De son affere bien mostrer."
> Si vus ne les volez regarder
> Ne volenters ou eux parler,
> Si averount mensounge trové
> Que vus estes descoillé!

[And I will show you by examples that are so general and compelling and so full of reason that one cannot fail to agree. If you are a simple and wise man, you are taken for a rogue . . . . If you like women and speak often with them, frequent them, and praise and honor them . . .

someone will say: "Look at that evil pimp who knows his work and shows it." If you do not look at them or willingly talk with them, they will find the lie to prove that you are castrated! *Recueil*, 2:249–65.]

The example with which we began, Jean de Meun's vision of women as overdetermined, is complicated by the fabliau's positing of the problem of overdetermination in terms of vision itself. There is, the anonymous poet asserts, no possibility of an objective regard upon the opposite sex and, therefore, no innocent place of speech. The mere fact of speaking to women makes one a pimp; a refusal to speak or even to look is the sign of a castrato.

This changes somewhat our paradigm, since the inadequacy of women to Being, expressed as an ever-present overdetermination, becomes, in the passage cited, indissociable from the inadequacy of words, or, as the anonymous author of *La Ruihote del monde* suggests, of speech:

> S'il se taist, il ne set parler;
> S'il parole, vés quel anpallier,
> Il ne cese onques de plaidier . . . .
> S'il cante bien c'est un jongleres;
> S'il dist biaus dis, c'est uns trouveres.

[If a man is quiet, he is accused of not knowing how to speak; if he speaks, of being a loudmouth who never shuts up. . . . If he sings well, he is taken for a jongleur; and if he uses nice phrases, for a trouvère.][8]

The riotousness of woman is linked to that of speech and indeed seems to be a condition of poetry itself. And if the reproach against woman is that she is a bundle of verbal abuses (*contenz, riotes, reprouches, requestes, plaintes*), such annoyances make her at least the fellow traveler of the trouvère. Because of the inadequacies of language that she embodies, she is in some fundamental sense always already a deceiver, trickster, jongleur. Here the king's attempt to buy the poet's horse and the image of the horse sale are central:

> Vendras tu ton roncyn à moy?
> —Sire, plus volenters que ne le dorroy.
> —Pur combien le vendras tu?
> —Pur taunt com il serra vendu.
> —Et pur combien le vendras?
> —Pur taunt come tu me dorras.
> —Et pur combien le averoi?
> —Pur taunt comme je recevroy.

[Will you sell me your horse? —Yes, more willingly than I would give it. —For how much will you sell it? —For as much as it will be sold. —And for how much will you sell it? —For as much as you will give me. —And for how much will I have it? —For as much as I shall receive; *Recueil*, 2.244–51.]

Woman, as deceiver, is like a horse that one cannot inspect before the sale; and, like language, she is, as Jean de Meun implies, pure cover who hides "that she might not displease before being wed."[9] Chaucer concurs: "Thou seist that oxen, asses, hors, and houndes, / They been assayed at diverse stoundes . . . . But folk of wyves maken noon assay, / Til they be wedded" ("Wife of Bath's Prologue," lines 285–91). Nor, as Innocent III contends, is it possible to separate the motif of horse trading from that of overdetermination: "There are three things," Innocent writes, "which keep a man from staying home: smoke, a leaky roof, and a shrewish wife. . . . If she be beautiful, men readily go after her; if she be ugly, she as readily after them. It is hard to keep what many want, and annoying to have what no one cares about. . . . When you buy a horse, an ox, a dog, clothes and a bed, even a cup and a pitcher, you get the chance to look them over. But no one displays a bride, lest she displease before the marriage."[10]

Reading Misogyny

If the above quotations seem repetitious to the point of monotony, it is because misogyny as a discourse is always to some extent avowedly derivative; it is a citational mode whose rhetorical thrust is to displace its own source away from anything that might be construed as personal or confessional and toward the sacred authorities whose own source, as often as not, is the absent (and possibly nonexistent) Theophrastus with which we began. The misogynist speaks of the other in terms that bespeak otherness, and this through the voice of the other. This defining tautology emphasizes the elusiveness of misogyny as well as the pertinence of the question of reading. To be more precise, I think that it can be shown that where antifeminism is concerned the question of reception is crucial, and work like the *Roman de la rose*, for example, may be less important for what it might actually contain than for what surrounds it. Indeed, the history of the reading of Jean's text not only offers a key to our understanding of misogyny at the end of the Middle Ages; it constitutes the most meaningful sense in which woman-hating can be historicized. The history of misogyny, as a citational mode, resides primarily in the radical difference in what has been said over time about such texts, or in the problem of interpretation. Hence the negotiation of the parameters for discussion of the misogynistic work is a map of a certain kind of sexually charged misreading that serves at any given cultural moment to define the permissible limits of gender relations.

It is, first of all, around the question of woman that questions of language and of literature are debated passionately between the thirteenth and fifteenth centuries. The so-called "Querelle de la rose" was not only France's first literary debate but one that turned specifically around the enmeshed issues of woman and interpretation which strike to the core of the issue at hand. Christine de

Pisan, for instance, poses the delicate questions of authorial intention, voice, and the relation of poetic representation to social base in a sarcastic response to Jehan Johannez a propos of the *Rose*:

Et la laidure qui la est recordee des femmes, dient pluseurs en lui excusant que c'est le Jaloux qui parle, et voirement fait ains comme Dieu parla par la bouche Jeremie. Mais sans faille, quelxque addicions mençongeuses qu'il ait adjoustees, ne peuvent—Dieu mercy!—en rien amenrir ne rendre empirees les conditions des femmes.

[And many say in excusing the ugly things that are said there of women that it is the Jealous Husband who talks, as if truly God were speaking through the mouth of Jeremiah. But without a doubt, whatever untruthful things he has added to the pile cannot—thank God!—either improve or render worse the condition of women.][11]

Or, as in the letter of Jean de Montreuil to Gontier Col, the questions of women and of reading are so thoroughly intertwined as to displace the phenomenon of misogyny away from any definable, stable, textual reality toward the reading subject:

Nonetheless our censors curse, hate, scorn, and attack him in a shameful way, having read him, studied, and understood him badly: this is what is intolerable! What arrogance! What rashness! What audacity! These people who admit themselves to only having read super-ficially, by bits and with no concern for context: here is how they rush in, like drunks arguing at the dinner table, to blame, reproach, and condemn arbitrarily and at their whim such an important work, conceived and edited in so many nights and days, at the price of so much effort and with such constant application, as if such an important text weighed no more in the balance than the song of a jongleur, the work of one day.[12]

Jean de Montreuil's concern is not only merely a rhetorical strategy; it poses what remains a key issue with respect to the study of misogyny: that is, how to recognize it, how to read it—which is not fundamentally different from the problem of how to read medieval literature or, for that matter, any literary text.

Is misogyny a matter of the portrayal of women or a more specific discourse? If a question of how women are portrayed, does one such portrayal suffice? Is it still misogyny if men are also so depicted? Is it misandry? Is there a masculine equivalent of misogyny? Are we still dealing with misogyny if good women are presented alongside of negative examples? Or, as some maintain, does such a balance constitute merely another misogynistic ruse? Is an obsession with women, in other words, misogynistic? Is the designation of misogyny as a topic for aca-demic discourse ultimately a misogynistic gesture?

In attempting to identify misogyny one is to some degree always dealing with a problem of voice, the questions of who speaks and of localizing such speech. If misogyny is a topos, a virtual element, found potentially in almost any work (including those that are overwhelmingly profeminine like *Aucassin et Nicolette*), how ascribable is it to something on the order of individual authorial intention? What does it mean to say that someone like Jean de Meun, about whom relatively little of a biographical nature is known, is a misogynist? Does it matter who speaks? How are we to read obvious delegations of voice as in the example cited by Christine? How are we to disentangle the assumed "truth of misogyny" from a literary topos that as often as not performs exactly what it ascribes to, projects upon, women—that is, seeks to deceive? Any answer to this question is, as we shall see, even further complicated by the association of women with writing and poetics.

Is misogyny an exclusively male phenomenon or is it part of a larger cultural discourse in which women also participate?[13] This in turn raises the question of whether or not there is an essential distinction between male and female writing. Is there, for instance, a difference in kind between the *Lais* of Marie de France (about whom little is known except that she was a woman) and the anonymous Breton *lais* written presumably by men, or between the writing of Marie and that of Chrétien de Troyes?

Is misogyny restricted to the domain of literature? What is its status in the other arts? Is the question of misogyny the same as that of woman? If so, we are forced to incorporate conflicting images of woman—Eve and Mary, woman as seducer and redeemer—within the essentially negative field of antifeminism and to deal with a paradox of history: that the periods of greatest misogynistic activity can also be periods of intense woman worship, as in the example of twelfth- and thirteenth-century mariolatry.[14] Then too, the mysticism current in the High Middle Ages would be unimaginable without such figures as Angela of Foligno, Bridget of Sweden, Catherine of Sienna, Saint Gertrude, Hildegard of Bingen, Juliana of Norwich, who were the equivalents of female prophets. It has been argued that the adoration of women, whether the Holy Virgin, the courtly lady, or the prophetess, is but another form of misogynistic investment. This returns us to the subject of whether or not idolatry is merely another form of misogyny, taking us in turn into complex issues of reading that are not fundamentally different from the interpretation of any text. What is different, and here the present essay departs from all previous discussion, is, as we shall see, the extent to which the practices of medieval hermeneutics and the discourse of misogyny are bound up in each other.

Any study of misogyny must, it seems to me, begin from two fundamental assumptions. The first is a recognition of the very real disenfranchisement of women in the Middle Ages. Such a premise is based upon careful work over the last fifteen years within the realm of social history. Few would dispute, for example, that there were from the fourth through the fourteenth centuries essential differences in men's and women's rights to possess, inherit, and alienate property; in their duties to pay homage and taxes; in their qualification for exemptions. To these are added differences in men's and women's civil and legal rights: in the rights to bear witness, collect evidence, represent oneself (or others) in judicial causes; to serve as judges or lawyers, as oath helpers; to bring suit or to stand for election. Legal penalties for the same crime often differed substantially, as, for instance, in the punishments for adultery, for bearing children out of wedlock, for beating one's spouse. Even the mode of execution was in certain cases not the same for women as for men. Social historians in conjunction with demographers have raised radically the question of whether sons were treated better than daughters to the extent of creating a higher infant mortality rate among females. Moreover, the questions remain of whether those who survived participated equally in urban privileges such as membership in guilds and opportunity of employment; whether, when employed, wages were equivalent; whether women were allowed a role in affairs of state and especially in those of the Church, which, its ideological commitment to the equality of all Christians notwithstanding, still excluded women from participation in certain offices like preaching or setting Church policy or doctrine.

All of these, and the list of material recrimination is by no means complete, are real and unavoidable issues. But they are not the same as misogyny, and one has to be careful not to move too easily between the domain of institutions and the discourse of antifeminism. For the risk, in neglecting the complicated series of intervening mediations, is entrapment in the movement of the very phenomenon one seeks to expose. The unqualified and unreflective equation of the two is tantamount to a ritual recitation of tort—yet another speaking or citation of the traditional topoi—that serves less to redress historical injustice than to naturalize it in terms of an ineluctable rule of relation between the sexes.[15]

Scandalous Excess

And the Lord God formed man of the slime of the earth, and breathed into his face the breath of life; and man became a living soul. . . .

And the Lord God said: It is not good for man to be alone; let us make him a help like unto himself.

And the Lord God having formed out of the ground all the beasts of the earth, and all the fowls of the air, brought them to Adam to see what he would call them: for whatsoever Adam called a living creature the same is its name.

And Adam called all the beasts by their names, and all the fowls of the air, and all the cattle of the field: but for Adam there was not found a helper like himself.

Then the Lord God cast a deep sleep upon Adam: and when he was fast asleep, he took one of his ribs, and filled up flesh for it.

And the Lord God built the rib which he took from Adam into a woman: and brought her to Adam.

And Adam said: "This now is bone of my bones and flesh of my flesh; she shall be called woman, because she was taken out of man."

—Gen. 2.7–23

What often passes unnoticed in the Genesis story is the degree to which the creation of woman is linked to a founding, or original, linguistic act. Adam is said to be the first to speak, the namer of things; woman—or the necessity of woman, her cause—seems to emanate, in turn, from the imposition of names.[16] The designation of things, or a primal instance of man's exertion of power over them, and the creation of woman are coterminous. Further, in this account of the *ad seriatim* creation of the genders, woman is by definition a derivation of man, who, as the direct creation of God, remains both chronologically antecedent and ontologically prior. This at least is how early commentators on Genesis—Augustine, Jerome, Philo Judaeus—understood things. "It is not good that *any* man should be alone," writes Philo. "For there are *two* races of men, the one made after the (Divine) Image, and the one moulded out of the earth. . . . With the second man a helper is associated. To begin with, the helper is a created one, for it says 'Let us make a helper for him'; and in the next place, is subsequent to him who is to be helped, for He had formed the mind before and is about to form its helper."[17] Thus, woman, created from man, is conceived from the beginning to be secondary, a supplement. Here the act of naming takes on added significance. For the imposition of names and the creation of woman are not only simultaneous but analogous gestures thoroughly implicated in each other. Just as words are the supplements of things, which are supposedly brought nameless to Adam, so woman is the supplement to, the "helper" of, man. She comes into being metonymically as a part of a body more sufficient to itself because created directly by God and to whose wholeness she, as part (and this from the beginning), can only aspire.

Adam's priority implies a whole set of relations that strike to the heart not only of medieval sign theory but to certain questions of ontology that make apparent that the Fall, commonly conceived to be the origin and cause of medieval misogyny, is merely a fulfillment or logical conclusion of that which is implicit to the creation of Eve. Woman, as secondary, derivative, supervenient, and supplemental, assumes all that is inferior, debased, scandalous, and perverse.

Adam, first of all, has what medieval philosophers called substance. His nature is essential; he possesses Being, Existence. "All good is from God," Augustine affirms, "hence there is no natural existence which is not from God."[18] Eve, as the byproduct of a part of the essential, partakes from the outset of the accidental, associated with a multiplicity of modes of degradation implicit to her coming into being as becoming.

If Adam exists fully and Eve only partially, it is because he participates in what is conceived to be an original unity of being while she is the offshoot of division and difference. And unity, another word for Being, is the goal of philosophy because it is also synonymous with truth. "Philosophy as a discipline," writes Augustine in the *De ordine*, "itself already contains this order of knowledge, and it need not discover more than the nature of one, but in a much more profound and divine sense."[19] The oneness that Adam once enjoyed, the uniqueness of singularity, is indistinguishable from the oneness that is the founding principle, the guarantor, of grammar, geometry, philosophy; and, implicitly, of theology, since God is defined as the nature of one, that which is universal and eternal. "Christ," writes Tertullian, "is everything which is once for all."[20]

This is another way of saying that Adam possesses form, is the equivalent of an Idea; for that which has unity and existence also has form. "All existing things would cease to be if form were taken from them, the unchangeable form by which all unstable things exist and fulfill their functions," asserts Augustine in a formula that appears almost everywhere in the discourse of misogyny.[21] That is, man is form or mind, and woman, degraded image of his second nature, is relegated to the realm of matter. Put in terms more appropriate to the Patristic tradition, man is spirit or soul formed directly by God, partaking of his divinity, while woman partakes of the body in which inheres, again, the principle of division.

Herein lies one possibility of reading misogyny: if man enjoys existence (substance), being, unity, form, and soul, woman is associated with accident, becoming (temporality), difference, body, and matter—and with all they imply by way of a secondariness that summons the more specific recriminations which constitute the discourse of misogyny.

Woman's supervenient nature is, above all, indistinguishable from that of all signs in relation to the signified and of representation. As Philo Judaeus maintains, her coming into being is synonymous not only with the naming of things but with a loss—within language—of the literal:

"And God brought a trance upon Adam, and he fell asleep; and He took one of his sides" and what follows (Gen. 2.21). These words in their literal sense are of the nature of a myth. For how could anyone admit that a woman, or a human being at all, came into existence out of a man's side?[22]

Since the creation of woman is synonymous with the creation of metaphor, the relation between Adam and Eve is the relation of the proper to the figural, which implies always derivation, deflection, denaturing, a tropological turning away. The perversity of Eve is that of the lateral: as the outgrowth of Adam's flank, his *latus*, she retains the status of *translatio*, of translation, transfer, metaphor, trope. She is side-issue.

This link between the derivative nature of the female and that of figural representation itself explains why the great misogynistic writers of the first centuries of Christianity—Paul, Tertullian, John Chrysostom, Philo, Jerome—were so obsessed by the relation of women to decoration, why they themselves were so fascinated by veils, jewels, makeup, hair style and color—in short, by anything having to do with the cosmetic. Such an obsession is evident even in the titles of the essays of, say, Tertullian: "On the Veiling of Virgins," "On the Pallium," "On the Apparel of Women." For the third-century apologist, woman is a creature who above all else and by nature covets ornamentation:

You are the devil's gateway: *you* are the unsealer of that (forbidden) tree: *you* are the first deserter of the divine law: *you* are she who persuaded him whom the devil was not valiant enough to attack. *You* destroyed so easily God's image man. On account of *your* desert—that is, death—even the Son of God had to die. And do you think about adorning yourself over and above your tunic of skins? Come, now; if from the beginning of the world the Milesians sheared sheep, and the Serians spun trees, and the Tyrians dyed, and the Phrygians embroidered with the needle, and the Babylonians with the loom, and pearls gleamed, and onyx stones flashed; if gold itself also had already issued, with the cupidity (which accompanies it), from the ground; if the mirror too, already had licence to lie so largely, Eve, expelled from paradise (Eve) already dead, would also have coveted *these* things, I imagine! No more, then, ought she *now* to crave, or be acquainted with (if she desire to live again), what, when she *was* living, she had neither had nor known. Accordingly, these things are the baggage of woman in her condemned and dead state, instituted as if to swell the pomp of her funeral.[23]

If man's desire for ornament, or for that which is secondary, is analogous to man's desire for woman, it is because woman is conceived *as* ornament. She is, by her secondary nature, automatically associated with artifice, decoration. The mildest version of such a paradigm is found in the often repeated licence for men to pray with head bare while women are enjoined to be veiled—and in its corollary, that woman is covering or veil: "But if a woman nourish her hair, it is a glory to her," writes Paul, "for her hair is given to her as a covering" (1 Cor. 11.15). Woman naturally decorates herself; and, according to Tertullian, is by nature decoration:

Female habit carries with it a twofold idea—dress and ornament. By "dress" we mean what they call "womanly gracing"; by "ornament," what is suitable should be called "womanly *dis*gracing." The former is accounted (to consist) in gold, and silver, and gems, and garments; the latter in care of the skin, and of those parts of the body which attract the eye. Against the one we lay the charge of ambition, against the other prostitution.[24]

The traditional reading of the above passage equates a certain hostility toward women with a more generalized horror of the flesh. And yet, it is not the flesh that Tertullian denounces. On the contrary, it is the draping of the flesh with "dress and ornament" that is the equivalent of seduction:

The only edifice which they know how to raise is this silly pride of women: because they require slow rubbing that they may shine, and artful underlaying that they may show to advantage, and careful piercing that they may hang; and (because they) render to gold a mutual assistance in meretricious allurement.[25]

To decorate oneself is to be guilty of "meretricious allurement," since embellishment of the body, a prideful attempt "to show to advantage," recreates an original act of pride that is the source of potential concupiscence. This is why Tertullian is able to move so quickly and naturally from the idea of dress to a whole range of seemingly unapparent associations—e.g., between transvestism and the monstrous; or between the toga and lust, adultery, cannibalism, intemperance, and greed.[26] It is as if each and every act of clothing an original nakedness associated with the sanctity of the body, and not the weakness of the flesh, were a corrupting recapitulation of the Fall entailing all other perversions.

If clothes are at once the sign, the effect, and a cause of the Fall, it is because, as artifice, they, like woman, are secondary, collateral, supplemental. Dress is unnatural since, like all artifice, it seeks to add to, to perfect, the body of nature or God's creation:

That which He Himself has not produced is not pleasing to God, unless He was *unable* to order sheep to be born with purple and sky-blue fleeces! If He was *able*, then plainly He was *unwilling*: what God willed not, of course, ought not to be fashioned. Those things, then, are not the best by *nature* which are not from God, the *Author* of nature. Thus they are understood to be from *the devil*, from *the corrupter* of nature: for there is no other whose they *can* be, if they are not God's; because what are not God's must necessarily be His rival's.[27]

A recreation, the artificial implies a pleasurable surplus that is simply inessential:

Thus (a thing) which, from whatever point you look at it, is in *your* case superfluous, you may justly disdain if you have it not, and neglect it if you have. Let a holy woman, if naturally beautiful, give none so great occasion (for carnal appetite).[28]

Tertullian does not, of course, seek to determine how something can be "naturally beautiful," much less to wrestle with the supervenient status of his own thought upon the superficial.[29] His indictment of the artificial condemns not only what we think of as the realm of the aesthetic, "adulteration with illegitimate colors," but extends to any investment of nature with human intention.[30] Thus the constant comparison of iron, the use value par excellence, with gold, which is perverse because its worth is extrinsic.[31] The affinity between gold, the product of excess labor, "the arts," and women constitutes an economic nexus taken as a given; their natures, by definition inessential and antinatural, attract each other because they partake cocvally in a scandalous excess that offends.[32]

Here we arrive at an idea that runs deep throughout medieval thought and that indeed can be considered to constitute the essence of a certain theologizing of the aesthetic. To wit, the artificial participates in a supervenient and extraneous rival creation that can only distract man's attention from God's original "plastic skill": "Whatever is *born* is the work of God," Tertullian concludes. "Whatever is *plastered* on is the devil's work. . . . To superinduce on a divine work Satan's ingenuities, how criminal it is!"[33] The decorative not only constitutes, as in the case of gold, an artificial investment of value, with all that such intention implies by way of potential concupiscence, but is a literal adding to the "weight" of creation:

The wonder is, that there is no (open) contending against the Lord's prescripts! It has been pronounced that no one can add to his own stature. *You*, however, *do* add to your *weight* some kind of rolls, or shield-bosses, to be piled upon your necks! . . . Nay, rather banish quite away from your "free" head all this slavery of ornamentation.[34]

From the always scandalous dressing of the naked body of nature emanates the entire range of perverse terms associated with "meretricious garbs and garments." In particular, the church fathers move quickly, by association, from the symbolic—artifice, idolatry—to the erotic—concupiscence, fornication, adultery, as if representation itself were, always and already, an offense. Verbal signs, in particular, stand as a constant reminder of the secondary and supplemental nature of all "the arts." "With the word the garment entered," Tertullian asserts, implying that language is a covering that, by definition and from the start, is so wrapped up in the decorative as to be essentially perverse.[35]

This nexus of ideas suggests that the representation of woman as ornamentation is an integral part of a broader paradigm, or that her perverse secondariness is the secondariness of all symbolic activity. The deep mistrust of the body and of the materiality of signs defined by their accessibility to the senses constitutes, in fact, a commonplace of what we know about the Middle Ages—yea, something that might be considered to constitute a cultural constant alongside of, indeed allied with, that of misogyny. God produced signs, Augustine writes, "in order to signify His presence, and to reveal Himself in them, as He Himself knows it to be fitting, but without appearing in that substance itself by which He is, and which is wholly unchangeable."[36] If, as Tertullian claims, "all things that are not of God are perverse," and if, as Augustine maintains, God is not in signs, then not only are signs perverse, but words or verbal signs stand as a particularly degraded excess. For where numbers signify permanence, reason, and order, language belies only corruption.[37] Words are to images in the mind as the corporeal or sensitive is to the domain of the spirit; they are secondary, derivative, supplemental, rival and potentially confusing semblances that rely upon the fallible function of sound. This is a well-known topos among Patristic writers. Where it becomes interesting for our purpose is in the explicit analogy between woman and the sensible; for, as Philo reminds us, the relation between the mind and the senses is that of man to woman:

To begin with, the helper is a created one, for it says, 'Let us make a helper for him'; and in the next place, is subsequent to him who is to be helped, for He had formed the mind before and is about to form its helper. In these particulars again, while using terms of outward nature, he is conveying a deeper meaning. For sense and the passions are helpers of the soul and come after the soul.[38]

The ontological status of woman is, then, analogous to that of the senses within the cognitive realm. Man as mind and woman as sensory perception are, as Philo explains, mutually exclusive: "It is when the mind (Adam) has gone to sleep that perception begins, for conversely when the mind wakes up perception is quenched."[39] Woman, formed of flesh from the rib, remains bound by the corporeal. "'He built it to be a woman' (Gen. 2.22)," Philo continues, "proving by this that the most proper and exact name for sense perception is 'woman.'"[40] Nor is it even necessary to distinguish between active and passive intellectual faculties.

Woman as sensitive soul is allied with the sensual; to perceive her, John Chrysostom maintains, is no less dangerous to men in general than the faculty of perception is to the soul of every man:

Hence how often do we, from beholding a woman, suffer a thousand evils; returning home, and entertaining an inordinate desire, and experiencing anguish for many days; yet nevertheless, we are not made discreet, but when we have scarcely cured one wound, we again fall into the same mischief, and are caught by the same means; and for the sake of the brief pleasure of a glance, we sustain a kind of lengthened and continual torment. . . . The beauty of a woman is the greatest snare. Or rather, not the beauty of woman, but unchastened gazing![41]

Here we arrive at a series of paradoxes within the discourse of misogyny. To wit, if woman is conceived to be synonymous with the senses or perception, then any look upon a woman's beauty must be the look of a woman upon a woman, for there can be no such thing as a male gaze or desire. This is why any answer to Saint Chrysostom's question "How is it possible to be freed from desire?" must be to be free of perception, or from the feminine altogether.[42] In this sense misogyny is bound to the desire to escape the senses, perception, the corporeal, or consciousness, which leads to the inevitable conclusion that it contains a desire for the absolute, or for a totality that is the unmistakable symptom of a death wish. Nor does the paradox end there, since the identification of misogyny with the desire for perfection is the site of another contradiction—a conflict between the keenness of the awareness of woman as flaw and the desire for wholeness, expressed in the persistent exhortation to virginity.[43]

Misogyny as Literature

The relation between vision—the seduction of a gaze—and the erotic lies at the source both of an idealization of women in literary texts and a corresponding antifeminism. For if a look engenders desire, desire, in turn, forecloses all future possibility of seeing. This is true not only for the church fathers but for the classic misogynists of the High Middle Ages as well. Love, for Andreas Capellanus, the architect of courtly and indeed of Western romantic love, represents "a certain inbred suffering caused by sight of and excessive meditation upon the beauty of the opposite sex, causing desire for embrace."[44] And yet love, identified with woman and the senses, is also synonymous with illusion, which makes it the cornerstone of the discourse of misogyny. As we shall see by way of conclusion, it is the equation of women with the illusory that serves to identify the misogynistic with the literary.

Mathieu, the antiheroic narrator of the *Lamentations*, laments less because he has married a woman who has been married before ("Le plus chetif de tous clamés / Pour ce que je suy bigamé" [I am called the most unfortunate because I am bigamous; book 1, lines 1074–75]) than because his intellectual functions have been troubled by a gaze:

> Je me plaing, car par la *veüe*
> Fu ma science deceüe.
> Beauté par ma l'uel mon cuer navra,
> Dont jamais jour repos n'avra. . . .
> Las! povre moy, quant tant amay,
> Que par amours me bigamay.

> [I complain, for by vision was my knowledge deceived. Beauty wounded my heart through my eye, and because of which I will never be at peace. . . . Alas! poor me, when I loved so much that by love I became bigamous; book 1, lines 647–58.]

Beauty, however, has turned to its opposite.[45] The difference between a happy former state and the present state of bigamous torture is a difference produced by the seductions of vision ("Je fuy seduis et afollés / Par doulx regars, par beau langage" [I was seduced and maddened by sweet looks, by beautiful language; book 1, lines 570–71]) that now has turned to its opposite: "Mon impotence est anoncie" (My impotence is made manifest; book 1, line 1349). It is impossible, in fact, to tell if it is a loss of beauty that has diminished desire or diminished desire that has troubled perception—or rather, whether it was or was not a trouble of perception that produced desire in the first place. For vision is certainly at stake in Mathieu's seduction:

> Mieulx me venist mes yeux bander
> Au jour que premier l'avisay
> Et que sa beauté tant prisay
> Et son doulx viaire angelique
> Dessoubs la fame sophistique.

> [I would have done better to shield my eyes the day I first saw her and so esteemed her beauty and her sweet angelic face covering sophisticated woman; book 1, lines 626–30.]

Here the connection is established between bigamy, seduction, and sophistication. Woman, feminine or sophisticated beauty, is that which seduces not only because it appeals to the senses but because it corrupts them, one by one:

> Mes cinq sens sont mortifiiés
> Mes yeuls ne peuent regarder . . . .
> Je ne puis a goust savourer
> Ne je ne puis rien odourer,
> Si ne sçay taster de mes mains

> Tant com je souloie, mais mains,
> Et de mes oreilles n'oy goute.

[My five senses are mortified, my eyes cannot see. . . . I cannot taste or smell anything, nor can I feel anything with my hands as I used to be able, but less; and my ears don't hear a thing; book 1, lines 1510–16.]

Thus we encounter a familiar paradox: before marriage the senses are seduced and distorted by desire, yet after marriage they are distorted by abuse, or by the tears of lamentation that distort vision. There is, then, no moment at which woman does not trouble vision, distort and destroy the senses. This is because the seducing sophistication of woman is that of illusion itself; she is by definition not only sophisticated (e.g., dirty, illusory) but is posited as that which exists in distinction to reason. If, as Mathieu admits, "By her sight my knowledge [*science*] was troubled," it is because woman is conceived as that which escapes logic. Rather, she is portrayed as a kind of false logic, the sophism that vanquishes both grammar and logic: "En ce fu grammaire traïe / Et logique moult esbaïe" (In this was grammar betrayed and logic greatly confounded; book 1, lines 1105–6). Together grammar and logic constitute within the medieval language arts the *trivium*, the sciences of the true, respectively of rectitude of expression and of correct propositions. Woman, however, is posited as the opposite of the truth: "Femme de verité n'a cure" (Woman cares not at all for truth; book 1, line 966). More precisely, she becomes, in the misogynistic thinking of the High Middle Ages, associated with the third element of the *trivium*—rhetoric, the art of persuasion that, by the thirteenth century, was synonymous with poetics. Woman is figured as the sophist, the dissimulator ("Faindre et dissimuler convient" ([To feign and trick comes naturally; book 1, line 1024]), the seducer with false arguments or subtlety: "Oultre les tençons et les limes / Par cinq manieres de sophismes / La femme meine l'omme a methe" (In addition to arguments and quarrels woman brings man to his end with five kinds of sophism"; book 1, lines 843–45). Here just before ending I would like to stop for a moment on the word *methe*, which from Latin *meta, metae* means "a mark or boundary, an end, period, or turning point." But the resonance of *methodium*, "a witty conceit, jest, or joke," is also there, as is that of *metus*, "fear." Moreover, the careful reader, aware of the extent to which medieval vernacular poets loved word play, cannot help but recognize in *methe* a part of the poet's name—Mathieu or Matheolus brought by woman to his end. But why not all four—end, joke, fear, and the name of the poet? After all, if woman is by definition the sign of an always present bigamy, she is also the very figure of ambiguity ("figure d'amphibolie"; book 1, line 1144): the one who through the ruse that is her power works against logic and grammar (*methodice*) to trouble the senses with sophisms: "Avec la langue est la veüe / Par le sophisme deceüe" (book 1, lines 903–4).

Here we have come full circle, since the alliance of women with rhetoric against grammar and logic places her on the side of the poet, whose interference with univocal meaning is equated with noise—noise, furthermore, specifically related to the defining secondariness with which we began:

Pourquoy sont femmes plus noiseuses,
Plaines de paroles oiseuses
Et plus jangleuses que les hommes?
Car elles sont d'os et nous sommes
Fais de terre en nostre personne:
L'os plus haut que la terre sonne.

[Why are women more noisy, full of foolish words, and more garrulous than men? Because they are made of bones and our persons are made of clay: bones rattle louder than earth; book 2, lines 241–46.]

More than mere encumbering ambiguity, woman is defined, above all, as embodying the spirit of contradiction: "Je ne sçai de chose passé / Ne du temps present rien retraire / Qu'elle ne die le contraire" (I know how to say nothing, past or present, that she does not say the opposite; book 1, lines 1300—1302). As man's copy or image, his double, she doubles perniciously everything he says: "Elle est de trop parler isnelle / Et en parlant a double ment, / Pourquoy je peris doublement" (She is too quick to speak; and in speaking she lies twice, by which I perish doubly; book 1, lines 1291–92). Nor is Jehan Le Fèvre's characterization unique. Andreas Capellanus, to cite another prominent example, concurs:

No woman can make you such a firm promise that she will not change her mind about the matter in a few minutes. . . . Woman is by nature a slanderer of other women, greedy, a slave to her belly, inconstant, fickle in her speech . . . a liar, a drunkard, a babbler, no keeper of secrets. . . . Even for a trifle a woman will swear falsely. . . . Every woman is also loud-mouthed. . . . When she is with other women, no one of them will give the others a chance to speak, but each always tries to be the one to say whatever is to be said and to keep on talking longer than the rest; and neither her tongue nor her spirit ever gets tired out by talking. . . . A woman will boldly contradict everything you say.[46]

Neither the portrayal of woman as endless garrulousness nor as contradiction would be so significant if it were not for the defining rhetorical context of all misogynistic literature, which seeks to dissuade from marriage and to do so precisely by speaking, often at great length. How, it may be asked, does the desire of women to speak differ from that of the writer who, like Walter Map, author of the "Dissuasion of Valerius to Rufinus the Philosopher That He Should Not Take a Wife," repeats in the space of only two pages: "I am forbidden to speak, and I cannot keep silence. . . . So I am forbidden to speak—I the prophet of truth. . . . I cannot keep silence. . . . I cannot keep silence . . . therefore I cannot keep silence. . . . I am forbidden to speak. . . . Therefore I cannot keep silence. . . . I am forbidden to speak. . . . You should make allowance for me who, in the impatience of my affection, cannot keep silence."[47]

If a woman is defined as verbal transgression, indiscretion, and contradiction, then Walter Map, indeed any writer, can only be defined as a woman; and the discourse of misogyny then becomes a plaint against the self or against writing itself. For Walter is no less fickle than Andreas accuses all women of being: "No woman ever makes up her mind so firmly on any subject that she will not quickly change it on a little persuading from anyone. A woman is like melting wax, which is always ready to take a new form and to receive the impress of anyone's seal."[48] And the very works that bemoan the instability of women are attempts to achieve what they denounce; they perform what in their own terms is the otherness of which hatred of the sexual other is the thematic analogue. Put another way, the author seeks to do to his interlocutor—whether the anonymous Walter or Rufinus—precisely that of which he accuses women: to deceive with words, to provoke contradiction, and to seduce with what is defined as the essence of the feminine: the ruses of rhetoric.[49] The misogynistic writer uses rhetoric as a means of renouncing it, and, by extension, woman; he "cheats," in the phrase of Andreas, "one trick with another" (*Courtly Love*, 205). This, perhaps, is the greatest ruse of all, for the confession of contradiction, which Walter Map equates with "the goodwill of the writer and the honesty of the written page" (*De nugis*, 164), is no less of an aporia than Andreas's concluding advice:

Now this doctrine of ours, which we have put into this little book for you, will if carefully and faithfully examined seem to present two different points of view. In the first part . . . we set down completely, one point after another, the art of love. . . . In the latter part of the book . . . we added something about the rejection of love.[50]

Thus the book is all that it claims to reject: contradiction, deceit, seduction, a source of mischief and of mistrust. "We know that everything a woman says is said with the intention of deceiving, because she always has one thing in her heart and another on her lips," Andreas inveighs in a phrase whose unreadability warns against nothing so much as itself (*Courtly Love*, 204).

This is a way of suggesting, by way of conclusion, that the reader's own strategy can only be one of mistrust of the writer and of the text—which returns us to the problem of reading. How do we distinguish, finally, persuasion from dissuasion? How do we mark the difference, for example, between Andreas's prescription, "If you want to get a woman to do anything, you can get her to do it by ordering her to do the opposite" (*Courtly Love*, 206), and the opening injunction to the reader, "Friend Walter": "Read this little book, then, not as one seeking to take up the life of the lover, but that, invigorated by the theory and trained to excite the minds of women to love, you may, by refraining from so doing, win an eternal recompense" (*Courtly Love*, 187). There is no way of determining with certainty Andreas's intent—whether to urge to convince or desist—and ultimately whether he wants us to take literally the warning against love or ourselves to be seduced by the letter. He, and any other author for that matter, performs that which he denounces Eve for having done—seduces, in the words of Tertullian, "by mere words," disobeys his own injunctions. The danger of woman, according to this reading of the phenomenon of misogyny, is that of literature itself.

Notes

1. See, for example, Thomas Aquinas, *Summa Theologiae* (New York, 1963), part 1, qu. 92; part 3, qu. 32. Innocent III is particularly virulent on the topic of woman. "Menstrual blood," he writes, "ceases in the female after conception so that the child in her womb will be nourished by it. And this blood is reckoned so detestable and impure that on contact with it fruits will fail to sprout, orchards go dry, herbs wither, the very trees let go their fruit; if a dog eat of it, he goes mad. When a child is conceived, he contacts the defect of the seed, so that lepers and monsters are born of this corruption"; *On the Misery of the Human Condition*, trans. Mary Dietz (New York, 1969), 9. In the misogynistic thinking of the Middle Ages, there can, in fact, be no distinction between the theological and the gynecological. Woman is a limit case of man who remains, as in Platonic thought, bound by the material, by flesh and lust. "Man was formed of dust, slime, and ashes, what is even more vile, of the filthiest seed. He was conceived from the itch of the flesh, in the heat of passion and the stench of lust, and worse yet, with the stain of sin"; ibid., 6.
2. It can be no accident, as Catherine Brown pointed out in my seminar, that the discourse of misogyny, which represents an attempt to speak of the other through the voice of the other, is so closely allied with the literary form or register whose very name implies "speaking otherwise."
3. *Le Roman de la rose*, ed. Daniel Poirion (Paris, 1974), lines 8561–70.
4. John of Salisbury, *Frivolities of Courtiers and Footprints of Philosophers*, ed. J. B. Pike (Minneapolis, 1938), 357.
5. Geoffrey Chaucer, "The Wife of Bath's Prologue," *The Canterbury Tales*, ed. F. N. Robinson (Cambridge, 1957), lines 248–52.
6. "Ce n'est pas merveille trop dure / Se le mari nul temps ne dure / Contre sa femme mal pitieuse, / Envers la tençon rioteuse / Que souvent li scet aprester" (It is no great wonder if the husband doesn't last very long against his pitiless wife, if he doesn't hold out against the riotous arguments that she knows how to prepare for him); Jehan Le Fèvre, *Les Lamentations de Matheolus*, ed. A.-G. Van Hamel (Paris, 1872), lines 829–33.
7. "Car um puet oyr sovent / Um fol parler sagement. / Sage est qe parle sagement"; *Recueil général et complet des fabliaux des XIIIe et XIVe siècles*, ed. A. de Montaiglon, 6 vols. (Paris, 1872), 2:256.
8. Cited by Victor Le Clerc, "Les Fabliaux," in *Histoire littéraire de la France*, vol. 23 (Paris, 1895), 98.
9.   Et cil qui font les mariages,
         Si ont trop merveilloz usages,
         Et coustume si despareille
         Qu'il me vient a trop grant merveille.
         Ne sai d'u vient ceste folie,

Fors de rage et de desverie.
Je voi que qui cheval achete
Ja n'iert si fox que rienz y mete,
Comment que l'en l'ait bien couvert,
Sil ne le voit a descouvert;
Par tout le regarde et descueuvre.
Mes la fame si bien se cueuvre,
Ne ja n'i sera descouverte,
Ne por gaaingne ne por perte,
Ne por solaz ne por mesese,
Por ce, sans plus, que ne desplese
Devant qu'elle soit espousee.

[And those who marry have a most unusual and unnerving way of operating that surprises me greatly. I don't know whence this foolishness can come except from madness and rage. For a man who buys a horse would not be so crazy as to put any money down if he had not seen it uncovered first, no matter how well covered it was in the first place. He looks it all over and uncovers it. But woman covers herself so well that she can never be uncovered—neither for gain nor for loss, neither for solace nor for grief; for this, and no more, that she might not displease before being wed; *Roman de la rose*, lines 8661–77.]

10. Innocent III, *Misery*, 20. Chaucer repeats the topos: "Thow seyst that droppyng houses, and eek smoke,/ And chidying wyves maken men to flee / Out of hir owene hous"; "The Wife of Bath's Prologue," lines 278–80.

11. *Le Débat sur le "Roman de la rose": Edition critique, introduction, traductions, notes*, ed. Eric Hicks (Paris, 1977), 15.

12. Ibid., 35.

13. Christine, whom no one would consider a misogynist, addresses the Provost of Lille in self-deprecating terms that, despite the possibility of sarcasm, would be taken as evidence of misogyny if from the pen of a man: "Bien est vray que mon petit entendement y considère grant joliveté . . . " (While it is true that my little understanding finds very amusing . . .). Then again, even so important a female figure as Hildegard of Bingen appropriates certain theological presuppositions that serve as the ontological basis of much of the misogynistic thinking of the Middle Ages: "When God saw man he saw that he was very good, for man was made in his image. But in creating woman, God was aided by man. . . . Therefore woman is the creation of man. . . . Man symbolizes the divinity of the Son of God and woman his humanity. Therefore man presides in the courts of this world since he rules over all creatures, while woman is under his rule and submits to him"; cited in Shulamith Shahar, *The Fourth Estate: A History of Women in the Middle Ages* (London, 1983), 57.

14. This is a historical aporia implicit to psychoanalytic explanations of misogyny in terms of male anger at rejecting mothers as well as to anthropological explanations involving the collective anxiety of males in dealing with the fear of feminine power. The difficulty of the former is that in biologizing misogyny it is at the same time naturalized, since there can be no escape from the basic cultural process expressed in the oedipal imposition of the father between mother and son and the son's concomitant anger. The problem with the latter is of a more logical order. To wit, if misogyny is the symptom of men's fear of the real power of women, then the more misogynistic a culture is, the stronger females can be assumed to be; in this way antifeminism represents not the derogation of women but an expression of their material enfranchise-

ment. See Katharine M. Rogers, *The Troublesome Helpmate: A History of Misogyny in Literature* (Seattle, 1966); H. R. Hayes, *The Dangerous Sex: The Myth of Feminine Evil* (New York, 1964).

15. Leaving aside the unknowable affective element of woman-hating, misogyny is a way of speaking about women as distinct from doing something to women, though speaking may be a form of doing and even of social practice, or at least its ideological component. Misogyny is a speech act such that the subject of the sentence is woman and the predicate is a more general term.

16. See my *Etymologies and Genealogies: A Literary Anthropology of the French Middle Ages* (Chicago, 1983), 37–44.

17. Philo, *On the Creation* (London, 1929), 227.

18. Augustine, *De libero arbitrio*, ed. J. H. S. Burleigh (London, 1953), 169.

19. Augustine, *De ordine*, ed. J. Jolivet (Paris, 1948), 444.

20. Tertullian, "On Exhortation to Chastity," in *The Ante-Nicene Fathers*, ed. Alexander Roberts and James Donaldson, vol. 4 (Buffalo, 1885), 54.

21. Augustine, *De libero arbitrio*, 163. This is also an important concept in the Aristotelian tradition according to which in procreation man supplies the form and woman the matter; see in particular *De la génération des animaux*, ed. P. Louis (Paris, 1961), 3–5, 39–43.

22. Philo, *On the Creation*, 237.

23. Tertullian, "On the Apparel of Women," in the *Ante-Nicene Fathers*, 4:14.

24. Ibid., 16.   25. Ibid.

26. Tertullian, "On the Pallium," in *The Ante-Nicene Fathers*, 4:9, 12.

27. Tertullian, "On the Apparel," 17.   28. Ibid., 20.

29. One of the salient ironies of misogynistic discourse is that it often becomes rhetorical or ornamental in direct proportion to the extent to which it denounces woman as ornament.

30. Tertullian, "On the Apparel," 17.

31. "So true is it that it is not intrinsic worth, but rarity, which constitutes the goodness (of those things): the excessive labour, moreover, of working them with arts introduced by means of the sinful angels, who were revealers withal of the material substances themselves, joined with their rarity, excited their costliness, and hence a lust on the part of women to possess (that) costliness"; ibid., 23.

32. "For they who rub their skin with medicaments, stain their cheeks with rouge, make their eyes prominent with antimony, sin against HIM. To them, I suppose, the plastic skill of God is displeasing! In their own persons, I suppose, they convict, they censure, the Artificer of all things. For censure they do when they amend, when they add to, (His work); taking these, their additions, of course, from the adversary artificer. That adversary artificer is the devil"; ibid., 20–21.

33. Ibid.   34. Ibid.

35. Tertullian, "On the Pallium," 8.

36. Augustine, *De trinitate* (Washington, D.C., 1963), 105.

37. "From that time forth she [Reason] found it hard to believe that the splendor and purity [of numbers] was sullied by the *corporeal matter of words*. And just as what the spirit sees is always present and is held to be immortal and numbers appear such, which sound, being a sensible thing is lost into the past"; Augustine, *De ordine*, 434.

38. Philo, *On the Creation*, 227.   39. Ibid., 237.   40. Ibid., 249.

41. Saint Chrysostom, Homily 15, in *Nicene and Post-Nicene Fathers*, ed. P. Schaff, vol. 9 (Grand Rapids, Mich., 1956), 441.

42. Saint Chrysostom, Homily 17, ibid., 10:116.

43. Virginity as such is obviously a concept crucial to the study of misogyny, one too vast for even superficial treatment within the limits of the present essay. Suffice it to say that virginity, like misogyny itself, is impossible to locate since the ever narrowing definitions given by the church fathers relegate it to the realm of a pure idea. To be more precise, virginity contains a historical reference to Adam and Eve and to a theological state of man, as in Augustine's notion of technical virgins who reproduce in paradise without desire or pleasure; it contains a doctrinal reference to Mary, the Virgin who redeems Eve; and it is associated on an individual level with a lack of personal sexuality. It is here that the concept of virginity becomes more interesting, since the more one seeks to fill the category, the more elusive it becomes; and the Patristics, in their desire for the absolute (which, as absolute, is synonymous with virginity), are not satisfied until the concept of virginity, like woman, is emptied of sense. It is not enough, for example, merely to be chaste; in order to be a virgin it is necessary never to have experienced desire. Nor is the absence of desire sufficient; the stimulation of desire in another impugns one's own chastity; see John Chrysostom, Homily 15, 443. And since desire is engendered by, and can consist in, a look, a virgin, seen, is no longer a virgin. "Every public exposure of an honorable virgin is (to her) a suffering of rape," Tertullian maintains ("On the Veiling of Virgins," 29). Jerome even wonders if it is licit for virgins to bathe since, in seeing their own bodies, there is always the potential for desire: "For myself, however, I wholly disapprove of baths for a virgin of full age. Such an one should blush and feel overcome at the idea of seeing herself undressed"; Letter 107, in *The Nicene and Post-Nicene Fathers*, 6:194. Thus there are only two possibilities: 1) virginity, as an absolute, a totality or Idea, does not exist; 2) the abstraction that virginity implies is destroyed by its articulation. This is another way of saying that the loss of virginity implied in its exposure is analogous to the loss of universality of an Idea implicit to its expression; or, there is no way of talking about virginity that does not imply a loss since the universal is always veiled by the defiling garment of words. In that case, virginity itself becomes a veil. (Jerome speaks of the "veil of chastity"; ibid., 192). Language becomes the ornament, the veil, that defiles the virgin by exposure, since the senses, equated with the body, have no direct access to an Idea, allied with the soul. "No one," John Chrysostom writes, "has anywhere seen a soul by itself stripped of the body"; "Letters to the Fallen Theodore," in *Nicene and Post-Nicene Fathers*, 9:104.

44. Andreas Capellanus, *The Art of Courtly Love*, trans. John J. Parry (New York, 1969), 28.

45.
> Las! or ay le cuer trop marri.
> Car orendroit est tant ripeuse,
> Courbée, boçue et tripeuse,
> Desfigurée et contrefaite
> Que ce semble estre une contraite.
> Rachel est Lya devenue,
> Toute grise, toute chenue,
> Rude, mal entendant et sourde,
> En tous ses fais est vile et lourde;
> Le pis a dur et les mamelles,
> Qui tant souloient estre belles,
> Sont froncies, noires, souillies
> Com bourses de bergier mouillies.

[Alas! now my heart is very sad, for she is now so mangy, stooped, humpbacked and pot-bellied, disfigured and undone that she seems to be a deformed person. Rachel has become Leah, all grey, white-haired, rough, senile, and deaf. In all she does she is heavy and vile; her chest is hard and her breasts that used to be beautiful are wrinkled, black, spotted like the wet bags of a shepherd; *Lamentations*, book 1, lines 672–84.]

46. Capellanus, *Courtly Love*, 201, 204, 207.

47. Walter Map, *De nugis curialium*, ed. Montague R. James (London, 1923), 160–61.

48. Capellanus, *Courtly Love*, 204.

49. How, one might ask, can the reader to whom the work is addressed be other than a woman as defined in Andreas's own terms as the one subject to persuasion: "Woman is commonly found to be fickle, too, because no woman ever makes up her mind so firmly on any subject that she will not quickly change it on a little persuading from anyone"; ibid., 204.

50. Ibid., 210.

JOEL FINEMAN

Shakespeare's *Will*:
The Temporality of Rape

There is a great difference, whether any Booke choose his Patrones, or finde them. This hath done both.
> —Editors' Dedication to *The Shakespeare First Folio*[1]

The loue I dedicate to your Lordship is without end: wherof this Pamphlet without beginning is but a superfluous Moity.
> —Shakespeare's Dedication to "The Rape of Lucrece"[2]

Lucius Tarquinius (for his excessive pride surnamed Superbus), after he had caused his own father-in-law Servius Tullius to be cruelly murd'red, and contrary to the Roman laws and customs, not requiring or staying for the people's suffrages, had possessed himself of the kingdom, went, accompanied with his sons and other noblemen of Rome, to besiege Ardea; during which siege, the principal men of the army meeting one evening at the tent of Sextus Tarquinius, the King's son, in their discourses after supper every one commended the virtues of his own wife; among whom Collatinus extolled the incomparable chastity of his wife Lucretia. In that pleasant humor they all posted to Rome, and intending by their secret and sudden arrival to make trial of that which every one had before avouched, only Collatinus finds his wife (though it were late in the night) spinning amongst her maids; the other ladies were all found dancing and revelling, or in several disports; whereupon the noblemen yielded Collatinus the victory, and his wife the fame. At that time Sextus Tarquinius being inflamed with Lucrece' beauty, yet smothering his passions for the present, departed with the rest back to the camp; from whence he shortly after privily withdrew himself, and was (according to his estate) royally entertained and lodged by Lucrece at Collatium. The same night he treacherously stealeth into her chamber, violently ravish'd her, and early in the morning speedeth away. Lucrece, in this lamentable plight, hastily dispatcheth messengers, one to Rome for her father, another to the camp for Collatine. They came, the one accompanied with Junius Brutus, the other with Publius Valerius; and finding Lucrece attired in mourning habit, demanded the cause of her sorrow. She, first taking an oath of them for her revenge, revealed the actor, and whole manner of his dealing, and withal suddenly stabbed herself. Which done, with one consent they all vowed to root out the whole hated family of the Tarquins; and bearing the dead body to Rome, Brutus acquainted the people with the doer and the manner of the vile deed; with a bitter invective against the tyranny of the King, wherewith the people were so moved, that with one consent and a general acclamation the Tarquins were all exiled, and the state government changed from kings to consuls.
> —The Argument, "The Rape of Lucrece"

I

Because the first sentence of Shakespeare's Dedication to Southampton speaks of "this Pamphlet without beginning" it is not altogether certain Shakespeare wrote "The Argument" that precedes the text of "The Rape of Lucrece": "without beginning" very likely refers to the fact that "the poem begins," as the glossing apparatus of the *Riverside* edition puts it, "in the middle of the action," but it might just as well refer to the absence of a conventional, prefatory, narrative summary.[3] In neither case, however, is there anything especially peculiar about the way the poem or, more precisely, "this Pamphlet," is lacking something from the start. With or without an Argument, no surprise attaches to the way the poem opens *in media res*, with Tarquin rushing "From the besieged Ardea all in post" (1), this being a conventional way to initiate the narration of such well-known, epically contexted, stories as that of the rape of Lucrece. So too, again because the rape story and its epic frame (the formation of the Roman republic) are both so famous and familiar, there is nothing very strange about Shakespeare having chosen to omit, if he did, what was a customary, but by no means an obligatory, introductory recapitulation. For this reason, however—because a shared literary history presumptively resumes the story before a reader reads it, because both within and without the poem a general literary context supplies the pretext of an Argument—it is striking that Shakespeare, looking back at "The Rape of Lucrece" from the distance of the Dedication, remarks the way "this Pamphlet" begins "without beginning," all the more so since, as it is written, "this Pamphlet without beginning" stands in complementary contrast to a dedicatory love "without end."

The absolute formality of this abstract opposition, plus the intricacy of the logical and syntactic hinge through which the opposition is coordinated— "wherof"—establishes a field or spectrum that at first appears to be exhaustive: a systematic completeness in between two interminable extremes, an enormity of everything extending forward, to begin with, to beyond the end, reaching backward, to conclude with, to before the beginning. And yet, at least in this first sentence of the Dedication of "The Rape of Lucrece," the entirety thus so blankly and encyclopedically imagined, specified neither in terms of space nor time, contains within it only that which is excessive to the wholeness it comprises: namely, the "superfluous Moity" Shakespeare advances as his judgment on or of his text's relation to his "love." "Moiety" is a word that for Shakespeare most often connotes a conflicted and contested, usually binary, portion of a larger whole—as at the opening of *King Lear* where "in the division of the kingdom, it appears not which of the Dukes he values most, for equalities are so weigh'd, that curiosity in neither can make choice of either's moi'ty" (1.1.4–7)—but here, because the dedicated "Moity" is "superfluous," it becomes a portion that exists as something surplus to the whole of which it is a part. And this is not altogether an abstraction. Precipitated out of the conjunction of an inconclusive "loue . . . without end" and a headless "Pamphlet without beginning," there emerges a poem that is "but a superfluous Moity." But Shakespeare knew enough Latin that we can be certain this textual superfluity contains for him a very vivid image: a liquid portion that runs over, a fluidity that overflows.

As it happens, this image is quite central to "The Rape of Lucrece," figuring not only the rape but also its motivation and consequences, so it is significant that Shakespeare, speaking in the authorial first-person of the patronizing Dedication, in this way associates his poem with the phenomenology of the spurt, with both the energy and the materiality of a liquified ejection, as though his text itself, as "superfluous Moity," were the objectification of an ejaculate suspense. It remains to determine why, here and elsewhere, the "superfluous Moity," both in its material fluidity and in its constrained directionality—thrusting outward from the aftermath of the pre-beginning toward the unreachable horizon of an ultimate inconclusivity; a movement, frozen in a static motility, between a departure always initiated *après coup* and an arrival prospectively postponed in anticipation of a forever deferred and receding destination: "Before, a joy propos'd, behind, a dream," to use the language of sonnet 129—so readily, frequently, and circumscribingly informs Shakespeare's imagination of what comes to pass when the erotic ("The loue I dedicate") and the poetic ("this Pamphlet") go together. That this happens here, in the first-person address to Southampton, suggests that this is partially a biographical question, a matter of what Shakespeare found convenient when he represents himself as speaking in his own subjective voice. That this happens elsewhere, however—in Shakespeare's poems, even when they are not in the first-person, as well as in the plays—suggests that this is not simply a personal but also a more general literary matter, having to do with the way Shakespeare imagines the literary presentation of subjective character as such, the way he constructs or achieves the literary effect of psychologistic, characterological subjectivity.

In what follows I want to show that the individually inflected cast of Shakespeare's character, on the one hand, and the varied cast of Shakespearean literary characterology, on the other—together, the personal and the personalizing Shakespeare, i.e., the person who creates literary personae—are related to each other in ways quite literally prescribed by the contours of the "superfluous Moity." More precisely, in what follows I want not only to show that there is something characteristically Shakespearean about the way Shakespeare summons up the figure of an interposed or intervening excess when he locates the endlessness of the sexual and the beginninglessness of the textual in relation to each other, but that, *because* there is so, this determines the formation and reception of the Shakespearean subject. Accordingly, because the large question I am concerned with is how the singularity of a contingent personality—the idiosyncratic Shakespeare—corresponds with, informs, motivates and is motivated by, a generic and highly determined subjective literary phenomenon—Shakespearean characterology—it is necessary to say clearly, before beginning, that the terms of my argument are at once more particular and more general than might at first appear: by "characteristically Shakespearean" I refer to that which literally marks out Shakespeare, Shakespeare's *"Will,"* not his name but its signature; by "the Shakespearean subject" I refer both to Shakespeare's biographical first-person—the one who writes "By me *William Shakespeare*" when he signs his will—and also to the subjectivity effect sometimes evinced by Shakespeare's literary representations of human character, where there are lyric and narrative as well as dramatic examples.[4] This is why "The Rape of Lucrece," though it is not usually recognized as a major work by Shakespeare, and though the subjectivity effect it generates is relatively feeble, is worth considering in considerable detail, for it provides a clear-cut illustration of the way the impression of psychologistic person in Shakespeare's texts characteristically effects and is effected by the mark of Shakespeare's person. Given the institutional force of Shakespearean characterology, given what goes on in Shakespeare's name, this is an important and not only literary issue.

I have elsewhere argued that in his sonnets Shakespeare invented a genuinely novel poetic first-person, one that comes to possess enormous power and authority in post-Shakespearean literature because, in a uniquely literary way, it reflects and responds to the conclusion or waning of the poetics and poetry of praise.[5] From antiquity to the Renaissance, in both literary theory and practice, the poetics of praise—i.e., epideictic or demonstrative oratory—defines the rhetorical mode not just associated with, but, more strongly, identified with the literary per se; accordingly, Shakespeare's registration or production of a difference in this long-standing tradition represents an important event in literary history, for it speaks to a significant rethinking of the means and meaning of literature as such. One necessary consequence of this rethinking or mutation of the literary, I have argued, is the arrival of specifically psychologistic literary subjectivity effects.

According to this argument, three large and related literary features mark the way Shakespeare's sonnets revise what until Shakespeare is taken to be an orthodox literariness. First, at the level of theme, Shakespeare's sonnets, situating themselves posterior to the poetry of praise, forswear the idealization of poetic language formally and historically endemic to the language of poetic idealization. Second, corresponding, at the level of motif, to this thematic recharacterization of the nature of poetic language, Shakespeare's sonnets give over a general imagery of vision, the homogeneous phenomenality of which traditionally materializes the ideality not only of the object of praise but also of the poet's epideictic language and desire, and, instead, develop an imagery of phenomenal hetero-geneity the conflicted physicality of which embodies an interruption in or wrin-kling of familiar imagery of visionary sameness, identity, reflection, likeness. Third, a change of poetic manner corresponding to these changes in poetic matter, Shakespeare's sonnets regularly develop a four-term tropic structure of cross-coupling chiasmus the complicated figurality of which works not only to redouble but thereby to introduce disjunction into typically two-term compari-sons and metaphorical identities developed in the poetry of praise.

Considered independently, any of these innovations—thematic, material, tropic—amounts to an important rewriting of orthodox epideictic literariness; taken together, however, these three features reciprocally corroborate each other in a decisive way, for the chiastic rhetoricity of Shakespeare's sonnets serves to foreground a specifically verbal duplicity that confirms the way poetic language, heard as language and invoked as such, is essentially discrepant to idealizing, unitary, visionary speech. In this way, the very languageness of language in Shakespeare's sonnets, sounded out, becomes both witness and performance of the belation and belying of linguistic idealization, with the result that poetic voice in Shakespeare's sonnets, to the extent it is registered as voice, not vision, estab-lishes the first-person speaker of the sonnets, whom the sonnets will sometimes call "Will," as the internally divided, post-idealist subject of a "perjur'd eye" (sonnet 152). It can be shown that this subject, "Will," again for purely formal reasons, possesses a specific characterological profile; e.g., he—for this subject is conceived as male—experiences his own phenomenal substantiality as a materi-alized heterogeneity; he is subject of an unprecedentedly heterosexual, and therefore misogynist, desire for an object that is not admired; he speaks a lan-guage that effectively speaks against itself and derives from the experience of such speaking a specific sense of space and time.

I summarize this argument regarding Shakespeare's sonneteering first-person not because in what follows I want to presuppose either its assumptions or its conclusions but because I want to bear its terms in mind as part, though only part, of my claim that what happens in "The Rape of Lucrece" is character-istically Shakespearean. Accordingly, it seems significant, in the light of Shake-speare's "perjur'd eye," that "The Rape of Lucrece" organizes at its beginning the very same literary features—again, thematic, material, tropic—as those that con-dition the formation of Shakespeare's lyric self, and does so so as to tell a story about what happens after praise. These are the opening stanzas of "The Rape of Lucrece":

> From the besieged Ardea all in post,
> Borne by the trustless wings of false desire,
> Lust-breathed Tarquin leaves the Roman host,
> And to Collatium bears the lightless fire,
> Which in pale embers hid, lurks to aspire,

> And girdle with embracing flames the waist
> Of Collatine's fair love, Lucrece the chaste.
>
> Happ'ly that name of "chaste" unhapp'ly set
> This bateless edge on his keen appetite;
> When Collatine unwisely did not let
> To praise the clear unmatched red and white
> Which triumph'd in that sky of his delight;
> Where mortal stars as bright as heaven's beauties,
> With pure aspects did him peculiar duties.
>
> (1–14)

As the first two stanzas introduce the story, there was a time, before the beginning of the poem, when things were as they should be, an originary time of ideal and specifically visual "delight," when "mortal stars as bright as heaven's beauties, / With pure aspects did him peculiar duties." This is how the poem initially images or imagines Collatine's initial happiness—what the third stanza of the poem will call "the treasure of his happy state"—as a primal shining moment in the past to which the poem's present-tense narrative now remembers back as absolute beginning of the diegetic story. At the same time, however, at least in opening narrative retrospect, this is a strange beginning in the sense that, as beginning, it may never have begun, as the fourth stanza explains:

> O happiness enjoy'd but of a few,
> And if possess'd, as soon decay'd and done
> As is the morning's silver melting dew
> Against the golden splendor of the sun!
> An expir'd date, cancell'd ere well begun.
>
> (22–26)

What puts a more or less immediate end to this ideal beginning, the reason why "the morning's silver dew" melts "against the golden splendor of the sun," or the reason why this happy beginning—and here we can think of "this Pamphlet without beginning"—is "cancell'd ere well begun," is the fact that, as the second stanza recalls, "Collatine unwisely did not let / To praise the clear unmatched red and white." This is a very precise and repeatedly emphasized narrative stipulation. The poem understands Collatine's praise of Lucrece, his "boast of Lucrece' sov'reignty" (29), as fundamental cause of Tarquin's rape of Lucrece; pointedly, it is not Lucrece's chastity but "that name of 'chaste'" that "set / This bateless edge on his keen appetite." And if it is Collatine's praise that motivates Tarquin's movement, at the opening of the poem, "From the besieged Ardea all in post" "to Collatium," the poem from its beginning consistently develops this movement as an oxymoronic clouding, a systematic complication, of the simple, lucid visuality of Collatine's praiseworthy past, so that, in contrast to "the clear unmatched red and white" and the "pure aspects" of "mortal stars as bright as heaven's beauties" that we hear about in the second stanza, "lust-breathed Tarquin," instead, in the first stanza, while he is "all in post," "bears the lightless fire, / Which in pale embers hid, lurks to aspire."

Reversing the narrative order in which the first two stanzas of the poem present this information, we can therefore reconstruct a serial chronology for the story as a whole: first there is or was an original moment of visual ideality that elicits Collatine's praise (this is "that sky of his delight," which, given the conventions of Renaissance poetry and the "clear unmatched red and white," we can provisionally take to be Lucrece's cheeks); in turn, Collatine's boasting leads on to Tarquin's posting, which in turn leads on to the rape of Lucrece. Generalizing, we can say that, according to the poem, in the beginning or, rather, in immediate response to the beginning—even more precisely, before or "ere" the beginning was "well begun"—was the word, specifically, Collatine's provocative epideictic word, "that name of 'chaste,'" that, when spoken, spelled an end not only to the beginning but also to the pure, clear vision in terms of which this beginning is now retrospectively conceived. Moreover, as the poem presents it, this focus on a fall, conceived or conceited as a corruption of vision, that follows from and after epideictic speaking is more than a merely thematic matter, since the poem itself performs or activates this same praising word of which it speaks when it speaks about the way "that name of 'chaste' unhapp'ly set / This bateless edge on his keen appetite."[6] Here, in the first line of the second stanza, the poem makes a point of mentioning its use of "chaste" in the last line of the first, but this remarking or citation of its own language, when the poem for the first time recalls its own speaking, is how the poem manages to raise a merely ordinary adjective into something extraordinary, effectively translating "chaste" into "'chaste'" within implicitly remarked quotation marks, or what the poem here properly calls a "name," as though the poem intended by such self-quotation to repeat or to reenact at its beginning the original event of epideictic designation it recalls.

Naming, we will see, is a central theme of "The Rape of Lucrece"—also the narrative climax of the poem, much more so than the rape itself—so it is significant that the first line of the second stanza, where the poem both blames and names "that name of 'chaste,'" is also where the poem first establishes for itself a rhetorically self-conscious narrative persona. By means of the poem's editorializing conjecture with regard to Tarquin's motive, and by quoting its own prior speaking, the poem acquires an immanent authorial agency appropriate to its own intentionality, a distinct poetic voice expressing the poem's or, rather, its narrator's point of view. For this reason, however, it should also be noted that the first line of the second stanza is also where the poem first introduces what we will learn to recognize as its most distinctive rhetorical trope: namely, the chiasmus of "Happ'ly that name of 'chaste' unhapp'ly set." This is an almost textbook illustration of the figure of speech that George Puttenham, the sixteenth-century theoretician of poetic rhetoric and ornament, called the "cross-coupler," which is the syneciostic trope that "takes me two contrary words, and tieth them as it were in a paire of couples, and so makes them agree like good fellowes."[7] Reading "hap'ly," on the one hand, as "perhaps," "by chance," on the other, as "in a happy manner," "gladly" (the two alternatives are, of course, already compact in each other, e.g., "fortune"-"fortunate"), the initially oxymoronic "Happ'ly"-"unhapp'ly" combination is transformed into chiasmus by the double correlation of two bivalent terms. The word play here is obvious, even, as is typical of "The Rape of Lucrece," ostentatious, which is why critics so frequently notice, even when they do not complain about, the poem's extravagant rhetorical manner, the brittle artificiality of the diction, its over-conceited style. But, even if they do so in a hyperrhetorical way, the four permuted propositions opened up by the line's positive and negative cross-coupling of two equivocations—blending happiness with sadness ("happily"-"unhappily") and the contingency of chance with the destiny of the determinate ("haply"-"unhaply")—together formulate the poem's official and explicit account of just why Tarquin is "all in post" to begin with. Putting a very fine point on it, this is precisely what "set / This bateless edge on his keen appetite."

The point is significant because, as when it names "that name of 'chaste,'" the stressed rhetoricity of the first line of the second stanza again enforces a strangely performative correspondence between the poem's matter and its manner. The heavy-handedly chiastic rhetoricity of "Happ'ly"-"unhapp'ly," to which the poem seems deliberately to draw attention, offers the motivation for Tarquin's movement "From the besieged Ardea" "to Collatium," i.e., the reason for his "posting." But if this describes the origin and constitution of Tarquin's rapacious desire, it is at the same time an origin mimicked, *ex post facto*, at the beginning of the poem precisely to the extent that the poem begins with Tarquin "all in post." Again, the poem starts off, very straightforwardly, with Tarquin rushing, "all in post," "From the besieged Ardea" "to Collatium." Moving in this way, in the first stanza, from one place to another, Tarquin, from the beginning, is geographically and thematically, as well as diegetically, *in media res*; specifically he is in between and in transit between a siege and rape. But this straightforward progress, though it goes in only one direction, becomes, as we hear more about it, to some considerable extent refractive, for not only is it defined as a movement from the public and foreign outside of Rome (Ardea) to Rome's private and familiar inside (Collatium) but, more precisely, as a movement from, on the one hand, an outside Rome surrounds for the purpose of violent entry to, on the other, an inside Tarquin enters so as therein to surround what turns out to be another or a second inside there within. Tarquin therefore, *in media res* at the beginning, as he follows out the path of "false desire," thus withdraws from the outside of the outside to an inside on the inside, but the imagery of encirclement with which this intrusion is initially imagined—"girdle with embracing flames the waist / Of Collatine's fair love, Lucrece the chaste"—makes his penetrating movement to and into the recesses of a deep internality inversely complementary to the way in which, when he "leaves the Roman host," he departs from and without the enveloped externality of the "besieged Ardea" (fig. 1).

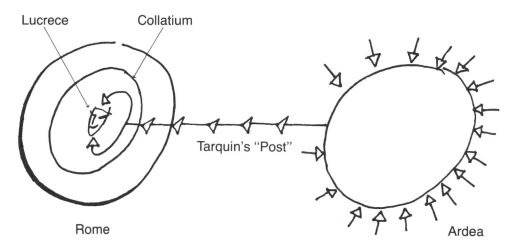

FIGURE 1.

This is how the poem first figures Tarquin on the road to rape, moving toward a conclusion that, as final destination, is nothing more than the Beginning in inverted form. And it is in the context of the more or less chiastic formation of this initial "bi-fold" posting journey—the vector of two reciprocally complicating movements, each conceived as the other inside out (a first movement of "from," defined as the extracurricular evasion of an external invasion; a second movement of "to," defined as an invasive and internal but yet circumferential and encapsulating penetration)—that the ostentatiously chiastic rhetoricity of "happ'ly"-"unhapp'ly" seems not only to explain but also to example both the motivation and the movement that leads Tarquin on to the rape of Lucrece.[8] Just as Tarquin, when he is "all in post," is in between an inside and an outside that are both turned inside out, so too "that name of 'chaste,'" which is the cause of Tarquin's desire, is located at the disjunct intersection formed by the cross-coupling of "happ'ly" with "unhapp'ly." And this becomes a more directed displaced place of in-betweenness when we discover later on that the very same inside-outside imagery of "post," as well as this chiastic formulation and formation, is also used to illustrate and explicate the rape toward which this "name" and posting lead. Summarizing, therefore, we can say that the end of Tarquin's desire (the rape), and the motivation of Tarquin's desire ("that name of 'chaste'"), and also the movement of Tarquin toward the satisfaction of his desire (Tarquin's "posting"), are all located in the same expulsive *in extremis* in-betweenness as is the

Dedication's "superfluous moity"; they are all intrinsically excessive to the boundaries that chiastically enclose them, boundaries folded over on each other in a way that leads what lies between them into an open-ended *cul de sac*.

I am looking so carefully at the way the poem thinks its way into the beginning of its story so as to guard against a variety of naturalistic or naturalizing accounts that might be advanced to explain both the causes and the consequences of Shakespeare's version of the rape of Lucrece. Given the boasting contest conducted by the Roman men around the military camp at Ardea, one might want to see the rape as Tarquin's deflected response to his implicitly homosexual relation to Lucrece's husband Collatine, as a version, therefore, of the kind of jealously paranoiac defense against homosexuality whose root propositional attitude Freud formulated, in a famous formula, as "I do not love him, she loves him."[9] There are surely many features of the poem that might support such a reading, as when Tarquin, for example, later on, trying to talk himself out of the rape, imagines Collatine repeating Tarquin's "post":

> "If Collatinus dream of my intent,
> Will he not wake, and in a desp'rate rage
> Post hither, this vile purpose to prevent?
> This siege that hath engirt his marriage."
> (218–21)

So too, less psychoanalytically, more anthropologically, but following out pretty much the same kind of reasoning, the story might be understood to exemplify René Girard's account both of the operation of mimetically mediated desire and of the mythographizing scapegoat mechanisms through which, according to Girard, societies formulate instances of effective difference with which to organize and to sustain culturally significant structures of hierarchical order; from the point of view of such a reading the achievement of just such grounding and orientating Difference would be the function both of the initial heroicizing boasting contest, where, as the Argument puts it, "the noblemen yielded Collatinus the victory, and his wife the fame," and also of its vilifying and victimizing outcome, on the one hand, the chastening and mortifying rape, on the other, the scapegoating expulsion of Tarquin from Rome to which the poem refers in its final couplet: "The Romans plausibly did give consent / To Tarquin's everlasting banishment" (1855–56).[10] In a similar mythographic vein, the story could be understood, in the manner of Lévi-Strauss, to package strong cultural oppositions in a reconciliatory, pacifying way—e.g., the way the martial violence of the siege at Ardea and the erotic intimacy of a domestic Collatium are married to each other in the principle of rape, where the desire for violence and the violence of desire each become, quite traditionally, expressions of the other; it would not be difficult to show how such representations work to resecure the force of larger social interdictions and demands, e.g., the operation of kinship laws, the exchange of women, etc.[11] All such accounts, which no doubt could be developed more elaborately, especially if eked out by relevant feminist or Marxist commentary (e.g., Eve Sedgwick's inflection of Girard's ungendered triangles in terms of more and less Freudian homophobic social patterns, or Pierre Macherey's Marxist analysis of ideology in terms of what is essentially Lévi-Straussian reflection theory), speak to various aspects of the poem, and it is also fair to say that the general story of "The Rape of Lucrece," the one Shakespeare inherits, in many respects invites such readings and responses, as could be seen by comparing in detail the terms and assumptions of such readings with traditional commentary and critical controversies attaching to the story, from St. Augustine on, e.g., whether Collatine has only himself to blame for the rape of his wife, or whether Lucrece is morally right or wrong to kill herself, or whether rape is a form of suicide or suicide a form of rape, etc.[12]

Shakespeare's poem, however, as distinct from the myth or story he inherits, is, as we have already seen, considerably more specific in its account of the motive of the rape, stipulating as its effective cause the fact that Collatine spoke his words of praise, as though it were this speaking that the poem holds responsible for the story it recounts. Again, it is because "Collatine unwisely did not let / To praise the clear unmatched red and white" that "that sky of his delight" will soon be clouded over, just as it is as a consequence of "that name of 'chaste'" that Tarquin is "all in post." And this is an explicit thematic claim of the poem as we discover soon enough, in the fifth stanza, when the narrator asks, in his own voice, the poem's first rhetorical question, to which he then responds with an equally and specifically rhetorical answer:

> Beauty itself doth of itself persuade
> The eyes of men without an orator;
> What needeth then apology be made
> To set forth that which is so singular?
> Or why is Collatine the publisher
>   Of that rich jewel he should keep unknown
>   From thievish ears because it is his own?
>
> Perchance his boast of Lucrece' sov'reignty
> Suggested this proud issue of a king;
> For by our ears our hearts oft tainted be.
>   (29–38)

The ideal visuality of "that sky of his delight" is here presented as a "beauty" that "persuade[s] / The eyes of men without an orator," just as desire is here said to be corrupted, as well as occasioned, by the language that it hears: "For by our ears our hearts oft tainted be." And, again, precisely because the poem thus makes thematic and incriminating issue out of "oratory," the poem's own rhetoricity is once again performatively implicated in the rape that it reports, as though the poem itself, *because* it speaks rhetorically, were speaking to its reader's "ear" so as to "taint" its reader's "heart."

All three features, therefore, that I previously characterized as characteristically Shakespearean—1) the evocation of a fallen language opposed to a clear vision, 2) a stressedly chiastic figurality, 3) the imagination of a material phenomenality folded over on itself—are not only present at the beginning of "The Rape of Lucrece," but they are also all operatively assimilated to the poem's own status as a verbal artifact, so that, in principle, from the very first oratorical word of the poem, from "From," we are situated in a present both successive to or "post" an ideal past at the same time as this present is directed toward a future that will end in rape. Moreover, the poem quite frankly adopts the rapacious point of view of this both retrospective and tendentious present, so that, in contrast to the way that Collatine, in the past, looked at Lucrece and praised "the clear unmatched red and white," both Tarquin and the narrator, in the poem's narrative present, instead regard her in an altogether different light, as when, a few stanzas later, we see what Tarquin and the narrator together see when they look at Lucrece:

> This heraldry in Lucrece' face was seen,
> Argued by beauty's red and virtue's white;
> Of either's color was the other queen,
> Proving from world's minority their right;
> Yet their ambition makes them still to fight,
>   The sovereignty of either being so great
>   That oft they interchange each other's seat.
>
> This silent war of lilies and of roses,
> Which Tarquin view'd in her fair face's field
> In their pure ranks his traitor eye encloses.
>   (64–73)

The "interchange" of red and white is, of course, a commonplace in Petrarchist lyric, but, as "The Rape of Lucrece" develops it, this chiastic color scheme—two colors systematically at odds not only with each other but with themselves as well: "Of either's color was the other queen"—specifically defines the point of view of rape, not only implicitly, as in the first stanza, where Tarquin "bears the lightless fire, / Which in pale embers hid, lurks to expire," but explicitly, as when, but this is only one example among many, Lucrece demands of Tarquin "Under what color he commits this ill" (475) and:

> Thus he replies: "The color in thy face,
> That even for anger makes the lily pale,
> And the red rose blush at her own disgrace,
> Shall plead for me and tell my loving tale. . . ."
>   (476–80)

We will see later on how emphatically, and, again, heavy-handedly, "The Rape of Lucrece" associates this particular conflict of colors not only with rape and wounding death but also with the way that language, being false, gives a subjectifying lie to the seeming truth of vision: according to the poem's color scheme, red and white, chiastically conjoined, yield a dappled purple that the poem not only imagines as the specific color of rhetoric but with which the poem also thematically colors its own purple rhetorical passages. For the moment, however, the only point important to insist on is that this particular color scheme, though nothing but conventional, is nevertheless something characteristically Shakespearean, at least insofar as Shakespeare organizes his two narrative poems around precisely such erotic war of red and white. Thus, Shakespeare's other and earlier narrative poem, "Venus and Adonis," also dedicated to Southampton, begins with a "purple"—its first line, "Even as the sun with purple-color'd face"—which it immediately presents as compact of the chiastic war between internally conflicted red and white, and then proceeds, as does "The Rape of Lucrece," to develop this "check'red" red-white combination, first, as image of the object of venereal desire—e.g., when Adonis "low'rs and frets, / 'Twixt crimson shame and anger ashy-pale. / Being red, she loves him best, and being white, / Her best is better'd with a more delight" (75–78)—then, as image of the castrating wound that marks the object of desire—the murderous boar "sheath[es]" his "tusk in his soft groin" (1116), thereby forming "the wide wound that the boar had trench'd / In his soft flank, whose wonted lily white / With purple tears, that his wound wept, was drench'd" (1052–54)—and, finally, as image of the conclusion of desire, when the dead Adonis, at the end of the poem, is transformed into "A purple flow'r sprung up, check'red with white / Resembling well his pale cheeks and the blood / Which in round drops upon their whiteness stood" (1168–70). Again, we will see "The Rape of Lucrece" develop, in a focused way, the same color imagery through the same topoi to the same end, but for now the simple point to notice is that this is something characteristically Shakespearean, first, because Shakespeare does the same thing in his two narrative poems, second, because he does it in so fixed and formulaic a fashion that it impresses itself on readers as a kind of identifying trait, as we can confirm from the fact that contemporary references to "Venus and Adonis," whether serious or parodic, fasten on and remark the poem's purple and chiastic red-and-white, as though the poem's first readers recognized in Shakespeare's handling of the motif something characteristically and characterizingly Shakespearean. Here is Gullio, in the third act of *The Return from Parnassus, Part 1*, paraphrasing "Venus and Adonis":

> Thrise fairer than my selfe, thus I began
> the gods faire riches, sweete above compare
> Staine to all Nimphes, [m]ore loueley the[n] a man
> More white and red than doues and roses are

Nature that made thee wth herself had strife,
saith that the world hath ending wth thy life
. . . .

Even as the sunn wth purple coloured face
had tane his laste leaue on the weeping morne. &c.;
(3.1.1006–21)

and here is Ingenioso, one act later, also intending an echo of "Venus and Adonis":

Faire Venus queene of beutie and of loue
thy red doth stayne the blushinge of the morn
thy snowy neck shameth the milke white doue
thy presence doth this naked world adorne.
(4.1.1189–92)[13]

At the very least, it is fair to say an enthusiastic reader of the first poem, "Venus and Adonis"—the sort who to "worshipp sweet M^r. Shakspeare, and to honoure him will lay his Venus, and Adonis under my pillowe"—who also notes the way "The Rape of Lucrece" begins with "clear unmatched red and white," might plausibly expect the poem to develop this image, as in fact it does, in a coherent and self-conscious way.

So too with the four-term chiastic rhetorical form, as distinct from the chiastic content of the red-white motif, for the structured criss-cross of this tropic feature—to which I have already referred in connection with "Happ'ly that name of 'chaste' unhapp'ly set"—is also equally prominently and stressedly evident in both "Venus and Adonis" and "The Rape of Lucrece." A short example from "The Rape of Lucrece" will serve to illustrate the way Shakespeare conceives the rhetorical structure of the cross-coupler at the level of the signifier, rather than at the level of the signified, at the same time as the example suggests how such a purely formal concatenation nevertheless calls forth from Shakespeare a specific ensemble of semantic, and specifically Shakespearean, associations. Here is Tarquin in his bedroom, a little later in the poem, mulling over whether he should or shouldn't rape Lucrece:

As one of which doth Tarquin lie revolving
The sundry dangers of his will's obtaining;
Yet ever to obtain his will resolving,
Though weak-built hopes persuade him to abstaining.
(127–30)

The rhetorical wit of these lines derives from the way, through the repetition of "re-"s, "re-volving" and "re-solving" are turned over or "re-turned" over on each other so that each is heard as near anagrammatic replication of the other. With "re-volving" and "re-solving" folded back upon themselves in this literal, and by no means subtle, fashion, the indecisive *volvere* of Tarquin's "revolving" turns out to be, because the sounding of "revolving" is audibly turned inside out, precise prefiguration of Tarquin's decisively rapacious "will resolving." In the same way, the hard rhyme of "ob-taining" and "ab-staining" works to sound out the "stain" that soon becomes the poem's dominant image of Lucrece's rape. Though local, the example possesses general interest because, as we will see, these are not, for Shakespeare, casual configurations. For example, we can think of these lines in the context of *Twelfth Night*, where just these signifiers control the characterological relations of the play, in the often remarked anagrammatic correlation of "Malvolio"-"Viola"-"Olivia," and where what is nominally at stake in the flamboyant, allegoricizing anagrammatics is the pointed pun on *voglio*—"will" or "badwill" ("Mal-volio"). We can add that in *Twelfth Night* all this is initially thought or presented through the sound associated with the purple flower called up in the opening lines of the play—"the sweet sound / That breathes upon a bank of violets" (1.1.5–6)—a violet, moreover, the play associates not only with "Viola" but also with the violence and violation of her imagined rape (*violare*).[14] I cite the example, and will return to it later, because the repetition of "re-"s in "re-volving" and "re-solving" in these lines from "The Rape of Lucrece" turns on the remarked repetition of "will"—"will's obtaining"-"will resolving"—which "The Rape of Lucrece" will give us good reason to consider a specifically and personal Shakespearean nominal repetition—as, of course, does *Twelfth Night*, if we recall the apposite alternative the play itself entitles: *or What You Will*.[15]

Leaving this Shakespearean "will" to the side, for the moment, the question raised by "The Rape of Lucrece," given the way the poem ostentatiously foregrounds its chiastic matter and manner, is why chiasmus—either the chiastic content of Lucrece's red and white or the chiastic rhetorical form of the crosscoupler—is understood to motivate desire in general and rape in particular. Specifically, why is it that "Happ'ly that name of 'chaste' unhapp'ly set / This bateless edge on his keen appetite," and why is it that Tarquin "posts" to Rome because Collatine "did not let / To praise the clear unmatched red and white?" We get the beginnings of an answer when the poem proceeds to elaborate Tarquin's indecision at the moment he decides upon his rape:[16]

> Away he steals with open list'ning ear,
> Full of foul hope, and full of fond mistrust;
> Both which, as servitors to the unjust,
> So cross him with their opposite persuasion,
> That now he vows a league, and now invasion.
> (283–87)

The interest of these lines derives from the way Shakespeare here makes a point of showing how a certain kind of tropic figurality is, as such, itself the figure of subjective motivation. We recognize, presumably, since the narrator makes the point explicit, that Tarquin is here "crossed" between two coupled oxymorons. The "foul hope" of his lust is poised off against the moral reservation of his "fond mistrust" in a conjunction that reverses the normal connotations of all four terms. As a result, because the positives become negatives and the negatives become positives, Tarquin is left suspended between a foul fondness and a hopeful mistrust, a rhetorical indeterminacy that serves, at least initially, to illustrate his hesitation between a peaceful "league" and an aggressive "invasion." Again, this is a general formal feature of "The Rape of Lucrece," as when Lucrece, resisting the rape, defensively appeals to Tarquin's better nature and tells him not to let a tiny spot of lust "stain the ocean of thy blood. / If all these petty ills shall change thy good, / Thy sea within a puddle's womb is hearsed, / And not the puddle in thy sea dispersed" (652–58), a conceit that asks us to imagine, as with Tarquin's "posting," the inside on the outside and the outside on the inside, as though the infinitely small were larger than the infinitely large and the "boundless flood" containable "within a puddle's womb"—a conceit whose titillating resonance and contours seem, under the circumstances, uniquely ill designed to accomplish Lucrece's chastening, prophylactic purpose. What the example indicates, however, is that this structure of chiastic indeterminacy, whereby Tarquin alternately "vows a league, and now invasion," itself determines a determinate desire—to rape—as we see if we follow out the movement of Tarquin's indecisive lust.

The poem does not give us a graphic description of Tarquin's rape of Lucrece, at least not of the actual "invasion," this being passed over by the poem in a single discreet line to which we will soon turn. Instead, beginning where the lines on "foul hope" and "fond mistrust" end, the poem projects the details of the rape onto a description of Tarquin's progress toward Lucrece's bedroom, his movement through the passageways of her castle to her "chamber door" (337) being developed as a kind of pornographic *effictio*. In the course of this movement—it is fair to say in the intercourse of this movement—three obstacles bar Tarquin's progress, three hindrances stand, as the narrator puts it, "between her chamber and his will" (302). First, there is a series of locked doors, "each one by him enforc'd retires his ward" (303). Then, "as each unwilling portal yields him way" (309) "the wind wars with his torch to make him stay" (311). Finally, there is "Lucretia's glove, wherein her needle sticks" (317), which, when Tarquin picks it up, "the needle his finger pricks" (319). All three of these items—the doors, the wind, the glove—slow Tarquin down, as though the material world conspired to retard the rape. All three, however, are at the same time, and very obviously so, precisely rendered images *of* the rape, its physical objectification: the doors whose locks are "enforc'd" and which "unwilling" "yields him way"; the wind, which "through little vents and crannies of the place" (310) "wars with his torch . . . And blows the smoke of it into his face" (311–12); the fetishistic glove "wherein her needle sticks." Moreover, not only is each one of these things, in the resistance that it offers, an image of the rape that it repulses, but so too does each one of these bars to Tarquin's desire manage also to spur the rapist on. The "his" of "retires his ward" refers both to Tarquin and the door. The wind that blows out Tarquin's torch also inspires "his hot heart, which fond desire doth scorch,/[To puff] forth another wind that fires the torch" (314–15). So too with the clitoral "prick" of the glove that "pricks" the rapist on: "This glove to wanton tricks/is not inured" (320–21).[17]

All this does not go by unnoticed, either by the narrator or by Tarquin. With regard to the hindrances to Tarquin's desire, the narrator observes:

> He in the worst sense consters their denial:
> The doors, the wind, the glove that did delay him,
> He takes for accidental things of trial;
> Or as those bars which stop the hourly dial,
>   Who with a ling'ring stay his course doth let,
>   Till every minute pays the hour his debt.
>
> (324–29)

The narrator's image is of a clock whose hour hand, connected to a spring mechanism, builds up potential energy when its movement is restrained by protuberant minute markers. At successive intervals the hour hand bursts past each momentary "let" in an explosive, jerky movement that measures time and brings the marker of the hours to its next repulsing and propulsing impediment. It is an image of inviting resistance, of an impetus derived from its frustration, and as such illustrates not only the way "the doors, the wind, the glove that did delay him" promote what they postpone, but also illustrates the rape itself, the way, that is, that Tarquin "consters" Lucrece's "denial."

It is perhaps an obvious point, for Tarquin draws the same moral for himself, immediately repeating—indeed, sharing—the narrator's image of the temporal "let":

> "So, so," quoth he, "these lets attend the time,
> Like little frosts that sometime threat the spring,
> To add a more rejoicing to the prime,
> And give the sneaped birds more cause to sing."
>
> (330–33)

However, even if the erotic psychology thus enunciated is proverbial, and its sententious phrasing makes it seem as though it is, it is important to notice that the erotic psychology of the "let," as well as the material phenomenology of the doors, the wind, and the glove, unpacks the cross-coupling formal rhetorical logic of "foul hope" and "fond mistrust."[18] That is to say, when Tarquin was initially indeterminately suspended between oxymorons, when he was "crossed" by "their opposite persuasion," he was already, by virtue of the very structure of this indeterminacy, embarked upon his rape. Speaking thematically we can say that Tarquin's indecision is decisive: its static framing is what thrusts him into the directed duration of erotic time. But this is also a significant point for Shakespearean poetics, because it shows us that the cross-coupler, at least as Shakespeare here employs it, is not a neutral trope; it is instead the trope of a specific desire whose hindrance is what gives it leave to go. Specifically, it is the tropological structure and expression of an eros whose *contrapposto* energy, the resistance to resistance, simulates the action of a rape—and of a rape, moreover, that, rendered genially pastoral by "the little frosts that sometime threat the spring,/To add a more rejoicing to the prime," offers itself as general model for the motivating and consummating *friction* of heterosexual desire per se. This, at any rate, seems to be both the erotic and the rhetorical logic of "let" that links Lucrece to Tarquin and that makes Lucrece responsible for her rape by virtue of the energetic and energizing resistance that she offers to it. Lucrece herself becomes a "let," because, as Tarquin says, in response to her cross-coupling entreaties:

> "Have done," quoth he, "my uncontrolled tide
> Turns not, but swells the higher by this let.
> Small lights are soon blown out, huge fires abide,
> And with the wind in greater fury fret.
> The petty streams that pay a daily debt . . ."
> (645–48)

These lines make swelling, overflowing, or "superfluous" water, along with the already erotically coded imagery of torch and wind, into a metaphor of the results of "let": "my uncontrolled tide/Turns not, but swells the higher by this let." But just a few lines later the metaphor is literalized or activated when Tarquin, for what is the final time—as though his dam had finally broken, or as though the moment for the movement of his hour hand had come round at last—inserts himself into or, rather, inter-rupts Lucrece's spoken "let":

> "So let thy thoughts, low vassals to thy state"—
> "No more," quoth he, "by heaven I will not hear thee."
> (666–67)[19]

This is the last instance of outspoken resistance in the scene of rape, after which there is no turning back. Given the dramatic staging, however, with the two principals acting out the "let" that they engage in, it is fair to say that this is how the poem *accounts* for rape: through this increasingly obtrusive sounding out of "let." Accordingly, we can better understand the constitutive energy built into the rape's initiating moment: "When Collatine unwisely did not let/To praise the clear unmatched red and white." As it echoes through the text of "The Rape of Lucrece," Collatine's original and originating "let," though voiced by the narrator, is heard to contain within itself, as its own provocation, the chiasticized formation and materialization of Tarquin's rapacious desire: "Happ'ly that name of 'chaste' unhapp'ly set/This bateless edge on his keen appetite." And, again, this is something the poem enforces not only thematically but also by means of its elaborated rhetoricity, so that both the poem's matter and manner, its cross-coupled signi-fieds along with its criss-crossing signifiers, together work together to establish the initial equi-vocation of Collatine's reverberating "let" as that which pro-vokes the rape of Lucrece. Moreover, we can now add, if this conjoined chiastic form and matter—the literal correspondence of Collatine's "let" with the phenome-nology of Shakespearean copulation: the wind, the torch, the glove, the swelling water—thus immanently characterize both the motive of the rape and Tarquin's movement toward the rape—either the obstructed movement of Tarquin's "will" through the passageways of Lucrece's castle to her "chamber door" or the opening rush of Tarquin toward Collatium when he is "all in post"—so too does it describe the very action of the rape, as it occurs, soon after Tarquin's interrup-tion, in one climactically chiastic line:

> This said, he sets his foot upon the light,
> For light and lust are deadly enemies;
> Shame folded up in blind concealing night,
> When most unseen, then most doth tyrannize.
> The wolf hath seiz'd his prey, the poor lamb cries,
>   Till with her own white fleece her voice controll'd
>   *Entombs her outcry in her lips sweet fold.*
>   (673–79)

"En-tombs her out-cry" replicates the same reciprocally complicated four-term topography of inside-outside invagination that we have already come upon sev-eral times. But if this appears to open up a space that folds the inside and the outside over on each other, the space itself, for all its aporetic complications, is firmly placed within the "in" of "her lips sweet fold."[20]

It is fitting that the rape, when it finally occurs, is figured in and as a simul-taneously emergent and recessive in-betweenness forming and informing the "fold" of Lucrece's lips, for the smirky collation of Lucrece's mouth with her vagina supports the formal implication that Lucrece is asking for her rape because her "no," as "no," means "yes." Hence the correspondence of the "sweet fold" of "her lips" with the "Shame" or "pudendum" "folded up in blind con-cealing night." Beyond that, however, this focus at the climax of the scene of rape on "her voice controll'd"—and the syntax of the line leaves undecided just who the agent of the verb is, Tarquin or Lucrece—brings out the fact that Tarquin and Lucrece both speak the *same* language, a point, already clear enough from the equivalent tonalities and diction, the shared motifs, the stichomythian back-and-forth rhythms, through which the two of them conduct their formal argu-ment, *in utramque partem*, pro and contra rape. Not suprisingly, this is something critics often complain about, on the grounds that the poem, a mere exercise in rhetoric, thus fails to individuate the characters of Tarquin and Lucrece. But such criticism misses a point on which the poem itself insistently insists: that Tarquin and Lucrece are inverse versions of each other, and for this reason *together* make the rape of Lucrece, as is no doubt suggested by the objective and subjective genitive of the poem's title.[21] Hence, too, the disjunctive conjunction of the rape itself, where Tarquin and Lucrece, because the two of them are both chiastically imagined, both come together "in her lips sweet fold."

This elaborated correspondence between Tarquin and Lucrece, which partially accounts for the oddly abstract and near comic inevitability the poem accords Lucrece's violation, is something the poem continues to develop in the aftermath of the rape, when Tarquin exits from the narrative and the poem turns its attention to Lucrece and to her lamentations. Thus, immediately after "Entombs her outcry in her lips sweet fold," the narrator forges a characteristically chiastic link, a "forced league," between the rapist and his victim:

> But she hath lost a dearer thing than life,
> And he hath won what he would lose again;
> This forced league doth force a further strife.
>
> (687–89)

So too, the poem continues to decorate Tarquin and Lucrece with the same motifs, so that, for example, Tarquin, as he steals away, "bear[s] away the wound that nothing healeth, / The scar that will despite of cure remain" (730–32), whereas Lucrece remarks her "unseen shame, invisible disgrace! / O unfelt sore, crest-wounding private scar!" (827–28; in this second section of the poem, which focuses on Lucrece and not on Tarquin, the poem establishes many such metaphoric correlations between Tarquin and Lucrece). So too, Lucrece herself anticipates a future in which, adding rhetorical insult to an already rhetoricized injury, "The orator to deck his oratory / Will couple my reproach to Tarquin's shame" (815–16).[22] Yet more powerful, however, in its effect, than any of these articulated correspondences between Tarquin and Lucrece is the way the outspoken oratory of Lucrece's own formally declaimed complaint reiterates with its chiastic manner the chiastic matter of the rape. Thus, addressing herself to a series of allegorical abstractions—just the sort of abstractions one expects to find in a Complaint poem—first Night, then Opportunity, Lucrece concludes her lamentation with a vilifying apostrophe to personified Time; for it is Time, imagined as a particular kind of person, whom she holds responsible for what has come to pass:

> "Misshapen Time, copesmate of ugly Night,
> Swift, subtle post, carrier of grisly care,
> Eater of youth, false slave to false delight,
> Base watch of foes, sin's pack-horse, virtue's snare!
> Thou nursest all, and murth'rest all that are.

> O hear me then, injurious shifting Time,
> Be guilty of my death, since of my crime."
>
> (925–31)

It is difficult to determine whether, as "Swift, subtle post," generic Time here emerges as a version, after the fact, of rapacious Tarquin rushing to Collatium "all in post" or, instead, whether Tarquin, from the beginning, is himself already a proleptic version of "Misshapen Time." In either case, "Misshapen Time" is presented as the initiating cause as well as the condition of the rape: "But some untimely thought did instigate / His all too timeless speed" (43–44). For this very reason, however, remembering that it is through a specific imagery of time—"those bars which stop the hourly dial, / Who with a ling'ring stay his course doth let, / Till every minute pays the hour his debt"—that the poem explicitly presents its logic of "let," and remembering how, according to Tarquin, "'these lets attend the time,'" the peroration of Lucrece's address to Time, with its symphony of reiterated, hortatory "lets," seems intentionally to call forth or to sound out, as much as it regrets and reviles, the same moment and momentum—Collatine's "let"—that potentiates her rape in the first place:

> "Thou ceaseless lackey to eternity,
> With some mischance cross Tarquin in his flight.
> Devise extremes beyond extremity,
> To make him curse this cursed crimeful night.
> *Let* ghastly shadows his lewd eyes affright,
>   And the dire thought of his committed evil
>   Shape every bush a hideous shapeless devil
>
> "Disturb his hours of rest with restless trances,
> Afflict him in his bed with bedred groans;
> *Let* there bechance him pitiful mischances
> To make him moan, but pity not his moans;
> Stone him with hard'ned hearts harder than stones,
>   And *let* mild women to him lose their mildness,
>   Wilder to him than tigers in their wildness.
>
> "*Let* him have time to tear his curled hair,
> *Let* him have time against himself to rave,
> *Let* him have time of Time's help to despair,
> *Let* him have time to live a loathed slave,
> *Let* him have time a beggar's orts to crave,
>   And time to see one that by alms doth live
>   Disdain to him disdained scraps to give.
>
> "*Let* him have time to see his friends and foes,
> And merry fools to mock at him resort;

Let him have time to mark how slow time goes
In time of sorrow and how swift and short
His time of folly and his time of sport;
   And ever *let* his unrecalling crime
Have time to wail th' abusing of his time."
                    (976–94)

    As with "Happ'ly that name of 'chaste' unhapp'ly set," the central fact about these stanzas is the way their insistently chiastic rhetoricity, drawing attention to itself, appears to determine what they say, as though the entire speech were programmatic explication or duplication of what the poem associates with "let." With chiastic flourishes—"ex-tremes beyond ex-tremity"—Lucrece demands that Time, the "ceaseless lackey to eternity," "with some mischance cross Tarquin in his flight." But the "mischance cross" that Tarquin is supposed to bear is constructed of the same conflicted intersection of contingent destiny and happy sadness as is packed into "Happ'ly"-"unhapp'ly": "Let there bechance him pitiful mischances." In such oblique and yet accented ways, Lucrece's speech, for all its force and fluency, ends up crossing itself, developing the rhetorical "cross" of the cross-coupler in so ostentatious a fashion that the chiastic content of the lines becomes the performative vehicle of their chiastic form, rather than the other way around. Again, for a rhetorically sophisticated Elizabethan reading audience this would define the oratorical "wit" of Lucrece's complaint, a wit that signals a rhetorical self-consciousness thoroughly suffusing and yet still distanced from Lucrece's imprecations. Repeatedly repeating individual words within a syntax that circles round upon itself—"Disdain to him disdained scraps to give," "Let him have time to mark how slow time goes / In time of sorrow and how swift and short / His time of folly and his time of sport," etc.—Lucrece's speech becomes, despite herself or her intentions, the systematic instrument and issue of the chiastic folds on which consistently it turns. Only a reader for whom rhetoric has no force or function could fail to notice this, and it is just such indifference to the effect of the poem's rhetorical effects that regularly produces critical complaints about the poem's declamatory style, its idly extravagant rhetoricity. What we must also note, however, is that such complaints about the poem's excessively rhetorical manner themselves repeat what Tarquin or Lucrece—the rapist and, as we have seen, his rhetorically willing victim—themselves will say about this very topic, as, for example, a few lines later, when Lucrece, tired of her formal railing, proclaims:

Out, idle words, servants to shallow fools,
Unprofitable sounds, weak arbitrators!
Busy yourself in skill-contending schools,
Debate where leisure serves with dull debaters
                    (1016–19)

lines that echo the way Tarquin earlier, when he grew tired of his own rhetorical indecision, resolved upon the rape: "'Why hunt I then for color or excuses? / All orators are dumb when beauty pleadeth . . . / Then childish fear avaunt, debating die!'" (267–74).

A long and familiar history of anti-rhetorical sensibility no doubt lies behind Lucrece's pejorative assessment of "unprofitable sounds," or what she calls a few lines later "this helpless smoke of words," so there is nothing in any way novel about either Lucrece's or Tarquin's stated thoughts about the issue of rhetoric. Neither is it surprising, given the structural symmetry the poem establishes between them, that this expressed concern for solid rhetorical matter as opposed to empty rhetorical manner is something that the rapist and his victim share: Tarquin's vice is consistently presented by the poem as reciprocal inversion and occasion of Lucrece's virtue, and vice versa, so the point of view that either one of them adopts on any topic whatsoever will likely be a version of the point of view adopted by the other. But, again, this is *not* the point of view of the poem itself, or at least this characterization of rhetoric as something "idle" or inexigent is not the point of view of the poem's personified narrator, who, from the first moment that a coded narrative voice enters the poem—i.e., from the moment of "Happ'ly that name of 'chaste' unhapp'ly set"—takes quite a different position with regard to the question of rhetorical effect, explicitly blaming the rape of Lucrece on Collatine's "oratory," and saying outright, as clearly and straightforwardly as possible, to ears willing to hear it, that "by our ears our hearts oft tainted be."

The point is worth stressing because it allows us to take the narrator at his own oratorical word and thereby to recapture a specifically Elizabethan reading experience of the poem's rhetoricity, one that is thereby attuned to, or responsive to, the effect of an author induced by the poem's rhetoricity. In ways that go, so to speak, necessarily without saying, "The Rape of Lucrece" calls out for a reading that attends to the different ways in which the poem's signifiers control its signifieds, to the way the poem's manner, *as* manner, determines its matter. This is a literal, *not* a metaphorical, way of putting things. When an Elizabethan reader reads Lucrece's apostrophe to Time and comes upon its reiterated "lets," he will hear them as performative climax of the way, for Tarquin, "these lets attend the time." But this performance, to the extent a reader registers it, is neither Tarquin's nor Lucrece's doing; it is instead a function of the immanent authorial agency governing the poem's rhetorical production, even though this authorial agency is itself an effect of the way the poem rhetorically unfolds. Similarly, when an Elizabethan reader reads Lucrece's apostrophe to Time and comes upon a couplet like:

> And let mild women to him lose their mildness,
> Wilder to him than tigers in their wildness.

the lines carry literary weight for him in good part because the criss-cross structure of "mild"-"mildness"-"wild"-"wildness" invites him to see how the *M* of "mild," thus cross-coupled with the *W* of "wild," literally enacts the chiastic "fold" of "her lips sweet fold": ⋈.[23] It is this porno-graphic staging of the literal letters in its lines, the way the chiasmus makes erotic *theater* of the poem's textuality, that gives the couplet its rhetorical spirit, at the same time as this raises such literal inversion to the level of a theme. But neither Tarquin nor Lucrece can ever be the authors of these letters that perform them, and so it is the very crossing of the letters that calls forth the figure of an author who can serve as the inscribing agent of the way the letters cross.

Taken by itself, this last example, the anacreontic *MW*, may at first sight seem a trivial example of what in the poem are more urgent or more telling thematic matters, but I want now to argue that the example does more than simply illustrate or exemplify how, as I said earlier, the characteristically Shakespearean determines the formation, on the one hand, of the subjectivity of the historical Shakespeare—Shakespeare, the person—and, on the other, the formation of Shakespeare's literary subjectivity effects, i.e., the impression of psychologistic person that we associate with some, though by no means all, of Shakespeare's fictional characters. To see why this should be the case, however, it is necessary, first, to understand in what way this chiastically acrostic *MW* collation is, in fact, characteristically Shakespearean, second, how, as such, it relates both to Shakespeare's person and to the subjectivity effects sometimes exerted by Shakespearean literary personae.

To begin with, simply as a matter of statistical frequency, we can again say, as with the red-white-purple motif, that this is something distinctively Shakespearean, for there are six such prominently chiastic typographic configurations of *MW* in "The Rape of Lucrece." Even by the measure of Elizabethan poetry, where such letter play is in fact rather common, this seems a striking, if not inordinate, number. Moreover, all six examples are not only thematically suggestive in themselves, but they also tend to form a coherent ensemble of cross-referencing associations. In the first instance, the narrator explains that Lucrece cannot "read the subtle shining secrecies/Writ in the glassy margents of such books" (i.e., Tarquin's eyes) and, in addition:

> Nor could she *m*oralize his *w*anton sight,
> *M*ore than his eyes *w*ere open'd to the light.
> (104–5)

The second example descibes what is erotic about Lucrece's hair:

> Her hair like golden thread play'd with her breath—
> O *m*odest *w*antons, *w*anton *m*odesty.
> (400–401)

In the third example Tarquin explains to Lucrece that:

> Thy beauty hath ensnared thee to this night,
> Where thou *w*ith patience must my *w*ill abide—
> *M*y *w*ill that *m*arks thee for *m*y earth's delight.
>
> (485–87)

In the fourth example Lucrece explains how she will kill herself to set a good example:

> How Tarquin must be us'd, read it in me:
>   *M*yself thy friend *w*ill kill *m*yself thy foe
>   And for *m*y sake serve thou false Tarquin so.
>
> This brief abridgement of *m*y *w*ill I make.
>
> (1195–98)

I have already cited the fifth example:

> And let *m*ild *w*omen to him lose their *m*ildness,
> *W*ilder to him than tigers in their *w*ildness.
>
> (978–79)

In the sixth example, the narrator explains the reason for Lucrece's tears, and why she is not "author" of her "ill":

> For *m*en have *m*arble, *w*omen *w*axen *m*inds,
> And therefore are they formed as *m*arble *w*ill,
> The weak oppress'd, th' impression of strange kinds
> Is form'd in them by force, by fraud, or skill,
> Then call them not the authors of their ill.
>
> (1240–44)

Taking these examples, somewhat artificially, together, we can say the criss-cross *MW* inversion, when it appears in "The Rape of Lucrece," seems to collate themes of reading and of marking with images of things that are either violent or erotic (it would be possible to look at these examples in more detail and discuss the way they relate to and support larger themes and images that run throughout the poem). At the same time, however, we can also note—even though it is very unlikely that a reader would in fact notice this as he reads through the poem—that either in or in a field adjacent to almost all the examples, and again in a way that seems statistically significant, there is a remarkably consistent remarking or foregrounding, either through repetition or through word play, of the word "will."[24]

Recognizing this, and recognizing also at the same time the bizarre particularity and apparent reductiveness of the claim, I want now to suggest that the chiastic typographic inversion of these letters, *MW*, is for Shakespeare a characteristic—indeed, *the* characteristic—indication of his own name, "Will," i.e., that it is a version, literally at the level of the letter, of the way earlier we saw "will" acquire a peculiar place and charge through its framed repetition in between the chiastic coordination of "will's obtaining" and "will resolving," a repetition or self-citation corresponding to the way that "chaste," in the first and second stanzas of the poem, is raised into "that name of 'chaste'" when it appears within the chiasmus of "happ'ly"-"unhapp'ly." I propose, therefore, that 𝕄, as formal and performative index of an internal revolving that turns turning or "revolving" inside out, possesses for Shakespeare the same nominalizing function; that it functions as a signature—like the proper-name determinative in Egyptian hiero-glyphs—that for Shakespeare, first, raises the ordinary word "will" into the proper name "Will," and, second, thereby "set[s]/This bateless edge on his keen appetite." Consciously or unconsciously, by happenstance chance or by designed destiny, for good or for bad—i.e., "Happ'ly"-"unhapp'ly"—*MW*, when it happens these letters or characters are chiastically staged in Shakespeare's texts, stand out for Shakespeare as sign of his own name, possessing the same kind of self-remarking function as is conveyed or gestured at by Shakespeare when he writes, on the last page of his will, "By me, *William Shakespeare*"—and we can now add that on the second page he shortens this to "*Willm Shakspere*," and that elsewhere, even shorter, in what we can call, using Lucrece's phrase, a "brief abridgment of my will," he writes yet more simply "*Wm Shakspē*."[25]

This is why I said before that by the "characteristically Shakespearean" I meant to refer to that which literally marks out Shakespeare, not his name but its signature. And I want now to add that this remarking of his own name, as a signature effect, possesses for Shakespeare—for Shakespeare, the person, the historical subject—a strictly circumscribed and circumscribing subjectifying func-tion. Specifically, I propose that the criss-cross conjunction of the two letters that mark the beginning and end of Shakespeare's name—"WilliaM"—*because* they serve as signature of Shakespeare's name, determine the experience of Shake-spearean subjectivity as psychological equivalent of the chiastically extracted "superfluous Moity," i.e., that Shakespeare's sense of his own bio-graphicized person is for him the subjective objectification of what stands between or, rather, ex-ists between the cross-coupling boundaries of a textualized beginning without beginning and an eroticized end without end. Yet more specifically, I propose that the cross-coupling orthographics of *MW*, when these two folded letters are thus folded over on each other, spell out for Shakespeare a structure of subjective constitution organized by the three post-epideictic literary features to which I earlier referred: 1) the evocation of a fallen language opposed to clear vision, 2) a stressedly chiastic tropic figurality, 3) the imagination of a material phenome-nality folded over on itself. In turn, I want also to propose that this explains why Shakespeare's literary characters, when it happens they give off a strong subjec-tivity effect, both evidence and are conditioned by a particular Shakespearean erotics and a particular Shakespearean sense of space and time. For example, I

say Shakespeare's person is itself marked out, and thereby subjectively constituted, by the literal chiasmus of *MW*:

$$\text{"Will"} \leftarrow \bowtie$$

and, moreover, that this touch of the personally Shakespearean latently informs
the formal disposition of:

> For *men* have *marble, women waxen minds,*
> And therefore are they formed as *marble will.*

Assuming the *MW* formation, as it is here deployed, effectively evokes the erotic
logic of chiastically conjoined man and woman that runs throughout "The Rape
of Lucrece"—as when Tarquin and Lucrece come disjunctively and "shamefully"
together in "Entombs her outcry in her lips sweet fold"—we can understand how
it happens that "The Rape of Lucrece," as do all of Shakespeare's literary writings,
recognizes the difference between the two sexes—as this difference emerges in
their violent, "bifold," and cross-coupling copulation—at the same time as it attributes subjectivity only to the "will" of man:[26]

$$\text{"Will"} \leftarrow \bowtie \frac{\text{(en)}}{\text{(omen)}}$$

Is it possible so much can come of the writing of letters? The question returns
us to the unfolding action of "The Rape of Lucrece," for, only a few stanzas after
the "waxen minds"-"marble will" example, Lucrece herself sits down to write a
letter, calling out for "'paper, ink, and pen'":

> "Bid thou be ready, by and by, to bear
> A letter to my lord, my love, my dear.
>   Bid him with speed prepare to carry it,
>   The cause craves haste, and it will soon be writ."
>   (1289–95)

The writing of this letter marks the end of Lucrece's formal lamentation, when
she stops complaining about the rape and begins to do something about it:
namely, informing her husband of what has come to pass. But, though "the cause
craves haste, and it will soon be writ," the writing of her letter is immediately
postponed, and this because, as she sits down to write, Lucrece's "wit" and "will"
engage in a protracted battle:

> Her maid is gone, and she prepares to write,
> First hovering o'er the paper with her quill.
> Conceit and grief an eager combat fight,
> What wit sets down is blotted straight with will;
> This is too curious-good, this blunt and ill:

> Much like a press of people at a door,
> Throng her inventions, which shall go before.
> (1296–1302)

With the fight they stage between "conceit and grief," these lines more than call up, they also thematize, all the issues of plain matter versus ornate manner, pro and con, that the hyperrhetorical diction of "The Rape of Lucrece" regularly elicits from its critics. But the poem does not evoke what is probably the most tired cliché of Renaissance poetics so as to take a stand, one way or the other, on the matter of matter versus manner but, instead, so as to focus on the way the writing of Lucrece's letter establishes within Lucrece an indecisive, though still "eager," fight between her "wit" and "will": "Hovering o'er the paper with her quill. / Conceit and grief an eager combat fight, / What wit sets down is blotted straight with will." Like the rape that comes of its obstruction, the writing of Lucrece's letter is thus presented as specific issue of Lucrece's writing block; it is a writing "let" that writes her "letter," spotting it with "blots" of "will."[27] If it seems too much to say that Shakespeare's own "Will" here marks his "wit," it remains the case that the poem here describes a scene of writing involving the same kind of heavy-handedly indeterminate, internal, rhetorical quarrel that earlier, just *because* it was something indeterminate, determined Tarquin, when he was "crossed" between "foul hope" and "fond despair," to embark upon the rape: Lucrece's "will," if not Shakespeare's, is figured through the same, specifically rhetorical, figure of ongoing indeterminacy that earlier prefigured Tarquin's "will," as well as its rapacity, in terms of a chiastic excess in "between her chamber and his will." So too, the liquid blot that now spills out of Lucrece's "will"—in the course of "eager combat," crossing out her "wit"—is no less undetermined than was the "superfluous Moity" of the Dedication or than was the little drop of Tarquin's lust that sought "to stain the ocean of thy blood"; it marks Lucrece's "wit" just as Tarquin put his willful mark upon Lucrece: "'Where thou with patience must my will abide—/ My will that marks thee for my earth's delight.'" And so too does Lucrece's letter, as a whole, bear the same distinctive willful mark. Because Lucrece now writes her letter to Collatine in the same chiastic way that Tarquin earlier raped Lucrece, because the writing of the letter is materially precipitated by the "let" that is its motive, her letter too turns out to bear the characteristic wrinkle of "her lips sweet fold":

> Here folds she up the tenure of her woe,
> Her certain sorrow writ uncertainly.
> By this short schedule Collatine may know
> Her grief, but not her grief's true quality.
> She dares not thereof make discovery,
>   Lest he should hold it her own gross abuse,
>   Ere she with blood had stain'd her stain'd excuse.
> (1310–16)

For the moment, it is true, folding up the letter, "her certain sorrow writ uncertainly," Lucrece postpones a full report; she keeps her secret to herself, choosing not to put her rape directly into words until her suicide will vouchsafe the truth of what she has to say. Her blood itself must "stain her stain'd excuse," and so, pending the final staining of her stain or the final blotting of her blot, we await the moment when Lucrece's bloody, visible matter will confirm her merely verbal manner:

> To shun this blot, she would not blot the letter
> With words till action might become them better.

> To see sad sights moves more than hear them told,
> For then the eye interprets to the ear
> The heavy motion that it doth behold,
> When every part a part of woe doth bear.
> 'Tis but a part of sorrow that we hear.
>> Deep sounds make lesser noise than shallow fords,
>> And sorrow ebbs, being blown with the wind of words.
>> (1322–30)

But this postponement—lest "sorrow ebb, being blown with the wind of words"— itself repeats the poem's already fully elaborated structure of rapacious delay, i.e., the way the poem turns watery and windy deferral into the experience of rape, as when Tarquin's "uncontrolled tide / Turns not, but swells the higher by this let," or as when "The doors, the wind, the glove that did delay him, / He takes for accidental things of trial; / Or as those bars which stop the hourly dial, / Who with a ling'ring stay his course doth let" (323–28). Accordingly, and not only etymologically (*post-ponere*), it seems to be precisely this temporal postponement—while the poem looks forward to a future when "the eye interprets to the ear"—that puts Lucrece's letter in the "post":

> Her letter now is seal'd, and on it writ,
> "At Ardea to my lord with more than haste."
> The post attends and she delivers it.
> (1331–33)

As conclusion to Lucrece's static, even tedious, lamentations, the dispatching of this letter amounts to a dramatic and decisive gesture. However "uncertainly" Lucrece now writes her "certain sorrow," however delayed her will to write the letter—"it will soon be writ"—the delivery of her letter to the "post" marks a turning point in the unfolding action of the poem: once posted, her letter bears the promise of her rape's eventual revenge. For this very reason, however, *as a turning point*, the posting of Lucrece's letter also returns us to the beginning of the poem and thereby to the way what I have called the characteristically Shakespearean determines the formation of a specifically Shakespearean subjectivity effect. We have seen that "The Rape of Lucrece" begins with Tarquin rushing "From the besieged Ardea all in post," and we have also seen that the poem makes elaborate issue of the fact that Tarquin sets out on this journey because "Collatine unwisely did not let / To praise the clear unmatched red and white." Quite literally—we can say, quite "characteristically"—according to the first two stanzas of the poem, it is Collatine's "let" that puts Tarquin "all in post," this "posting" being the unintended consequence of Collatine having praised Lucrece's "chastity." Given the postal or epistolic motif the poem now introduces, as well as the variety of heavy-handed correspondences the poem has hitherto established between the "let" and rape, we can say "The Rape of Lucrece," as it now rhetorically unfolds, here retroactively directs its reader to conceive of Tarquin, in his first "posting" movement, as a letter initially dispatched by Collatine—more precisely, by Collatine's "let"—to his own address: "From the besieged Ardea all in post" "to Collatium." Correspondingly, when Lucrece now explicitly addresses her letter to Collatine—"'At Ardea to my lord with more than haste.' / The post attends and she delivers it"—the poem seems to make a point of relaying Collatine's letter back to where it came from, back to Collatine, by return "post." Taking these two movements together—Tarquin's "post" and its reversed repetition by Lucrece's "post"—we can say the poem looks forward to a moment in which Collatine will eventually receive a version of the very letter he himself initially had posted. But our reading of the poem already tells us in advance that the meaning of this letter is inverted, not repeated nor reversed, in the course of its transmission, since the letter that Lucrece now writes will once again assert Lucrece's "chastity" but in the unexpected, inverse form of rape.

This complicating structure of repetition, reversal, and inversion—which works to add a new corroborating wrinkle to Collatine's original praise of Lucrece's "clear unmatched red and white"—explains why the "posting" of Lucrece's letter not only marks a turning point in the poem but one that will turn out, as such, to be conclusive. As repetition of Tarquin's "post," Lucrece's epistolic gesture first serves to reverse the directed movement of the poem, returning Collatine's "let" and letter to their original author. But this reversal thereby serves to complete, *by* inflectively inverting, the poem's directed movement, folding Tarquin's "post" back upon itself so that Collatine's first "let" and "letter," in this way ex-plicated and re-turned to sender, concludes a comprehensive circuit "From the besieged Ardea" "to Collatium," and then back again, "'At Ardea to my lord with more than haste'" (fig. 2).

It is, of course, a merely formal circuit—first one "post," Tarquin's, and then, now, with Lucrece's letter, another—thus traced out by "a certain sorrow writ uncertainly." But the complete trajectory of the letter—a narrative trajectory composed, like the literal formation of chiastic *MW*, of two folded letters folded over on each other—turns out in "The Rape of Lucrece" to enforce a precise literary consequence. For the only anthropomorphic figure in the poem who pos-

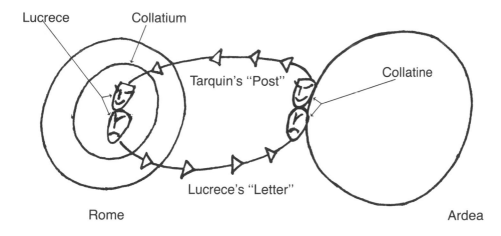

FIGURE 2.

sesses, at least a little, some of the characteristic density, textured internality, and affective pathos we associate with Shakespeare's fully developed psychologized characters is neither Tarquin nor Lucrece—both of whom seem, throughout the poem, both tonally and structurally, like abstract, allegorical versions of each other—but, instead, Lucrece's husband, Collatine, whom the poem at its beginning describes as author of the rape—because he is the "orator" and "publisher/ of that rich jewel" (30–34)—and to whom at its conclusion the poem will turn its full attention when Collatine at last receives his "let" and "letter" back by postponed "post." Anticipating this conclusion, as well as the way in which Collatine is transformed into a recognizably Shakespearean literary character when his letter finally arrives at what is both its first and final destination, I propose that the constellation of the "let," the "letter," and the "post," as this is developed in "The Rape of Lucrece," shows us in simple, reductive, skeletal form how Shakespeare conceives the formation of literary subjectivity in general, so that the poem's particular elaboration of a postal circuit whereby Collatine becomes a sender who receives his message back in an inverted form (inverted by the movement of re-turning or re-versing repetition) describes the way in which *all* Shakespeare's strong literary characters acquire their specifically psychologistic literary power.

It takes time, however, for a letter, even one transmitted "with more than haste," to reach its destination, and so, before turning to the end of the poem and to a discussion of Collatine, it is necessary to pause, as does "The Rape of Lucrece," to consider what takes place within the temporal interval separating the letter's dispatch and its delivery. This brings us, following the poem's expository development, to the long section the poem now devotes to a description of a "skillful painting" that depicts illustrative scenes from the *Iliad*. This ekphrastic digression, which is of course a convention of Complaint poems, is explicitly presented as that which passes "time" while Lucrece's messenger and message enact a movement of "return":

> But long she thinks 'til he return again,
> And yet the duteous vassal scarce is gone;
> The weary time she cannot entertain.
> (1359–61)

At the same "weary time," however, while her letter follows out the circle of its circuit, it is as something understood as novel that Lucrece, "Pausing for means to mourn some newer way" (1365), turns to examine the visual image of her own complaint:

> At last she calls to mind where hangs a piece
> Of skillful painting made for Priam's Troy,
> Before the which is drawn the power of Greece,
> For Helen's rape the city to destroy.
> (1366–69)

In some obvious ways, the Homeric story, because it collates the military siege of Troy with the rape of Helen, fits Lucrece's situation to a T. In other ways, equally obvious, the Homeric story is to some extent ill chosen, since for Shakespeare, if not for Homer, it is the rape of "strumpet" Helen—as Lucrece soon calls her: "show me the strumpet that began this stir" (1471)—that occasions the siege, rather than, as happens with the chaste Lucrece, the other way around.[28] In either case, however, appropriate or not, the poem's citation of the Homeric story gives an exemplary dimension to Lucrece's situation, making it another instance of the primal "rape" (or cuckolding) with which our literary tradition historically begins, another version of the same old story. So too, because "Beauty itself doth of itself persuade / The eyes of men without an orator," or because "to see sad sights moves more than hear them told," the "skillful painting" promises to function as powerful eye-witness to Lucrece's plight. And indeed, it is for just this reason, because "the eye interprets to the ear," that the poem now thematically emphasizes the specifically visual modality of the "skillful painting," not just because the painting, as a painting, is something to be seen, but because, for the most part, what the "skillful painting" movingly depicts is eyes, and looks, and gazes, as though the painting were primarily concerned, by focusing on such images *of* vision, to illustrate the visual itself. Consider, to take just a few examples, the painted details mentioned in the first two stanzas of the narrator's description:

> A thousand lamentable objects there,
> In scorn of nature, art gave liveless life:
> Many a dry drop seem'd a weeping tear,
> Shed for the slaught'red husband by the wife;

> The red blood reek'd, to show the painter's strife
> And dying eyes gleam'd forth their ashy lights,
> Like dying coals burnt out in tedious nights.
>
> There might you see the laboring pioner
> Begrim'd with sweat, and smeared all with dust,
> And from the tow'rs of Troy there would appear
> The very eyes of men through loop-holes thrust,
> Gazing upon the Greeks with little lust.
> Such sweet observance in this work was had,
> That one might see those far-off eyes look sad.
>   (1373–86)

Perhaps yet more emphatic, we are told a stanza later that:

> In Ajax and Ulysses, O what art
> Of physiognomy might one behold!
> The face of either cipher'd either's heart,
> Their face their manners most expressly told:
> In Ajax's eyes blunt rage and rigor roll'd,
> But the mild glance that sly Ulysses lent
> Showed deep regard and smiling government.
>   (1394–1400)

Moreover, even when the painting paints the act of speaking, it does so by making language into something visual, into something more or less directed to the eye, as when, a stanza later, it illustrates "Nestor's golden words" (1420):

> There might you see grave Nestor stand,
> As 'twere encouraging the Greeks to fight,
> Making such sober action with his hand,
> That it beguil'd attention, charm'd the sight.
>   (1401–4)

At stake in all this, of course, or what is being presupposed throughout, is the perennial aesthetic of the "speaking picture," the idea, as well as the ideal, of a visual verisimilitude, a specular mimetics, so effective and affective as to erase the difference between representation and that which representation represents. And this familiar visionary aesthetic, an aesthetic of transparent imitation, of presentational representation—which is traditionally applied to all the referential arts, not just to painting, as in the doctrine of *ut pictura poesis*—in turn entails or presupposes, as the narrator now points out, an equally perennial and equally visionary semiotics, one whereby a signifier, conceived as something visually iconic, is so fixedly and unequivocally related to its signified that by itself it can present its meaning or its referent to the "eye of mind":

> For much imaginary work was there,
> Conceit deceitful, so compact, so kind,

That for Achilles' image stood his spear,
Grip'd in an armed hand, himself behind
Was left unseen, save to the eye of mind:
A hand a foot, a face, a leg, a head
Stood for the whole to be imagined.

(1422–28)[29]

This eloquent language of the "speaking picture," because it can "persuade /
The eyes of men without an orator," is what powers Lucrece's empathetic
response to the "skillful painting," whether that response is sympathetic, as when
with pity she beholds the look of Hecuba "Staring on Priam's wounds with her
eyes" (1448), or antipathetic, as when she looks disdainfully at Helen's lascivious
eye: "Thy eye kindled the fire that burneth here, / And here in Troy, for trespass
of thine eye, / The sire, the son, the dame, and daughter die" (1475–77). And the
same essentially visionary motives and motifs also govern Lucrece's mouth, such
that even what Lucrece will say about the painting is but the evoked image of the
way the painting looks: "Here feelingly she weeps Troy's painted woes . . . / To
pencill'd pensiveness and color'd sorrow; / She lends them words, and she their
looks doth borrow" (1492–98).

And yet, despite the way the poem here presupposes and calls forth the entire
system of specular ideality as this is conventionally deployed in the Renaissance,
despite the power of the painting to address itself directly to "the eye of mind,"
the poem's ekphrastic description seems to stress the ideal visuality of the painting
only for the purpose of immediately belying it, and this it does by pointing to the
one thing in the Homeric story that the painting, precisely because it is an artifact
of vision, cannot truly represent. Lucrece now "throws her eyes about the
painting round, / . . . [and] At last she sees a wretched image bound, / That piteous
looks to Phrygian shepherds lent" (1499–1501). This "wretched image" is the
figure of Sinon, the betrayer of Troy, and he is pictured through the same check-
ered combination of red and white with which from its beginning the poem consistently imagines the chiastic end of what is visually pure:

In him the painter labor'd with his skill
To hide deceit, and give the harmless show
An humble gait, calm looks, eyes wailing still,
A brow unbent, that seem'd to welcome woe,
Cheeks neither red nor pale, but mingled so
That blushing red no guilty instance gave,
Nor ashy pale the fear that false hearts have.

(1506–12)

Unlike Ulysses and Ajax, whose "face their manners most expressly told," Sinon's
face, specifically, the "mingled" colors of his cheeks, disguises what he is, and this

is something very different from the way, before, a single part "Stood for the whole to be imagined." "Neither red nor pale," but, rather, "mingled," Sinon's cheeks do not betray the telltale blush of guilty red nor "ashy pale" of fearful white, and so his cheeks become demonstrative icon of the failure of visionary iconography, an image of the clouding of the clarity of vision. Sinon's very appearance, therefore, his "mingled" look, displays a blind spot in "imaginary work," showing forth an image of the way a visual appearance fails to be, or to stand for, the meaning of the way it looks. And the poem, returning to its initial claim that "by our ears our hearts oft tainted be," explains this disruption or distortion of specular transparency by seeing it as illustration of the lying "words" of "perjur'd Sinon":

> The well-skill'd workman this mild image drew
> For perjur'd Sinon, whose enchanting story
> The credulous old Priam after slew;
> Whose words like wildfire burnt the shining glory
> Of rich-built Ilion, that the skies were sorry,
>   And little stars shot from their fixed places,
>   When their glass fell wherein they view'd their faces.
>   (1520–26)[30]

There is something momentous, both thematically and tonally, about the way this stanza calls up the loss of everything the English Renaissance self-servingly identifies with the bright light of Troy, something genuinely epic, not mock epic, in the stanza's elegiac retrospection. But the stanza also carefully repeats the terms with which, at its beginning, in the second stanza, the poem accounts for the loss of Collatine's ideal vision, "the clear unmatched red and white." Sinon's "words" spark a "wildfire" that burns "the shining glory of rich-built Ilion" just as Collatine's "praise" inspired Tarquin's "lightless fire." So too, the "little stars shot from their fixed places, / When their glass fell wherein they view'd their faces" fulfill the fall of Collatine's original "delight," which is imagined in the second stanza as a "sky" "Where mortal stars as bright as heaven's beauties, / With pure aspects did him peculiar duties." These repetitions work both to memorialize and to generalize the way in which "Collatine unwisely did not let / To praise the clear unmatched red and white"; they make the burning of "the shining glory of rich-built Ilion" into the mythic precursor of the loss of Collatine's "delight," but they do so at the cost of identifying the lying "words" of "perjur'd Sinon" with Collatine's equally catastrophic "praise," as though it were the very act of speaking, true or false, that spells an end to the ideality of vision.

What is remarkable about all this—especially if we remember that ekphrasis is a literary device designed to put the visual into words—is that the poem, now, at the conclusion of its description of the picture, makes explicit thematic issue of this displacement of ideal vision by language, so that Lucrece herself, gazing on the picture's portrait of Sinon, will now observe the structural limits of the "skillful painting":

> This picture she advisedly perus'd,
> And chid the painter for his wondrous skill,
> Saying, some shape in Sinon's was abus'd:
> So fair a form lodg'd not a mind so ill.
> And still on him she gaz'd, and gazing still,
> Such signs of truth in his plain face she spied,
> That she concludes the picture was belied.
> (1527–33)

It is as though the long digression of the ekphrasis had been developed only so as to articulate this paradox: that the picture, not despite but because of its "wondrous skill," is "belied" by its very honesty, that the "skillful painting," because it is composed of truthful images, "signs of truth," cannot represent the spoken lies of Sinon. Moreover, having formulated the theme, the poem now strives to put this paradoxical moral yet more literally into words, so that Lucrece's own speaking—remarked as such, cited as something verbal rather than visual, of the "tongue" and not the eye—now mimics and performs the way in which the "lurking" "look" of vision is revealed by a specifically linguistic and, therefore, re-visionary "turn."

> "It cannot be," quoth she, "that so much guile"
> She would have said, "can lurk in such a look";
> But Tarquin's shape came in her mind the while,
> And from her tongue "can lurk" from "cannot" took:
> "It cannot be," she in that sense forsook,
> And turn'd it thus, "It cannot be, I find,
> But such a face should bear a wicked mind.
> (1534–40)

In the context of the unfolding action of the poem, this ekphrastic movement, from "imaginary work" to "the picture was belied," from the imagination of true vision (the "skillful painting") to the performance of equivocating language (she "turn'd it thus"), defines what goes on in the time, both narrative and thematic, it takes for Lucrece's letter to reach its destination: "Thus ebbs and flows the current of her sorrow,/And time doth weary time with her complaining" (1569–70). Accordingly, since this is what enables the "return" of "post," it seems all the more important that when Lucrece's letter is now finally delivered, i.e., when "the mindful messenger, come back,/Brings home his lord and other company" (1583–84), this same imagery of time, along with everything the poem has here-tofore associated with it, is reapplied to Collatine in what are increasingly explicit ways. This is what I want to look at now—the ways in which, in the final section of the poem, time takes place in Collatine—for this is how the poem builds up to and arrives at what is structured as its strong, subjectifying climax.

After the ekphrasis, when Collatine has returned to Collatium, Lucrece begins to tell her story, though she begins and will continue its narration through a process of delay: "Three times with sighs she gives her sorrow fire, / Ere once she can discharge one word of woe" (1604–5). Drawing out the story, through a series of deferments that heighten its suspense, Lucrece first reports the fact of her rape but does not reveal her rapist's name. Collatine's response to this first segment of Lucrece's story is carefully described:

> But wretched as he is he strives in vain,
> What he breathes out, his breath drinks up again.
>
> As through an arch the violent roaring tide
> Outruns the eye that doth behold his haste,
> Yet in the eddy boundeth in his pride
> Back to the strait that forc'd him on so fast
> (In rage sent out, recall'd in rage, being past),
>   Even so his sighs, his sorrows, make a saw,
>   To push grief on, and back the same grief draw.
>   (1665–73)

It is evident the poem here makes a point of importing into Collatine the imagery of eddying wind and tidal water with which it not only imagines the rape—"'my uncontrolled tide, / Turns not, but swells the higher by this let'"—but so too the promise of the rape's final revelation, as when Lucrece decided "she would not blot the letter / With words till action might become them better". "Deep sounds make lesser noise than shallow fords, / And sorrow ebbs, being blown with the wind of words." Yet more precisely, as though the stanza were describing how it feels to be subjected to chiasmus, this back and forth movement, of wind and water, is imagined as a "saw," made up, we can suppose, of little x's or crosses, that carves a groove in Collatine while with his grieving sighs he draws it back and forth across himself.[31] This imagery, along with the whole thrust of the narrative, serves to focus attention on Collatine; we await his response to the conclusion of Lucrece's story, which should occur, we have been promised, when Lucrece reveals her rapist's name. Once again, however, there is another moment of delay, while Lucrece extracts from the assembled company a promise of revenge:

> "But ere I name him, you fair lords," quoth she
> (Speaking to those that came with Collatine),
> "Shall plight your honorable faiths to me
>   With swift pursuit to venge this wrong of mine."
>   (1688–91)

And then, a few stanzas later, in what would seem to be the climax of the story:

> Here with a sigh as if her heart would break,
> She throws forth Tarquin's name: "He, he," she says,
> But more than "he" her poor tongue could not speak,
> Till after many accents and delays,
> Untimely breathings, sick and short assays,
>   She utters this, "He, he, fair lords, 'tis he,
>   That guides this hand to give this wound to me."
>
> Even here she sheathes in her harmless breast
> A harmful knife, that thence her soul unsheathed.
>   (1716–24)

What is surprising about this, of course, and specifically ante-climactic, is that—despite the traditional version of the Lucrece story, and despite what is announced in the poem's Argument: "She, first taking an oath of them for her revenge, revealed the actor, and the whole manner of his dealing, and withal suddenly stabbed herself"—Lucrece here fails to name her rapist. The poem explicitly insists upon the fact that Lucrece does not "throw forth Tarquin's name," but throws out, instead, as prologue to her suicide, this series of anony-myzing, deictic "'he'"s: "But more than 'he' her poor tongue could not speak." Again, therefore, we are obliged to await the naming of Tarquin, the straightfor-ward and outspoken speaking of his name, which, if ever it occurs, will function as conclusion to the theme of naming introduced at what the poem at its begin-ning stipulates *as* its beginning: when, again, "Happ'ly that name of 'chaste' unhapp'ly set / This bateless edge on his keen appetite; / When Collatine unwisely did not let / To praise the clear unmatched red and white."

The poem will not let Tarquin's name remain anonymous—Collatine himself will pronounce it in a moment—but before the name is mentioned it is significant that the poem allows itself two further moments of delay. First, there is the matter of Lucrece's death, which is described thus:

> And from the purple fountain Brutus drew
>   The murd'rous knife, and as it left the place,
>   Her blood, in poor revenge, held it in chase.
>
> And bubbling from her breast, it doth divide
> In two slow rivers, that the crimson blood
> Circles her body in on every side.
>   (1734–39)

As at the end of "Venus and Adonis," where Adonis is transformed into "A purple flow'r, check'red with white," the poem here resolves the red-white color scheme through which its vision has consistently been filtered by imagining a "purple," like the chiastically colored cheeks of "perjur'd Sinon," which is the poem's iconic image of what puts an end to vision. In addition, this "purple" manifests its own material or phenomenal formation, a "divided" flowing of "two slow rivers" that spill out from the inside of Lucrece so as to surround her on the outside with a wrinkled or a folded "circle" in whose circuit Lucrece figures as both source and center. If we try to picture this complicated image of tangential circumscription, it looks something like the way we draw a heart (fig. 3).

FIGURE 3.

Surrounded, therefore, by her liquid inside, encircled by her broken heart, Lucrece becomes, at the moment of her dying, the fixed and permanent objectification of an overflowing spurt, the fleshed out incarnation of the etymological fluidity of the Dedication's "superfluous Moity." In the erotic terms developed by the poem, she embodies Tarquin's inside-outside movement when he "posts" from Ardea to Collatium for the purpose of her rape, and she also replicates the "fold" with which her two lips came together at the moment of her rape: "Entombs her out-cry in her lips sweet fold." At the same time, as she promised when she folded up her letter, her "crimson blood," as it "circles her body in on every side," now "stains her stain'd excuse."

The second moment of delay is equally recapitulatory and equally conclusive. Seeing his daughter dead upon the ground, Lucrece's father starts to speak his own memorial lament:

> "Daughter, dear daughter," old Lucretius cries,
> "That life was mine which thou hast here deprived.
> If in the child the father's image lies,
> Where shall I live now Lucrece is unlived?

Thou wast not to this end from me derived.
　　If children pre-decease progenitors,
　　　We are their offspring, and they none of ours.

"Poor broken glass, I often did behold
　In thy sweet semblance my old age new born,
　But now that fair fresh mirror, dim and old
　Shows me a bare-bon'd death by time outworn.
　O, from thy cheeks my image thou hast torn,
　　And shiver'd all the beauty of my glass,
　　　That I no more can see what once I was!

"O Time, cease thou thy course and last no longer,
　If they surcease to be that should survive."
　　　　　　　　　　　　　　　(1751–66)

Again the poem foregrounds chiasmus—e.g., "'If children pre-decease pro-genitors'"—and again the poem unfolds the trope so as to formulate the breaking both of ideal vision—"'Poor broken glass'"—and of the mimetic logic of succes-sive, imitating repetition: "'I often did behold / In thy sweet semblance my old age new born, / But now that fair fresh mirror, dim and old / Shows me a bare-bon'd death by time outworn.'" In personal terms, the dead Lucrece, enveloped by her "wat'-ry rigol [i.e., a watery 'ring']" (1745), displays to her father his dis-tance from his ideal image of himself; like father, like daughter, her "'broken glass'" reflects the breaking, or the having-been-broken, of his specular identity: "'O, from thy cheeks my image thou hast torn, / And shiver'd all the beauty of my glass, / That I no more can see what once I was!'" And this in turn determines for Lucrece's father an infinite "old age," since Time itself, "'by time outworn,'" is now supposed to be chiastically suspended between the death of life and life of death: "'O Time, cease thou thy course and last no longer, / If they sur-cease to be that should survive.'"

These two final moments of delay, therefore—Lucrece's death, her father's lament—together recapitulate the themes, motifs, and movements—the mixed-up red and white, the loss of ideal vision, the inside-outside in-betweenness—that control the exposition of "The Rape of Lucrece" from its beginning, from "From the besieged Ardea all in post." Taken together, *as* moments of delay, they now potentiate the poem's climax, the naming of Tarquin by Collatine. First (and the gesture repeats the way Venus purples her face by kissing Adonis' castration—"With this she falleth in the place she stood, / And stains her face with his con-gealed blood"; 1121–22), Collatine awakes and "mingles" his own cheeks:

By this starts Collatine, as from a dream,
And bids Lucretius give his sorrow place,

And then in key-cold Lucrece' bleeding stream
He falls, and bathes the pale fear in his face.
(1772–75)

And then, no longer mute, Collatine "at last" pronounces Tarquin's name:

The deep vexation of his inward soul
Hath serv'd a dumb arrest upon his tongue,
Who mad that sorrow should his use control,
Or keep him from heart-easing words so long,
Begins to talk, but through his lips do throng
   Weak words, so thick come in his poor heart's aid,
   That no man could distinguish what he said.

Yet sometime "Tarquin" was pronounced plain,
But through his teeth, as if the name he tore.
This windy tempest, till it blow up rain,
Held back his sorrow's tide, to make it more.
At last it rains, and busy winds give o'er.
(1779–90)

This is how the poem conceives the way that Collatine "begins to talk," stressing the at once climactic and inaugural momentum through which speech becomes articulate—"Yet sometime 'Tarquin' was pronounced plain"—as it rises out of babble, "Weak words . . . That no man could distinguish." It is a speaking whose pronouncing is specifically provoked, like the rape, by the logic of the "let," so that what precipitates the "raining" of "the name" is the way the "windy tempest" "Held back his sorrow's tide, to make it more." Accordingly, the swelling force of pent-up sorrow now spills forth as the ejaculation of a name—"At last it rains, and busy winds give o'er"—and thereby introduces into Collatine the liquid temporality of rape: erotic Time (*tempus*) takes place within him when the "windy tempest" (*tempestas*) overflows.[32] Rather systematically, therefore, the end of the poem, focusing on the person of Collatine, returns to its beginning with a climactic but specifically revisionary recapitulation. When he "tears" the name between his teeth, Collatine repeats the way "Happ'ly that name of 'chaste' unhapp'ly set / This bateless edge on his keen appetite," but now "that name of 'chaste'" has been transformed into the name of "'Tarquin.'" This is why I said before that there is something final or conclusive in the way that Collatine receives the letter he initially transmits—Tarquin's "post"—in the inverted form of Lucrece's folded "letter." With the "pale fear" of his face bathed in Lucrece's "bleeding stream," Collatine himself becomes the unintended consequence of the way he "did not let / To praise the clear unmatched red and white," just as he becomes the "post" by means of which "Lust-breath'd Tarquin leaves the Roman host." And this "let," because it is now finally delivered, is what situates in Collatine the tidal overflow of a tendentious but yet retrospective time whose passing only comes to pass precisely at or as the very moment in which Collatine first speaks.

It is fair to call all this characteristically or typically Shakespearean because, from the beginning to the end of Shakespeare's career, the images, motifs, and themes through which Collatine arrives at speech also control Shakespeare's theatrical imagination of dramatic, characterological destiny. This is the case, for example, in a quite simple way, in an early, reconciliatory comedy like *The Comedy of Errors* where whatever is first "splitted in the midst" (1.1.103) by windy storm— e.g., the father who is "sever'd from my bliss" (1.1.118) or the twins "who could not be distinguish'd but by names" (1.1.52)—is only brought together after registration of a torn paternal "voice": "Not know my voice!—O time's extremity, / Hast thou so crack'd and splitted my poor tongue" (5.1.308–9). And so too is this the case, though far more complicatedly, in a late romance such as *The Tempest*, where windy storm again initiates division—"Blow till thou burst thy wind" (1.1.7); "We split, we split, we split" (1.1.62)—where "time," which is a central theme because it is "sea-swallow'd," "performs an act / Whereof what's past is prologue, what to come" (2.1.251–53), and where concluding union only comes when Prospero delivers to assembled ears his strange but calming story: *Alonso*: "I long / To hear the story of your life, which must / Take the ear strangely"; *Prospero*: "I'll deliver all, / And promise you calm seas, auspicious gales" (5.1.313–15). In the middle tragedies, where Shakespeare develops his most famously and powerfully psychologistic characters, the Collatinian terms of such dramatic personal formation are yet more evidently pronounced, whether we think, for example, of the storm in *Othello*—"The desperate tempest hath so bang'd the Turks, / That their designment halts" (2.1.21–22) and of the play's denominating, self-evacuating climax—"That's he that was Othello; here I am" (5.2.284)—or of the storm in *King Lear* that "germinates" the king's disseminated tragedy—"Blow, winds, and crack your cheeks! blow! / You cataracts and hurricanoes, spout / Till you have drench'd the steeples, drown'd the cocks! . . . And thou, all shaking thunder, / Strike flat the thick rotundity o' the world! / Crack nature's moulds, all germains spill at once / That makes ingrateful man" (3.2.1–9)—or of the mixed-up letters through which *Hamlet*'s time and being are subjected to the "leave" of "let": "If it be now, 'tis not to come; if it be not to come, it will be now; if it be not now, yet it will come—the readiness is all. Since no man, of aught he leaves, knows what is't to leave betimes, let be" (5.2.220–24). In all these plays, to which of course I now can only gesture, characters enact the same misogynist erotics as is developed in "The Rape of Lucrece"; they discover the same internal sense of present broken self and retrospective temporality as is summed up in "I no more can see what once I was"; and they all turn into textured subjects when they learn first-hand how "by our ears our hearts oft tainted be."

However, beyond such shorthand references to what is characteristically, in the sense of typically, Shakespearean about the construction of Shakespeare's various *dramatis personae*, I have also suggested, with what I said about *MW*, that for Shakespeare, the person, there is something yet more literally "characteristic" about Collatine's receipt, in inverse form, of the letter he dispatches, for Shakespeare's "*Will*" is also implicated in the writing of two criss-crossed literary letters. The question that remains, therefore, is why, for Collatine or Shakespeare, the writing of a letter is related to the registration of a name.

Our reading of "The Rape of Lucrece" at least allows for a schematic answer, for, as we have seen, the poem associates the act of naming both with writing and with speech. Collatine's "let" puts Tarquin "all in post," but so too does it "praise the clear unmatched red and white." In either case, a name results, first "that name of 'chaste,'" and then the name of "'Tarquin,'" but the latter name, when it is spoken, bespeaks the final mix-up of Lucrece's pristine "red and white." As we have also seen, when Collatine, at the end of the poem, at what I have called its climax, "pronounces 'Tarquin' plain," he exemplifies what happens to a person when he "begins to talk," something the poem amplifies as an inaugural moment of constitutive, subjectifying transition in which the truth and clarity of vision is supplanted and belied by verbal speech. This corruption of ideal vision by spoken language, the reason why "by our ears our hearts oft tainted be," serves to motivate the erotic and temporal movement of the poem, establishing desire as a longing for a visionary origin that the very act of speaking renders lost, introducing successivity into Time by making "now" the aftermath of what has come before. But the speaking of the name with which the poem in this way brings itself full circle is itself provoked by Collatine's originary "let," as though Collatine can only say the name of "Tarquin" and thus become a person, when the epistolic "post" that he himself initially dispatched completes its complicated circuit.

Putting, as the poem does, all these movements and motifs together, we can say that writing in "The Rape of Lucrece" is what leads its subject into speech. The "let" that "posts" a "letter" is the instrumental medium by means of which "that name of 'chaste'" is translated into "'Tarquin.'" In large thematic terms, therefore, writing functions in "The Rape of Lucrece" as that which marks off, but thereby produces by remarking, the difference between what the poem associates with vision and what the poem associates with speech. More precisely, writing is the complication that stands between a language understood as something visual (e.g., the "praise" of red and white), a language that is therefore truthful image of its meaning or its reference (e.g., the semiotics of "imaginary work"), and a language understood, instead, as something spoken (e.g., she "turn'd it thus"), which is a language, therefore, that by virtue of its verbal essence is fundamentally discrepant both to meaning and to reference (e.g., the lies of "perjur'd Sinon"). Poised, however, in between the image and the word, writing does not stand apart as something that is neutral; its complication is no more undecided than was Tarquin when, "with open list'ning ear," he was "crossed" between "foul hope" and "fond despair." As something intermediate, writing introduces difference into what ideally is the same, and in this way makes the movement of the poem, from Collatine's first "let" to "sometime 'Tarquin' was pronounced plain," into a coherent and inexorable progress. As with the implicit quotation marks that indicate, without pronouncing, the way a word becomes a name when use turns into mention (e.g., the remarked repetition whereby "chaste" turned into "'chaste'"), writing thus not only registers but also warrants the unhappy destiny the poem associates with names.

But this returns us to the way the poem theatrically performs its letters, for the typographic gestures to which I have referred make the poem's own textuality—the literal letters that are seen upon the page—into an example of what stands between the image and the word. Accordingly, if Shakespeare's own *"Will"* is graphically inscribed at the criss-cross of *MW*—and four of the examples directly call up images of writing, reading, marking—this reflects the way Shakespeare's own authorial voice is called forth by what belies it. The signature of Shakespeare's name—the letters that chiastically circumscribe his name's beginning and its end—in this way authorizes the subjective content of what, to paraphrase Juliet's famous question, is in and what goes on in a Shakespearean name when it is made such *by* remarking: between the *W* and *M* Shakespeare too can read the provocative difference between an ego of full being and the designated subject of a name, for the very fact that they are written is what proves that Shakespeare's "Will" is different from "I am."

It is, of course, an altogether contingent fact that Shakespeare's name was "William," and I do not mean to argue that if Shakespeare had been called by any other name he could not have written what he wrote. If I insist upon the particular importance of the *"Will"* ← 𝕎 formation, it is in part because there are a remarkable number of examples of it in the poem (and also elsewhere in Shakespeare's writings), in part because "The Rape of Lucrece" makes such a vivid issue of the relation between "Will" and "writing" ("What wit sets down is blotted straight with Will"), but most of all it is because this reminds us that the name of Shakespeare is nothing but contingent.[33] It is in this sense, as something that occurs "Happ'ly"-"unhapp'ly," that we should understand how it happens the "superfluous Moity" of the Dedication turns out to materialize the poem's demonstration of the inexorable return of subjectifying letters. On the one hand, we can see this as a personal effort, on Shakespeare's part, to adapt the tradition of the dedicatory epistle to the logic of the "let," as though by writing to his patron Shakespeare means to put himself in "post." On the other hand, to account for the popular success of so personal a gesture, we can see it as a consequence of and a response to the increasingly acute perception and experience in the Renaissance of a specifically textual quality attaching to writing in general, and to letter writing in particular—what Claudio Guillén, speaking of the revival and invention of epistolic genres, has called "the Renaissance awareness of the letter."[34] This explains how the idiosyncratic inflection of Shakespeare's individuated character subsequently becomes the governing model for literary subjectivity as such, for soon enough, when Shakespeare writes for the theater, he will turn this private structure of author-patron epistolic exchange into something public, and his "*Will*," because its letters are addressed to everyone, will come to seem generic. But this remains a thoroughly contingent fact within our literary history, as contingent as is the accident of Shakespeare's name, and a contingency that will only seem inevitable within a *literary* history of self-remarking, self-performing names. This is why we should read what the editors write to William, Earl of Pembroke, in the Dedicatory epistle to *The First Folio* as a thoughtful caution rather than a boast: "There is a great difference, whether any Booke choose his Patrones, or finde them: This hath done both." At a moment when contemporary theoretical debate about the relation of psychology to literary letters simply repeats, without inverting, the topoi and the story of "The Rape of Lucrece," at a moment when the resignation of Shakespearean designation claims the authority of an extra-literary force, at a moment when moralizing contextualizations of literature illiterately reinscribe the characters of master texts, it is all the more urgent to recognize, by reading, the specifically literary formation of the subjective "appetite" occasioned by "Happ'ly that 'name' of chaste unhapply set."[35] For this is the only way to break the legacy of Shakespeare's "*Will*," the only way to open up a time outside the temporality of rape. It is now about time to think ourselves outside the Shakespearean constellation of the "let," the "letter," and the "post."

Notes

1. John Heming and Henry Condell, eds., dedicatory epistle to William, Earl of Pembroke, and Philip, Earl of Montgomery, *The Shakespeare First Folio* (1623).
2. The Argument, "The Rape of Lucrece"; Shakespeare citations will be to *The Riverside Shakespeare*, ed. G. Blakemore Evans et al., (Boston, 1974); references to the original edition (1594) will be to the facsimile edition published by the Scolar Press (London, 1968). Citations of poems will give line numbers within parentheses in the text.
3. T. W. Baldwin discusses the influence on The Argument of Ovid's *Fasti* and Livy's *Historia* in *On the Literary Genetics of Shakespeare's Poems and Sonnets* (Urbana, Ill., 1950), 108–12. James M. Tolbert argues The Argument to the poem is not by Shakespeare, "The Argument of Shakespeare's 'Lucrece': Its Sources and Authorship," *Studies in English* 29 (1950): 77–90.
4. There are six attested Shakespeare signatures; "By me *William Shakespeare*" is on page 3 of Shakespeare's will. For discussions, not always persuasive, and reproductions of Shakespeare's handwriting, see Charles Hamilton, *In Search of Shakespeare* (New York, 1985), esp. 38–47.
5. Joel Fineman, *Shakespeare's Perjured Eye: The Invention of Poetic Subjectivity in the Sonnets* (Berkeley, 1986).

6. Facsimile edition, "Hap'ly that name of chast, unhap'ly set."

7. George Puttenham, *The Arte of English Poesie* (1589; facsimile ed., Kent, Ohio, 1970), 216.

8. "Bi-fold" is from *Troilus and Cressida*; this is Troilus' response to Cressida's duplicity: "O madness of discourse, / That cause sets up with and against itself! / Bi-fold authority, where reason can revolt / Without perdition, and loss assume all reason / Without revolt. This is and is not Cressid!" (5.2.142–46). The passage is relevant to the Troy ekphrasis the poem develops later on, especially Troilus' dumbfounded response to "how these two did co-act": on the one hand, "Shall I not lie in publishing a truth," on the other, the hope "that doth invert th' attest of eyes and ears" (5.2.118–22).

9. Sigmund Freud, "Certain Neurotic Mechanisms in Jealousy, Paranoia, and Homosexuality" (1922), in *Sexuality and the Psychology of Love*, ed. Philip Rieff (New York, 1970), 162. Freud sees this as the logic of projective jealousy, and footnotes Desdemona's "Willow song" as evidence: "'I called my love false love, but what said he then? / If I court moe women, you'll couch with moe men,'" 161; see note 33, below.

10. René Girard, *Deceit, Desire, and the Novel* (Baltimore, 1965); *Violence and the Sacred* (Baltimore, 1977).

11. Claude Lévi-Strauss, *The Elementary Structures of Kinship* (Boston, 1969). Patricia K. Joplin discusses the rape of Philomela in Girardian and Lévi-Straussian terms in "The Voice of the Shuttle Is Ours," *Stanford Literature Review* 1 (1984): 25–53. Nancy Vickers discusses the rhetoric of praise in "The Rape of Lucrece" in much the same terms, "'The blazon of sweet beauty's best': Shakespeare's 'Lucrece,'" in *Shakespeare and the Question of Theory*, ed. Patricia Parker and Geoffrey Hartman (New York, 1985): 95–115.

12. Eve Kosofsky Sedgwick, *Between Men: English Literature and Male Homosocial Desire* (New York, 1985), esp. 161–79. Pierre Macherey, *Pour une théorie de la production littéraire* (Paris, 1970). Traditional commentary on the story of the rape of Lucrece is usefully reviewed in Ian Donaldson, *The Rapes of Lucretia: A Myth and Its Transformations* (Oxford, 1982). Moralizing discussions of the ethical questions raised by the rape and suicide of Lucrece rapidly become formulaic "themes for disputation." Accordingly, aspects of her story provide convenient topical commonplaces through which to display and to teach rhetorical skills; hence, the purely rhetorical tradition of arguing on both sides of the question, *in utramque partem*, *Pro Lucrecia* and *Contra Lucreciam*, e.g., Coluccio Salutati, George Rivers, et al.; see Donaldson, *Rapes of Lucretia*, 38. As I argue in connection with Tarquin's "cross," the story of the rape of Lucrece systematically activates essentially, and therefore interminably, contestable questions so as to elicit from readers a suspended investment in the story that, as something suspended, determines the inevitability of rape.

This is why triangulating characterizations of the relation of desire to violence in literature, such as those to which I refer above, regularly promote, whatever their explicit intentions, an erotics that conduces to rape. The tradition behind this literary strategy is an old one, which is why I say above that the desire for violence and the violence of desire are traditional expressions of each other. A paradigm for this, one that is quite important to Shakespeare, comes at the end of Chaucer's *The Knight's Tale*, which seems to resolve and to defuse the opposition between a violent Mars (represented by Arcite, who is nevertheless a lover) and a desiring Venus (represented by Palamon, who is nevertheless a warrior) in the figure of Emeleye, the representative of Diana who, as goddess both of the hunt and of childbearing chastity, is image of the domesticated integration of violence and desire. The terms of this happy reconciliation go back to Homer, from whom derives the medieval tradition according to which the legitimate marriage of Mars and Venus spawns as its issue the child-god Harmonia (spelled "Hermione" in the Middle Ages, a point relevant to *The Winter's Tale*). In *The Knight's Tale* (and elsewhere) the harmonious resolution of the chiastic conjunction of a venereal Mars and a martial Venus is accomplished through the exigently accidental violence that puts an end to the public fight for love conducted by Palamon and Arcite. But this harmonious and triangulated resolution of the two lovers' quarrel is staged for a fourth point of vantage, that of amazon Hippolyta and warrior Theseus, who thus come to occupy, by virtue of their witness to triangularity, the place in which violence and desire come together in chiastic disjunction, the vantage point, therefore, of rape. "Hippolyta, I woo'd thee with my sword," says Theseus at the opening of *A Midsummer Night's Dream*, "And won thy love doing thee injuries" (1.1.16–17):

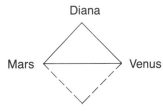

Diana

Mars ⟷ Venus

Hippolyta and Theseus

Since Chaucer is the most eminent rapist in our literary tradition (thanks to the Cecily Champagne episode in which he was accused of *raptus*), there are anecdotal, biographic grounds with reference to which we can understand why it is so regularly the violent case in Chaucer that *Amor Vincit Omnia*—usually with the help of Cupid's arrows. Chaucer consistently induces from the chiastic concatenation of violence and desire a specific form and substance of literary desire, e.g., the way, at the opening of *The Canterbury Tales*, a male Aphrodite (April) "pierces" a female Mars (March) or the way his/her liquidity spills forth to surround the parched channels through which it is supposed to flow: "Whan that Aprill with his shoures soote, / The Droghte of March hath perced to the roote, / And bathed every veyne is swich licour . . . / Thanne longen folk to goon on pilgrimages." I discuss the way the criss-crossed invaginations informing these lines derive from a general literary logic of erotic yearning in "The Structure of Allegorical Desire," in *Allegory and Representation: Selected Papers from the English Institute, 1979–80*, ed. Stephen Greenblatt (Baltimore, 1981). I discuss the tradition behind the Mars-Venus topos in my forthcoming book on Shakespeare's plays, *Shakespeare's Will* (University of California Press). We can note here, however, that *The Knight's Tale* occupies a central place in Shakespeare's dramatic imagination; e.g., he concludes his career by retelling the story in *The Two Noble Kinsmen*. I mention this because, though this essay on "The Rape of Lucrece" is primarily concerned to establish the poetics of Shakespearean rape, the argument it develops is intended to serve as a basis for a discussion of how the *theatrics* of rape functions in Shakespeare's plays. Again, though Shakespeare's use, in narrative and drama, of the chiastic concatenation of violence and desire is nothing but traditional, there is something novel and historically significant about the way he uses the commonplace to produce powerful literary subjectivity effects, rather than the abstract, allegorical agents through which the commonplace is motivated in pre-Shakespearean literature.

13. Cited in *Riverside Shakespeare*, 1837.

14. Compare with *Twelfth Night*'s purple "violet," the magic flower of erotic mix-up in *A Midsummer Night's Dream*, which is turned purple by Cupid's erring arrow: "Yet mark'd I where the bolt of Cupid fell. / It fell upon a little western flower, / Before milk-white, now purple with love's wound" (2.1.165–67); also "The forward violet" of sonnet 99. Purple is the color, and violets "breathe" the odor, of Shakespearean rape.

15. A full discussion of the relation of *Twelfth Night* to "The Rape of Lucrece" would require an account of the way the false letter of *Twelfth Night*, written by a woman's hand, leads Malvolio to sport "cross-garter'd" stockings. With regard to what I argue above, it is important that the "signature" of the letter emerges from the literal connection of "cut" and "cunt": "By my life, this is my lady's hand. These be her very c's, her u's, and her t's, and thus makes she her great P's" (2.4.86–88). This is the same signature system as is developed in "The Rape of Lucrece," as Malvolio himself remarks: "And the impressure her Lucrece, with which she uses to seal" (2.4.93–94).

16. The following four paragraphs are adapted, with some revisions, from *Shakespeare's Perjured Eye*, 39–41, where I used this stanza to example Shakespeare's use of rhetorical chiasmus; I want here to consider how chiasmus functions thematically in "The Rape of Lucrece."

17. Cf. the inside-outside glove in *Twelfth Night*: "A sentence is but a chev'ril glove to a good wit. How quickly the wrong side may be turn'd outward!" (3.1.11–12). Referring to gynecological tradition, Stephen Greenblatt gives a naturalizing account of this love-glove in "Fiction and Friction," in *Reconstructing Individualism: Autonomy, Individuality, and the Self in Western Thought*, ed. Thomas Heller, Morton Sosna, David Wellbury (Stanford, Calif., 1986), 30–63.

18. The proverb survives through Freud: "Some obstacle is necessary to swell the tide of libido to its height; and at all periods of history, wherever natural barriers in the way of satisfaction have not sufficed, mankind has erected conventional ones in order to be able to enjoy love," "A Special Type of Object Choice Made by Men" (1910), in *Sexuality and the Psychology of Love*, 67.

19. *Riverside Shakespeare* prints a dash, but the facsimile edition a comma.

20. The next stanza continues, "For with the nightly linen that she wears / He pens her piteous clamors in her head" (680–81); compare these "folded" "lips" and "pen" with *King Lear*: "If I had thee in Lipsbury pinfold, I would make thee care for me" (2.2.9–10).

21. The title on the frontispiece is *Lucrece*, but the running title at the head of all the pages of the facsimile edition is *The Rape of Lucrece*.

22. Cf. Lucrece's "'Let my good name, that senseless reputation, / For Collatine's dear love be kept unspotted: / If that be made a theme for disputation, / The branches of another root are rotted'" (820–24).

23. The relevant Freudian parallel is the Wolfman's "W-espe," which, on the one hand, at the level of the signifier, spells out the Wolfman's initials, "S. P.," on the other, as "wasp," at the level of the signified, calls up the image of the butterfly that determines the Wolfman's erotic object-choice (*coitus a tergo*) through its associations with castration and the primal scene, *From the History of an Infantile Neurosis* (1918), in *Three Case Histories*, ed. Philip Rieff (New York, 1970), 286–87. As I argue above, it is only within a specific literary tradition that the visualization of letters necessarily entails this kind of subjectifying erotic designation.

24. Example 1 does not play on "Will," but leads immediately to a thematization of epideictic "name": "He stories to her ears her husband's fame, / Won in the fields of fruitful Italy; / And decks with praises Collatine's high name" (106–8). Two stanzas

after example 2: "And in his will his willful eye he tired./With more than admiration he admired" (417–18). A play on "will" occurs within example 3, but this is further amplified in the following stanza, where it is developed in terms of the logic of the "crossed," pricking "let": "'I see what crosses my attempt will bring,/I know what thorns the growing rose defends,/I think the honey guarded with a sting:/All this beforehand counsel comprehends./But Will is deaf and hears no heedful friends'" (491–95). A play on "will" occurs within example 4, with "'Myself thy friend *will* kill myself. . . . This brief abridgement of my *will* I make.'" In example 5 redoubled "will" appears in the doubled "wil-dness." Example 6 imports the doubleness of "will" into the ambiguities of "marble will"; see footnote 26.

25. *"Willm Shakspere"* appears on page 2 of Shakespeare's will; also, *"Willm Shakp"* appears in a document relating to a legal suit. *"Wm Shakspē"* occurs on the mortgage deed of Blackfriars house.

26. This corresponds to thematic ambiguities raised by the syntax of example 6, which allow the "as" of the couplet to coordinate both male and female "will": with male will "forming"—either molding by encircling or engraving by carving—the waxy minds of women, as it chooses; and with female will, thus doubly "styled," the simulacrum— "as" as the likeness or masquerade—of the marble minds of men. In either case, Lucrece is not the "author" of her "will."

27. Cf. Tarquin's argument: "Then for thy husband and thy children's sake,/Tender my suit; bequeath not to their lot/The shame that from them no device can take,/The blemish that will never be forgot,/Worse than a slavish wipe, or birth-hour's blot;/For marks descried in men's nativity/Are nature's faults, not their own infamy" (533–39).

28. Cf. Thersites' judgment in *Troilus and Cressida*: "All the argument is a whore and a cuckold" (2.3.72–73).

29. The synecdochical procedure that allows a part to stand "for the whole to be imagined" presupposes a figurality that works by visually imaging the trope's signified (e.g., to take the standard example, fifty sails for fifty ships); this is quite different from a figurality based on the linguistic substitution of one signifier for another signifier, which is how Jacques Lacan understands the general operation of metaphor. Lacan explains this, and points up the nominalist folly informing a synecdochical understanding of poetic trope, in "The Agency of the Letter in the Unconscious or Reason Since Freud," in *Ecrits*, trans. Alan Sheridan (New York, 1977), 146–78.

30. This blind spot *in* vision is thematically present in the poem from the very beginning; hence the book-reading context for the first *MW* example: "But she that never cop'd with stranger eyes,/Could pick no meaning from their parling looks,/Nor read the subtle shining secrecies/Writ in the glassy margents of such books./She touch'd no unknown baits, nor fear'd no hooks,/Nor could she moralize his wanton sight,/More than his eyes were open to the light" (99–105).

31. Note that, at the level of the signifier, the "tide" which "outruns the eye" is articulated as "saw" and "draw," the past tenses of "to see" and "to draw."

32. Though this marks its climax, the poem does not end right here, but continues on for a short while, first, developing a rivalry in grief between Lucrece's father and Collatine—"Then son and father weep with equal strife,/Who should weep most, for daughter or for wife" (1791–92)—then, gesturing, very briefly, toward the promised revenge. The father-in-law versus husband competition is central to Shakespeare's understanding of a structural contradiction energizing patriarchal marriage. When, in marriage, the daughter substitutes her husband for her father, her passage from the one male to the other amounts to a forswearing of the father, e.g., Brabantio in

Othello: "Look to her, Moor, if thou hast eyes to see; / She has deceiv'd her father, and may thee" (1.3.292–93). For this reason, for Shakespeare, the woman has always already committed adultery by virtue of her having entered into marriage. The way the poem's conclusion scants the political consequences of the story—the expulsion of the Tarquins from Rome and the institution of the republic, events to which the Argument gives more weight—suggests that Shakespeare was more concerned with the personalizing consequences of the rape, i.e., the way the "let" returns to Collatine, than with the rape's historical significance. For this reason, the poem leaves some of its readers wanting more, but more of the *same*, e.g., J. Quarles's extension of the story in *Tarquin Banished; or, the Reward of Lust,* which concerns itself with what happens to Tarquin after the rape; this was published as an appendix to a 1665 edition of Shakespeare's poem; see Donaldson, *Rapes of Lucretia,* 179.

33. Shakespeare plays, famously, on his own name in the so-called "Will" sonnets, where, since "will" refers to both male and female genitals, his lyric first-person is designated by disjunctive copulation, e.g., sonnet 136: "Make but my name thy love, and love that still, / And then thou lovest me for my name is *Will*"; see *Shakespeare's Perjured Eye,* chap. 5. There are many "*Will*" ← 𝕄 examples in the plays, e.g., the vocative "will" of William Page in the M*erry W*ives *of W*indsor: *Evans*: "What is the focative case, William?"; *William*: "O—*vocativo,* O" (4.1.50–51), or the "Will" of Desdemona's "Willow song": "'The fresh streams ran by her and *m*urmur'd her *m*oans, / Sing *w*illow, *w*illow, *w*illow'" (4.3.44–45); "'Sing *w*illow, *w*illow, *w*illow; If I court *m*oe *w*omen, you'll couch *w*ith *m*oe *m*en'" (4.3.56–57). I discuss the theme of naming in *Othello* and its relation to Shakespeare's name in "The Sound of *O* in *Othello*: The Real of the Tragedy of Desire" (forthcoming, *October,* Spring 1988).

    More generally, it can be shown that Shakespeare regularly finds the same old story in the remarked designation of a name. Consider, as a small example, but one relevant to "The Rape of Lucrece," what Titus says in *Titus Andronicus* when he sees his daughter, the raped Lavinia, making inarticulate gestures because her arms have been cut off and her tongue has been torn out: "Mark, Marcus, mark! I understand her signs" (3.1.143–44). Later, Lavinia will successfully reveal her rapists' names when, after first pointing to a passage about Philomela in "Ovid's Metamorphosis," "She takes the staff in her mouth, and guides it with her stumps, and writes" (4.1.76, stage direction).

34. Claudio Guillén, "Notes Toward the Study of the Renaissance Letter," in *Renaissance Genres: Essays on Theory, History, and Interpretation,* ed. Barbara Lewalski (Cambridge, Mass., 1986), 70–101. Guillén argues that the diffusion of printing technology, the Humanist revival of classical epistolary modes (neo-Latin and vernacular prose and verse epistles), the incorporation of fictional letters in literary works, the publication of letter manuals, plus an increase in private correspondence, leads to the formation of a specifically literary stylization of voice: a written voice that strives to seem conversational, spontaneous, individuated, intimate. Guillén sees this as an important factor behind the rise of the novel. In a larger historical context, we can say, as Brian Stock implicitly suggests in *The Implications of Literacy: Written Language and Models of Interpretation in the Eleventh and Twelfth Centuries* (Princeton, N.J., 1983), that an oral culture only becomes such after the fact of diffused literacy: a writing culture looks back to an authentic orality that exists only as a function of retrospective nostalgia. This is how the writing "post" of "The Rape of Lucrece" works to establish "The golden splendor of the sun" as "An expir'd date, cancell'd ere well begun"; in the terms proposed by

the Dedication, this is why "this Pamphlet without beginning is but a superfluous Moity."

35. I refer here, of course, to some of the consequences arising, directly and indirectly, from the by now well-known debate between Lacan and Jacques Derrida, which centers around this claim at the end of Lacan's seminar on Poe's "The Purloined Letter": "The sender, we tell you, receives from the receiver his own message in reverse form [*une forme inversée*]. Thus it is that what the 'purloined letter,' nay, the 'letter in sufferance' means is that a letter always arrives at its destination"; Jacques Lacan, "Seminar on 'The Purloined Letter,'" trans. Jeffrey Mehlman, *Yale French Studies* 48 (1972): 72 (a full version of the seminar appears in Lacan's original *Ecrits* [Paris, 1966]); in French, the message is inverted, not reversed (41). For Lacan, this is a shorthand way of summarizing his understanding of how it happens a subject comes to be a desiring subject when he accedes to speech, passing (though Lacan means to describe a structural, not a chronological, staging process) from an "Imaginary" register of visual identification and idealization to a different register that Lacan calls "Symbolic," which he associates with a necessary slippage of meaning inherent in subjective speech, and by reference to which he accounts for the subject's insertion into the cultural order. Derrida objects to this Lacanian claim on the grounds that it universalizes a "logocentric" determinism; he summarizes his objection by pointing out that a letter does not always arrive at its destination since it sometimes goes astray. On these grounds, Derrida proposes to oppose, deconstructively, "writing," "*écriture*," to Lacan's sexist, spoken "logos"; a short version of Derrida's argument appears in "The Purveyor of Truth," trans. Willis Domingo et al., *Yale French Studies* 52 (1975), but the argument is considerably amplified in *La Carte postale* (Paris, 1980).

What I have tried to suggest through the above reading of "The Rape of Lucrece"—with its account of a subjectifying progress from true vision to false language, via the intermediating circle of Collatine's "let"—is that this debate gains its charge because it repeats a familiar literary story; this is why "The Rape of Lucrece" seems so precisely to predicate the topoi and argumentative terms of the debate. As we know from *Romeo and Juliet*, where a "purloined" (i.e., post-poned) letter is what causes the lovers' tragedy, literary letters *always* arrive at their destination precisely because they *always* go astray. Derrida's powerful critique of Lacan, therefore, is readily assimilable to Lacan's general claim (as is apparent in Lacan's late introduction of a third term, the "Real," to function as disjunctive supplement to the Imaginary-Symbolic dialectic). This is why it is so dangerous to rewrite literary stories in an extra-literary register, for, when one does so, one ends up acting out a Shakespearean tragedy. The point is especially important when erotic intentionality is at issue. One contemporary example will have to stand for many. In a translation of a portion of Luce Irigaray's "When Our Lips Speak Together," we read "I love you: body shared, undivided. Neither you nor I severed. There is no need for blood spilt between us. No need for a wound to remind us that blood exists. It flows within us, from us. It is familiar, close. You are quite red, and still so white. . . . The whiteness of this red appropriates nothing. It gives back as much as it receives, in luminous mutuality"; trans. Carolyn Burke, *Signs* 6, no. 1 (1980): 70. Commenting on this portion of the text, the translator adds an approving footnote: "Irigaray's use of 'red' and 'white' differs consciously from the traditional Western opposition of these terms as symbols of passion and purity. In general, she tries to locate a locus in writing where such 'opposites' may coexist, in a new way" (70). As we have seen, however, the Western tradition does not "oppose" red and white; quite the inverse: "when our lips speak together" in Irigaray's text, therefore, they may call out in a thematic way for "luminous mutuality," but their literary effect is to replicate the inside-outside in-betweenness of "her lips sweet fold," a replication that opens up "a locus in writing" that invites the intrusive interjection of the footnote. This is a model of "reader-response," and the example suggests why it is very dangerous to underestimate the seductive subtlety of Western literariness.

JACQUELINE LICHTENSTEIN

Making Up Representation: The Risks of Femininity

> *What is art? Prostitution.*
> —Baudelaire

WRITING IN the seventeenth century, Jean de La Bruyère remarked:

For a woman to paint herself red or white is, I admit, a smaller crime than to say one thing and think another; it is also something less innocent than to disguise herself or to go masquerading, if she does not pretend to pass for what she seems to be, but only thinks of concealing her personality and of remaining unknown; it is an endeavor to deceive the eye, to wish to appear outwardly what she is not; it is a kind of "white lie." We should judge of a woman without taking into account her shoes and head-dress, and, almost as we measure a fish, from head to tail.[1]

The severity toward women demonstrated by this text was highly uncharacteristic of classical France. In a century in which the majority of authors paid homage to the sovereignty of women—whether in politics, during the Regency or the Fronde, or in the worldly society of the salons—La Bruyère undeniably appears as an exception. On the whole, the men of the *Grand Siècle* were "feminists," if we can use such an anachronistic term, and they said as much. From Corneille to Perrault via the Libertines, from the Jesuits to the Jansenists of Port Royal, the majority of writers indefatigably celebrated the acuteness and discrimination of "feminine reason." Even Descartes recognized its superiority, as his letters to Elisabeth and Christine de Suède eloquently testify. The fineness of women's judgment and the intelligence of their conversation were universally admired. There were no terms flattering enough to describe the pleasing turns that women alone knew how to give to thought. This talent attested to a politeness of understanding that contemporaries took as a sign of the highest moral distinction.[2] The discourse of misogyny in authors such as Molière was an isolated phenomenon, and, if made subject to generalization, easily leads to false conclusions about the "spirit of the age."

However, La Bruyère's text can be seen as exemplary of a certain discourse *on* femininity, even if it cannot serve to prove the existence, in the seventeenth century, of a discourse *against* femininity. In associating a critique of women with a condemnation of makeup, La Bruyère extends a topos already clichéd by this time; his thought takes place within a long tradition that had never separated the problematic of ornament from that of femininity. This tradition consistently joined the dissipation of an ever deceitful sex and the excess of overly made-up representation in the same aesthetic-moral condemnation. From antiquity to the classical age, the seductions of makeup were thought to correspond, in the hierarchy of representations, with the aberrations of femininity. It was as if the luster added to appearances could only be thought through categories designating a sex whose essence, it was said, consists precisely of the deprivation of essence—since its nature, ontologically deficient, is necessarily exhausted in its simulation of appearances. *Makeup, woman*: two terms signifying the same substance, or rather the same absence of substance—as La Bruyère wrote, "a kind of white lie."

Such an analogy clearly played a decisive role in the history of theories of representation. All analysis of representation that poses the question of ornament must determine the proper importance of the artifices that embellish appearance. If adornment is necessary for beauty, too much ornament distorts nature and truth: we can summarize thus an aesthetic principle, current until France's classical period and still shaping our own discourse. This principle implies an essential distinction that constitutes all metaphysical aesthetics, allowing one to separate the wheat from the tares: a distinction between ornament and makeup, between a regulated and unregulated use, between lawful employment and abuse. Used to excess, ornament becomes makeup, which conceals rather than elucidates truth. This distinction, the secret of cosmetics as taught in the schools of metaphysics since Plato, was applied in the same manner to language and to the image.[3] In the case of language, it was addressed to the din of hyperbole, the indulgence of metaphor, the glut of tropes that were charged with overwhelming content and obscuring the purity of the idea. In the case of the image, the distinction concerned coloration, whose brilliance was accused of hiding the figure, of shrouding the line and corrupting its efficacy. The analogy is often explicit in medieval rhetoricians: "Employed sparingly, rhetorical figures enhance style just as colors bring out a drawing; when used too lavishly, they obscure it and cause the clear line to disappear."[4]

In the rhetorical tradition, Latin authors from the beginning represented excessive ornamentation through metaphors of femininity. In the immense repertoire of corporeal images used to define qualities of style, those referring to the feminine body clearly occupied a privileged place. Thus, when Cicero attempted to describe a simple style, he compared it to a woman "without trappings," whose naturalness "suits her well." He recommended leaving aside overly gaudy ornament and excessively bright colors, and taking as a model those beauties whose simplicity has no need for enhancement by pearls and makeup. Like an honest woman's tresses, this style should unfurl with the movement of a natural wave: "One will even eschew the curling iron."[5] But we should remember that this modest genre does not correspond, according to Cicero, to the sublime style, which must be passionate and majestic, solemn and ornate, richly colored and violently moving. Even so, the majority of criticism addressed to Cicero's orations specifically attacked their abundance of ornament as a sign of Asiatic bad taste. If we believe Tacitus, Brutus reproached Cicero for his "enervated" and "emasculated" eloquence, and Quintilian reported criticism of his "almost effeminate" style. The innumerable critics of rhetoric, in fact, have generally condemned such Asiatic stylistic figures in a vocabulary borrowed from the lexicon of the prostituted body, from the indecent attire and the profligate sexuality of women, as if every manifestation of an excessive taste for images could only be thought through the aesthetic-moral category of perversity, of a culpable seduction that originates in a certain femininity. Here, Dionysius of Halicarnassus' descriptions are particularly revealing. He depicts Asiatic rhetoric as a prostitute who is now installed in the house of language after having ousted the legitimate bride, the sweet and virtuous Attic muse:

In the epoch preceding our own, the old philosophic Rhetoric was so grossly abused and maltreated that it fell into a decline. . . . Another Rhetoric stole in and took its place, intolerably shameless and histrionic, ill-bred and without a vestige either of philosophy or any other aspect of liberal education. It was altogether vulgar and disgusting, and finally made the Greek world resemble the houses of the profligate and the abandoned: just as in such households there sits the lawful wife, freeborn and chaste, but with no authority over her domain, while an insensate harlot, bent on destroying her livelihood, claims control of the whole estate, treating the other like dirt and keeping her in a state of terror.[6]

Debauched, vulgar, seductive, and excessively made up, such wanton eloquence decidedly bore the stigmata of dissolute femininity, or rather of a dissoluteness which is that of femininity itself. For a further demonstration, it suffices to read the long analyses dedicated by Quintilian to the question of ornament in which he contrasts "made-up," emasculated rhetoric, corrupted by effeminacy, with the healthy eloquence of the virile orator.[7]

These figures and analogies were first used to designate the perverted forms of a rhetorical style that delights in the infinite play of discourse's manner at the expense of its matter. They soon invaded the analysis of painting, where they served to denounce certain "corrupt" practices of pictorial representation: an indulgence in the refinements of the brush stroke and the immoderate pleasures of color. The same metaphors played a decisive role in the quarrel that opposed the followers of Poussin, the defenders of drawing, to those of Rubens, the partisans of color, in seventeenth-century France. In painting, such a metaphorization of makeup acquired even more resonance to the degree that its object, coloring, appeared in the work as a physical fact. *Coloring*, when applied to painting—the preeminent and essential cosmetic art, consisting of both "staining" (*teindre*) and "feigning" (*feindre*)[8]—became no longer just a word but sensible, tactile, and visible, made of paste and ointments, genuine pigments like those used in women's cosmetics. The seductive artifice of the coloring praised by the colorists partook of the courtesan's and prostitute's allures. Here, love is not very different from art; in both cases, cosmetic illusion must be seen as a promise of illicit pleasures.

Just as the magical attractions of coloring were found to be similar to the charms of feminine seduction, they also became a focus for the same moral reprobation. If a picture's embellishments could be seen as "makeup," the painting becomes a woman, and one of the most dangerous sort: illegitimate, like the pleasure for which she serves as a metaphor. Neither virgin nor wife but single and therefore libertine, such women had already been accused by Dionysius of Halicarnassus of intruding into the house of eloquence in order to evict the Attic muse. Asiatic when she overwhelms the citadel of language, this figure of the courtesan becomes a colorist when she takes on painting in order to banish drawing. In 1662, several years before the *disegno-colore* quarrel that had occupied the Italians during the previous century was taken up in the setting of the French academy, Fréart de Chambray published *The Idea of the Perfection of Painting*, a slight volume of rather violent tone. In it, he denounced the corruption of the visual arts: those responsible for painting's decadence are the colorists, "who have introduced through their cabal an unheard-of libertine painting that is entirely free from all the constraints that formerly made that art so admirable and so difficult." These conspirators, he continued, "have made themselves a new mistress, coquettish and waggish, who asks only for some makeup and colors in order to please at the first encounter, without worrying if she will please for very long."[9]

We know that this warning had hardly any effect, as the power of the "cabal" continued to grow stronger in the following decade. During this period, the colorists found a remarkable leader in Roger de Piles. In 1668, twenty years after the founding of the Royal Academy of Painting and Sculpture, de Piles retook the initiative against the partisans of drawing who reigned at the Academy, with the goal of conquering the doctrinal and institutional terrain. This battle lasted almost half a century, ending with the victory of the colorists, at least on the institutional level, when de Piles was elected Amateur Counselor of the Academy on 25 April 1699. Even so, on 26 April 1697, or only two years before de Pile's election and therefore at a time when the partisans of drawing were already weakened, Noel Coypel took up the accusation again in similar terms, telling the Academy "that it would be of grave consequence to the progress of the arts of drawing . . . if one authorized such license and attributed the essence of painting to coloring"—a statement in which the word *and* clearly plays a decisive role.[10]

Of all the metaphors for makeup, that of the courtesan, the woman of easy virtue and venal loves, was doubtless the most frequently invoked. It offered the advantage of a focus for any criticism likely to be addressed to representation, whether concerned with the truth of the image or with the legitimacy of one's pleasure in it. The metaphor of the courtesan provided a transhistorical rallying point where protagonists of the most heterogeneous philosophies could unite. Here the Platonic criticism of the cosmetic met the Pauline condemnation of women's hair and joined with diverse accusations against all forms of libertinism, both moral and sexual. Coloring was reproached not so much for pleasing as for leading the spectator astray from the correct path, luring him to the ruin of illegitimate pleasure, enticing him onto the paths of aesthetic adultery. Once again painting resembles love: the only authorized pleasure is to be one permanently inscribed in time that preserves pleasure from momentary fluctuations and unforeseen occasions of desire.

Thus, the charge most frequently addressed to the charms of color was that of "pleasing at the first encounter," as Fréart de Chambray said, the immediacy of seduction invalidating both the qualities of the object and the pleasures of the spectator. Immediacy pertains to the same category as ephemerality and chance, one that metaphysics obliges us to think of as ontologically deficient. Color, likewise, is as evanescent in its material nature as in its effects. Are not its charms, accused of engendering an insubstantial pleasure, equally accountable for painting's material fragility, for its deterioration and, indeed, for its ultimate loss? Is not color unstable by definition, responsible as well for the difficult problems of conservation? And finally, is not its beauty, which pleases too easily, simply the result of a contingent gesture by the painter, a gesture just as immediate as the regard of the spectator it seduces? Pictorial color is initially, in fact, a spot: the *macchia* whose secrets Leonardo deciphered, an effect of the instant if not of chance, as the often cited history of Protogenes demonstrates. Unable to succeed at representing the foam in the nostrils of the horse he was painting, this painter angrily threw his sponge against the canvas, spotting it with a stain that instantly produced the pictorial effect he had so desperately sought.

Since Plato, an identification between the problematics of color and of chance has been a constant in the analysis of painting. Color belongs to the universe of unstable matter and contingent effects. It is the most variable aspect of the shifting illusion of appearances, and it is that part of a representation which is completely immersed in the sensible. As opposed to drawing, which assumes the course of a line and the skeleton of a design, color hurls its flames blindly, instantaneously, and by chance. For Aristotle, "a painter who smeared on the most beautiful colors at random would give less pleasure than he would by making a likeness of something in black and white."[11] And, as if language were in complicity with metaphysics, this conception of color, thought through the diverse modalities of temporal contingency, chance, ephemerality, and immediacy, is reinforced through the common origin of the French words *dessein* and *dessin*, both deriving from *disegnare*, which means simultaneously "to draw" and "to make a plan" (as *design* in English).

Only in these terms can we understand the general suspicion provoked by all that appeared as makeup. This mistrust bore witness to an undoubtedly archaic fear, one that was sustained by a long tradition that condemned all that appeared unstable, fugitive, and transitory, and that denounced both their images and the pleasure they aroused; the world of the heterogeneous, the ephemeral, and the qualitative that is often characterized as feminine—because the feminine has often been portrayed by these attributes. Paradoxically, the most explicit discourse on this subject in the seventeenth century can be found in the writings of the Chevalier de Méré, a Libertine whom we might have expected to defend colorism. This connoisseur of fugitive pleasures, of chance encounters and opportune delights, should have appreciated the immediate seductions of painting as well as those of love. However, his arguments indicate an absolute resistance point at which epicurianism is strangely confounded with puritanism. A compliment he addressed to one of his correspondents is revealing in this regard: "It seems to me that you are not like those beauties who initially surprise, but only at first sight." Certainly, such flattery is a commonplace of masculine gallantry, and it is not devoid of ambiguity. This appreciation, however, which could have been written by a moralist, is justified by de Méré through an aesthetic of distance, indeed one of the most salient features of the Libertine's ethics, in which desire refuses to let itself become attached to any object. The flaw of such dazzling beauties, said de Méré, is that they obsess one because they please in excess. "That radiant beauty is almost always false; and what ensures that you eventually detest her, although she initially enraptured you, is . . . that she absorbs too much, and you do not want to be dazzled for too long." At its basis, the Libertine's taste remained very classical. After all, he was a rationalist whose philosophy was inscribed in a Cartesian heritage. He also required beauty to please without (too much) seduction in order to maintain the distance necessary to keep control over representation. Should we be surprised that our author continued his letter with an analogy to painting? "I am certain that an excellent painter, of the finest craft, would not use it thus, if he wished to make the beauty of a woman or goddess appealing. He would take extreme care not to place on her person, or anywhere in the painting, a brilliance that would affix the sight or the thought."[12]

If Fréart de Chambray condemned the "makeup" of painting because it excited only momentary pleasure, de Méré reproached it for arousing a pleasure that was too intense. However, both these discourses expressed, in their own ways, identical desires for mastery and equal fears of dissolving, for an instant, in a fascination with their object. Not durable enough for one critic, too powerful for the other, simultaneously too trifling and too violent, the beauties of coloring are decidedly refractory to signification and rebellious to all determination. And, in order to exercise its power, consciousness wants its conceptual distinctions to correspond to real ones—so that the pleasure of appearance would *only* be inessential, and that the artificial *never* be confused with the natural. Fundamentally, the Libertine maintained a system of traditional distinctions, even if he inverted its values. He demanded that the accidental be the object of a merely superficial pleasure and innocuous desire. Whether in the name of virtue or pleasure, the grievance against makeup was always that it did not respect the distinctions necessary for the subject to be master of himself; it was criticized for effacing the boundaries introduced by thought between different orders—between appearance and reality, surface and depth, necessity and contingency, heaviness and lightness, gravity and ephemerality.

If tyranny, as Pascal said, consists in a desire for domination "beyond its scope,"[13] the seductions of coloring are surely tyrannical. Their powers violate the limits that the subject imposes on representation and carry him away in a pleasure that is not controlled by any rule and not obedient to any law. Here pleasure exceeds the limits of discursivity. Like the passions, the beauties of pictorial coloring escape from the determination of the linguistic order. The Italian and French colorists were frequently reproached for their wish to define painting by a quality that cannot be the object of any discourse, thus jeopardizing the liberal dignity, so dearly acquired, of painting. How does one name a pleasure that eludes all signification? Since the Renaissance, the defenders of the nobility of painting had deplored such pleasure: the emotion that seized the spectator—enraptured by the charms of coloring, dazzled by the gleaming embellishments of the vision offered to him—always showed itself in a difficulty of enunciation, in a privation of speech and the faltering of language. How could one theorize this aspect of depiction, subordinated to chance and not obedient to any rules? If the pleasure of color is impossible to describe, the practice of color is impossible to teach.

The colorists' task, as we have seen, was not easy. In taking up the defense of color, they attacked the domination of discourse as well as the superiority of drawing, the hegemony of a mimetic and therefore metaphysical conception of the image along with the privilege of the idea for representation, the principles of morality at the same time as the pedagogic virtues of rules. They insolently defended the purely sensible qualities of painting, indecently vindicating makeup, pleasure, and seduction. They libertinely praised color for the confusion into which its semblances threw its spectators. In this way, the force of the colorists' attack was not only aesthetic but theoretical as well, since it affirmed the nobility and dignity of painting while refusing to submit to the traditional discourses of legitimation. This rebellion was already evident in the writings of the Italian colorists, although their defiance was timid and often cautious. Perhaps still too much caught up in metaphysics, the Italians were beneficiaries as well of a political climate that encouraged subtle alliances and delicate compromises. The French critics, however, obliged by the existence of the Academy and the resulting institutional conflicts to systematize their aesthetic orientation, abandoned this reserve. Thus de Piles, without hesitation or doubt, proposed an audacious, philosophically unprecedented apology for the beauty of makeup while taking up the defense of what could be called an erotics of painting. His theory borrowed the majority of its terms from that hitherto vilified image of culpable femininity which had previously served to characterize the artifices of seduction. In doing so, de Piles was the first to take up a radically new discourse on seduction. How to please without seducing: to this question, which had never ceased to obscure the analysis of representation and to embarrass all who tried to escape from the norms of a puritan aesthetic, de Piles responded without ambiguity. From his point of view, it was simply impossible: in order to give pleasure, one must seduce. And since one cannot seduce without recourse to the allures of artifice, it is necessary to use makeup in order to please.

Indeed, Rubens's painting could be seen as only "beautiful makeup,"[14] but it would be naive or stupid to criticize him for this. "It is true that this is makeup, but we should wish that all current paintings were made up in this way. We already know that all painting is only makeup, that it is part of its essence to deceive, and that the greatest deceiver in this art is the greatest painter."[15] The same idea, in many variations, traverses all of de Pile's texts: painting should seize the spectator, strike him at first glance, attract him violently, force him to stop, take him by surprise, reduce him to silence—in brief, seduce him (in its proper sense) by obliging him to interrupt his course and turn his gaze. Accepting without reticence this analogy of painting with passion, de Piles describes the spectator's relation to the painting in a vocabulary drawn from the lexicon of amorous discourse. In the case of both painting and passion, seduction is immediate and acts in a brutal and unexpected manner. The spectator must be seized by the surprises of coloring just as the lover is victimized by the surprises of love: his pleasure must literally take the form of a ravishment. Like those beauties who are "fatal" because all succumb to their charms, true painting is irresistible. The theme is repeated in a number of passages taken at random from de Pile's *Cours de peinture par principes*:

True painting must call its spectator . . . and the surprised spectator must go to it. (4)

A painting in which the drawing and the detail of coloring are mediocre but enhanced by the artifice of chiaroscuro will not let its spectator pass tranquilly; it will call him and at least occasionally stop him. (301)

The true painting is thus that which calls us (so to speak) by surprising us; and it is only through the power of this effect that we are forced to approach it, as if it had something to tell us. (3)

But if, seen from afar, the image seduces and unsettles the spectator to the point of making him speechless, the painting itself, when seen up close, condemns him to a still greater silence. When, finally regaining his spirits and becoming master of himself again, he succeeds in tearing himself away from the power of the image and approaches the painting in order to describe those qualities that have imposed silence on him, it is only to discover that his recovered speech is of no help. This same spectator who, an instant earlier, stood dumbfounded at the sight of the image, now, before the density of pictorial matter, discovers the impotence of habitual procedures of language. How can he speak of coloring? What can he say about a painting that would be a discourse on painting, and not just a discourse on the image? He does not know what to say of the painting *as* painting, except that it exerts a specific effect that consists of the ruin of all possible articulation. Of the painting's beauty, he could say, like Nero before Junia, "Transported by the sight, / I wished to speak to her but lost my voice."[16]

Feminine, indecent, unnameable, and illicit, makeup gives itself over to the gaze in the dissolution of speech. The beauties of coloring are those of the Medusa. And this Medusa of abundant and terrifying hair occurs in painting with the features of a woman who has often been represented by painters as holding the head of a man by his hair: the figure of Judith. We should not be surprised that the story of Judith has had such success in painting from the time of the Renaissance. Whatever her other meanings—and we do not pretend to any scientific or iconographic truth—Judith seems also an allegory of makeup, an allegory of painting in its essence and in its effects. If Narcissus, as Alberti found, was the inventor of painting, it was of painting as mimetic representation, an illusive double where the "I" projects itself, and not as a blinding representation of the other. After all, Narcissus had only succumbed to the charms of an image, his own image, while Holofernes died from having been seduced by the gleaming finery of femininity, from having desired the opposite sex in its brilliance and having met it in its reality.

We learn from reading the Jesuit works on rhetoric from the period of the Counter-Reformation that Judith was indeed considered to be an allegory of makeup. In the frontispiece of *La Doctrine curieuse des beaux esprits de ce temps* by Father Garasse (1622), a vignette representing Judith cutting off Holoferne's head figures as an emblem for eloquence. Earlier, in 1599, Father Possevino had used this same image to allegorize the triumphant eloquence of the Christian church.[17] As Marc Fumaroli writes, "These images of murder and war, this allegory of Judith-as-priest, an ascetic adapting herself to the role of a courtesan in order to trick and destroy her adversary, were characteristic of a book full of the zeal of the *reconquista*."[18] Rather than a "made-up," "permanent-waved" eloquence, a "courtesan overflowing with feminine artifice, wrapped in a multicolored robe,"[19] as characterized by Father de Cressoles, certain Jesuits preferred a simpler eloquence, less colored, of more modest beauty, which, while seeking to please, refused to resort to the sensual artifices of seduction. To the made-up rhetoric allegorized by Judith, Father Louis Carbone opposed the chaste eloquence best allegorized by the virtuous beauty of Esther.[20]

Esther or Judith? Pleasure or seduction? We recognize the same debate that in antiquity set the defenders of Atticism against the partisans of Asiaticism, and whose concern, we recollect, was the role and the importance of makeup in representation. But if the debate is the same, the terms and the balance of forces have changed—first, because Asiatic influence incontestably triumphed during the Baroque era; and, second, because these two "styles" of discourse, simple or ornamental, were now inscribed in a different system of metaphors. Where the Latin authors opposed healthy and virile rhetoric against the eunuchlike eloquence of an emasculated language—or masculinity to femininity—the French authors at the end of the sixteenth century and especially during the seventeenth century contrasted two feminine figures, two equally heroic images of women. As Fumaroli notes again, "For the men of the seventeenth century, the figures of sacred and profane history were often feminine allegories."[21] This indeed demonstrates that during the seventeenth century, as we have shown, women were very much loved. Doubtless this is because, at the court of the French kings, makeup was also very much appreciated.

—Translated by Katharine Streip

Notes

1. *The Characters of Jean de La Bruyère*, trans. Henry Van Laun (London, 1929), 59–60.
2. Thus, when Saint Evremond wished to portray an accomplished individual, he naturally employed the features of a woman because it was "less impossible," he said, "to find a strong and healthy masculine judgment in a woman than it was to find the charm and the natural grace of women in a man."
3. The application of this rule extends, of course, to the face. At cosmetic counters and makeup studios, customers are taught that makeup should enhance the features rather than stand out as a separate feature.
4. Cornificius, cited by Edgar De Bruynes, *Etudes d'esthétique médiévale* (Bruges, 1946).
5. Cicero *De oratore* 23.79.
6. Dionysius of Halicarnassus 1.415; in *Dionysius of Halicarnassus: The Critical Essays in Two Volumes*, trans. Stephen Usher (Cambridge, Mass., 1974), 5, 7.
7. Quintilian *Institutio oratoria*, esp. preface, 2.5, 5.12, 8.3
8. Hence the insistence with which the Italian and French colorists distinguished natural from artificial color. In this sense, Dolce, in his *Dialogo della pittura*, differentiated the *colorito* of the painting from the color, *color*, as it emerged from the tube and whose beauty owed nothing to the talent or knowledge of the artist but only to the technique of its fabricators. In the same way, one century later, Roger de Piles distinguished the material color "that makes objects sensible to the sight" from *coloris*, which is the work of the painter and which includes the knowledge of chiaroscuro. "It is true that the dyers understand something about color, but they don't understand anything about *coloris*," he wrote in his *Dialogue sur le coloris* (Paris, 1673). This distinction between color and *coloris* is untranslatable in English.
9. Roland Fréart de Chambray, *Idée de la perfection de la peinture démontrée par les principes de l'art* (Le Mans, 1662).
10. Noel Coypel, "Sur le rang que le dessin et le coloris doivent tenir entre les partyes de la peinture," Academic lecture of 26 April 1697, in *Revue universelle des arts* 18 (1863): 188–211.
11. Aristotle *Poetics* 6.50a.38ff.; in *Aristotle's Poetics*, trans. James Hutton (New York, 1982), 51.

12. Antoine Gombauld, Chevalier de Méré, *Des agrémens* (Paris, 1677).

13. Blaise Pascal, *Pensées*, trans. W. F. Trotter (New York, 1958), 5.332, p. 93. Pascal means by this that the political chief, for example, who claims to govern not only public acts but private sentiments becomes tyrannical because he exceeds his scope—as when passion tries to govern reason, or vice versa.

14. Gabriel Blanchard, the only colorist of the Academy, used the expression *le beau fard* to characterize Rubens's paintings in a lecture delivered at the Academy on 7 November 1671, "On the Merit of Color," in response to Philippe de Champaigne's lecture of 12 June 1671, on a painting by Titian whose coloring de Champaigne severely criticized.

15. Roger de Piles, *Cours de peinture par principes* (Paris, 1708), 10.

16. Jean Racine, *Britannicus*, 2.1; in *Five Plays*, trans. Kenneth Muir (New York, 1960), 78–79.

17. Antonio Possevino, *Biblioteca selecta* (Rome, 1593). The two examples of Father Garasse and Father Possevino, like those of Father de Cressoles and Father Louis Carbone, are taken from Marc Fumaroli, *L'Age de l'eloquence: Rhétorique et 'res literaria' de la Renaissance au seuil de l'époque classique* (Paris, 1980), an inexhaustible mine on this subject.

18. Fumaroli, *L'Age de l'eloquence*, 181, note.

19. Louis de Cressoles, *Theatrum veterum rhetorum* (Paris, 1620); cited in Fumaroli, *L'Age de l'eloquence*, 310.

20. Louis Carbone, *Divinus orator vel de rhetorica divina libri septem* (Venice, 1595); cited in Fumaroli, *L'Age de l'eloquence*, 184.

21. Fumaroli, *L'Age de l'eloquence*, 184, note.

FRANCES FERGUSON

Rape and the Rise of the Novel

THE TRIAL OF ANY CRIME may raise a variety of skeptical questions: what does it mean to take X as evidence of Y? What is involved in taking an act as evidence of someone's intention? What is credibility, and how does it attach itself to particular persons? The crime of rape raises these questions in the way that any crime might. As crimes go, however, it is remarkable for focusing attention on mental states and their apprehension. While the intention to do harm is requisite for conviction for a number of crimes, the legal debates surrounding rape claim that the mental states of two persons are crucial—the intention of the accused and the consent or nonconsent of the victim. Since one cannot have an intention to engage in nonconsensual sexual intercourse if the other party is consenting, the presence or absence of the other party's consent becomes crucial in the determination of criminal intent.[1]

Equally crucial is the question of the parties' understandings of one another's intention and consent. If a man believes that a woman consents to sexual intercourse but is mistaken in that belief, can he be said to have had the intention to have nonconsensual sexual intercourse? If a woman believes that a man intends to override her nonconsent and have intercourse with her but is mistaken in that belief, can he be said to be guilty of attempted rape? While the statutory definitions of rape consistently revolve around the violation of the victim's will, around the perpetrator's disregard for her nonconsent, that apparent unanimity masks an ongoing debate about what consent is and how it manifests itself in the world. This is to say, in part, that the issue of consent itself reflects a question about who or what counts as a person who can consent, whose consent is significant.

To frame the question in this way is, however, to suggest an answer. For it implies that rape victims (whom I will hereafter refer to as women not because men are not raped but because the crime itself has historically been depicted as a crime committed by a man upon the person of a woman) must inevitably be perceived as deficient persons, inasmuch as women are generally "by our society" seen as deficient versions of men. From this perspective, rape victims are violated first by the actual, physical act of rape and then by a legal system that does not take them at their word but demands further proof.[2] However sympathetic or plausible this account may be, it tends to imply that truthfulness and reality are, first, easy to identify in an alleged crime of rape and, second, that they are continually suppressed. Thus, many writers who are critical of rape laws as they have been framed and enforced focus on the question of credibility; they see credibility less as a matter of a jury's decision about the relative credibility of the various witnesses than as a matter of the victim's credibility in the eyes of the law. As evidence of the law's suspicion of the testimony of rape victims, they frequently cite Sir Matthew Hale's warning in his *History of the Pleas of the Crown* that, though "rape is a most detestable crime . . . it must be remembered, that it is an accusation easily to be made and hard to be proved, and harder to be defended by the party accused, tho never so innocent."[3] For Hale's lack of certainty that every charge of rape is directly tied to an act of rape, Susan Brownmiller dismisses him with the observation that he "assured himself of immortality" when he wrote the words quoted above.[4] She proceeds to argue that "since four out of five rapes go unreported, it is fair to say categorically that women do not find rape 'an accusation easily to be made'" (413–14). That is, all accusations of rape ought to be believed either because all women are truthful or because the difficulty of bringing the charge itself must count as evidence of its veracity. For her, it is easily assimilable to "male fear of the false rape charge brought by a lying woman—the old syndrome of Potiphar's wife" (414). The concern over the false rape charge thus operates more as a cover than as an expression of real fear; it justifies male disbelief in female testimony. The fear of the lying woman, on Brownmiller's account, renders a woman's testimony trivial, because it can never be seen to count as true even when it is. If a writer like Susan Brownmiller refers to Hale's cautionary remark with a certain scorn, Susan Estrich sees it as both symptomatic of male views and as productive of them. In her thoughtful book *Real Rape*, she traces the difficulties that women have in making their experience of rape come to look real in the framework of the legal system, and she notes that Hale's words have been adopted as something like the formulaic warning to a jury that they not be too quick to assume the guilt of the accused.[5] If the customary standard is that "one must be considered innocent until proven guilty beyond a reasonable doubt," and if this standard appears to suffice for murder, robbery, and burglary cases, why does it need to be supplemented in a case of rape? There is, as the New York Supreme Court opinion in People v. Linzy (1972) put it, "no cogent reason why . . . [the usual cautionary words] should fail when the crime charged is a sex offense."[6]

The doubled warning to the jury—not merely "Are you sure?" but "Are you sure you're sure?"—had served until the 1970s to mark rape as particularly difficult to determine and had identified it for some two and a half centuries as the charge most likely to provoke skepticism. For while the possibility of convicting an innocent person is always inherent in any legal system, the charge of rape has historically involved the possibility that an innocent person might be condemned to death on the basis of someone else's word alone. And it was in illustration of this point that Matthew Hale had told a story immediately after pronouncing his now notorious warning. A man of about sixty-three, having been charged with the rape of a girl of fourteen on her sworn statement, protested that "his very age carried a great presumption that he could not be guilty of that crime" and then went on to offer evidence of his innocence that was taken as conclusive. He had "for above seven years last past been afflicted with a rupture so hideous and great, that it was impossible he could carnally know any woman," he said, and he proceeded to introduce his rupture as evidence before the jury, displaying his body to give proof of his necessary innocence of the charge.[7] Hale uses this case, in which the sworn testimony of the complainant and the physical evidence of the defendant are at odds, to suggest both the superiority of physical evidence over testimony and the dangers implicit in any legal situation where different sets of testimony compete with one another without any check or support from physical evidence. A judge and jury may, he fears, be transported "with so much indignation" over "the heinousness of the offense" that "they are over-hastily carried to the conviction of the person accused" (636).

Actions—or the physical manifestations of inability to act—should, Hale implies, speak louder than words, and the display of a mutilated body trumps testimony every time. Thus, rape has historically been easiest to prove when it is most nearly identical with battery and mayhem; by the same logic, Hale's innocent accused is most easily exonerated by a rupture that speaks more convincingly than any words. And when figures like Hale, William Blackstone, and Cesare, the marchese of Beccaria, discuss the grounds of evidence for crimes generally, as for rape specifically, they continually seek evidence of an action that will be separable from the transmission of words. As Beccaria puts it, in assessing the relative weight one should give different sorts of testimony:

Finally, the credibility of a witness is null, when the question relates to the words of a criminal; for the tone of voice, the gesture, all that precedes, accompanies and follows the different ideas which men annex to the same words, may so alter and modify a man's discourse, that it is almost impossible to repeat them precisely in the manner in which they were spoken. Besides, violent and uncommon actions, such as real crimes, leave a trace in the multitude of circumstances that attend them, and in their effects; but words remain only in the memory of the hearers, who are commonly negligent or prejudiced. It is infinitely easier then to found an accusation on the words, than on the actions of a man.[8]

In finding evidence in actions stronger than evidence in words, commentators on the law were inevitably restricting the capacity of the law to deal with crimes like rape in which the evidence of actions necessarily involved considerable verbal supplementation. The physical similarity between an intention to have consensual intercourse and an intention to have nonconsensual intercourse, in fact, meant that the only way one could communicate a difference between consensual intercourse and rape was by testifying about mental states. And only the intention to have sexual intercourse has any nonverbal clarity. The law has repeatedly maintained that the capacity for sexual penetration in the act of intercourse establishes intention (although at least one defense maintained that intercourse had been "accidental").[9] The act itself thus indicates intention. But because sexual intercourse is not in itself legally culpable, evidence of penetration is necessary but not sufficient to establish criminal intent. The crime, that is, only becomes a crime on the level of mental states. The victim's nonconsent revalues the shape of the act of intercourse, and converts what could conceivably be merely an intention to have intercourse into a criminal intention to have intercourse despite the nonconsent of the other party. Thus, while critics of rape law have plausibly objected that victims are more aggressively interrogated than rape suspects themselves, that very attention to the victim bespeaks the fact that rape has progressively been defined as a crime that is constituted as one by the victim's nonconsent.

Moreover, since rape was, for the eighteenth century as for the present, a crime that was "in its nature commonly secret," according to Sir Robert Chambers, laws governing the prosecution of rape acknowledged that "the party injured is . . . an admissible witness."[10] That is, the secrecy of the crime inevitably led to the necessity that "part of the proof must always be circumstantial" (1:406). The crime, being secret, was often assumed to have no history apart from that provided by the competing testimony of the victim and the accused, supplemented by the jury's sense of the relative credibility of these accounts. And, as Chambers's assimilation of the victim's testimony to circumstantial evidence suggests, the process of proving the crime had a tendency to displace the crime itself, as the accessory or additional information about circumstances became all-important in lending plausibility or probability to a charge. Thus, the "good fame" or "evil fame" of the woman bringing charges, the promptness of her complaint or her concealment of her "injury for any considerable time after she had opportunity to complain,"[11] and her outcry or her silence become the central elements for scrutiny.

As the circumstances surrounding the rape displace the act as the subject of the account, the legal effort to deduce individual intention about the act itself from surrounding behavior and from general "character" begins. The victim's apprehension of the perpetrator's act becomes more important than the perpetrator's account of his intention, and her physical manifestations of that intention become the signal marks of that intention. Her body is thus converted into evidence, having become the text that bespeaks not only her intention not to have consented but also the perpetrator's intention to have overridden that refusal to consent.

The emphasis on the victim's body as a text, for all its intrusiveness, shifts the focus of inquiry into mental states. If the assailant can claim a kind of refuge in the ambiguation that any formal construct is susceptible to, the manifestation of nonconsent always occurs as a disambiguating gesture—an insistence that the form (in this case, the body) is not large enough to accommodate radically diverging views of the mental state it represents. And the debate between those who emphasize male intention and those who stress female nonconsent thus revolves around the question of how persons should relate to symbolic structures.

The progress of rape law in the Western tradition suggests a persistent competition between two strategies of interpreting the crime. One embraces ambiguity by insisting that diametrically opposed views of the same action be accommodated in that action; the other attempts to desynonymize actions by stipulating what they mean.

According to modern accounts of rape law, ancient Hebrew law was committed to preserving the structures of consent by insisting that persons take intercourse as synonymous with marriage and consent as synonymous with non-consent. The law, that is, tended to produce the form if not the substance of an agreement between the parties in insisting that the parties make the outrage into a way of life. Jewish law thus commanded that a rapist pay an unbetrothed girl's father "fifty silver shekels in compensation for what would have been her bride price" and that the rapist and the victim simply marry.[12] Similarly, Henry of Bratton (Bracton) reported that Saxon law offered a raped virgin the possibility of extending retroactive consent to her rape; she could extricate her attacker from his sentence of death by agreeing to marry him. If rape parodies the formal features of happier sexual relations by disposing the same sets of body parts, Hebraic and Saxon law in their earlier phases were committed to the assumption that intention and consent were so far derivable from the forms of actions that there essentially could not be a form that did not imply consent. Thus, the problem of consent became less a problem about consent and more a problem about the synchronization of one party's intention and another party's consent in a particular form of action. Consent, it was assumed, would always ultimately follow from the ongoing operation of the form. Only with such an assumption could the legal recompense for rape turn out to be marriage, which formally (in this case, legally) implies the consent to intercourse that was previously lacking. Marriage recasts rape, so that marriage is a misunderstanding corrected, or rape rightly understood.

The insistent legalism of the ancient Hebrews and Saxons, then, subordinates the parties and their understandings to the form of the act. A resisted act and an intended act come to be the same thing—at least, eventually, and rape simply ceases to exist because it has been, by definition, absorbed into marriage. Moreover, marriage itself has been formally defined to preclude the possibility of disagreement between spouses.

Although such an extreme subordination of individual will to formulaic definitions of it may seem alternately brutal and anachronistic, various feminist critiques of the patriarchal law of rape have framed their argument in similarly formal terms. Thus, writers like Brownmiller and Andrea Dworkin, for example, challenge the particular content of the stipulations of ancient law, but they also follow the procedure of stipulating inexorable connections between the form of an action (intercourse) and the mental state of the individuals involved. But while ancient law tended to stipulate that consent is implicit in the act of intercourse, they argue that the form of that act, and even the form of gendered bodies, implies the impossibility of consent. Thus Brownmiller derives the intention to rape from the physical capacity to do so:

Man's structural capacity to rape and woman's corresponding structural vulnerability are as basic to the physiology of both our sexes as the primal act of sex itself. Had it not been for this accident of biology, an accommodation requiring the locking together of two separate parts, penis and vagina, there would be neither copulation nor rape as we know it. . . . This single factor [that in terms of human anatomy the possibility of forcible intercourse incontrovertibly exists] may have been sufficient to have caused the creation of a male ideology of rape. When men discovered that they could rape, they proceeded to do it.[13]

In this conjectural history of the origins of human society, Brownmiller moves from the claim that the penis has the capacity to be a weapon to the assertion that that very potentiality itself constitutes an intention. The discovery of the capacity to rape may have begun in a kind of accident, in that it was, she imagines, "an unexpected battle founded on the first woman's refusal." Yet in her account, rape continued by conscious design: "The second rape was indubitably planned." The accident of man's early "discovery that his genitalia could serve as a weapon to generate fear" is for Brownmiller analogous to the discovery of "the use of fire and the first crude stone axe," a discovery of the potential of a tool, and the crucial point in her conjectural history is that she takes the potential of the penis to be used for rape as synonymous with men's intentions to rape: rape "is nothing more or less than a conscious process of intimidation by which *all men* keep *all women* in a state of fear" (5).

If for early Hebrew and Saxon law, all rape might be marriage, for Andrea Dworkin all marriage—and for that matter, all intercourse—is rape. That is, even when women may see themselves as consenting to intercourse, the very notion of their being able to extend or deny consent is itself illusory: "Physically, the woman in intercourse is a space inhabited, a literal territory occupied literally: occupied even if there has been no resistance, no force; even if the occupied person said yes please, yes hurry, yes more."[14] Consent, in these terms, is a byproduct of the structural relationships that obtain (in, for instance, the specification of intercourse as the male occupation of a woman's body). Thus, the structures carry with them an intention, a willingness to consent or to deny consent, and the person who operates within those structures can only be in relatively good or relatively bad faith in imagining that she can have a view of those structures that is separable from them, and from her behavior.

Thus, Brownmiller and Dworkin share with ancient rape law the tendency to specify the male injury to the female in terms of formally identified and stipulated mental states. And they thus recapitulate, even though in a reversal of those early legal codes, the tendency of the law to negate particular psychological states and to substitute formal states for them. In other words, the process of reading an action as evidence of intention confines itself to stipulated states that are specifically detached from the notion of individual, actualizable psychological states. For ancient Hebrew law the act of sex carries with it the inevitability of consent. For Brownmiller and Dworkin, it carries with it the impossibility of consent: women, because they are women, never consent; men, because they are men, always rape.

The similarity of these two opposed positions is more than merely ironic, for it suggests that both the legal system and the majority of its critics have agreed at least in seeing rape as a problem that can be addressed on formal grounds. This is to say that the legal system has been most successful—for good and for ill—when rape approaches most nearly to a formal definition. In fact, the law of rape continually draws and redraws its terms, as if to underscore the desire to identify the crime as a project of stipulating formal criteria ever more precisely, ever more thoroughly in an effort to minimize the problems that can arise in the effort to identify psychological states. Questions about such issues as the requisite age for consent become, therefore, particularly important. Consent or nonconsent as mental states may be unspecifiable, but defining legal infancy as the necessary inability to consent makes the determination of any mental state irrelevant. If psychological states like intention and consent frequently look inaccessible, the statutory definition of them solves the problem created by their inaccessibility by making them irrelevant. The law enables itself to identify rape, then, by denying the possibility that a very young woman could ever have the psychological state that would count as consent. Even if she explicitly employs all the words and gestures of consent, she cannot consent.

Hale defines rape as "the carnal knowledge of any woman above the age of ten years against her will, and of a woman-child under the age of ten years with or against her will" in a way that marks the age of ten as the functional boundary of what we have come to call statutory rape.[15] And after such a gesture, there can be no point to debates over consent as such; there can only be dispute over where the age of consent falls. Thus, even after having produced this definition that makes the age of ten the determining factor in distributing the ability to consent, Hale proceeds to account for decisions in various cases by resolving certain inconsistencies in the numbers.

It was doubted, whether a rape could be committed upon a female child under ten years old, *Mich. 13 & 14 Eliz. Dy. 304 a.* By the statute of *18 Eliz. cap. 7* it is declared and enacted, 'That if any person shall unlawfully and carnally know and abuse any woman-child under the age of ten years, it shall be felony without the benefit of clergy.'

My lord *Coke* adds the words, *either with her will or against her will*, as if were she above the age of ten years, and with her will, it should not be rape; but the statute gives no such intimation, only declares that such carnal knowledge is rape.

And therefore it seems, if she be above the age of ten years and under the age of twelve years, tho she consents, it is rape. 1. Because the age of consent of a female is not ten but twelve. 2. By the statute of *Westm. I. cap. 13. Roy de end, que nul ne ravise ne prigne a force damsel deins age, ne per son gree ne sans son gree*; and my lord *Coke* in his exposition upon that statute declares, that these words *deins age* must be taken for her age of consent, *viz.* twelve years, for that is her age of consent to marriage, and consequently her consent is not material in rape, if she be under twelve years old, tho above ten years old, altho those words are by some mistake crept into my lord *Coke's* definition of rape, *Co.P.C. cap. II*. (630–31)

Without pausing to wonder at the fact that Coke might have meant to establish the possibility of consent for different kinds of acts at different ages, Hale moves to clean up the conflict, to eliminate the period between the ages of ten and twelve as a limbo for the possibility of consent to carnal knowledge.

Moreover, the consistent inclination of the statutes and their interpreters to focus on formal categories that abolish the possibility of certain mental states becomes more apparent when we realize that the law formally distributed not only an age of consent to sexual intercourse but also an age of intention to rape. It was statutorily impossible for a male under the age of fourteen to commit a rape, even if he were physically capable of it:

An infant under the age of fourteen years is presumed by law unable to commit a rape, and therefore it seems cannot be guilty of it, and tho in other felonies *malitia supplet aestatem* in some cases as hath been shewn, yet it seems as to this fact the law presumes him impotent, as well as wanting discretion. (630)

The laws governing rape, then, distribute both statutory guilt (for sexual intercourse with a female under the age of ten or twelve or sixteen) and statutory innocence (for sexual intercourse that a male under the age of fourteen may have had in defiance of the law's assertions of possibility).[16] And even on the most sympathetic and apologetic account, the intense formality of the law of rape seems designed to substitute the reliability of invariable formulae for the manipulable terms of psychological states.

The desire for invariable formulae was so strong that it could produce both extraordinary wrangling over a young woman's age and the possibility of stipulating that even a theoretically conceivable and verifiable act, rape by a young man under the age of fourteen, could not occur. This is to say that even the occurrence of such an act could not, by definition, erode the assertion of its impossibility. The terms of these rigidly articulated accounts of consent and intention, thus, clarify psychological states by producing formal criteria that will not so much represent psychological states as replace them. For the statutory definitions establish the possibility—and indeed the inevitability—that consent and intention will be self-contradictory, or impossible, notions. They thus create the categories of consent that is not consent (for some hypothetically consenting female who has not reached the age of consent) and intention that is not intention (for some hypothetically intending and physically competent male who has not reached the age of legal discretion and competence). And these categories, in the very process of functioning as solutions to potential interpretative dilemmas, replicate exactly the kinds of problems that appear in any jury's deliberations concerning a charge of rape. They solve a certain conundrum that appears in the interpretation of testimony about rape—did he/she really mean or want what he/she said he/she wanted?—by insisting upon it, by saying that even where there might appear to be consent, even where there might appear to be intention, there can be none.

Thus, while Susan Estrich very powerfully argues for the right of a woman to be taken as meaning "no" when she says *no* in the "simple rape" that can involve one woman and one man who know each other, that effort to disambiguate the interpretation of a woman's intention runs counter to the form of rape law.[17] For the form of statutory rape, the kind of case least open to interpretation and therefore easiest of proof, establishes a model of internal self-contradiction that is not set aside but merely reversed in the cases involving other kinds of rape. If in statutory rape *yes* is always taken to mean "no," in other kinds of rape *no* is frequently taken to mean "yes." Thus, rape law continually suggests as a paradigmatic interpretative strategy the reversibility of the terms that seem to be asserted by the charge of rape itself.

The paradoxes that govern the laws of rape, then, include an apparent contradiction between an almost unfailing historical depiction of rape as one of the most serious possible crimes and a relatively low conviction rate for felony rape. Rape therefore appears to be a crime that is serious but rare. And the essence of the feminist critique of rape law is that such law denominates rape as a very serious crime but relegates any charge of rape to the level of the possibly fictitious. Thus, Estrich identifies in American case law a recurrent "distrust of vindictive, lying women who might use a rape charge as a weapon" (72). As Brownmiller puts it, "The famous story of Potiphar's wife is an important morality lesson in Hebrew, Christian, and Moslem folklore, and it expressed the true, historical concern and abiding fear of egocentric, rapacious man: what can happen to a fine, upstanding fellow if *a vengeful female lies* and cries that she has been assaulted."[18] In these accounts, the stigma attached to false appearances falls particularly, and virtually exclusively, to women, and skepticism in general is easily assimilable to distrust of women.

The accounts of Brownmiller and Estrich take a general male distrust of women as inevitably producing a law that regards any female victim with suspicion. But however credible these views may be, they suffer from a similar difficulty: they can only effect change by converting this particular line of analysis into a stipulation. Where the legal system has repeatedly said, "Disbelieve her, because she is a woman," Brownmiller and Estrich, for all their differences, would say, "Believe her, because she is a woman." For them a rape trial is thus a gendered version of the class competitions that occur in trials in Jacobin novels. The end result of the trial in those novels is always predetermined; the competition between narrators will always eventuate in an unjust victory for the member of the gentry, or the higher-class male, whose very ability to manipulate the fictions of the powerful enables him to pass for the more truthful party. Credibility revolves around the credit of the person rather than around the facts of the narrative, and the "lesser" person will always lose. Thus, Beccaria feels that he must argue for a change in the standards for assessing the credibility of witnesses when he proposes that those with less to lose be seen as preeminently convincing witnesses:

> But the credibility of his evidence will be in proportion as he is interested in declaring or concealing the truth. Hence it appears how frivolous is the reasoning of those, who reject the testimony of women on account of their weakness; how puerile it is, not to admit the evidence of those who are under sentence of death, because they are dead in law . . . and how irrational, to exclude persons branded in infamy, for in all these cases they ought to be credited, when they have no interest in giving false testimony.[19]

Weakness—having nothing to lose—in one sense is, for Beccaria, strength, not needing to tailor your account of the truth to the preservation of your place, rank, and station. But this logic, for all its apparent distance from the tendencies of rape law, in fact recapitulates the tension everywhere apparent in that network of statutes and cases. For Beccaria is basing his argument for women's truthfulness entirely on their lack of independent status, on the similarity between women in their weakness and those "under sentence of death" who are thus "dead in law." And in this equation of women's truthfulness and their weakness, he recreates the preferences we have already traced in rape law for stipulating forms that will guarantee meaning by applying even in despite of the person whom they represent. For he, like the statutory formulations of consent and intention, traces the source of women's veracity to their being nonpersons, just as a female under the age of ten or twelve or sixteen or a male under the age of fourteen is a nonperson for the purposes of consent and discretion.

Even as the political and fictional logic establishes the woman's truthfulness, the link between her truthfulness and her powerlessness itself comes to function as an inevitably self-contradictory formula. It thus imposes a limiting term on the very capacity for subversion or compensation that political reform and visionary fiction might hope to provide. Were a woman to become powerful, she would lose the weakness that is the very condition for the strength of her testimony. That is, her very lack of power guarantees her truthfulness; her not counting makes her words count. The question of authentic testimony about rape thus approaches something of the paradox of statutory rape in which the possibility of radical self-contradiction is defined as the easiest case, the most determinate and determinable reality.

We can summarize the various treatments of the history of rape in the following manner:

First, there is a formal stipulation of truthfulness by gender, so that all men always mistrust all women's charges of rape, and thereby relegate them to the status of the merely fictitious, or, conversely, so that all women always speak truly about rape and thereby make the countertestimony or suspicions of men simply false.

Second, the law generates a fictitious certainty—or the certainty of fiction— by defining rape in formal terms that specifically involve the possibility of self-contradiction. Thus, the illusion of certainty is created by making self-contradiction, an assent to unreality in the form of an assertion that $A \neq A$. The model of statutory rape thus establishes consent and intention as potentially self-evacuating terms, so that "more complicated" cases of rape, where intention and consent are required to manifest themselves without the statutory mechanism of age, occur under the formal skepticism about them that statutory rape creates.

Third, there is the argument that establishes an economy between the reality of the story of rape and the relative unreality of the victim before society or the world. While it is conceived in a spirit of political change, it is essentially trapped by the formal structures of stipulation that emerge in both the ancient law of rape and its modern critics. For although this view appears to involve a competition between male and female narrators in specifically political terms, it quickly collapses into itself with a competition between the story and the narrator. That is, the power of the story, the story's claim to truthfulness, relies so exclusively on the weakness of the storyteller that any recognition of the narrator's increased strength involves a corresponding loss for the story, and vice versa.

This view of the law of rape argues that its mechanisms for defining rape in terms of formally stipulated states continually operate to reduce mental states to potentially or actually self-contradictory constructs. That is, the constructs that make it possible to secure justice for an injured party themselves become an affront, an implicit trivialization of the very subjectivity that they are, at least heuristically, designed to protect. That is, the importance of the notion of a mental state, the importance of the notion of subjectivity itself, may be guaranteed precisely by eradicating its relevance in an actual situation, precisely by denying the capacity of a particular individual to have a meaningful mental state.

This particular interpretation of the law of rape may, moreover, lead us toward a revised understanding of the psychological novel and the importance that Samuel Richardson attaches to rape in producing, in *Pamela* and *Clarissa*, the first full examples of the psychological novel. We know from Margaret Doody's useful discussion that Richardson was drawing on imagery and techniques developed in earlier eighteenth-century rape narratives and novels of "love and seduction,"[20] but a question about the particular resonance of rape for depicting individual psychology remains. In the terms of Michael McKeon's excellent recent study of the origins of the English novel, a crime like rape would represent one element of the intersection between eighteenth-century skepticism and prose fiction.[21] Rape, that is, dramatizes a problematic about the relationship between the body and the mind; although a rake like Lovelace may imagine that carnal "knowing" includes knowing someone else's mind, a character like Clarissa—virtuous even in her violation—suggests that one knows about mental experience as much in despite of the body as through it.

Two models of intersubjective understanding are in competition here. The one, emphasizing a split within the individual, provides the model of internal confusion that has always left Pamela open to charges of self-deception at best and duplicity at worst. Pamela's marriage both bespeaks her ability to reread Mr. B's attempted rape as seduction and also works to make her virtue look like an instrument in a marriage campaign rather than an end in itself. The individual changes situations—and stations—by discovering the unreliability of the self in determining what one really wants. The other model, emphasizing a split between private experience and its public apprehension, suggests that the psychological novel arises to demonstrate the superiority of individual perception to the world of social forms. The strength and pride of the individual, in this account, rest in being misunderstood. Thus, the psychological novel seems to be psychological either by virtue of being either resolutely confused or resolutely unconfused. While the conduct books and model letter-writers that Richardson had earlier written might have suggested that there was a straightforward technology for producing upright and efficient individuals, *Pamela* and *Clarissa* appear to be psychological novels precisely because they continually pose the confusions or resolutions of the self as an alternative to social engineering. *Clarissa*, indeed, seems to provide a more satisfying model of the psychological novel because it rests more squarely on psychology as interiority, the individual's inalienable rights in herself, than does *Pamela*, with its reconciliation with Mr. B. and society.

Thus, in Ian Watt's *The Rise of the Novel*, *Clarissa* epitomizes the novel of private experience.[22] And the occurrence of rape within a novel like *Clarissa* represents the novel's ability to convey, as the stage could not, private aspects of experience such as sexuality. Moreover, the rape becomes the vehicle for the contrast between what could be said in public and proved and what is said in private and believed. As Watt comments on Clarissa's decision not to take Lovelace to public trial, the issue of rape comes to dramatize the primacy of psychological states for the novel:

A bare summary of the events might suggest that Clarissa courted her fate; only a full knowledge of her sentiments and aspirations, and the certainty that Lovelace understood them well enough to realise the enormity of his offence, enable us to understand the real nature of the story. (198)

As an act that cannot really be understood in public, the rape in *Clarissa* bespeaks the primacy of the psychological states that Richardson was continually trying to transcribe with greater and greater accuracy (194).

Richardson's presentation of the rape in *Clarissa* would seem, then, to criticize the limitations inherent in the formal criteria by which the publicly recognizable laws of rape function. For it is not so much the particular laws as their inevitable reduction of psychological states to formal states that makes them both public and problematic. Likewise, recent criticism of the novel has continued to prefer the psychological in discussing the rape. For Terry Castle and Terry Eagleton the rape becomes the occasion for protest against the forced alienation of the individual's meaning. The psychological novel, as fully initiated by *Clarissa*, thus appears to be a confrontation between other people's accounts of one and one's own account. For Castle the psychological novel affirms Clarissa's right not to mean anything she does not want to mean, her right not to be "interrupted" in her course of seeking to mean.[23] For Eagleton it revolves around the woman's resistance to hegemonic forms, her "rebuffing of all patriarchal claims over her person."[24]

One crucial difficulty with seeing the rape as illustrating the primacy of the psychological, however, is that it occurs while Clarissa is unconscious. If the question in any rape case is, "What was the victim's mental state? Did she consent?" then the answer *Clarissa* seems to give is, "She had no mental state." The very fact that the rape counts as rape necessarily depends not on Clarissa's mental state but on a formal account of that state. It therefore looks as if *Clarissa*, like rape law and unlike the "psychological novel" that it is supposed to represent, argues for the primacy of form by framing the rape so that it cannot depend upon the victim's mental state. On the one hand, Clarissa's unconsciousness during the rape eliminates her capacity not to consent to her rape. Therefore, her resistance to the rape has been made impossible. On the other hand, her resistance has been made inescapable. For the law of rape specifically stipulates that unconsciousness (along with states like idiocy, insanity, and sleep) "negatives" consent.[25] Thus, although Clarissa's unconsciousness deprives her of the capacity to resist and even of the capacity to know exactly what happened to her, it also ensures that her nonconsent will be inescapable. The stipulation that unconsciousness is nonconsent—even though it necessarily cannot manifest itself as physical resistance—thus provides that Clarissa's nonconsent continues even in her absence, even in her unconsciousness.

But if it then appears that *Clarissa* bespeaks the primacy of forms—a primacy designed to ensure the legibility of mental states by deriving them from forms—that very legibility itself carries within it the constant possibility of internal contradiction. For it stages the possibility that one's actual mental state will conflict with one's stipulated mental state—that which one is held to have by virtue of age, mental capacity, or lack of consciousness. It recapitulates the contradiction that we earlier discovered in the very form of the law of rape and the feminist critique of it—that one might never consent even if one wanted to consent, that the form might itself oppose the very mental state it was designed to represent. What Clarissa's unconsciousness establishes for the psychological novel, then, is a pattern of psychological complexity that does not at all directly express mental states but rather relies on the contradiction built into the formal stipulation of them. Psychological complexity, that is, pits the stipulated mental state against one's actual mental state, so that one is able to resist without resisting, can have a mental state even in unconsciousness, and is unable to consent even if one wants to.

The contradiction that establishes psychological complexity, then, enables us to reread Lovelace's aesthetic detachment. For Lovelace has appeared in the role of the artist who is committed to a proliferation of meanings, and, in the terms of William Warner's deconstructive account of him, he has continually dispersed and recreated himself to acknowledge the absurdity of the connection between any particular form and any particular significance.[26] In this he seems to doubt both the ability of forms to determine mental states and the ability of mental states to determine forms. But his very boldness in trying out different roles represents not so much an escape from connections between intentions and forms as a reversal of what might seem their usual sequence. He can thus distance himself from forms, but only by insisting that the form be completed by a mental state. Always proceeding as if there could be no such thing as an unclaimed form, a form detached from someone's mental state, he cannot himself exercise the freedom he prides himself on until someone else has fulfilled the form. As becomes clear from his bafflement at Clarissa's continuing resistance to the rape, form for Lovelace implies a mental state. Lovelace's account of himself is that he will discover what it was that he intended when he sees how things turn out, so that his account of his intentions is that they are infinitely variable precisely because they are defined as arbitrary, operating as a fictional code in which he assumes different parts at the will of the imaginary text that he is elaborating. This apparent suspension of representational will, however, is equivalent to the greatest possible confidence that the very perception of a form or an act involves the perceiver's assent. Whatever is, is made right by the perceiver rather than the initiator of the form. After the rape, however, it becomes clear that he has imagined, like Brownmiller and Dworkin, that the forms of actions—however fictitious—carry mental states like intention and consent within them. Form, in this account, can never really be contradicted, only replaced or outdistanced.

From Lovelace's standpoint, then, the chillingly brief letter that announces the rape to Belford is not so much a confessional or even a triumphant one as a bizarre kind of birth announcement: "And now, Belford, I can go no farther. The affair is over. Clarissa lives."[27] Lovelace, having followed out the logic of his plottings and his plot, sees them as having resulted in the annihilation of the affair and the creation of Clarissa. That is, the rape for him is at least as much the transfer of intention as it is an attempt to "know" Clarissa. He must "know" her not only to know what she knows, but also so that he will be able to have a sense of how his plottings have come out—so that he will know what it was that he meant.

When Lovelace's intention does not get translated into consent, his rape of her is rendered perpetually incomplete. Thus he writes with gloomy self-pity to Belford:

Caesar never knew what it was to be *hypped* [depressed], I will call it, till he came to be what Pompey was; that is to say, till he arrived at the height of his ambition: nor did thy Lovelace know what it was to be gloomy, till he had completed his wishes upon the charmingest creature in the world, as the other did his upon the most potent republic that ever existed.

And yet why say I, *completed*? when the *will*, the *consent*, is wanting—and I have still views before me of obtaining that? (888)

In Lovelace's terms, the rape remains incomplete, because the only evidence that would count as the apprehension of the rape is Clarissa's consent. He can, thus, never discover the shape of his own intention, as long as the rape remains self-canceling—which it inherently becomes in two senses. Without Clarissa's consent, the rape remains incomplete, and it therefore seems, in Lovelace's account, not a rape. Were the rape to be validated by Clarissa's consent, however, it would cease to be rape and would instead count as seduction (or marriage, according to Brownmiller's account of Hebrew law)—intercourse as the act of discovering what one really wanted all along.

Just before the rape, Lovelace, having noticed Clarissa's suspicion of the legion of fictitious agents he has planted in the world he has substituted for her bourgeois home, writes to Belford that "her mistrust is a little of the latest to do her service" (882). Having mistrusted too late, she is, he thinks, no longer in a position to imagine that she can set the conditions of her liking or her trust. And it seems that Clarissa fully emerges as an individual in her insistence that she can continue to refuse to accept Lovelace's valuation of her, that she thinks she can always continue to deny her consent. The question of consent comes to be framed, alternatively, by the Lovelacean view that "the action" is already over and that consent has always implicitly been given, and by Clarissa's view that consent can only be given freely and thus that the act of deciding the value of an action—the interpretation of it—is itself a kind of prospectiveness, a claim that "the action" is never over.

Lovelace, trying to gain his point that Clarissa's consent is already contained within the events that have already transpired, thus offers a series of ways of domesticating the rape. First, he suggests, in an echo of rape law as it was established prior to the Statutes of Westminster of 1285, that Clarissa should redeem him through marriage. If his marrying her will redeem her reputation, her marrying him will redeem him from the crime that she charges him with (if only outside the legal system). The appeal of marriage for Lovelace, then, is that it establishes the wife's consent as a stipulated state, and one that of necessity exonerates him. He imagines that Clarissa's consent to marriage, once given, amounts to a wife's irrevocable consent—so irrevocable even as to apply before it was given. To the man who has said "*A wife at any time*," the fixity of the implications of marriage allows considerable latitude in the timing of a woman's consent (915); the form of consent will count as having always existed. Thus his first stratagem after the rape is to convince Clarissa that they are already married: "I would at first have persuaded her, and offered to call witnesses to the truth of it, that we were actually married" (889; cf. 896).

What Lovelace wants, then, is not so much consent as the effect of consent. He therefore repeatedly misses the point of Clarissa's having been unconscious at the time of the rape. Thinking that her unconsciousness merely preserves her honor, he archly writes to Belford, "I know thou hast such an high opinion of this lady's virtue, that thou wouldst be disappointed if thou hadst reason to think that she was subdued by *her own* consent, or any the *least* yielding in her will" (888). Clarissa's unconsciousness is, for him, merely the absence of her consent, a deficiency that will be retrospectively repaired. This is why he imagines it would serve his purposes just as well to convince Clarissa that she had married him while she was unconscious, and why he imagines that he can point to the fact that other people take them to be married as an argument that Clarissa should think them married. In the same spirit, he fantasizes that Clarissa will discover herself to be pregnant from the rape:

Were I to be sure that this foundation [Clarissa's pregnancy] is laid (and why may I not hope it is?), I should not doubt to have her still (should she withstand her day of grace) on my own conditions: nor should I, if it were so, question that *revived* affection in *her* which a woman seldom fails to have for the father of her first child, whether born in wedlock or out of it. (917)

Pregnancy would provide a reason for Clarissa to consent, to set things right; a child would represent in little the society whose version of things Lovelace is continually asking Clarissa to consider and to accept as her measure. Moreover, he can speak significantly in this fantasy of Clarissa's *revived* affection, because he is clearly taking the imagined pregnancy as a sign of consent. For while commentators like Sir Matthew Hale specifically denied "that it can be no rape if the woman conceive with child,"[28] Hale was directly responding to legal commentators in the formalist tradition I have outlined who had claimed that conception was presumptive evidence of consent.

Lovelace, while not worrying particularly about whether he would or would not be acquitted in a trial for rape, thus continually presents the evidence that would make it look as though Clarissa had consented to their relationship. She had created the conditions that resembled consent not just in running off with him but in appearing to agree to live in the same house with him, in appearing to be his wife, and her pregnancy might have appeared as just the final formal version of consent, her body speaking truly in open opposition to her voice.[29] Although Clarissa rails against the misrepresentations involved in seeing any of these appearances as expressions of consent, Lovelace goes further than merely answering her when he argues that some version of consent is implicit in participating in any appearance at all. Clarissa would invent independence "at the latest," he argues to Belford: "And as to the state of obligation, there is no such thing as living without being beholden to somebody. Mutual obligation is the very essence and soul of the social and commercial life—Why should *she* be exempt from it?" (760).

On this account, persons are persons not because they preexist society but because they are continually produced by their sociability, their coming into view and contact with other persons. From Lovelace's perspective, then, there can be no such thing as the falseness, the false personation, that Clarissa accuses Lovelace of. For the falseness involved in his impersonating a husband is, on his account, necessarily redeemed by the fact that it can produce true persons. To send the false impression out into the world is to set up a part of that structure of obligation which is "the soul of social and commercial life." Falseness is then truth, because it is instrumental in producing truth. Lovelace's falsehood is a falsehood he continually justifies as fundamentally truthful, because its aim was to produce forms that would tell both Clarissa and him what it was they really wanted, who it was they really were.

The Lovelacean apology for his act of rape continually equates his role in relation to Clarissa with the role of society in relation to any newborn infant. For him, individual existence thus involves an acknowledgment of events and forms that preexist the individual. Identity is forged in the process of the individual's adjusting to make the text of the past event whole, to make it come out right. Thus the notion of agency is transferred from the rapist to the victim, from the active party to the passive one, as Lovelace's continuing complaints and self-pity over Clarissa's bad reaction to the rape suggest. *Caveat lector.* Like the letters that circulate in authentic or forged form throughout the novel, the truth or falsity of any transfer of meaning becomes the responsibility of the recipient.

For Lovelace, however, the greatest impediment to the project of transferring responsibility to Clarissa lies in his having resorted to "art," his having drugged her to effect the rape. Lack of consciousness, both in the law and in the logic of the novel, always counts as nonconsent. While there may be two bodies—Lovelace's and Clarissa's—involved in the rape, only one person is present. The central argument that Lovelace has been making is that responsibility is always to be dispersed, diffused among a number of persons other than himself, and his entire defense must rest on the desperate effort to multiply himself retroactively to make it look as though there was anyone at the rape except him. This is why he needs the formulae of consent—the marriage, the pregnancy—that would belie

Clarissa's resistance and establish that she was there—and why he continually frames the rape that she did not consent to with the events that she did participate in—the elopement, residence in the same house.

From Lovelace's standpoint, then, Clarissa's unconsciousness at the time of the rape ought to be a matter of complete indifference, because he imagines that the form of the act should make consent implicit. Clarissa's derangement after the rape is, therefore, particularly troubling to him because it indicates that his effort to make states of consciousness derive from the forms of action has not taken. The mad papers that Clarissa writes after resuming consciousness seem designed to cast doubt on the capacity of any written form to connect with a mental state. As Terry Castle has observed, "Clarissa's mutilation of her own discourse suggests not only an impulse toward self-destruction, but also a massive, indeed traumatic loss of faith in articulation, and the power of the letter to render meaning."[30] But while Castle sees "the mutilation of sense and syntax" in the mad letters as being "linked to a loss of selfhood" (120), one might want to modify that implicit claim about the link between the self and the representation of it. For the disruption physically wreaked on the letters itself establishes a representational homology with the stipulated state that may or may not correspond with one's mental state.

In the representational conventions of the epistolary novel, the convention of reading acts as a kind of stipulation. The characters repeatedly claim that they are writing, in the famous Richardsonian phrase, "to the moment," that they are setting down for each other accounts of events that have just transpired. Readers, likewise, do not pause to wonder that what they accept as an up-to-the-minute account of what just happened could already have been written about and could have been returned from the printer's in orderly lines that do not look at all like anyone's handwriting. Convention prescribes that the characters' script always looks like a printed page. To call attention to this stipulation, however, is to indicate the discrepancy between the handwriting that the printed page has been defined to be and the print that it so palpably is. Richardson produces this effect particularly strikingly in the tenth paper that Clarissa writes after the rape, in which the lines of writing run at off angles on the page. Various critics have noted that this paper shows, in Ronald Paulson's phrase, "the printed page itself" becoming "a form of mimesis."[31] The very impulse of using the printed page to ape Clarissa's mental derangement with skewed and unjustified lines of print is, however, both mimetic and antimimetic at the same time, for it calls attention to the fact that one has dutifully been reading for hundreds of pages as if the printed page counted as handwriting. Thus, the tenth mad paper operates as a kind of failed ostensive definition; the typographical arrangement of the words converts the letter into a kind of display of itself, a sign announcing "this is handwriting," but the very announcement of what the letter is—or would be—acts to point to the obviousness of the fact that the type is not handwriting. It is a mimesis of distinction rather than of similarity, a pitting of stipulation against its internal self-contradiction.

More than a fiction of nature or truth, more than the representation of epistolarity as a matter of "writing to the moment," Richardson's formal insistence here upon a mimesis of distinction represents something like his invention of a new aesthetic. For it represents in formal terms the negative that Clarissa continually deploys against what comes to look like Lovelace's complacent acceptance of forms. Perhaps nothing else epitomizes Lovelace so much as his sense of the capaciousness of forms, his susceptibility to the notion of reformation in the purely pagan terms of metamorphosis, in which matter is never lost but merely converted into a new shape. If he thus imagined that Clarissa would recognize herself in a new form as a result of the rape and would become what she had been made, he did not count on her capacity continually to produce a negative that leaves the business of forms appear to be unfinished. He did not, that is, count on her reforming herself into a version of the disorderly letter. For the force of her negative is not merely to oppose Lovelace but to see his effort at converting her nonconsent into consent not as making her a woman but as returning her to girlhood, to the legal infancy that means that she could not consent even if she wanted to. Clarissa makes her body, the body that Lovelace had hoped to convert into a form of consent, into a slowly wasting sign of the inability of a form to carry mental states in anything but excessively capacious (that is, ambiguous) or potentially self-contradictory stipulated forms. Thus her notoriously slow-paced death is itself a way of calling attention to the states like consent that seem illusory to a character like Lovelace. For from the moment after the rape, when Clarissa begins dying and Lovelace begins longing for her consent, the novel is literally haunted by the specter of psychology, in which mental states do not so much appear as register the improbability of their appearing. The psychological novel arises by registering the enormity of Lovelace's sophisticated but absolutely unquestioning belief in representation, in thinking that a body with its blushes can represent an interior state like consent or that a printed page can announce itself as handwriting.

For what Lovelace had merely taken as the absence of consent—Clarissa's unconsciousness during the rape—turns out to be for Clarissa the condition for the impossibility of consent. In the law unconsciousness "negatives" consent, in much the same way as being ten years old—or twelve or sixteen—"negatives" it. Thus, although Lovelace expects Clarissa's unconsciousness to be over when it is over, Clarissa recognizes it as something like a stipulated state—an ongoing condition of the impossibility of consenting whether one consents or not. She had said, on Lovelace's account, that she was "cast from a state of *independency into one of obligation*" (760), and her progressive reduction of her body mimics a return to the body of a ten-year-old, in which one's actual consent (or nonconsent) and one's ability to consent potentially contradict one another. In such a stipulated state as legal infancy, there is no inevitability that the difference between one's mental state—what one wants—and one's stipulated state—what one must want—will appear. But the contradiction makes the difference between mental states and their formal stand-ins, stipulated states, visible. To Lovelace's effort to read the form of the act of rape as stipulating consent, Clarissa thus responds with her own persistent impersonation of stipulated nonconsent. For him, lack of consent will (eventually) carry consent, become its opposite; for her, not having consented establishes a condition of dependency that makes nonconsent inevitable (no matter what she might want). In her white dress and increasingly childlike body, she represents the difference between the *Bildungsroman*, with its project of maturation, and the psychological novel, which can never get ahead, because its way of manifesting itself in the world is to make apparent its own subjection to a stipulated state—a legal infancy—that its conditional likings and wishes can strain against and contradict but never escape.

Much of the most powerful recent criticism of *Clarissa*—particularly that of Warner, Castle, and Eagleton—suggests an equivalence between the violence enacted by Lovelace in the act of rape and the violence of any interpretative gesture. Thus, Warner can write that "Clarissa's narrative letters work to give the 'subject' (as a center of consciousness) dominion over several more passive and compliant 'subjects'"[32] and can see Clarissa's intention to reform Lovelace as being essentially as violent as the rape, his effort to reform her. And Castle can very powerfully align Lovelace's physical penetration of Clarissa with his interpretative penetration of her. Clarissa is, for Castle, "a hermeneutic casualty" because she "remains the subject of his interpretation," but she is also a victim in any situation in which another character thinks ill of her.[33] Clarissa is, for example, a cipher available for mere projection when she is subjected to "Arabella's lurid reading of her behavior and her part in family history," which is part and parcel of the "linguistic oppression instituted by the Harlowes" (62). Similarly, Eagleton can claim that Clarissa's victimization in rape amounts to political victimization, her having become a figure in someone else's game:

Sexuality, far from being some displacement of class conflict, is the very medium in which it is conducted. In one sense, the novel does indeed sharply counterpose social relations and sexuality: Clarissa has the unenviable choice of becoming a pawn in the Harlowe's property game or Lovelace's erotic object. Yet this contradiction between bourgeois property and aristocratic anarchy conceals a deeper complicity. Both display a form of possessive individualism.[34]

The privileged position in all of these accounts is the position of relative inactivity, and the critics differ primarily in assigning different degrees of interpretative activity—and thus violence—to Clarissa. For Warner, Clarissa is more violent than Lovelace; for Castle, she is less so. Through the logic that equates knowledge of things with sexuality in the language of "penetration" and "probing" and "knowing," the best is not to know. What I have been arguing, however, is that Richardson's achievement in *Clarissa* is to insist on a fundamental mistake in the idea of equating epistemology and psychology.

Were we to construct a conjectural history of the rape story we would describe it in terms of a narrative about symbolic systems themselves, a narrative in which the distance between objects and persons is progressively increased. Thus, Rousseau in the *Essay on the Origin of Languages* tells the story of the rape of the concubine or wife of the Levite of Ephraim in illustration of the claim that "if the only needs we ever experienced were physical, we should most likely never have been able to speak."[35] We would, he says, "have been able to establish societies little different from those we have, or such as would have been better able to achieve their goals" (9), if we had had only a language of signs and gestures. The efficiency of such a language emerges when he describes how the Levite communicated the story of his wife's rape by sending her mutilated body to the tribes of Israel:

When the Levite of Ephraim wanted to avenge the death of his wife, he wrote nothing to the tribes of Israel, but divided her body into twelve sections which he sent to them. At this horrible sight they rushed to arms, crying with one voice: *Never has such a thing happened in Israel . . . !* And the tribe of Benjamin was exterminated. (7)

Violation precedes mutilation, which in turn leads to extermination. The efficiency of the symbolic system here is its absolute murderousness. The sense that there is nothing that needs to be said to explicate the twelve sections of the woman's dead body is what it means for this symbolic system to be completely effective—and what it means for it to be a system that eliminates ambiguity as it eliminates persons.

The story of the rape of Philomela might represent the second stage in the progressive account of rape and symbols. The account of Philomela eventuates in something like the same structure of outrage for outrage, retaliation for violation, that the biblical story does. Yet it does so by foregrounding the indirection of the means of revenge. Philomela, having been raped by her brother-in-law Tereus after he took her from her father's care, is silenced when Tereus cuts out her tongue to prevent her speaking of the violation. She then weaves a tapestry that recounts the story, using "the voice of the shuttle" to replace the voice she has lost and to prompt her sister Procne to join her in avenging the crime, by tricking him into eating the flesh of his own son Itys. The story retains the revenge plot of the biblical story, but it both gauges the revenge more precisely—the death of Tereus' son for the rape of Pandian's daughter—and makes the process of weaving emphasize the protraction and suspension of that plot. In some sense the story becomes the story of suspension itself as it becomes an account of the origin of poetry in the nightingale's leaning on a thorn to dictate to poets its song.

It is not so much that the art of poetry operates as a compensation for the reality of suffering; it is that the very process of searching for equivalences becomes an account of overcompensation, of Philomela's being able to tell her story by weaving when she had no voice and then of gaining a new voice with which to sing, if only in a speech that must be translated. As the story is elaborated, Philomela has both revenge and, then, poetry. If the basic assumption of the metamorphic tradition is that nature is created directly out of human culture and human event, the story of Philomela uses a catastrophic event—rape—to provide an origin for poetry. The specific technological advantage of poetry in this account is that it makes the process of remembering even more important than what is remembered. Philomela, as someone whose story is continually recast or decanted, translates event into tapestry into event, but the process of recasting seems to outlive the matching of act for act, revenge for rape. Memory in excess of action is what remains in the form of the nightingale and her song.[36]

If the story of Philomela presents itself as a kind of technical and technological improvement over the story of the rape of Levite's wife, then the story of the rape of Clarissa similarly declares itself to be inaugurating a new genre. While the metamorphic account of rape gives the shape of memory to the story of an unspeakable act, Richardson rewrites the rape story to create the psychological novel.[37] The novel is psychological, moreover, not because it is about the plausibility of its characters but because it insists upon the importance of psychology as the ongoing possibility of the contradiction between what one must mean and what one wants to mean. In fact, it is psychological precisely for the implausibility of a character like Clarissa, whose actions always seem precipitous to the point of unpredictability (as in her elopement with Lovelace, which looks now as if it is, now as if it isn't, going to succeed). For it sets itself up against the metamorphic account of form that insists that forms can never be outrun, that they only, possibly, can be redeemed through recycling, by exposing the self-negations of the very stipulations that seem to make it possible to interpret them. For as soon as the existence of a particular form is taken as stipulating a mental state like consent, the possibility of contradiction within the stipulated state makes it clear that that stipulation has not so much resolved the more general problem of interpretation as recreated it in a form that guarantees some meaning but not necessarily *anyone's* meaning. *Clarissa* becomes a psychological novel, then, not just in representing the ambiguity of forms and the struggles inherent in interpretation. In adapting the spirit of the Lovelacean stipulation that nonconsent can be consent, Clarissa answers Lovelace not just by refusing her retroactive consent to the act of rape but by living the stipulated contradiction that his act and his construction of it have made visible. Stipulation, trying to put a limit to ambiguity by defining the understanding of a term or a situation, is potentially infinite. But what *Clarissa* argues is that all the negotiations in the world cannot supply the deficiency in stipulation that is made apparent when a thing may be its opposite. Stipulation may be from one standpoint a way of securing agreement and a way of allowing for ambiguity; I make a statement, I make a statement but cross my fingers, I make a statement but cross my fingers and say that crosses don't count. But from Clarissa's standpoint, it has become simultaneously infinite and irrelevant at the moment when the price of ambiguity turns out to be the possibility of internal contradiction. If Lovelace's act of rape essentially stipulates that nonconsent can be—or become—consent, Clarissa's achievement—and her plight—is to become the living embodiment of a legally stipulated state of infancy in which the contradiction can never be overcome and not even consent itself can count to override nonconsent.

Notes

My thinking on the issue of rape and its relationship to symbolic structures has been, at every stage, challenged and refined by my discussions with Walter Benn Michaels, who has read and commented on various drafts of this essay. I am also grateful to Carol Clover and Lynn Hunt for their scrupulous readings of the penultimate version.

1. Susan Estrich focuses on the issue of consent and nonconsent in the third chapter of her powerful book on rape and the legal treatment of it; *Real Rape* (Cambridge, Mass., 1987), esp. 29–41.
2. Ibid., 8–26; Susan Brownmiller, *Against Our Will: Men, Women, and Rape* (New York, 1975), 1–22; Camille E. Le Grande, "Rape and Rape Laws: Sexism in Society and Law," in *Forcible Rape: The Crime, the Victim, and the Offender*, ed. Duncan Chappell, Robley Geis, and Gilbert Geis (New York, 1977), 67–83.
3. Matthew Hale, *Historia Placitorum Coronae: The History of the Pleas of the Crown*, ed. Sollom Emlyn (1736); rev. ed. George Wilson (Dublin, 1778), 635.
4. Brownmiller, *Against Our Will*, 413–14.
5. Estrich, *Real Rape*, 28–29. See also Frederick J. Ludwig, *Rape and the Law: The Crime and Its Proof* (New York, 1977), 37–38. Characterizing Hale as "an unusually literate English jurist," Ludwig points to Hale's classification of the criminal law and proceeds to cast some doubt on his reliability in the following description:

   > Sir Matthew was the inventor three centuries ago of the nomenclature employed today in the criminal law: felony and misdemeanor and the single-word symbol for the composite elements of behavior constituting a crime, such as burglary and rape. But Sir Matthew also presided at trials of females resulting in their conviction for witchcraft. Protection of innocent males, of course, depends upon the state of mind of the victim at the time of the alleged act of the male, and it is desirable to consider revenge, blackmail, and hallucination of the female victim. Sir Matthew perpetuated the syndrome of "a woman's revenge" in rape.

6. Ludwig, *Rape and the Law*, 1–2.
7. Hale, *History of the Pleas of the Crown*, 636.
8. Cesare Marchese de Beccaria, *An Essay on Crimes and Punishments* (1764; Albany, N.Y., 1872), 50–51.

9. R. v. Billingsley, *The English and Empire Digest* 15, part 17 (1947), 1210, no. 7751.

10. See Robert Chambers, *A Course of Lectures on the English Law, 1767–1773*, ed. Thomas M. Curley, 2 vols. (Madison, Wisc., 1986), 1:406.

11. Chambers provides a remarkably lucid and compact narrative history of the legal treatment of rape generally; ibid., 1:405–7. His account of the circumstantial nature of evidence appears on 1:406. See also Charles Viner, *A General Abridgment of Law and Equity* (Dublin, 1793), 153–55, esp. 154, for a discussion of the circumstantial evidence of rape.

12. Brownmiller, *Against Our Will*, 11.

13. Ibid., 4.

14. Andrea Dworkin, *Intercourse* (New York, 1987), 133.

15. Ludwig provides a brief history of the historical development of the notion of an age of consent; *Rape and the Law*, 7–10. As he notes, "The age of consent for rape, which is usually identical with that of consent for marriage, has advanced in most states by statutes which have fixed the age usually at either eighteen or at sixteen" (8).

16. See also Chambers, *Lectures on English Law*, 1:406.

17. Estrich, *Real Rape*, 100–104.

18. Brownmiller, *Against Our Will*, 12–13.

19. Beccaria, *Essay on Crimes and Punishments*, 47–48.

20. Margaret Doody, *A Natural Passion: A Study of the Novels of Samuel Richardson* (Oxford, 1974), 128 and passim.

21. Michael McKeon, *The Origins of the English Novel, 1600–1740* (Baltimore, 1987), esp. 21–22.

22. Ian Watt, *The Rise of the Novel* (Berkeley, 1967), 194.

23. Terry Castle, *Clarissa's Ciphers: Meaning and Disruption in Richardson's "Clarissa"* (Ithaca, N.Y., 1982), 16 and 57–80.

24. Terry Eagleton, *The Rape of Clarissa: Writing, Sexuality, and Class Struggle in Samuel Richardson* (Minneapolis, 1982), 62.

25. Thus, the law of rape is less equivocal in siding with Clarissa than many literary critics have been. See the passage cited above from Watt and particularly Judith Wilt, "He Could Go No Farther: A Modest Proposal About Lovelace and Clarissa," *PMLA* 92, no. 1 (1977): 19–32, which argues that the rape may well not have occurred.

26. William Beatty Warner, *Reading "Clarissa": The Struggles of Interpretation* (New Haven, 1979), 50–52.

27. Samuel Richardson, *Clarissa; or, The History of a Young Lady*, ed. Angus Ross (Harmondsworth, Eng., 1985), 883. I follow the text of the Penguin edition, which offers the complete text of the first edition. Although the obvious disadvantage of this text is that it omits the material that Richardson added in the second and third editions, its advantage is its ready availability. Further references to this edition of *Clarissa* will appear in parentheses in the text.

28. Hale, *History of the Pleas of the Crown*, 631.

29. I have found no full legal articulation of the view that conception could only occur if a woman achieved orgasm and that orgasm itself had to be consensual, but, as Carol Clover pointed out to me, one would imagine that this particular line of argument was connected with eighteenth-century medical accounts of a link between female orgasm and conception. For a discussion of such views and their decline, see Thomas Laqueur, "Orgasm, Generation, and the Politics of Reproductive Biology," *Representations* 14 (Spring 1986): 1–41.

30. Castle, *Clarissa's Ciphers*, 43.

31. Ronald Paulson, *Emblem and Expression: Meaning in English Art in the Eighteenth Century* (Cambridge, Mass., 1975), 51.
32. Warner, *Reading "Clarissa,"* 90.
33. Castle, *Clarissa's Ciphers*, 16.
34. Eagleton, *The Rape of Clarissa*, 88.
35. Jean-Jacques Rousseau, *Essay on the Origin of Languages*, trans. John H. Moran, in *On the Origin of Language* (New York, 1966), 9.
36. Patricia Joplin's suggestive "The Voice of the Shuttle Is Ours," which I am grateful to have had the opportunity to read in typescript, argues that the rape narrative provides an occasion for a specifically female claim to articulation.
37. Carol Clover has suggested to me the possibility of tracing this representational history of rape through a film like *Birth of a Nation*, which, arguably, uses the question of rape in the service of a statement of its own establishment of a new representational mode.

NAOMI SCHOR

The Portrait of a Gentleman: Representing Men in (French) Women's Writing

I want to know
your true opinion
which one you prefer, and what's
the mirror where you stare

For the mirror with no image so disrupts
my rhyme that it almost interrupts it
but then when I remember what my name records,
all my thoughts unite in one accord
—Lombarda

IN 1980 AN EXHIBITION was held in London that, according to its organizers, "aroused enormous controversy and attracted record attendances."[1] The theme of the exhibit was "Women's Images of Men." Not surprisingly, male critics responded with particular outrage to this attempt on the part of women to "look back," to reverse the centuries-old model-artist relationship, just as some hundred or so years earlier the impudent gaze of Manet's *Olympia* had aroused the ire of a primarily male bourgeois spectatorship.

What made the London exhibit so shocking was not merely its display of images of men produced by women, for after all women artists have been producing male imagos for centuries. Nor was it the fact that these images, informed by the feminist revolution of the second half of the twentieth century, were overtly political. What created the scandal and drew the crowds was that the women artists who displayed their work in various media at the Institute of Contemporary Arts, in a manner unimaginable to women artists of earlier times—who were, as we know, barred from the figure drawing classes of the Academy—dared to depict the male nude, indeed the penis in every state from the limp to the erect. Now the transgression of the secular taboo on women representing the male sexual organ is, as Sarah Kent reminds us, a very recent phenomenon: "With a few notable exceptions like Suzanne Valadon and Alice Neel, the male nude is a subject that women have turned to only during the last twenty years—a minute length of time when compared to the illustrious history of its female counterpart."[2] To subject the penis to representation is to strip the phallus of its empowering veil, for—and much of what follows turns on this aporia—while the phallus can be said to draw its symbolic power from the *visibility of the penis*, phallic power derives precisely from *the phallus's inaccessibility to representation*. Again in the words of Sarah Kent: "This points to a fundamental problem in depicting the penis. For as a symbol of masculine power, authority, and potency within the patriarchy the phallus has to carry an enormous burden of significance. That bulge in the trousers on which the hero's sexual identity depends and on which pop stars, like Elvis, focused their fans' attention to such good effect, cannot withstand exposure to view."[3]

Clearly it is a far cry from the risqué visual representations of male sexual organs by late-twentieth-century women artists to the non-sexually-explicit textual representations of male characters by such women writers as Mme. de Lafayette, Mme. de Staël, and George Sand, but I will want to argue here that at least in France—and the question of national difference will have to be considered—the representation of men by women writers has been every bit as subversive of phallic hegemony over the symbolic as the unveiled penises on view in the "Women's Images of Men" exhibit. But, because of the constraints of a representational system coterminous with patriarchy, the women writers I have in mind were obliged to resort to complex strategies to lay bare the source of both male power and female powerlessness. My argument is based on the close analysis of a recurrent scene, a female topos, that links up Mme. de Lafayette's *The Princesse de Clèves*, Mme. de Staël's *Corinne*, and George Sand's *Indiana*. Briefly stated: the scene stages the violation by the male gaze of the female protagonist's private space and the male protagonist's discovery therein of a portrait, his own and/or that of another masculine figure.

But, as a preliminary to the detailed examination of this recurrent "portrait of a gentleman" scene, I want to raise the larger theoretical issue at stake here, that is, the representation of men in women's writing, a question neglected by feminist critics (myself included) more concerned with the urgent question of the representation of women first by male writers and, more recently, by women writers.[4] Though the field has hardly been exhausted, it seems opportune now to turn to the question of the representation of the Other's other, and some of the questions before us then are: what strategies do women writers enlist to represent men? Are they different from those at work in men's writings about women? Do they cut across national boundaries and constitute a specificity of women's fiction?

That the representation of men is problematic for the female novelist is stated very clearly by George Sand in the preface to one of her early woman-centered novellas. Responding to the criticism that in her writings she systematically foregrounds and favors her female characters, Sand writes:

It is very difficult for a woman to successfully define and depict a fully worthy man and above all to *employ* him as the active protagonist in a novel. For a woman writer to know well the causes and the play of man's moral forces, she must with time, observation, and some studies unjustly reputed useless to her sex and estate become not man himself, for that would be impossible, but somewhat less of the child she was left by her early education. She will then be able to understand certain intellectual preoccupations foreign to her and not restrict the masculine role to his relationship to love or the family.

Lest these remarks appear to suggest that male writers experience no difficulty in representing women, Sand goes on to say:

To be fair, let us say that men writers also experience great difficulties when it comes to entering with delicacy and impartiality into woman's heart and mind. In general they make her too ugly or too beautiful, too weak or too strong, and those who have met the rugged challenge of this work of divination know that it is no small thing.

Yet, for all her attempts at evenhandedness, Sand goes on to conclude: "Thanks to his more complete education and more practiced reasoning, man can more easily depict woman than woman can depict man."[5]

Sand's problematization of gender-bound representations is itself characteristically problematic, in that it stops well short of contesting the system of values that accords less prestige to depictions of the domestic and erotic spheres inhabited by women than to the supposedly wider spheres in which men traditionally deploy their activities: commerce, the professions, war. No lover of the homely details of everyday life, Sand does not valorize the world of home and family. And yet, despite Sand's implicit endorsement here (and elsewhere) of the ideology that attaches more value to representations of public than private spaces, despite her explicit privileging of men's writing, her remarks install a significant and potentially subversive dissymmetry between gentlemen and lady novelists. For whereas women writers are prevented from creating well-rounded protagonists by their infantilizing education, men writers fail in their depictions of women for reasons less amenable to remediation: lack of tact and fairness. Their representations are distorted by a seemingly congenital blindness; theirs is a failure not of education but of vision. Thus, while recognizing the advantages enjoyed by her male contemporaries in representing the Other, Sand implies that in the long run, when women are given equal access to higher education, it is the men who will be at a disadvantage. It will require a complete overhaul of the curriculum—the introduction of women's studies, perhaps?—to enable men to represent women without indulging in the twin excesses that are the hallmarks of male misogyny: idealization and demonization.

Male critics who have recently raised the specter of misandry, a sort of woman writers' revenge, would, I am well aware, want to take issue with the scenario I have teased out of Sand's text. They would argue, as does K. K. Ruthven, that it is only for lack of opportunity that women have not produced a volume of misandrous representations to rival the proliferation of misogynous representations produced by men:

If men appear to have spent more time abusing women than women men (which is what the textual evidence suggests), this is not because misandry is a more rare phenomenon than misogyny, but because for several centuries most printed books were written by men. "If wommen hadde writen stories," Chaucer's wife of Bath points out, "They wolde han writen of men moore wikkednesse / Than al the mark of Adam may redresse"—to which one can only add that feminist writing published during the last fifteen years or so has been doing what it can to ensure that misandry will eventually be as well represented in print as misogyny now is.[6]

That there have been excesses committed in recent women's writings about men is open to debate, providing, of course, that specific examples of offending texts are cited in place of such unverifiable references as "feminist writing published during the last fifteen years or so." But the unquestioned assumption that misandry simply *mirrors* misogyny is, arguably, only another avatar of phallocentrism's "old dream of symmetry," to quote Luce Irigaray, and as such is highly suspect. The important question, however, lies elsewhere and it is: can men, who have for centuries enjoyed a virtually undisputed monopoly on the means of representation—the pen, the brush, and the chisel—so surely distinguish between misandry and women's talking, looking, and writing back? The discourse of misogyny, let us recall, has throughout the centuries singled out for unique scorn women who, refusing to be mere signs to be exchanged among men, have sought instead to become producers and circulators of signs in their own right: the *précieuse* in seventeenth-century France, the bluestocking in nineteenth-century France and England.[7] To put the question another way: can men who have for centuries, as Virginia Woolf so memorably phrases it in *A Room of One's Own*, consigned women to the role of magnifying mirrors so surely distinguish between life-size representations and caricatures? In her unendingly prescient book, Woolf suggests that when women do write, they provide their male readers with a view of "the spot the size of a shilling at the back of the head [which one can never see for oneself]."[8] Finally, the question is: can men stand the sight of their blind spot, or, having caught a glimpse of it, will they hastily turn their gaze back on Woolf's reassuring "female looking glasses," which possess "the delicious power of reflecting the figure of man at twice its natural size"?[9] It is with these questions in mind that I would like to turn now to my reading of *The Princesse de Clèves*, *Corinne*, and *Indiana*.

That *The Princesse de Clèves* is the inaugural text of the French psychological novel is a matter of historical record, and Mme. de Lafayette's place in the canon—unlike those of Mme. de Staël and George Sand—is secure. And yet it is only now, in the wake of pioneering feminist studies of the novel by such critics as Nancy K. Miller, Peggy Kamuf, Marianne Hirsch, and Joan de Jean, that *The Princesse de Clèves*'s role as the matrix of French *women's* fiction can begin to be fully grasped and assessed.[10] French women novelists well into the nineteenth century appear to have inscribed themselves into a specifically female literary tradition by endlessly rewriting and refashioning the story of the beautiful young princess who loves a man who is not her husband, implausibly confesses her illicit love to her husband, and still more implausibly refuses to marry the object of her passion when her husband dies of grief, leaving her free to wed whomever she pleases. My concern in what follows, however, is with *The Princesse* as a model not for fictions of avowal and renunciation but for representations of men in a manner that calls into question what Nancy K. Miller has described as the "subject in power['s] . . . fascination" with "his own representation."[11] What the discovery of the intertextual relationship linking *The Princesse de Clèves*, *Corinne*, and *Indiana* demonstrates is the persistence in French women's writings of representations of men that work to unsettle man's secure relationship to his own image and the representational system it underwrites.

After both her husband and her would-be lover, M. de Nemours, depart from the court at the king's bidding, the Princesse de Clèves decides to go to Coulommiers, her country estate. In retreating to her private space, the princess does not leave Nemours altogether behind because her baggage includes some paintings of historical scenes in which the duke figures prominently:

> She went to Coulommiers, taking with her two big pictures which had been copied for her from originals painted for Madame de Valentinois's beautiful house at Anet and which represented all the outstanding events of the King's reign. Among others there was the siege of Metz, with portraits of all those who had distinguished themselves there; M. de Nemours was one of these and *perhaps* that may have been the reason why Madame de Clèves was so anxious to own these paintings.[12]

The use of the word *perhaps* here is distinctly at odds with the omniscient stance of the "knowing narrator"[13] throughout the story and thus serves to draw the reader's attention to these paintings and to the princess's interest in them well before they are foregrounded in the narrative. Indeed it is only several pages later that the doubt cast by the narrator on the princess's motives for transporting these bulky works of art—a doubt that does not so much diminish the narrator's omniscience as underscore the princess's unawareness of her own feelings—is lifted. Alone at night in the pavilion where she is at last able to give free rein to her erotic fantasies, the princess contemplates the portrait of Nemours with rapt adoration:

> She took a candlestick and went up to a big table which stood before the picture of the siege of Metz in which was a portrait of M. de Nemours. She sat down and gazed at this portrait with a far-away look that only love can give. (168)

There is in *Pride and Prejudice* an analogous scene, where on a visit to Darcy's estate Elizabeth Bennet stands similarly transfixed before a portrait of her suitor. However, as one critic has remarked: "Elizabeth can accept the hand of the man who steps out of the frame: the princess cannot."[14] Whereas Elizabeth's intense study of Darcy's portrait causes her to view him in a new and more favorable light and eventually to marry him, the princess's dreamy contemplation of Nemours's portrait presages her final refusal to marry him and her retreat into a new and inviolable space of erotic reverie: the convent. This difference in outcome depends on another difference between the two scenes: whereas Elizabeth looks at Darcy's portrait in his absence, at the very moment when the princess gazes rapturously at the portrait of the duke, the portrait's model is gazing equally rapturously at her. For the second time in the novel—the first is when he over-hears the princess's avowal to her husband—the duke has sneaked onto the secluded property to spy on the princess. As he, unbeknownst to her, watches her from his hiding place in the garden, he experiences something verging on that supreme form of sexual pleasure known in French and now also in English as *jouissance*.

How to express the feelings of M. de Nemours at this moment? What lover can ever have seen, at night, in the most perfect spot imaginable, the person he adored, have seen her without her knowing it and have seen that she was only occupied with things which had to do with himself and the love she kept hidden from him? Such things had never been enjoyed or imagined by any other lover. The Prince was beside himself, so much so that he forgot the precious minutes were ticking away as he stood there looking at Madame de Clèves. (168)

What makes this voyeur's pleasure so uniquely, so hyperbolically gratifying is not only that he holds the object of his desire prisoner of his gaze, not only that his gaze violates her most intimate secret, but rather and above all that what he beholds is his own likeness as viewed through the eyes of an adoring woman. *Jouissance* for Nemours is being the spectator of his own desirability. When but moments later he comes to his senses, the duke arrives at the sobering realization that his image and the fantasies it enables are his most powerful rivals for the princess's affections. But the portrait scene unfolds outside of the relentless flow of narrative time, for the moment of narcissistic contemplation suspends tem-porality; it is a moment of eternity. I want then to stay with this timeless scene for just a little while longer, to scrutinize it at leisure, for in it Mme. de Lafayette offers us conjointly a representation of a male protagonist and *en abîme* a com-mentary on man's relationship to his own representation. By training, as it were, her spotlight on the spectacle of the duke's ecstatic vision of the princess's no less ecstatic vision of his image, Mme. de Lafayette places the reader in a position to discover the voyeur's secret, a secret far less innocent than the princess's. Lest we doubt that what we have here under the cunning guise of a supremely romantic episode is a devastating exposure of the male subject's fascination with the evi-dence of phallic power, we must now turn away from this captivating scene to the scene that immediately precedes it and from which it cannot be separated except for heuristic purposes. Moments before the princess takes up her candle to go over to the duke's portrait, she is engaged in an activity whose fetishistic signifi-cance was first pointed out some years ago by Michel Butor:[15]

She lay on a day-bed and on a table beside her there were several baskets full of ribbons. She was picking over these ribbons and choosing out certain ones, and M. de Nemours saw that these were the very colours he had carried at the tournament, and then he saw that she was making knots and bows to go on the unusual malacca cane which, having used it for some time, he had given to his sister. Madame de Clèves had taken it from her without seeming to recognize it as having once been his. She worked away with a grace and a look of pure goodness which reflected the state of her soul. (167–68)

The duke's blissful vision of the princess's occupation with "things that had to do with himself" both confirms and exploits the metonymic and metaphoric links between the portrait and the cane. The double scene that the duke beholds stages the generally hidden, should I say veiled relationship between the phallus and representation in a society ruled by men. In other words, what the diegetic contiguity of these two objects lays bare is *the phallicity of the representation* and *the iconicity of the phallus*. In a scopic economy, the idolator worships indifferently at the altar of the image and the phallus, for there is at least in the "rhetoric of iconoclasm," recently studied by W. J. T. Mitchell, a pervasive symbolic equation between these two icons of the visible.[16]

If we now replace the portrait scene in the narrative, it becomes clear that the princess's ultimate enigmatic refusal is motivated not only by her fear of falling victim to the "poetics of abandonment," not only by her privileging of desire over satisfaction, but by her unwillingness to support a representational system so intimately bound up with male narcissism. The portrait scene, as noted earlier, repeats an earlier scene that unfolds in the same spot in the hidden presence of the same trespasser: I allude to the princess's celebrated avowal to her husband of her love for another man, a man the eavesdropping duke recognizes to be himself. Unable to keep this story so flattering to his person to himself, the duke proceeds to communicate it to his friend and traveling companion, the Vidame de Chartres. In recounting this episode the narrator is at her perfidious best, first by minimizing the seriousness of the duke's indiscretion, second by parrying the widespread assumption that women's writing is indistinguishable from autobiography. For Nemours's narrative, his sole attempt at fiction, is a flimsily disguised autobiographical fragment that fools no one:

M. de Nemours, obsessed with his passion and the surprise of what he had overheard, now fell into a not unusual indiscretion, that of talking in general terms of one's own experience, and narrating one's own adventures with fictitious names. During the journey he brought the conversation round to the subject of love, emphasizing the pleasure of loving a person really worthy of it. He spoke of the curious manifestations it sometimes produces and finally, unable to bottle up his amazement at what Madame de Clèves had done, he told the Vidame the whole thing, without mentioning any names or saying that it had anything to do with him. However, the Vidame guessed this at once. (135)

Given the laws that govern the circulation of fictions of female desire in this novel, dispossessing women, as Joan de Jean has shown, of the exclusive rights to their own stories, the vidame cannot resist repeating the duke's secret to his mistress, Mme. de Martigues, who tells it to the queen-dauphine in the presence of the princess. After initially accusing her husband of having put the story into circulation, the princess comes to the inescapable conclusion that the indiscretion was Nemours's and that realization is devastating to her love for him:

How mistaken I was when I thought there existed a man capable of hiding anything which flattered his vanity [*ce qui flatte sa gloire*]. And it is for the sake of this man, who seemed to me so different, that I find myself on a level with other women, I, who used to be so different indeed. (151)

The only man worthy of the love of a princess deeply marked by a maternal discourse that enjoins her to be different from other women is a man who would be similarly distinct from the other members of his sex. There is, however, a notable difference between male and female difference: to be unique among her sex a woman must practice an exemplary virtue and thus avoid, in Mme. de Chartres's dying words, "descending to the level of other women" (*tomber comme les autres femmes*, which is more accurately translated as "falling like other women"; 70), whereas to rise above his peers a man must refrain from advertising his conquests. In short, vanity and the indiscretion it provokes are to masculinity what easy virtue and the fall it entails are to femininity. In refusing to accept the duke's proposal of marriage and by placing herself beyond the reach of the irremediably specular male gaze—retired behind the walls of the convent and her country estate, the princess becomes in the end literally and quite spectacularly *invisible*—the princess engages, as has been pointed out by Dalia Judovitz, in the elaboration of a "new concept of ethical and aesthetic representation."[17] Judovitz locates the novelty of the princess's representation in its affirmation of the power of fiction over the real; for her the princess's is an "aesthetics of implausibility." For me, on the other hand, the princess's aesthetics is one of *discretion*, an extreme rarefaction of representation.

Discretion is hardly a virtue one would think of associating with Corinne, perhaps the most exhibitionistic female protagonist in the history of women's writing. Actress, improvisationalist, conversationalist, Corinne is constantly engaged in spectacularizing her life. From her first appearance in the novel, being crowned poet laureate on the steps of the Roman Capitol, to her last, staging her swan song, Corinne plays out her story on the public stage. Coming from England, which functions in this novel as the evil empire of patriarchy, Lord Oswald Nelvil, Corinne's lover, is both attracted to and repelled by her very public success. The attraction poses no challenge to our understanding or expectations. Nineteenth-century French fiction is full of male protagonists whose desire is mediated by the desiring gaze of other men—hence the erotic prestige enjoyed by the actress or indeed by any beautiful woman who ventures into the polyfocal space of the theater. Less common in the French tradition is the reversal of this scenario, where instead of swelling male desire, the spectacle of female success irritates the lover's jealousy, arouses his desire for exclusive possession of the admirable love object. Oswald's typically ambivalent oscillation between these two contradictory desires is given full play in chapter 3 of book 7, when he watches Corinne act the part of Juliet in a production of *Romeo and Juliet*. Before the play begins, Oswald looks forward to the event with mixed emotions:

Oswald felt at once disquiet and delight; he enjoyed Corinne's success, by anticipation; but even thus grew jealous, beforehand, of no one man in particular, but of the public, who would witness an excellence of which he felt as if he alone had a right to be aware. He would have had Corinne reserve her charms for him, and appear to others as timid as an Englishwoman.[18]

As the play unfolds, however, Oswald's regressive fantasies of exclusive possession are for one brief moment replaced by the sense of omnipotence that comes from being loved by a star: "He thought himself the king of the world since he held sway over a heart which contained all life's treasures" (197; my translation). This triumphant moment coincides with Oswald capturing Corinne's gaze at the very instant when she is declaring her love to Romeo. For Corinne, on the other hand, the supreme pleasure she experiences in performing the role of Juliet in front of Oswald would not be enhanced by having Oswald step onto the stage and play Romeo to her Juliet. If for her (and for the narrator) the event constitutes the high point of her doomed love affair with Lord Nelvil, it is because it constitutes a unique synchronization of their analogous but disparate desires: his to occupy Corinne's gaze exclusively and hers to have her success witnessed by Oswald. Hers can only be a reflected glory. Both Corinne and Oswald seek then in different ways for visible proofs of the *effect* they produce on others: he on her and she on the crowd. He can experience power over Corinne only by capturing her gaze and she can measure her success only by seeing it reflected in Oswald's eyes. Theirs is a battle of the gaze and, one might add, though Corinne wins many of the skirmishes, she does lose the war: in a dysphoric reversal of the *Romeo and Juliet* sequence, going to the theater in London she becomes a spectator to her own loss of effect as she watches how Lord Nelvil's gaze, once fixed on her, is transferred onto a rising star, her own half sister Lucile, whom Lord Nelvil eventually marries:

Suddenly, in an opposite box, she perceived Lord Nelvil, whose gaze was fixed on Lucy. What a moment for Corinne! She once more beheld that face, for which she had so long searched her memory every instant, as if the image could be effaced—she beheld it again—absorbed by the beauty of another. (318)

Corinne differs then strikingly from *The Princesse* in that it lays bare *the specularity of both male and female desires.* How then does the portrait scene function in this very different context? Though not foregrounded as it is in both *The Princesse* and *Indiana*, the portrait scene in *Corinne* serves as what Michael Riffaterre, borrowing from C. S. Peirce, has called an "interpretant," an intertext that stands literally between two other texts and mediates their relationship.[19] The portrait scene in *Corinne* rewrites the one in *The Princesse* even as it anticipates the one in *Indiana*.

Corinne has gone off to a convent for her annual pre-Easter retreat. Although forewarned of her absence, Oswald is shocked to discover her departure and is overcome by a feeling of abandonment that revives his grief for his father, whose recent death hangs like a pall over him and the entire novel. To comfort him, Theresine, Corinne's faithful maidservant, says:

"My lord, for your consolation, I will even betray a secret of my lady's: I hope she will forgive me. Come to her bedroom, and you shall see your own portrait!" —"My portrait!" he repeated. —"Yes; she drew it from memory, and has risen, for the last week, at five in the morning, to have it finished before she went to the convent." The likeness was very strong, and painted with perfect grace. This evidence of the impression he had produced on Corinne filled him with a most agreeable feeling. (161; translation modified)

Two related innovations serve to differentiate this scene from its homologue in *The Princesse*: Corinne is absent from the encounter between Oswald and his faithful likeness, and Corinne is herself the author of the portrait. In fact, one difference acts to cancel out the other, for the time and pains lavished by Corinne on the execution of the mimesis of her lover compensate for her absence. And yet, Corinne's absence and the noncoincidence it determines between the scene of the painting and the scene of self-contemplation introduce a time lag into the portrait scene that works to mute the emphasis on male narcissism. Indeed, though deeply touched by this "proof" of Corinne's love for him, Oswald is far less excessive in his response to the sight of his representation as produced by his lover than Nemours is to the sight of his as viewed by his beloved. And yet it is of the essence that Oswald is shown looking at the portrait signed by Corinne. Here again a brief comparison with an analogous scene in a work by an English woman writer serves to underscore the specificity of the insistently specular French tradition. While away from Thornfield on a visit to her Aunt Reed's, Jane Eyre draws a likeness of Rochester from memory.

One morning I fell to sketching a face: what sort of face it was to be, I did not care or know. I took a soft black pencil, gave it a broad point, and worked away. Soon I had traced on the paper a broad and prominent forehead, and a square lower outline of visage: that contour gave me pleasure; my fingers proceeded actively to fill it with features. . . .
   "Is that the portrait of some one you know?" asked Eliza, who had approached me unnoticed. I responded that it was merely a fancy head, and hurried it beneath other sheets. Of course, I lied: it was, in fact, a very faithful representation of Mr. Rochester. But what was that to her, or to any one but myself?[20]

Not only is Jane's portrait of Rochester a far more spontaneous creation—it is done quickly and as though her hand were being guided by a force independent of her will—but its significance is purely personal: Rochester never sees it.

But the major difference between the portrait scenes in *The Princesse* and *Corinne* lies elsewhere: in penetrating illicitly into Corinne's bedchamber, Oswald discovers an unexpected secret: the bedchamber is in fact a miniature gallery, containing other images, notably the portrait of another man. The scene is worth quoting in full:

His looks strayed tenderly through this chamber, where he stood for the first time. At the head of the bed he beheld the miniature of an aged man, evidently not an Italian; two bracelets hung near it, one formed by braids of black and silver hair, the other of beautiful fair tresses, that, by a strange chance, reminded him of Lucy Edgermond's, which he had attentively remarked three years since. Oswald did not speak; but Theresine, as if to banish any jealous suspicion, told him, "that during the eleven years she had lived with her lady she had always seen these bracelets, which she knew contained the hair of Corinne's father, mother, and sister." (162)

At first glance there is something odd about Oswald's response to his latest discovery: rather than focusing on the portrait of the mysterious old man, he is seemingly fascinated by the sight of the two hair bracelets contiguous with the painting. It is the sight of these bracelets and not of the other man's portrait that awakens the jealousy Theresine seeks to forestall; given the custom of lovers exchanging locks of hair, the presence of the bracelets suggests sexual intimacies that Oswald can only guess at. If, however, we superimpose this scene on the like scene in *The Princesse*, the logic at work in the displacement of Oswald's attention becomes apparent: the tressed bracelets stand in the same relationship to the portrait of the old man as the beribboned cane stands to that of the Duke of Nemours. There is in these novels—and *Indiana* will only serve to confirm this observation—a persistent association between the representation of the representation of men and fetishism, the perversion, that is, that enshrines the centrality of the phallus. What is troubling to Oswald is the uncanny doubling of the fetish, for this multiplication works to undermine the uniqueness of the phallus, and to underline its infinite substitutability. The doubled hair bracelet is in fact symptomatic of what Mme. de Staël sets out to do in *Corinne*, namely to ruin the foundation of man's relationship to his own image by a strategy of proliferating images. Indeed, often classified as a guidebook, *Corinne* has bewildered, not to say dismayed, many readers by its seemingly aberrant generalization of description. Leaving aside the masterworks on view in the churches, monuments, and galleries (both private and public) that Corinne visits with Oswald, the novel features a small collection of portraits: in addition to the portraits of Oswald and Corinne's father, there are the two portraits of Corinne, during and after her relationship with Oswald. Significantly, on her deathbed Corinne asks the attending priest to remove Oswald's portrait and to replace it with the image of Christ, as though only what René Girard once termed "transcendental meditation" offered a way out of this universe marked by a deliberate and spectacular *excess* of representation.[21]

Texts published anonymously or under a pseudonym constitute a supreme test for theories of sexual specificity in writing: a test critics of French literature have famously failed to meet in the celebrated cases of *The Letters of a Portuguese Nun* and *The Story of O*. *Indiana*, the first major novel George Sand published under her new masculine pseudonym, briefly obliged critics—for the biological sex of the suddenly famous author quickly became known—to articulate their assumptions about what it meant to write like a woman or a man. Most of these critics resorted to conventional ideas about gender to make their case, arguing, for example, that men write better of sensual love; women, of refined feeling—hence, this love story, both sensuous and delicate, must be a collaborative effort, on the model of George Sand and her lover Jules Sandeau's *Rose et Blanche*.[22] Sainte-Beuve, however, goes beyond the predictable clichés and locates the femininity of the writing of *Indiana* precisely in the unsparing representation of one of its male protagonists, the vile seducer Raymon. According to Sainte-Beuve, "This disappointing character, exposed and unveiled [*dévoilé*] in detail in his miserable egotism, as never a man, were he a Raymon, could have realized it and would have dared to say it,"[23] is the surest giveaway of the author's sex. Writing like a woman for Sainte-Beuve is in this instance bound up with a literal unveiling of the full horror of male egotism, the pre-Freudian term for narcissism. Now this gesture of unveiling is figured *en abîme* as it were in the portrait scene of *Indiana*. Raymon de Ramière, a dashing young aristocrat whose country home borders on that of Indiana and her husband, M. Delmare, has (unbeknownst to Indiana) become the lover of Noun, Indiana's maidservant and foster-sister. In a pathetic attempt to revive Raymon's flagging desire for her, Noun hits upon the idea of making love with him in Indiana's bedroom, while the Delmares are away in Paris. This arrangement suits Raymon fine for two reasons: first, it enables him to imagine that in making love to the sensual Noun he is possessing the unattainable Indiana, to whom (unbeknownst to Noun) he is attracted; second and perhaps more important, it allows him to penetrate into the private space of Indiana's curiously shaped circular bedroom. When, on the morning after their lovemaking, Noun hides Raymon in the bedroom, he continues to explore his surroundings with a mixture of reverence and ill-concealed curiosity:

When Noun left him to go and find something for breakfast, he set about examining by daylight all those dumb witnesses of Indiana's solitude. He opened her books, turned the leaves of her albums, then closed them precipitately; for he still shrank from committing a profanation and violating some feminine mystery. At last he began to pace the room and noticed, on the wooden panel opposite Madame Delmare's bed, a large picture, richly framed and covered with a double thickness of gauze.

Perhaps it was Indiana's portrait. Raymon, in his eagerness to see it, forgot his scruples, stepped on a chair, removed the pins, and was amazed to see a full-length portrait of a handsome young man.[24]

This scene, toward which, as I have tried to show, an entire literary tradition has been tending, is remarkable in its complexity. The gesture of tearing away the doubled gauze veil doubles back upon itself, for in uncovering the portrait of the other gentleman—here no harmless old man as in *Corinne*, rather a most threatening young one—Raymon exposes his own egotism, even as Sand demonstrates the functioning of what Eve Sedgwick has termed the "homosocial" bond.[25] Beyond or bound up with male representational narcissism is an aggressive fascination with the imaginary Other. When Noun returns, carrying the breakfast tray, Raymon can barely contain the "violent flame of wrath" (67) the sight of the portrait kindles in him. He rants:

"Upon my word!" he said to himself, "this dapper young Englishman enjoys the privilege of being admitted to Madame Delmare's most secret apartment! His vapid face is always there, looking coldly on at the most private acts of her life! He watches her, guards her, follows her every movement, possesses her every hour of the day."(68)

And he goes on to say to Noun that were he in Delmare's place, "I wouldn't have consented to leave it [the picture] here unless I had cut out the eyes." Not surprisingly, then, given the violence of Raymon's reaction to the fancied voyeuristic privileges enjoyed by the man in the portrait, the rivalry between Raymon and Sir Ralph, the portrait's model, will be entirely ocular, a struggle over who shall possess the exclusive right not to be gazed at by Indiana but to gaze at her:

She exchanged a meaning[ful] glance with Raymon but, swift as it was, Sir Ralph caught it on the wing, and Raymon was unable, during the rest of the evening, to glance at her or address her without encountering Monsieur Brown's eyes or ears. A feeling of aversion, almost of jealousy, arose in his heart. (117)

Clearly at these moments, as Leslie Rabine has phrased it, "the heroine is the space within which Ralph and Raymon look at each other."[26]

In the earlier versions of the portrait scene, the possibility of a misreading is carefully inscribed. Both Mme. de Lafayette and Mme. de Staël do allow the male protagonist and the male reader who identifies with him some measure of narcissistic gratification, even as they condemn the specularity of male desire and its representations. Sand's rescripting of this scene allows the resisting male reader no recourse to the comforts of misprision. In the event that the meaning of the portrait scene should have escaped the reader, male or female, it is doubled by another scene that takes place in Indiana's bedroom. This time it is Indiana who, giving in to Raymon's insistent pleas, has invited him to a midnight rendezvous in her room. Alerted by Ralph, Indiana has begun to suspect the truth about Raymon's affair with Noun and the part he played in driving the pregnant and abandoned Noun to commit suicide by drowning. Racked by doubts as to Raymon's guilt, Indiana is suddenly inspired to devise "a strange and delicate test against which Raymon could not be on his guard" (161). As Raymon approaches Indiana, she points to a "mass of black hair" (162) she holds in her hands. At first, believing that the hair is Indiana's, Raymon is beside himself with joy:

"O Indiana!" cried Raymon, "you know well that you will be lovelier than ever to me henceforth. Give it to me. I do not choose to regret the absence from your head of that glorious hair which I admired every day, and which now I can kiss every day without restraint. Give it to me, so that it can never leave me." (163)

But when he takes "that luxuriant mass" of hair into his own hands, Raymon realizes that it is not shorn from the scalp of the living Indiana but rather from the corpse of the dead Noun. Upon which, he faints away. When he comes to, he exclaims:

"You have inflicted a horrible wound on me," he said, "a wound which it is not in your power to cure. You will never restore the confidence I had in your heart; that is evident to me. You have shown me how vindictive and cruel your heart can be." (164)

The diabolical trap set for Raymon works in ways unforeseen by Indiana, though not, of course, by Sand. The sudden and irreversible death of Raymon's love for Indiana is caused less by the confirmation of his heartless seduction of Noun than by the supplementary revelation of his fetishism. Once again, as in our earlier examples, male narcissism and fetishism are shown to be inextricably linked; to unmask the one is to unmask the other, and to unmask both is to attack the very foundations of the representational system elaborated by patriarchal society. Or, perhaps more important: to attack representation is to attack patriarchy and its distributions of power. For it is a central intuition of postmodernist thought that "representation stands for the interests of power."[27] An impassioned condemnation of the barbarous "laws which still govern woman's existence in wedlock, in the family and in society" ("Preface of 1842"), *Indiana* has long been recognized as the most feminist of Sand's early feminist fiction, so it is surely no accident that in this novel the subversive intent of the portrait scene, so artfully camouflaged in the works of Lafayette and Staël, should be stripped of its protective veil and revealed in something like its truth.

At this juncture several questions arise, two of which I will raise only in passing: the first concerns the reasons for the difference between the French and the English traditions in women's writing. To begin to answer this question one would have to risk venturing onto the slippery terrain of national character, to speculate on the historical, social, economic reasons why French culture seems more self-consciously visual than the English. This I have neither the inclination nor the competence to do. The second question concerns not national but sexual difference and could be formulated as follows: what features distinguish exposures of male narcissism in men's writings from those in women's writings? While I am not yet prepared to answer that important question, the implication of the preceding analysis is that that difference is bound up with the recurrence of the portrait scene in women's fiction, that is with the persistent linkage in female-authored texts between representations of men and representations of representation. Ultimately what is at stake in women's representations of the specularity of male desire is representation itself. This brings me to a third question and one that I will attempt to answer: what becomes of the portrait scene in French women's writing of the twentieth century? Does it simply disappear, suggesting that it is historicizable, bound up with a social organization that being neither natural nor eternal has changed significantly over the years? The portrait scene recurs, but it does so in a guise so new and unfamiliar that it is at first unrecognizable. It recurs of all places in an early novel by Nathalie Sarraute, aptly entitled *Portrait of a Man Unknown*. What makes this example so compelling from my perspective is that over the years Sarraute has consistently and vigorously denied the impact of gender on (her) writing. The following response to a journal questionnaire on the fictional inscription of sexual difference is typical:

On the level on which the interior dramas I strive to bring to light are produced, there is, I am firmly convinced, no difference between men and women, just as there is none in their respiratory or circulatory systems. . . .

Consequently, I have never asked myself if it [the text] had qualities or defects said to be masculine or feminine.

I think these distinctions are based on prejudices, on pure conventions. They are unverifiable assertions which rest only on a very small number of examples, examples where the male or the female author claims to possess certain qualities he believes proper to his sex.[28]

Sarraute's refusal to be read as a woman writer extends far beyond her public statements about her own work. In *Portrait of a Man Unknown* it takes the form of a denial of female intertextuality; in a novel replete with literary allusions—e.g., *War and Peace*, *The Notebooks of Malte Laurids Brigge*, *Madame Bovary*—one would be hard pressed to find any reference to a literary foremother; if there exists any conscious link between *Portrait* and the tradition we have been tracing all material evidence of it has been completely expunged.[29] To further complicate my effort to appropriate Sarraute's novel for my argument, *Portrait* is a first-person narrative whose narrator is male and whose story, to the extent he tells one, is a deliberate rewriting of Balzac's *Eugénie Grandet*, entirely focused on the father-daughter struggle to the complete and significant exclusion of the mother and Charles, the love-object. Though the novel does end with the daughter's engagement to be married, Sarraute writes from beyond the erotics of the conventional marriage plot in which the previous portrait scenes function. Consequently, what I will nevertheless call the portrait scene takes place not in a woman's boudoir but in the very public space of a museum somewhere in Holland. I want now to compare Sand's description of the portrait of Sir Ralph, an example of academic portraiture of the school of Ingres or better Gainsborough, with Sarraute's description of a Dutch painting of the school of Frans Hals or Rembrandt:

The peaceable baronet was represented in hunting costume . . . and surrounded by his dogs, the beautiful pointer Ophelia in the foreground, because of the fine silver-gray tone of her silky coat and the purity of her Scotch blood. Sir Ralph had a hunting-horn in one hand and in the other the rein of a superb, dapple-gray English hunter, who filled almost the whole background of the picture. It was an admirably executed portrait, a genuine family picture with all its perfection of detail, all its puerile niceties of resemblance, all its bourgeois minutiae; a picture to make a nurse weep, dogs bark and a tailor faint with joy. (67)

The lines of the face, the lace jabot and waistcoat, as also the hands, seemed to present the kind of fragmentary, uncertain outlines that the hesitant fingers of a blind man might come upon haltingly, feeling his way. It was as though all effort, all doubt, all anxiety had been overtaken by a sudden catastrophe, and had remained congealed in action, like corpses that have petrified in the position they were in when death overtook them. The eyes alone seemed to have escaped the catastrophe and achieved fulfillment. It was as though they had attracted and concentrated in themselves all the intensity, all the life that was lacking in the still formless dislocated features.[30]

What we have here are two instances or stages of what I will call "female iconoclasm," a peculiarly feminine form of antirepresentationalism.[31] Sand's description of the portrait of a true English gentleman is a witty send-up of a sex, a class, a nation, and, above all, an aesthetic ideal: bourgeois realism. The butt of the humor is clearly the male human figure, here singularly diminished by being sandwiched between the foregrounded canine and the backgrounded equine figures, and further by being reduced to a mere clotheshorse. And yet, however clever the pastiche, by definition the portrait of Sir Ralph obeys the very convention it mocks.[32] The same cannot be said of the portrait of a man unknown. The extraordinary *disfiguration* of the anonymous gentleman bodies forth the radical assault on representation Sarraute undertakes in what Sartre in his preface to *Portrait* describes as her "antinovel." Visiting an exhibit with the novel's female protagonist later in the novel, the narrator elaborates on the aesthetic ideal embodied in his favorite painting:

"I believe that rather than the most perfectly finished works I prefer those in which complete mastery has not been attained . . . in which one still feels, just beneath the surface, a sort of anxious groping . . . a certain doubt . . . a mental anguish . . ." I was beginning to sputter more and more . . . "before the immensity . . . the elusiveness of the material world . . . that escapes us just when we think we have got hold of it . . . the goal that's never attained . . . the insufficiency of the means at our disposal." (201)

That the painting of the man unknown represents *en abîme* Sarraute's fictional universe with its celebrated *tropismes*—those multiple, minute stirrings that lie midway between the inchoate formlessness of the semiotic and the rigid armature of the symbolic—is hardly cause for surprise, given the relentlessly self-reflexive nature of the modernistic new novel. Further, one might argue that there is nothing particularly feminine about Sarraute's attack on the figure in an era when figurative art was giving way to abstraction. And yet the terms in which Sarraute's attack is formulated resonates with feminist critiques of representation. The main thrust of Sarraute's assault on traditional modes of figuration is significantly double: the visual and the whole. The morcelizing of the masculine imago works here to dethrone the visual from its hegemony over representation in favor of the tactile. And the promotion of the tactile in the arts leads inevitably to an end to mastery.

Sarraute's deconstruction of masculine representation does not end there. As the narrator stands transfixed before the portrait of the one he calls "The Man with the Waistcoat," he experiences a lyrical moment of total identification with the figure in the painting:

And little by little, I became aware that a timid note, an almost forgotten strain from long ago, had sounded within me, at first, hesitantly. And it seemed to me, as I stood there before him lost, dissolved in him, that this faltering note, this timid response he had awakened in me, penetrated him and reverberated inside him, that he seized it and gave it back to me increased and magnified as though by an amplifier; it began to rise from him and from me, louder and louder, a song filled with hope that lifted me up and bore me along. (85)

Though the narrator's ecstatic fusion with his alter imago calls to mind the duke of Nemours's *jouissance*, it arises from a curious form of mutual resonance that bypasses the specular in favor of the vocal. And, as though to seal the end of the reign of the specular, the operatic merging of the two male figures—with its vestigial male narcissism—is brutally undercut by the narrator's description of his reflection:

As I trotted along beside her, I avoided looking at the fellow "beyond his prime," with the bedraggled air and short legs, balding and slightly pot-bellied. But occasionally, I was unable to avoid him. He sprang forth from a mirror just opposite me, as we crossed the street. Never had my weary lids, my dull eyes, my sagging cheeks, appeared to me so pitilessly, as at that moment, beside her reflection, in that garish light. (198)

Unsupported by an adoring female gaze—the narrator's female companion registers no surprise on catching sight of his sorry figure in the glass; "She had seen me like that for a long time," he remarks ruefully—the male figure appears here in its un- or de-idealized form, in its all-too-human contingency. The mirror has turned on Narcissus.

I began this piece by evoking an exhibit entitled "Women's Images of Men," suggesting that what would follow would deal by analogy with "images of men" in women's writing, as though feminist criticism were somehow condemned to revert always to its origins, the now largely discredited pioneering work on "images of women" in men's writings. If I hope to have demonstrated anything in the course of this paper it is that one of the major differences between men's and women's writing, at least in France, is that *there are, so to speak, no "images of men" in women's writing* because that writing is marked from the outset by a profound suspicion of the image and its grounding phallicism. Rarefaction, multiplication, pastiche, and disfiguration are some of the operations to which the image, the male image that is, is subjected in French women's fiction from Lafayette to Sarraute. My final question then becomes: can there be misandry where there are no unproblematized images, where representation is from its very inception in crisis? For cannot it be said that misogyny, like all forms of discrimination, relies on the power of the subject in power to fix the Other in a static image, a stereotype or better yet a cliché. And cannot it be further said that the subject in power's ability to do so derives from his own possession of a secure, larger-than-life self-image? If the answer to these questions is affirmative—and that is, of course, a rather big if—then we can better understand why it is that for women writers, for whom the mirror has for centuries remained empty, the representation of men is bound up with the death of the image of man.

Notes

This paper is gratefully dedicated to the students in my course on French women's writing from the seventeenth century to the present at Brown University, Fall 1984, and University of California, Berkeley, Spring 1986. Special thanks to Carolyn Duffey for bringing to my attention the text quoted in the epigraph. Lombarda was a woman troubadour of the thirteenth century. The text is drawn from part 2 of her *tenson* with Barnat Arnaut d'Armagnac.

1. Sarah Kent and Jacqueline Morreau, preface to *Women's Images of Men* (London, 1985), 1.
2. Sarah Kent, "Looking Back," in ibid., 62.   3. Ibid., 72.
4. A very recent exception to this rule is Jane Miller's *Women Writing About Men* (New York, 1986). Though our approaches to the topic could not be more different—at no point does Miller problematize the very issue of representation—a disclaimer she makes in her introduction points to an odd resonance between our analyses: "My book will be a disappointment, I expect, for anyone hoping for a gallery neatly hung with the portraits women have painted of men" (3). Indeed, despite a typological organization largely informed by the categories of kinship—chapter headings include "Fathers and Gentlemen," "Brothers," and "Sons"—Miller's book frustrates any expectation of an exhaustive taxonomy of male imagos in (Anglo-American) women's writing. Unfortunately, it also disappoints in other ways, notably by its lack of theo-

retical rigor. Nevertheless, it is a pioneering study of the ways in which women's disempowerment in modern Western societies translates into their writing about men.

5. Janis Glasgow, *Une Esthétique de comparaison: Balzac et George Sand* (Paris, 1977), 44–45. Translations in the text are mine except where otherwise noted. The awareness of a special handicap in portraying men is shared by other women writers. Charlotte Brontë, for example, writes to a friend: "In delineating male character, I labour under disadvantages; intuition and theory will not adequately supply the place of observation and experience. When I write about women, I am sure of my ground—in the other case I am not so sure"; quoted by Miller, *Women Writing About Men*, 39. Writing about the same issues some one hundred years later, Virginia Woolf is, if anything, more pessimistic in her conclusions than Sand: "It remains obvious . . . that a man is terribly hampered and partial in his knowledge of women, as a woman is in her knowledge of men"; *A Room of One's Own* (New York, 1957), 87.

6. K. K. Ruthven, *Feminist Literary Studies: An Introduction* (Cambridge, 1984), 86. The recent polemic over the representation of the male protagonists in Alice Walker's *The Color Purple*—though it is, of course, immensely complicated by the tension between racism and sexism—provides a telling current example of the violence unleashed by women artists' attacks on male privilege. See, for example, Mel Watkins, "Sexism, Racism and Black Women Writers," *The New York Times Book Review*, 15 June 1986.

7. On the subject of misogyny through the ages, see Katherine M. Rogers, *The Troublesome Helpmate: A History of Misogyny in Literature* (Seattle, 1966).

8. Woolf, *Room of One's Own*, 94.   9. Ibid., 35.

10. The references here are in turn to Nancy K. Miller, "Emphasis Added: Plots and Plausibilities in Women's Fiction," in *The New Feminist Criticism*, ed. Elaine Showalter (New York, 1985), 339–60; Peggy Kamuf, "A Mother's Will," in *Fictions of Feminine Desire* (Lincoln, Neb., 1982), 67–96; Marianne Hirsch, "A Mother's Discourse: Incorporation and Repetition in *La Princesse de Clèves*," *Yale French Studies* 62 (1981): 67–87; Joan de Jean, "Lafayette's Ellipses: The Privileges of Anonymity," *PMLA* 99 (October 1984): 884–902. The connection between *The Princesse de Clèves* and *Indiana* is the subject of an article by Mario Maurin, "Un Modèle d'*Indiana*," *French Review* 50 (1976): 317–20. Noting the numerous echoes of *The Princesse* in *Indiana*, including the portrait scenes, Maurin concludes: "It is not implausible . . . that at the point of inaugurating an independent career as a novelist, George Sand should have unconsciously placed herself under the patronage of her illustrious predecessor" (320).

De Jean's article can be seen as part of a growing trend in feminist literary criticism to refine and rethink the universalist assumptions of pioneering work on "women's writing." Arguing that feminist literary criticism must take into account contextual particularities, especially the historical, de Jean writes: "Writing 'elsewhere' always takes place somewhere" (884), which is also to say someplace. Women writers in seventeenth-century France operate not within an "uncharted utopian space but a territory clearly and self-consciously defined by its creators." The "dream of a common language" (Adrienne Rich) that enabled and informed much early feminist criticism in America corresponded to the hegemony of feminists working within the dominant field of English. As the differences within difference (sexual, racial, ethnic) make their pressures felt, the continuing search for the specificities of women's writing must be coupled with the recognition of the diversity of women. My concern here is with what Miller refers to in passing as "the national constraints on the imagination" (347).

11. Nancy K. Miller, "Parables and Politics: Feminist Criticism in 1986," *Paragraph* 8 (October 1986): 46.

12. Mme. de Lafayette, *The Princesse de Clèves* (Harmondsworth, Eng., 1982), 164, emphasis added. Page numbers given in the text refer to this edition; citations in French refer to *La Princesse de Clèves* (Paris, 1966).

13. Jean Fabre, as quoted by Kamuf, "A Mother's Will," 68. Kamuf's reading interestingly likens narratorial and maternal omniscience.

14. Nancy K. Miller, "Emphasis Added," 350.

15. Michel Butor, "Sur *La Princesse de Clèves*," in *Répertoire I* (Paris, 1960), 74–78.

16. W. J. T. Mitchell, *Iconology: Image, Text, Ideology* (Chicago, 1986), in particular p. 113. Symmetry dictates that elsewhere in the novel the scenario we have been tracing is "reversed," if only to show that it is irreversible. I refer to the scene where the princess sees M. de Nemours steal a portrait of her belonging to her husband. The differences between the two portrait scenes are telling: first, the princess's moral dilemma—should she say something to prevent the theft, thereby publicizing Nemours's love for her or, by silently acquiescing to it, encourage Nemours's passion—arises precisely from her inability to occupy the voyeur's position: she knows that Nemours knows that she has witnessed his appropriative gesture. Even in this instance, the male gaze supersedes and recontains the female. Second, rather than experiencing bliss at witnessing Nemours's desire for her portrait, the princess is embarrassed and "very much upset" (97).

17. Dalia Judovitz, "The Aesthetics of Implausibility: *La Princesse de Clèves*," *Modern Language Notes* 99 (1984): 1053.

18. Mme. de Staël, *Corinne; or, Italy*, trans. Isabel Hill (New York, 1887), 122–23. The page references in the text are to this edition. When the French text is used, the reference is to *Corinne; ou, l'Italie* (Paris, 1985).

19. Michael Riffaterre, *Semiotics of Poetry* (Bloomington, Ind., 1978), 81–114.

20. Charlotte Brontë, *Jane Eyre* (London, 1924), 231–32.

21. A clear distinction must be drawn here between Mme. de Staël's ruining of representation and Corinne's more ambivalent relationship to the image, which is clearly bound up with the law of the father she would both transgress and reinscribe. Thus, when the portrait of Oswald's father (the posthumous lawgiver who prohibits the marriage of Oswald and Corinne) is nearly destroyed by water, Corinne restores it. In *Corinne*, female masochism and mimesis are shown to be inseparable.

22. See notes by Béatrice Didier in her edition of George Sand, *Indiana* (Paris, 1984), 359. Subsequent references to the French are to this edition.

23. Sainte-Beuve, *Les Grands Ecrivains français: XIXe Siècle, les romanciers* (Paris, 1927), 45.

24. George Sand, *Indiana*, trans. George Burnham Ives (Chicago, 1978), 66. The page references in the text are to this edition.

25. Eve Kosofsky Sedgwick, *Between Men: English Literature and Male Homosocial Desire* (New York, 1985).

26. Leslie Rabine, "George Sand and the Myth of Femininity," *Women and Literature* 4 (1976): 8.

27. Brian Wallis, "What's Wrong with This Picture: An Introduction," in Brian Wallis, ed., *Art After Modernism: Rethinking Representation* (New York, 1984), xv. A central theme of this anthology is the politics of representation, its complicities with all forms of power, especially the patriarchal.

28. Nathalie Sarraute, as quoted in *La Quinzaine Littéraire* 192 (August 1974): 29.

29. This remark raises the question of the "consciousness" of the tradition I have been tracing. In her early *Essai sur les fictions* (Paris, 1979), Mme. de Staël lists *The Princesse* among the masterpieces written not so much *by* women as *on* women for their moral

instruction (48). As for Sand's affiliation with Staël, this celebrated lyrical evocation of her youthful readings attests to Sand's keen awareness of her great predecessor: "Happy time! oh my Vallée Noire! Oh Corinne!"; *Lettres d'un voyageur* (Paris, 1971), 207.

30. Nathalie Sarraute, *Portrait of a Man Unknown*, trans. Maria Jolas (London, 1959), 84. The page references included in the text are to this edition.

31. The very notion of a "female iconoclasm" is iconoclastic in that, as Mitchell points out, the great iconoclastic discourses of both Lessing and Burke align painting and beauty with the feminine. In a very different perspective, Elizabeth Berg, in an essay titled "Iconoclastic Moments: Reading the *Sonnets for Helene*, Writing the *Portuguese Letters*," interrogates a certain feminist need to constitute secure self-representations, otherwise known as "images of women." She argues, iconoclastically, for a shattering of these "univocal images" in favor of a dissolution of all identities, especially the sexual. In Nancy K. Miller, ed., *The Poetics of Gender* (New York, 1986), 208–21, in particular 218.

32. When, later on in the novel, Raymon's new wife, Laure de Nangy, signs her paintings, she writes "Pastiche" next to the signatures; *Indiana*, 286. This crucial word is lost in the translation, which substitutes "copy" (267). Didier reads this scene as a sort of private joke, an ironic allusion to Sand's mentor's (Henri de Latouche) initial dismissal of her novel as a mere pastiche of Balzac. For more on Sand's relationship to the then dominant representational mode embodied by Balzac, see my "Idealism in the Novel: Recanonizing Sand," forthcoming.

GILLIAN BROWN

The Empire of Agoraphobia

"BARTLEBY THE SCRIVENER, A Tale of Wall Street" puts into circulation the story of a man about whom "nothing is ascertainable." Because "no materials exist for a full and satisfactory biography of this man," the "few passages in the life of Bartleby" related by the narrator represent the life of Bartleby. Transforming this very impediment to biography into biographical copy, Herman Melville's 1853 story of the "unaccountable Bartleby" both thematizes and reproduces a market-economy ontology: Bartleby's history is a tale of the marketplace and, like other market productions, significant because circulating, effective because communicative and commercial.[1] Melville's entry into mass-magazine circulation after the commercial failures of *Moby Dick* and *Pierre*, the tale exemplifies the mechanisms by which life in and of the marketplace is forwarded.

Unlike the moving copy the tale creates and disseminates, Bartleby himself is "a motionless young man" (45), "singularly sedate" (46), "stationary" (69). The curiosity "the inscrutable scrivener" provokes and the story he thus provides issue from this mysterious immobility, from "his great stillness" (53), his affinity to what is static in Wall Street: the walls of the buildings and offices where the circulation of property is ratified in deeds and titles, where changes in proprietorship are codified and copied. Amidst this conveyancing, Bartleby remains in his partitioned office cubicle—walled in, facing more walls through his window, in his own "dead-wall reveries" (56). This enigmatic stance by which Bartleby removes himself from circulation also occasions his biography; "Bartleby the Scrivener," a tale of a stationary man, thus includes within its commerce a protest against commerce, and moreover makes commerce of that protest, translating a wall into a scrivener, the scrivener's inscrutability into market reproduction.

Reiterating the market imperative to move, the circulatory fate of Bartleby demonstrates the crucial productivity of immobility. In the tautological procedures of the marketplace, Bartleby's static, even ahistorical, status, when transposed into literary currency, reprises life in the marketplace where movement is all. Melville's tale describes an itinerary of what might be called the immobility principle, the reproduction of circulation through tableaux of the stationary. Bartleby's arrested motion is one such tableau in the nineteenth-century American iconography of stillness featuring invalidism, woman, and home (and conflations of these) as predominant figures of restfulness.[2] The frail, sentimental heroine whose domestic angelicism marks her for death, imprinted in the American imagination by Harriet Beecher Stowe's 1852 invention of Little Eva—reproduced on the stage for the rest of the century—inaugurates and sustains this idealization of worldly retreat by a commercial society. Resembling the retreat of the invalid heroine into her home (Eva speaks of dying as going home to heaven), Bartleby's withdrawal invokes the domestic tableau in order to investigate its commercial peregrinations. How Bartleby's immobility moves is thus the story of how American culture deployed domestic stations and spaces of seclusion.

In order to understand how Bartleby's resistance ultimately enters and typifies commerce, or, to put it another way, how walls move, it is necessary first to see how and why, in nineteenth-century America, ordinarily mobile humans might become "dead-walls." The preeminent figure of immobility for the nineteenth century is the hysteric, whose strange postures freeze normal bodily motion and activity.[3] While Freud derived a theory of female sexuality from hysteria, American doctors focused upon the characteristic hysterical symptoms of paralysis and nervous exhaustion. Nervous attitudes and hysterical presentations fit into a recurrent imagery of paralysis and exhaustion in American medical literature on nervous disorders. This discourse of immobility treats nervous poses and symptoms as social practices, as variant implementations of a customary iconography. Postulating an evolutionary psychology in which mental diseases accidentally resuscitate formerly useful animal instincts, William James in 1890 associated "the statue-like, crouching immobility of some melancholiacs" with the "death-shamming instinct shown by many animals," the self-preservative immobility of "the feigning animal." This instinctual etiology, James believes, explains "the strange symptom which has been described of late years by the rather absurd name of *agoraphobia*." "When we notice the chronic agoraphobia of our domestic cats, and see the tenacious way in which many wild animals, especially rodents, cling to cover, and only venture on a dash across the open as a desperate measure," we are witnessing a prototype of the agoraphobic, who in "terror at the sight of any open place or broad street which he has to cross alone . . . slinks round the sides of the square, hugging the houses as closely as he can."[4]

This concern with the protection of walls and enclosures recurs throughout nineteenth-century case histories of agoraphobics appearing after the classification of agoraphobia as a nervous disease in 1873.[5] A Connecticut man treated by Dr. William A. Hammond "would not go out into the street unless he went in a carriage," and, "in passing from the vehicle to the door of a house, he required the support of two men—one on each side of him."[6] The agoraphobic dependence upon walls of some kind is epitomized in nineteenth-century medical literature by a story about Pascal. After a 1654 carriage accident in which he was thrown into the Seine, Pascal "had the morbid fear of falling into a large space." To protect himself from chasms he imagined at his side, Pascal ever afterward kept a screen beside him. Nineteenth-century French doctors posthumously diagnosed Pascal as agoraphobic. The agoraphobic dependence on enclosures or adjacent fortifications kept most sufferers within the walls of houses, safe from their terror of the street, where "everything was in motion."[7]

Many observers of the nineteenth-century American scene did not find such anxious house-hugging the anachronism James theorized but rather a symptom specific to the conditions of American economic life. The democratic opportunity and competition for economic advancement, the very mobility of American society, Alexis de Tocqueville worried in 1835, was apt to render the individual "stationary."[8] Agreeing with this evolution of anxiety from economic freedom, Dr. George M. Beard declared in 1881 that the recent inventions of steam power, the periodical press, and the telegraph, as well as developments in the sciences and the increased mental activity of women, "must carry nervousness and nervous diseases." New technologies of transportation and communication enable "the increase in amount of business" that has "developed sources of anxiety."[9] In the case of the agoraphobic man from Connecticut, Dr. Hammond noted that "there had been excessive emotional disturbance in business matters."[10] The anxieties and responsibilities of commerce, the famous Dr. S. Weir Mitchell believed, explain the "numerous instances of nervous exhaustion among merchants and manufacturers." According to Mitchell's notebooks of the 1880s, "manufacturers and certain classes of railway officials are the most liable to suffer from neural exhaustion"; merchants and brokers are the next most likely sufferers.[11] In the latter half of the century, the railroad figured prominently in American, German, and French lawsuits for mental health damages; it appeared to have created a fear of itself, the new phobia of railway traveling.[12]

In these accounts of nervousness and anxiety, the mechanisms and modes of commerce ultimately immobilize the individual. Beard and Mitchell's association of such conditions with economic developments in nineteenth-century life reflects anxieties about the effects of commerce notable in literature ranging from medical advice books to popular magazines such as *Putnam's* where "Bartleby" first appeared. In this context agoraphobia, the anxiety and immobility occasioned by the space and scope of streets, by the appurtenances and avenues of traffic, is an anticommercial condition—literally, fear of the marketplace. The nosology of the condition as it emerged in America in the latter half of the century suggests, contrary to James, the aptness of the term *agoraphobia*; what inhibits the agoraphobe is the commerce that inhabits American life.

From the symptomatology of immobility observed in nervous cases, an agoraphobic disposition emerges in social and medical discourse as a hallmark of American personal life. The agoraphobic recourse when outside the house to the protection of interiors or companions or shielding edifices represents an effort to retain the stability and security of the private sphere. Reproducing the enclosure and stillness of home in the deportment of the individual, agoraphobia approximates domesticity, often proclaimed the nineteenth-century antidote to commercialism.[13] The antagonism between self and world manifest in agoraphobia reflects and replays the opposition between home and market upheld by domestic ideology. By maintaining the integrity of the private sphere, this opposition sustains the notion of a personal life impervious to market influences, the model of selfhood in a commercial society. In his propinquity to walls and in his preference for his own impenetrable postures, Bartleby presents an extreme version of such a model: in "his long-continued motionlessness" he achieves an "austere reserve," the ideal of domesticity within Wall Street.

Just as hysteria translated into an anatomy of the self and its desires in Victorian society, agoraphobia furnished Victorian America with a paradigmatic selfhood associated with female experience—or more specifically, summarized and reproduced the tradition of selfhood established by domestic ideology. For nineteenth-century America, women signified the stability of the private sphere that Bartleby's wall-like stance exhibits, the standard of self-containment that the hysteric melodramatized. Thus the physicians who worried about the immobilizing effects of commerce direct much attention to preserving the tranquility of women and home, treating market-stricken men by attending to the maintenance of domestic womanhood. Both Beard and Mitchell decried nondomestic activity by women; Mitchell's *Wear and Tear; or, Hints for the Overworked* treats the deleterious effects of commerce with advice on women's health. "It will not answer to look only at the causes of sickness and weakness which affect the male sex," Mitchell believes, because "if the mothers of a people are sickly and weak, the sad inheritance falls upon their offspring." To strengthen mothers for the American future, Mitchell designed his famous rest cure for nervous diseases. After undergoing a regimen of constant bed rest and severely restricted activity, women patients were to return to tranquil lives as wives and mothers. The rest cure countered the marketplace with a fortified domesticity.[14]

This fortified domesticity finally fortified the marketplace. The interest of physicians in the immobilizing effects of the marketplace signifies not an antimarket program but a foregrounding of domesticity from other images of the stationary. As the symptomatology of immobility proliferates domestic attributes, its cure reiterates and recommends conventional domesticity. The aim of the rest cure, then, is not to limit market mobility but to reinforce a select domestic stillness, to underscore the healthy function of the stationary. In restricting women to bed, the rest cure in a sense demobilizes the domestic in order to recharge it for reproductive service to the market. This interdependence of domesticity with the market emerges with greater specificity in nineteenth-century feminist critiques of the rest cure.

Women like Charlotte Perkins Gilman and the autobiographical narrator of her "The Yellow Wallpaper," whose nervous prostration did not benefit from the rest cure, used immobility to parody and protest against domestic confinement, to withdraw from household business. The protagonist of "The Yellow Wall-paper" withdraws into the world she sees in the wallpaper; oblivious to all else, she becomes indistinguishable from the paper and the woman she imagines behind it. It is impossible to distinguish where the woman "creeping" around the walls of her room is; her association with the wallpaper involves a traversal of boundaries in which she simultaneously creeps along the walls of her room on both sides of the wallpaper and outside the house in "the long road under the trees."[15] The uncertainty of this woman's place, her identification with both the woman she imagines creeping behind the paper and the woman she imagines "creeping along" "in the open country" suggest that domestic borders vary and waver, that walls and women move (30–31).

In Gilman's portrait of its intensive domesticity, the rest cure results in changing and disappearing walls, in a marketlike domesticity. It is this delivery from home to market that nineteenth-century feminists from Charlotte Brontë to Charlotte Gilman explicated and elaborated in their reinterpretations of domesticity. The feminist point of "The Yellow Wallpaper," and of other madwoman-in-the-attic figures, is that domestic confinement ultimately destroys not only the woman but also the house; the real curative property of domesticity, then, would seem to be its elimination of barriers to the outside.[16] The final situation of the woman in "The Yellow Wallpaper" as she creeps "around the path by the wall" (36) is continual circulation.

That the domain of female circulation is madness would appear to reaffirm the etiologies of the doctors who treated men suffering from the deleterious effects of commerce. The chronology unfolded by "The Yellow Wallpaper," however, illustrates a different movement: the domestic appropriation of the market, the mapping of its space within the interiors of home. The nervousness manifest in moving walls and in the dislocation of self replicates the conditions of commerce from which those walls customarily and ideally barricade the individual. Woman's nervousness thus bypasses the market outside, proceeding to a circulation of her own.

Gilman's subversion of domesticity launches a utopian transformation of the market, elaborated in the socialist-feminist redesigns of domesticity and collective households she advocated in her subsequent writings.[17] Raising market nervousness to a feminist power, "The Yellow Wallpaper" exploits the negative logic of commerce chronicled in accounts of American nervousness, revealing the market reflected and lodged in the walls of home. This extenuation of the mechanics of immobility delineates and summarizes developments already visible in late-nineteenth-century domestic architecture: the accentuation of open space within the domestic interior, the de-emphasis on fixed enclosures in Frank Lloyd Wright's innovative windows, walls, and floor plans. Before Wright's new homes appeared in the 1890s, the century's best-known domestic ideologue, Catharine Beecher, had advocated in the 1840s the advantages housekeepers might enjoy from open rooms and moveable walls by which they could change the organization of domestic space to suit their various activities.[18] So the mutability of domestic walls and the embrace of unbordered space described by "The Yellow Wallpaper" realize the value of mobility, the ethos of the market, already present in the domestic blueprint.

"The Yellow Wallpaper" and "Bartleby" are key moments in and representations of the mobilization of immobility that characterizes nineteenth-century American culture. If Gilman's story images both a consonant and revisionary conclusion to an agoraphobic definition of selfhood, Melville's tale predicts and protests the circulation of the stationary that allows for such a conclusion. In the case of Bartleby, who doesn't creep and whose walls don't move, Melville depicts an intransigent agoraphobia that admits no entry to the market, a tableau of the stationary in which walls stand still. The scrivener's motionlessness removes him from all forms of circulation, not even achieving the mobility of the woman who creeps around her room. To forestall the return of the agoraphobic to circulation, to circumvent the border movements of "The Yellow Wallpaper," Bartleby images an agoraphobia recalcitrant to the publicity in which the reformative discourses of disease would place it. At the threshold of the American women's movement and the economic expansion of the latter half of the nineteenth century, "Bartleby" presents an anxiety about the market anxieties that would propel physicians and feminists, as well as other commentators on American life, in the succeeding decades.

In the following exposition of nervousness about American nervousness, it will become clear that the agoraphobic model of self-integrity instantiates the market destiny of domesticity. The informing principle of domestic sanctuary, agoraphobia epitomizes the structure of individuality in a market economy. What finally makes agoraphobia paradigmatic, however, is not the domestic stillness it reproduces but the home/market circuit its theatrics of interiority restage. Agoraphobia's incarnation of commerce thus assures the market's future, the acceptance of its natural movements.

The logic animating Bartleby's motionlessness emerges with greater clarity in another nineteenth-century discourse inspirited by the agoraphobic imagination, the antifeminist rhetoric of home protection. Nineteenth-century advice literature, sentimental novels, and women's magazines defined the home as a refuge from commercial life, an antithesis to the masculine marketplace.[19] Domestic literature such as *Godey's Lady's Book*, the century's most popular women's magazine, dedicated itself to the consolidation and cultivation of "the empire of home." Against men's struggle "for the mastery of the world," editor Sarah Josepha Hale urged women to stay home and engage in "a higher pursuit than the industrial arts afford," their "mission" as "guardians of whatsoever is good, pure, and lovely." Concurrent with the emergent consumerist role of women in the American economy, *Godey's* circulated an anticommercial rhetoric on the virtues of staying home; stories celebrated heroines who eschewed the glamors of social life and the pleasures of shopping for their "quiet office" and frugal economies in "the empire of home."[20]

Like the physicians Beard and Mitchell, the *Lady's Book* worried about women's part in contemporary economic revolutions, about the proliferation of commerce in women's work in the extradomestic world. Antifeminist polemics of the late nineteenth century amplify this concern in their scientistic characterizations of women as mentally inferior to men and subject to their reproductive function. This claim of biological determinacy advocates one form of reproduction over another; in opposition to the reproduction of commerce displayed by women's exercise of mental capacities and mobility, domestic traditionalists stressed "woman's nature" and "ministry at home."[21] Woman's participation in other occupations signals a degenerative movement, *Godey's* warned; "It is as though a star should strive to come down from its place in the calm sky and take the station of a gaslamp in a crowded city street."[22]

To keep women from the crowded city streets, *Godey's* promoted domestic values and "never admitted any article . . . which is not intended to instruct either by example, sentiment, hints, or warnings."[23] As the American market economy developed and expanded, and as women entered nondomestic situations, the magazine's instructive articles continued to hint and warn against the dangers of the business domain. These anxieties about women in the marketplace surfaced most strikingly in an anonymously authored story of 1870 entitled "My Wife and the Market Street Phantom."[24] The stereotypical other woman opposed to the wife in the title is not a romantic rival, not a mistress or previous wife, but a "lady capitalist." The scandal is not sexual indiscretion but indiscreet business affairs.

George, the narrator, relates the story of the strain placed on his marriage by his reliance on creditors in his merchant business. He takes out a ninety-day loan to carry him over what loan offices now call a cash-flow problem, until he can collect on his own extensions of credit. His loan is passed on by one creditor to the dreaded Market Street Phantom, a "lady capitalist" notorious as much for her business methods as her success. The lady's notoriety follows not only from the fact that she "is definitely a woman out of her sphere" but also from what the narrator calls her "peculiar style of doing business." When she buys up a loan note, she investigates the debtor:

She would look with the keenness of a merchandise broker at a stock of goods, count the boxes on the pavement before a store, inquire into the bank account of the drawer or city endorser, ascertain whether he was married or single, find it out if he kept a fast horse, and get a good look at him to see if he himself seemed to be a fast man. (340)

Then she enters into a familiar relation with the debtor, persistently calling on him to remind him of the due date on the note, assuming terms of "the most annoying cordiality" with him on every possible occasion. The worst of the Phantom's habits was "that she recognized all her debtors when she met them, that she spoke of them as her friends." For the duration of the loan period, the debtor is plagued by her presence—he is "under the spell of the Phantom." George compounds his predicament by not telling his wife the truth about his business affairs. The Phantom pays a call at the man's office the same day his wife is there. The wife immediately perceives her husband's embarrassment and is further disturbed when her husband refuses to tell her the truth about the Phantom's identity and her relation to him. Until the loan is repaid the marriage is in trouble and "agony." Finally, George pays his debt, confesses to his wife and brother-in-law, and "all the clouds that lowered upon our house were lifted." The three laugh over the misunderstanding and in the future the husband goes to his brother-in-law for business loans.

The narrator has learned his lesson—the perils of credit in the marketplace and the perils of withholding in the marriage. His mistake was to conduct business affairs he could not reveal to his wife; he should have entrusted his business problems to domestic care. The conflict between credit and family is resolved not by the termination of the credit economy, as one might expect in a moral tale about the dangers of credit, but by the domestic circle's absorption of credit relations. So the story finally rejects not the principle of credit against which it protests but the extrafamilial phenomena that credit represents. That is, credit relations within the family are fine but on Market Street are scandalous, akin to adultery. The narrator triumphs over his situation when he is able "to cut the Phantom dead!"—when he is able to extricate himself from exogamous relations. Domesticity withstands the impingement of marketplace immorality by simply nullifying the existence of extradomestic phenomena. The story thus consolidates the family state.

But while the story domesticates credit, it does not domesticate the lady capitalist. The lady capitalist is a homebreaker because she threatens to reverse the power relations that uphold domesticity. In a culture where woman can only be recognized as domestic, the lady capitalist is not merely aberrant but subversive. The story reconciles the opposition between home and market in the home's acceptance of credit as a component of domestic life. The Phantom reverses the order of this accommodation: she brings the home under the aegis of the market. In assuming intimacy with her business relations, the Phantom behaves as if the market were the home; she insists upon a chain of relations normally governed by domestic etiquette. She represents an untenable premise—not merely a woman out of her sphere but domesticity outside the home.

Making the domestic an integral part of market relations, the Phantom makes explicit the continuity between home and market that domestic rhetoric disguised. And she does this by subsuming the home into the market, familiar relations into credit checks. When George's brother-in-law replaces the Phantom as family creditor, the proper hierarchy is restored. Instead of the home being invaded by the market, the home annexes the market.

But this domestic campaign itself risks the disappearance of domestic boundaries in the family's incorporation of credit practices. In order to safeguard against this blurring of distinctions between home and market, the story fortifies the domestic by scapegoating the lady capitalist. Imaged as a state of being besieged, domesticity appears under attack from the female creditors who advance commerce, yet the ultimate enemy this domestic defense strategy addresses is the home's own undomesticity. When poltergeists haunt the marketplace, they are following the excursions of the home into the world. Thus, the goal of the effort to ostracize the lady capitalist is to deny both the Phantom's and the home's excursions, to affirm domestic integrity and isolationism. Home protectionism reaffirms domestic borders by disseminating fears of market manifestations.

For readers of *Godey's*, the "cutting dead" of the Phantom eliminated anxieties raised by their consumer role about the integrity of the domestic sphere; exorcising the Phantom meant purifying the home. In this fear of the marketplace, this literal agoraphobia, the Phantom is a bogeyman whose expulsion enforces the division between home and market. Like bogeymen in the closet or under the bed, the Phantom's potential reappearance offers a continual opportunity for reasserting domestic safety and tranquility. Although she figures as the credit economy's threat to the family, the lady capitalist in fact ensures the family's acceptance of credit. In this way she functions as the facilitating anxiety of the home's accommodation of change. The Market Street Phantom is thus the agoraphobic spirit governing consumerist domestic ideology.

What *Godey's* cautionary tale provided its reader was a reassurance of the existence of a frightening exterior world from which to preserve herself, reaffirming the need for domesticity. The tale circulates the production of domesticity as a state of anticipatory defense. This construction of a vigilant domesticity that absorbs exterior threats is of course a model of capitalist consumption: the realization and reinforcement of personal life in the acquisition of things believed to be necessary for self-sufficiency. What is sold by the story of a threatened domesticity is reinforced domesticity. This marketing of domesticity, the *raison d'être* of magazines like *Godey's*, shapes the consumer role of women in the American economy. In order that the domestic remain a principle of stability, domestic consumerism requires the remapping of the home's boundaries, their extension into commercial spaces.

Reenacting this implementation of domesticity against its own changeability, the department store first attracted late-nineteenth-century women shoppers by designing and advertising itself as a magnified model home, as the unlimited possibilities of domestic space.[25] *Godey's* performed a similar negotiation: the magazine introduced women to products and established continuity between consumerism and housekeeping. The market thus seemed in service to domesticity. The woman at home, Thorstein Veblen's model of conspicuous consumption, came to represent the foundation of the market economy, her demands and needs its motivating purpose—or, in the more positive, progressive version, her virtues signified the economy's idealist aims: philanthropy, comfort, progress.[26]

The institutionalization of women as consumers accomplished by the incorporation of consumerist sites into women's sphere established the primarily public nature of women's new domestic performances, the visibility denoted in Veblen's "conspicuous consumption."[27] So now, more than a century after the invention of the department store, the store itself figures as the dreaded open space in agoraphobic episodes. And women, who traditionally frequent shops and markets, predominate among agoraphobic cases. Most agoraphobic attacks take place within the walls of department stores or in vehicles on the way to stores. What might seem an environment more inducive of claustrophobia creates the same anxieties nineteenth-century agoraphobes associated with streets and open areas, and similarly causes retreat into houses. Staying home, "playing a paragon of Victorian femininity," the female agoraphobic identifies and fears the store's quintessential market character.[28]

Recognizing the refusal to leave home as a refusal to shop, contemporary behaviorist treatments of agoraphobia conclude with a celebratory shopping spree at a department store. The behaviorist aim to make women shop reinforces as it remarks the market agenda inscribed in domesticity during the nineteenth century. In returning women to the market, the behaviorist treatment updates Mitchell's rest cure to suit a consumerist domesticity; returning women to the department store is identical to returning women to their domestic sphere. These rearrangements of domestic space in the treatments of agoraphobia and nervous diseases are reflected in the strategically changing geography traced by contemporary agoraphobics. The agoraphobic lives according to a world map delineating safe and dangerous zones; often she will alter the boundaries of safe spaces so that she might venture beyond home to a friend's house or some other selectively domesticated hostile territory—for example, one side of an unsafe street. Conversely, and as usually happens in the debilitating process of the agoraphobic condition, the danger zones in the outside world multiply and eventually include even activities that connect the home and external world, such as telephoning and correspondence.[29]

Expansions and contractions of safety sites, agoraphobic manipulations of domestic borders continually manufacture the certainty of safe places, thereby reproducing domesticity. This productive circulation of domesticity elaborated in home-protectionist rhetoric consolidates not only home but the marketplace where home is sold. The alternate house-hugging and border crossing in agoraphobic practice manifest an uncertainty about where the market is, suggesting that what is most terrifying about the market is its ubiquity, its inescapability. With each new retrenchment of barriers, the marketplace advances ever nearer. For, if home in fact embraces the world, there is finally no place for the agoraphobic to go except to market. A continual border operation, agoraphobia always assumes the traversal of the boundaries it sets, always presumes that the limits can or will change. Mirroring the market economy's circulatory generativity, agoraphobia ultimately multiplies and magnifies the marketplace. Through its logic, through the productive persistence of domestic threats like the Market Street Phantom, the market circulates and expands.

A scenario of besieged domesticity, "My Wife and the Market Street Phantom" demonstrates this market-economy expansion. The economy associated with the Phantom triumphs when the family welcomes credit practices, reconstituting market relations as domestic ones. The wife takes the place of the Phantom in her husband's thoughts and, in resuming that place, offers him credit from her brother. In this transposition, domesticity subsumes the business of the ubiquitous lady capitalist, an assimilation perhaps most tellingly represented in Gilman's image of domesticity as woman's creeping confinement.

Replaying the mechanics of market expansion demonstrated in the *Godey's* story, the circulation of the woman "round and round and round and round" her room also reiterates the agoraphobic association between selfhood and domestic enclosure. The woman in "The Yellow Wallpaper" finally doesn't "want to go outside"; having locked herself in her room, she prefers to stay where her "shoulder just fits in that long smooch around the wall" (35). Declaring "you don't get *me* out in the road there!" she continues creeping on her "path by the wall" (35), just as Bartleby continues his agoraphobic behavior in prison, taking up a "position fronting the dead-wall" (72). These agoraphobic figures of self-preservation exemplify a more tenacious house-hugging than domesticity recommends; both retain their absolute interiority by identifying with and preserving themselves in the walls. But Bartleby's self-possession is more assured: when confined in prison (for the supremely ironic charge of vagrancy), "his face toward a high wall," he emphatically states "I know where I am" (71). This is a knowledge the woman cannot, and need not, claim because her attachment is to the moveability of walls; attaching herself to the wallpaper that changes and moves, she identifies with the wall she traces and traverses. Gilman's regrounding of female identity in unstable domesticity, in the uncertainty of a female form of commerce, imagines the benefits of not knowing where you are. Once the wall the woman becomes disintegrates in her domestic demolition project, she doesn't need to go out because she has already attained a sphere of selfhood, however bizarre.

Gilman is offering this female circulation as a feminist *point d'appui*, as the situation from which to reimagine female roles. In her later utopian *Herland* stories, the idea of female circulation culminates in the vision of a self-generating, all female culture.[30] The exorcism of the Market Street Phantom by the *Godey's* parable precludes such an alternative relation between women and economics. What haunts the agoraphobic imagination in its management of the market, however, is not specifically the feminist appropriation of circulation but the terminus of circulation an alternative economy might institute. This is the real fear in the agoraphobic imagination: circulations beyond even those of the female agoraphobic and "The Yellow Wallpaper" heroine, the prospect of a utopian circulation, which amounts to circulation nowhere, or no circulation, the immobilization of mobility.

Against this possibility of an altogether different form of life, the capitalist agoraphobic imagination summons the specter of the lady capitalist, a woman out of her sphere. The home-protectionist elimination of the lady capitalist limits and stabilizes the expansionist market; eliminating the lady capitalist is an intervention that prevents the eventual evolution of the market into something different, to check mobility from its own possible extremes. The feminist progress suggested by the Phantom—her market perambulations—signifies the chaos and unfamiliarity of not only a woman but a market unmoored from the modulations of immobility. Without the tableaux of the stationary performed by women and domesticity, the market approaches the uncertain state of the woman in "The Yellow Wallpaper." Against its own transformation into a feminist or foreign circulation, the market economy incorporates feminism as a regulatory mechanism for its own continuity. Premised as another threat to domesticity, feminism becomes the phantasm inspiring home defense. The *ménage à trois* husband, wife, and Phantom other woman—or market, home, and feminism—thus perpetuates the hegemony of consumerist domesticity.

At stake in this stabilization of circulation is the maintenance of a domesticity in which one knows where one is. The dizzying circulation "round and round and round and round" the room in "The Yellow Wallpaper," an extreme version of the domestic enclosure of the Market Street Phantom's perambulations, marks the uncertainty of a self defined by walls that inevitably move. A self dislocated by permutations in the standard tableau of the stationary signifies the continual risks to and relocations of selfhood induced by the capitalist agoraphobic imagination. The regulation of market progress introduced by the *Godey's* story stems the advance of the wall-moving woman of "The Yellow Wallpaper," which reveals in turn that the greater risk in capitalist agoraphobia runs through its own regulatory movements: that its propensity to change borders undermines the construct of a stable self. Shifting the walls that situate the self, agoraphobia is inevitably not agoraphobic enough. The emblematic market mechanism, it swerves too far from house-hugging to sustain the ideal of self-preservation its postures of immobility suggest. This is why the most thoroughgoing resistance to nineteenth-century consumerist domestic ideology and market operations comes from a figure antithetical to movement—the stationary, radically agoraphobic Bartleby.

It is within these politics of agoraphobia, the dynamic between home and world manifested by consumption, that the meaning of Bartleby's negations and mysterious isolationism emerges. Bartleby, who in Elizabeth Hardwick's paraphrase "shuns the streets and is unmoved by the moral, religious, acute, obsessive, beautiful ideal of Consumption," insists upon a noncommercial domesticity.[31] In preferring "to be stationary" (69), Bartleby achieves an impenetrability the lawyer narrator cannot alter or enter. What the lawyer recognizes as Bartleby's complete self-possession—"his great stillness, his unalterableness of demeanor under all circumstances" (53)—obviates the very notion of exchange or intercourse, denying any form of commerce, including the conversation and charity the lawyer would readily extend.

In his agoraphobic responses, or rather lack of responsiveness, Bartleby follows female agoraphobic modes of evading domestic consumerism and repudiating intercourse between private and public realms.[32] The encounter between the lawyer and the scrivener is one between two competing models of domesticity: commercial and truly agoraphobic.[33] In this context, the narrator appears as a kind of Wall Street housekeeper; however, his domesticated business practices are undermined by Bartleby's renunciation of the domestic pretensions of the "eminently safe man" in his "snug business" on Wall Street (40).

Although the lawyer belongs "to a profession proverbially energetic and nervous, even . . . turbulent," he permits "nothing of that sort . . . to invade [his] peace." He attributes to his office "the cool tranquility of a snug retreat" (40). The business of the lawyer's domestic commercial sphere chiefly involves overseeing and compensating for the unhealthy gestatory habits of his copyists. Turkey drinks and cannot perform his duties during the afternoon; his fellow worker Nippers suffers from morning indigestion and doesn't work efficiently until afternoon. The office boy Ginger-nut seems to function mainly as "cake and apple purveyor for Turkey and Nippers" (45). For the lawyer, these concerns with food and drink are labor/management issues: what his employees consume directly affects what they produce. In this office in the image of home, the eccentricities of appetite are incorporated into the business routine.

Into this domestic colony on Wall Street comes the "motionless young man" Bartleby (45), who initially seems to suit perfectly and even optimize the narrator's domestic economy. The lawyer thinks "a man of so singularly sedate an aspect . . . might operate beneficially upon the flighty temper of Turkey and the fiery one of Nippers" (46). Bartleby's habits "at first" appear the model of balance between work and diet, consumption and production—his work *is* ingestion. "As if long famishing for something to copy," the lawyer notes, "he seemed to gorge himself on my documents . . . without pause for digestion" (46).

Indeed, Bartleby so much epitomizes for his employer the successful union of economic and individual attributes that his place in the office— in a screened corner of a partition, facing a window with a view only of a brick wall—makes a "satisfactory arrangement" in which "privacy and society were conjoined" (46). The lawyer thinks of Bartleby's office carrel as "his hermitage" (50), and Bartleby literalizes this domestic fantasy. His insistent denial of every request directed at him, his removal of himself into his "dead-wall reveries" (52), effectively achieves the hermitage and privacy that the lawyer imagines his establishment provides. Making the "office his constant abiding place and home" (56), Bartleby purifies his employer's domestic economy. While the lawyer attempts to domesticate business, to accommodate the fluctuations of production and consumption within the walls of his establishment, Bartleby seeks to empty the domestic of the economic, to establish an impregnable privacy. Counter-spirit to the Market Street Phantom, the "apparition of Bartleby" "haunting the building" (53, 68) enforces the rhetorical boundaries of the private sphere.

Making the office home in fact, Bartleby is a missionary agoraphobic, incongruously claiming the walls of Wall Street as the protective borders of the private domain, preferring to the congenial agoraphobia of the narrator a doctrinaire, absolute one whose primary feature is not so much that he "never went anywhere" but that, as the lawyer observes, "he never went to dinner" (50). Rather than follow, in the fashion of the lawyer, the logic of agoraphobia, which ultimately admits and embraces the market, Bartleby "lives without dining" (73), perfecting the agoraphobic condition in anorexia, where the borders between world and self are traced (and ultimately erased) on the individual body. This radical refusal to partake of, and participate in, the world makes Bartleby "self possessed" (54) and impenetrable, the traditional goal of domestic life. Simultaneously fulfilling and negating the logic of agoraphobia—establishing selfhood in the extinction of commerce—anorexia secures the agoraphobic division of self from world, home from market. A strict and rigid observance of this division, anorexia realizes the hermitage agoraphobia cannot obtain; eliminating consumption, it halts agoraphobia's inevitable progress into the marketplace.

The anorexic, almost always a woman, avoids the world by refusing the most basic form of consumption. By starving herself she suppresses her menstrual cycle, shutting down the process of her own reproductive functions. She maintains in her body the fantasy of domesticity Bartleby enacts: a perfect self-enclosure. While anorexia hardly seems an ideal condition, it is the fulfillment of the ideal of domestic privacy, a state in which complete separation from the demands and supplies of the world is attained.

Anorexia, somewhat contrary to its name, is not the condition of being without desire but the enterprise of controlling desire. That is, the anorexic wants to not want and to this end tries not to consume, or to undo consumption. She devotes all her energy and efforts to regulating the passage of food to and from her body. Most anorexics do in fact succumb to eating binges and become bulimic, inducing expurgation after every meal. Or they adopt intensive exercise regimens and ingest large amounts of laxatives and diuretics. One anorexic reported to her therapist that she masturbated one hundred times each evening, believing the constant pressure would strengthen her sphincter muscles, thereby facilitating release of food through defecation.[34]

This effort to eliminate or control food frequently involves preoccupation with the buying, preparation, and serving of food. An anorexic will insist upon cooking for the family and produce elaborate meals whose consumption she supervises but herself forgoes. One anorexic was brought to treatment by her mother who was concerned about the weight gain her daughter was inflicting upon her. In this dedication to others' consumption, the anorexic bizarrely imitates the mother's housekeeping role. She thus controls the desire to consume that she recognizes as essential to the family. Another anorexic so insisted on having dominion over food that her wealthy father built her her own kitchen, separate from the kitchen where the family cook worked. Here the girl maintained her perfected domestic province, where she performed the central housekeeping role without consuming.[35] This case makes clear the anorexic's radical claim to domestic space, her Bartleby-like insistence on a privacy without commerce. The anorexic kitchen literalizes domestic ideals, perfecting domesticity in antidomesticity.

Anorexic practices, like agoraphobic strategies, manifest domestic functions in extreme forms. Not surprisingly, some recent analysts and interpreters of anorexia read in this hyperbolic condition a radical realization and indictment of cultural dictates upon women's bodies and functions. Anorexic body ideals seem to coincide with the contemporary valuation of female slenderness (another marketing of domesticity), prompting observers of anorexia to note the current "popularity" of this disease, its distinctive appeal to adolescent, middle-class girls.[36] While cases of anorexia in the latter half of this century clearly reflect and address specific cultural values, the anorexic strategy in "Bartleby" stresses another agenda: the rejection of consumerist domesticity. Bartleby's anorexia would remove agoraphobia from domestic commerce, making impossible the connection between these diseases and domestic consumerism that nineteenth- and twentieth-century feminists and physicians variously register.

First recorded in a 1689 treatise on tuberculosis as "A Nervous Consumption," anorexia nervosa did not become a specific clinical entity until 1873, the same year agoraphobia was first classified, twenty years after the publication of "Bartleby."[37] The difficulty nineteenth-century doctors encountered in diagnosing anorexia, in identifying it as a specific disease, lay in the similarity between the symptoms of anorexia and consumption, now remembered as the great nineteenth-century disease. Though an incorrect paradigm for anorexia nervosa, the initial clinical classification of anorexia with consumption unwittingly points to the connection between these illnesses as metaphors, to the way the diseases, or the descriptions of the diseases, both exemplify economic models. Susan Sontag has pointed out the isomorphism between the economies of tuberculosis and nineteenth-century expanding capitalism. Tuberculosis exhibits "the negative behavior of nineteenth-century *homo economicus*: consumption; wasting; squandering of vitality."[38] The fluctuations characteristic of the illness—dramatic variations in appetite and energy—aptly reproduced marketplace disequilibrium and concomitant anxieties about saving and spending. Tuberculosis mysteriously consumed the body from within; the consumptive sufferer seemed to replicate upon the body an apocalyptic view of economic progress, a state of simultaneous voraciousness and exhaustion. No Camille-like martyred heroine to this economy, the anorexic chooses illness as a repudiation of the marketplace and an expression of self-control. A refusal to replicate the economy in the body, anorexia is the paradoxical antidote to consumption, the negative behavior of *femina economica*.

The anorexic enactment of the self-destructiveness of self-denial surpasses the deaths of angelic, tubercular heroines like Stowe's Little Eva and Louisa May Alcott's Beth, translating domestic angels into skeletal women. Taking to the limit the sentimental ideals of true womanhood, the anorexic appears the sentimental self-denying heroine par excellence. A macabre mockery of domesticity, anorexia, like agoraphobia and hysteria, appears to offer another figure of resistance to domestic ideology, another feminist type of the madwoman in the attic.[39]

But since the anorexic opposes the economy of consumption of both feminist and traditional versions of domesticity, the anorexic resists canonization as a sentimental or feminist heroine. Indeed, feminist visions of women in the world epitomize the commercial possibility in home/market relations from which the anorexic retreats. The circulation of the woman in "The Yellow Wallpaper" exhibits the tendency to mobility in agoraphobia that anorexia would eliminate. Unlike agoraphobic or hysteric stances, anorexic body language refuses to represent any form of commerce. A purging of agoraphobia, anorexia replaces the economy of consumption with abstinence. Disappearing from sight and space, the anorexic creates her own purified version of nineteenth-century tableaux of the stationary, an approach to complete privacy and stillness.

It is finally death, the termination of self, rather than self-circulation through the elimination of cultural obstructions, that anorexia seeks. This cult of death differs from popular sentimentalist celebrations of death like Harriet Beecher Stowe's glorification of Little Eva's consumption that circulated in nineteenth-century domestic literature.[40] Whereas sentimental death seeks the world and an audience, demanding a public space in the world, anorexic death flees the world; the anorexic economy of self-denial redefines death as divestment from the marketplace. To realize the fantasy of controlling desire—to deny the existence of an outside, of anything exterior to the self—the anorexic inevitably must want to die. By rejecting the body she hates for its contiguity with the world, for its reminder of the desire to consume, the anorexic finally triumphs over desire. Paradoxically, her abstinence permits pure selfishness. Preferring not to eat, like Bartleby, she detaches herself from the world and finally from the body that borders it, the last semblance of walls contiguous with the world. In the logic of anorexia's perfection of agoraphobia, death best preserves the self.

These are the anorexic politics of Bartleby's radical employment of immobility. Stringently restricting the agoraphobic imagination to its ethic of immobility, Bartleby elaborates death as the best method of self-preservation. He leaves the world in order to keep himself. If properly understood, this choice of divestiture, despite the obvious disadvantages of the disappearing self, is a powerful one. What better critique of domestic difficulties than the decision to live no longer? But as inevitable as the cult of death is for the anorexic is the sentimentality of interpretation to which death is submitted and consequently misread. When Bartleby, entombed within the Tombs, sleeps "with kings and counsellors" (73), the narrator attempts to account for the bizarre life and death of his scrivener. In telling the scrivener's story, he accepts the invitation to investigate and interpret this successful agoraphobic. The "vague report" (73) he offers as an epilogue satisfies *his* curiosity about Bartleby's motivations. If Bartleby worked in the Dead Letter Office in Washington, then his condition might be understood as a response to such close association with death. For do not dead letters "sound like dead men?" (73). Bartleby's condition seems to the narrator an intensified experience of human mortality. He therefore commemorates Bartleby's passage as a testament of the human tragedy, joining the man and the crowd in his closing lament, "Ah, Bartleby! Ah, humanity!" (74).

The narrator's sentimental closure to Bartleby's story links Bartleby with the very chain of existence he preferred to avoid. This conjunction of Bartleby with humanity—the agoraphobic's nightmare—also elides the differences between the domestic preferences of Bartleby and of his employer, thus diffusing the force of Bartleby's renunciation of commercial domesticity. By ignoring the alignment between circulation, life, and death that Bartleby signifies, the narrator's solution preserves the commerce his version of domesticity tacitly transacts. The narrator would have us believe that Bartleby, continually witnessing letters on doomed errands of life, speeding to death, suffered from an overexposure to death, when death is precisely what Bartleby sought. The very idea of an errand—of letters reaching their destination—is anathema to Bartleby, who evades every form of intercourse, whose preferences cannot even attach to an object. The anorexic tries to deny food and body of any relation by transforming objects of consumption into threatening, alien forces; she asserts the body's independence from the objects of its desires. Similarly, Bartleby detaches himself from things and all activities involving things, refusing even to commit himself to predicates that would signify subject-object relations, that would connect his negation to something external to himself. Bartleby hardly exemplifies the tragedy of death; his anorexia attests to the tragedy of circulation. What impels him, or rather what inters him, are not the disconnections caused by death but the connections produced by life.

The success of suicide missions depends on the proper interpretation of the suicidal intention. Bartleby's final act of refusal secures him no recognition for his cause, no canonization by fellow adherents. Despite the intended enunciation of the scrivener's death, the lawyer interprets the tragedy as a confirmation of his own sentimentality. Whereas Bartleby sought to dissociate himself from all forms of economy, the narrator returns the copyist to the sentimental economy. Imagining Bartleby among kings and counselors, the lawyer invokes Job's artificial death wish. In his lament on the misfortunes of his life, Job cries that he would have been at rest with kings and counselors if he had died in the womb, or if his birth and nurturance had been prevented by the knees and breasts.[41] This lament almost comically shifts both the responsibility for Job's unhappy life and its points of termination; the logic of his wish delivers him to a resting point only imaginable in history, only possible for having lived. So Job doesn't wish that he had never been born—but that is precisely what Bartleby wishes when he prefers not to. The lawyer would return Bartleby to history when Bartleby would prefer not to have sucked, to have aborted his existence altogether.

The lawyer's interpretation of Bartleby's death, the tale's circulation of Bartleby's life, subsumes the radical act into the chain of existence and chronicle of history, into literary currency. This final domestication implies that the elimination of the body achieves only partial secession from the commercial. Interpretation invades death's privacy, taking death as a communiqué. Bartleby's imagination of an aborted self, a broken circuit, offers to the sentimental imagination an annexation of the unknown, the widening boundaries of what we think of as the world and women's sphere. In the agoraphobic imagination structuring selfhood in a market economy, death becomes another province, another border to be crossed—the final domestic station to be mobilized. The narrator's attempt to find a transcendent meaning in the Bartleby enigma is thus precisely the triumph of sentimentalism and consumerism: the perpetuation of the preoccupation with private property and personal provinces.

Even death, whether imagined as an escape by Bartleby or invoked as a principle of coherence by the lawyer, repeats the expansion and contraction patterns of the various sects of domestic perfectionists. The agoraphobic structure of domestic ideology, which Bartleby takes to the limit, includes and utilizes mortality within the logic of home protection. The life and death of Bartleby recirculates the imagination of being besieged that persists in shaping and defining the economies of capitalism and of private life. Even in death, commerce continues; this is the errand of life on which letters speed to and from death.

Notes

This essay is part of a larger project generously supported by a Henry Rutgers Research Fellowship at Rutgers, the State University of New Jersey. I would also like to thank Howard Horwitz, Myra Jehlen, and Lynn Wardley for their helpful readings.

1. Herman Melville, "Bartleby the Scrivener: A Tale of Wall Street," in *Great Short Works of Herman Melville*, ed. Warner Berthoff (New York, 1969), 39–40. Subsequent references are cited in parentheses in the essay.
2. For an account of the icons of home and mother in popular nineteenth-century discourse see Mary Ryan's discussion of the 1850s rhetoric of domestic isolation and rest in *The Empire of the Mother: American Writing About Domesticity, 1830–1860* (New York, 1982), 97–115.

    The invalid, housebound Alice James, who welcomed the "divine *cessation*" (her emphasis) of death, represents *in extremis* the ethic of immobility recommended by the nineteenth-century American cult of true womanhood; *The Diary of Alice James*, ed. Leon Edel (New York, 1964), 232. The resemblance between female invalidism and the domestic ideal of woman at home is explored in Jean Strouse, *Alice James* (New York, 1979); and Ruth Bernard Yeazell, *The Death and Letters of Alice James* (Berkeley, 1981).
3. The images of hysterical postures became publicly available with the publication of Désiré M. Bourneville and Paul Reynard's *Iconographie photographique de la Salpêtrière*, 3 vols. (Paris, 1877–80). On the discourse of hysteria in America, see Carroll Smith-Rosenberg, "The Hysterical Woman: Sex Roles and Role Conflicts in Nineteenth-Century America," *Social Research* 39 (Winter 1972): 652–78, reprinted in *Disorderly Conduct: Visions of Gender in Victorian America* (New York, 1985), 197–216. While paralysis represented only one symptom in the multivarious symptomology of hysteria that includes aphonia, depression, fatigue, nervousness, numbness, and epilepticlike seizures, it is preeminently emblematic of hysteria, I am suggesting, because of its continuity with domestic prescriptions. Hysteria in nineteenth-century America, in Smith-Rosenberg's words the disease of the Victorian bourgeois family, caricatures domesticity; in the sociological account of hysteria developed by American doctors and recently politicized by feminist investigators such as Smith-Rosenberg, the hysteric suffers mainly from reminiscences of that domesticity. While current feminist reformulations of hysteria, such as the provocative rereadings of Dora collected in *In Dora's Case: Freud/Hysteria/Feminism*, ed. Charles Bernheimer and Claire Kahane (New York, 1985), identify hysteric gestures as a female language, I am more interested in how the visibility of hysteria historically underscores what is already visible about woman: her removal from the public sphere. In this exposition, the dynamics of motion and stasis in the photographs of hysterical seizures and poses elaborate the antinomy between movement and repose upheld by nineteenth-century domestic ideology.

4. William James, *The Principles of Psychology*, 2 vols. (1890; reprint ed., New York, 1950), 2:421–22.

5. Dr. D. C. Westphal coined the term in an article discussing a case of fear of open places; *Journal of Mental Sciences* 19 (1873): 456. An earlier version of this article appeared in Germany in *Archiv für Psychiatrie* 1 (1871).

6. William A. Hammond, *A Treatise on Insanity* (1883; reprint ed., New York, 1973), 419–22.

7. Charles Bossut, ed., *Préface aux oeuvres de Blaise Pascal* (Paris, 1819), xxxii; and Louis-Françisque Lelut, *L'Amulette de Pascal* (Paris, 1846), quoted in Hammond, *A Treatise on Insanity*.

8. Alexis de Tocqueville, *Democracy in America*, ed. Phillips Bradley, 2 vols. (New York, 1945), 2:146.

9. George M. Beard, *American Nervousness, Its Causes and Consequences* (New York, 1881), 96–129.

10. Hammond, *A Treatise on Insanity*, 422.

11. S. Weir Mitchell, *Wear and Tear; or, Hints for the Overworked* (1887; reprint ed., New York, 1973), 63.

12. See George Frederick Drinka's chapter on railway neuroses in *The Birth of Neurosis* (New York, 1984), 108–22.

13. For example, the popular domestic architect Andrew Jackson Downing declared "the true home" a "counterpoise to the great tendency toward constant changes" in American social and economic life. His house and landscape designs accordingly stressed privacy and isolation, the home as a retreat from the world; *The Architecture of Country Houses* (1852, reprint ed., Cambridge, 1972).

14. S. Weir Mitchell, "The Evolution of the Rest Cure," *Journal of Nervous and Mental Diseases* (1904): 368–73. On the sexual politics of the rest cure, see Ann Douglas's pioneering essay "The Fashionable Diseases: Women's Complaints and Their Treatment in Nineteenth-Century America," *Journal of Interdisciplinary History* 4, no. 1 (Summer 1973): 25–52; and Ellen L. Bassuk, "The Rest Cure: Repetition or Resolution of Victorian Women's Conflicts?" in *The Female Body in Western Culture*, ed. Susan Suleiman (Cambridge, Mass., 1985), 139–51.

15. Charlotte Perkins Gilman, *The Yellow Wallpaper* (Old Westbury, N.Y., 1973). Subsequent references to this text are cited within parentheses in the essay. Gilman recorded her nervous illness and unsuccessful experience of Mitchell's rest cure in her autobiography *The Living of Charlotte Perkins Gilman* (1935; reprint ed., New York, 1963), 90–106. Walter Benn Michaels offers an intriguing analysis of the relations between "The Yellow Wallpaper," hysteria, and selfhood in a market economy in *The Gold Standard and the Logic of Naturalism* (Berkeley, 1987), 3–28.

16. As Sandra Gilbert and Susan Gubar explore the rebellion implicit in Charlotte Brontë's madwoman-in-the-attic figure, feminist historians similarly trace a history of feminism from the subversive or protofeminist features within domesticity. See, for example, Barbara Berg, *The Remembered Gate: Origins of American Feminism; The Woman and the City* (New York, 1980); Ellen Carol Dubois, *Feminism and Suffrage* (Ithaca, N.Y., 1978); Barbara Epstein, *The Politics of Domesticity: Women, Evangelism, and Temperance in Nineteenth-Century America* (Middletown, Conn., 1981).

17. Charlotte Perkins Gilman, *Women and Economics* (1898; reprint ed., New York, 1966); *The Home: Its Work and Influence* (New York, 1910).

18. Catharine Beecher, *A Treatise on Domestic Economy* (1841; reprint ed., New York, 1977), 268–97. Beecher and Gilman's contributions to architectural history are described in

Dolores Hayden, *The Grand Domestic Revolution: A History of Feminist Designs for American Homes, Neighborhoods, and Cities* (Cambridge, 1981).

19. In nineteenth-century sentimental literature, Nina Baym writes, "Domesticity is set forth as a value scheme for ordering all of life, in competition with the ethos of money and exploitation that is perceived to prevail in American society"; *Woman's Fiction: A Guide to Novels by and About Women in America, 1820–1870* (Ithaca, N.Y., 1978), 27.

20. Sarah Josepha Hale, "Editor's Table," *Godey's Lady's Book*, February 1852, 88.

21. Ibid. For an informative analysis of biological models invoked by late nineteenth-century antifeminism, see Rosalind Rosenberg, *Beyond Separate Spheres: Intellectual Roots of Modern Feminism* (New Haven, 1982).

22. Hale, "Editor's Table," 88.

23. Ibid.

24. By a Retired Merchant, "My Wife and the Market Street Phantom," *Godey's Lady's Book*, September 1870, 339–42.

25. Alan Trachtenberg, *The Incorporation of America* (New York, 1982), 130–39. In *The Bon Marché* (Princeton, N.J., 1984), Michael Miller interestingly treats the emergence of kleptomania as an effect of the department store's display of abundant goods; in "selling consumption," the department store seemed to incite theft by offering "apér-itifs du crime." Cases of kleptomania escalated with the emergence of the great store, and the store itself became the most common site of kleptomaniac thefts. I am stressing a similar complementarity between agoraphobia and the escalation of con-sumerism; both agoraphobia and kleptomania might be considered as diseases of sen-timentalism: conditions arising from desires in a sense invented and institutionalized by market capitalism, conditions linked to woman and her sphere, the repository of selfhood within consumerist culture.

    In focusing on the association of agoraphobia with consumerism, I do not mean to suggest a market determinism, but rather to trace one internalization of market capitalism that is neither simply a commodity nor a site of resistance to commodifica-tion. The agoraphobic imagination both produces and is produced by capitalism. Like any commodity, it might also serve other purposes—such as feminist resistance to domesticity.

26. Thorstein Veblen, *The Theory of the Leisure Class* (New York, 1899). On the transfor-mation of housekeepers into consumers, see Susan Strasser's indispensable study of housework, *Never Done: A History of American Housework* (New York, 1982), 243–62; Julie Matthaei, *An Economic History of Woman in America: Women's Work, the Sexual Division of Labor, and the Development of Capitalism* (New York, 1982); Ruth Schwartz Cowan, *More Work for Mother: The Ironies of Household Technology from the Open Hearth to the Micro-wave* (New York, 1983).

27. Philip Fisher brilliantly elaborates the features of this "conspicuousness" in late-nineteenth-century American culture in "The Life History of Objects: The Naturalist Novel and the City," in *Hard Facts* (New York, 1985), 128–78.

28. Robert Seidenberg and Karen DeCrow, *Women Who Marry Houses: Panic and Protest in Agoraphobia* (New York, 1983), 22–30; Alexandra Symonds, "Phobias After Marriage: Women's Declaration of Independence," *Psychoanalysis and Women*, ed. Jean Baker Miller (New York, 1978), 288–303.

    These studies of agoraphobia depart from standard psychoanalytic accounts that, following Freud's analysis of Little Hans, view agoraphobia as a form of castration anxiety. According to Freudian analyses, agoraphobia in women also signifies an unre-solved Oedipus complex—the anxiety of repressed libido manifest as "promiscuous urges in the street." The traffic and publicity of streets evoke in the agoraphobic her fears of her illicit incestuous desire. Helene Deutsch notes in female agoraphobics a "dread of parturition"—a dread of being "away from home and outside in the world" that masks a dread of defloration or parturition. More recently, Julia Kristeva rereads psychoanalysis and the case of Little Hans, viewing Hans's anxiety as the surfacing of the fear underlying castration anxiety: "the frailty of the subject's signifying system." Kristeva is critiquing and redefining the meaning of castration in the Freudian formulation of the subject, identifying castration anxiety as representative of an ever-present threat to the symbolic order from the unconscious. She characterizes the unconscious as pre-Oedipal and maternal. It is thus a relation to the primacy of the mother that castration, or agoraphobia, marks.

See Sigmund Freud, "Analysis of a Phobia in a Five-Year-Old Boy" (1909), in *The Sexual Enlightenment of Children*, ed. Philip Rieff (New York, 1974), 47–184; Milton Miller, "On Street Fear," *International Journal of Psychoanalysis* 34 (1953): 392–411; Helene Deutsch, "The Genesis of Agoraphobia," *International Journal of Psychoanalysis* 10 (1929): 51–69; Julia Kristeva, *Powers of Horror: An Essay on Abjection* (New York, 1982).

In both traditional and revisionary psychoanalytic accounts, agoraphobia involves a particular association with the mother, the prototypical woman. I am concentrating on the relation between agoraphobia and a nineteenth-century ideology of womanhood. The account of agoraphobia I am developing in this essay (from the imagery of public and private space recurring through psychoanalytic as well as pre- and post-psychoanalytic representations of agoraphobia) locates agoraphobia in the social rather than psychic register; I am not exploring agoraphobia as a disease but as an organization of specific social anxieties, as the structure of domestic ideology, and thus as the structure of selfhood in a market economy. In this account, the psychoanalytic exegesis of agoraphobia, staking out a psychic territory, would be another instance of how the agoraphobic imagination works—a denial of the agora in agoraphobia to advance a radically privatized model of self.

29. Seidenberg and DeGrow, *Women Who Marry Houses*, 47–48.
30. The self-sustaining female culture of Gilman's 1915 *Herland* is also the goal of earlier feminist elaborations of domesticity such as Catharine Beecher and Harriet Beecher Stowe's vision of "the Christian Neighborhood" in their popular manual *The American Woman's Home* (New York, 1869).
31. Elizabeth Hardwick, "Bartleby in Manhattan," in *Bartleby in Manhattan and Other Essays* (New York, 1984), 217–31. Another interesting aspect of "Bartleby" as an urban tale is its contemporaneous appearance with articles describing the emerging phenomenon of the urban poor and homeless. I am indebted to Hans Bergmann for this point.
32. For a different interpretation of Bartleby's feminine position in the tale, see Patricia Barber, "What If Bartleby Were a Woman?" in *The Authority of Experience*, ed. Arlyn Diamond and Lee Edwards (Amherst, Mass., 1977), 212–23. The possibilities of a "what if" school of literary criticism are limitless; I am suggesting that nineteenth-century culture defines the scrivener's mode as feminine. Bartleby's femininity, insistently encamped in the public sphere, draws attention to the public performance of the domestic. That Bartleby is a man makes his discontent with Wall Street an especially strong critique of both the market and domesticity. That is, though free to be in the world, Bartleby prefers not to. "The Yellow Wallpaper" suggests that if Bartleby *were* a woman, she would prefer to be in her own world, where she would circulate. Whereas Bartleby imagines pure domesticity, the woman in Gilman's story welcomes

its ultimate transformation. This is the difference between Bartleby's borrowed femininity and a nineteenth-century woman's given femininity.

33. Another reading of the lawyer-copyist relationship particularly suggestive to my own is Michael Rogin's interpretation of the tale as an exposé of false familial claims of employers of wage labor. In Rogin's reading, Bartleby attacks the lawyer's attempt to establish worker-employer bonds; Bartleby resists the boundaries of a sham familial relationship. In my reading, Bartleby redresses the falsity of the family not because he is "boundaryless and insatiable" as Rogin characterizes him but because the family, like the economy, is voracious and irrespective of boundaries. Bartleby insists upon the set boundaries and self-sufficiency associated with an ideal domestic economy. See Michael Paul Rogin, *Subversive Genealogy: The Politics and Art of Herman Melville* (New York, 1983), 192–201.

34. Ira L. Mintz, "Psychoanalytic Therapy of Severe Anorexia: The Case of Jeanette," in *Fear of Being Fat: The Treatment of Anorexia Nervosa and Bulimia*, ed. C. Philip Wilson et al. (New York, 1983), 217–44.

35. Hilde Bruch, *The Golden Cage: The Enigma of Anorexia Nervosa* (Cambridge, Mass., 1978), 75–77.

36. The anorexic case against the coda of conventional femininity is persuasively presented by Kim Chernin, *The Obsession: Reflections on the Tyranny of Slenderness* (New York, 1981); Susie Orbach, *Fat Is a Feminist Issue* (New York, 1978), and *Hunger Strike: The Anorectic's Struggle as a Metaphor for Our Age* (New York, 1986); Seidenberg and DeCrow, *Women Who Marry Houses*, 88–97; John Sours, *Starving to Death in a Sea of Objects* (New York, 1980).

37. Hilde Bruch, *Eating Disorders* (New York, 1973), 211–25. Before William Gull and Charles Lasegue introduced the nomenclature *anorexia nervosa* to eating disorders in 1873, Gull had recorded cases of female refusals to eat in 1868. Reports of similar cases date back to medieval times; Rudolph Bell and Caroline Bynum have identified anorexic behavior in the fasting of saints. See Rudolph M. Bell, *Holy Anorexia* (Chicago, 1985); Caroline Walker Bynum, "Fast, Feast, and Flesh," *Representations* 11 (Summer 1985): 1–25; and Bynum, *Holy Feast and Holy Fast: The Religious Significance of Food to Medieval Women* (Berkeley, 1987).

38. Susan Sontag, *Illness as Metaphor* (New York, 1979), 5–41, 60–62.

39. Sandra Gilbert treats the literary representation of the feminist politics of anorexia in "Hunger Pains," *University Publishing*, Fall 1979. Two more recent feminist analyses link anorexia to the problematics of female identity following from mother-daughter relations. In *Starving Women: A Psychology of Anorexia Nervosa* (Dallas, 1983), analyst Angelyn Spignesi characterizes the anorexic as "our twentieth-century carrier" of the repressed female psyche. In denying the "principles of matter . . . she enacts in her disease the interpenetration of the imaginal and physical realms." This lack of demarcation between body and psyche, self and others, returns her to "the realm of the mother." Similarly focusing on the relation of the anorexic to the maternal, Kim Chernin reads anorexia as matricidal act, "a bitter warfare against the mother," enacted on the daughter's body; *The Hungry Self: Women, Eating, and Identity* (New York, 1985). Taking the anorexic as protagonist in a history of female experience, or placing anorexia in a maternal tradition, in a chronology of the constitution of identity and difference, suggests a fundamental relationship between maternity, anxiety, and the definition of bodily borders. My purpose here is not to dispute or advance the claim of archetypal female anxiety but rather to demonstrate how a nineteenth-century cult of motherhood and domestic mythology shaped particular discourses of border anx-

iety: the nullifications of Bartleby, the negotiations of agoraphobia, and the negations of anorexia.

40. Ann Douglas has aptly termed this sentimental cult of death "the domestication of death" and characterized it as a gesture by which women claimed a real estate society denied them; *The Feminization of American Culture* (New York, 1977), 240–72.

41. Job 3.11–16.

CHARLES BERNHEIMER

Degas's Brothels:
Voyeurism and Ideology

IN EVOKING THE WORLD OF DANCE to which Degas devoted so many of his images, Paul Valéry offers a personal anecdote to confirm Mallarmé's paradox that "a danseuse is not a woman who dances, because she is not a woman, and she does not dance."[1] The truth of this enigmatic observation was demonstrated to him, Valéry says, by a film he once saw of giant, floating medusas, "not women at all, but beings of an incomparably translucent and sentient substance,"[2] as fluid as the liquid surrounding them, ideally mobile and elastic, requiring no solid ground, boneless yet not without form. The dance of the medusas embodies Valéry's conception of dance in its absolute state as pure movement aimed at nothing outside itself. According to this view, a ballerina's sexual identity plays no role, for she makes her body into "an object whose transformations necessarily recall the function a poet gives to his mind."[3] Her body, in other words, is a metaphor for the leaps, swerves, inversions, and pirouettes of the poet's own verbal creativity, "a corporeal writing" in Mallarmé's phrase.[4]

Dance becomes a figure for the symbolist aesthetic—nothing terribly surprising about this, one may say. The surprise comes in Valéry's second paragraph about the medusas, in which what was repressed by the symbolist idealization returns with a vengeance:

No human ballerina, inflamed woman, drunk with movement, with the poison of her own overwrought energy, with the ardent presence of gazes charged by desire, ever expressed the imperious oblation of sex, the mimic summons of the urge to prostitution, like the giant medusa, which, with an undulating shudder of flowing festooned skirts that she lifts and lowers with a strange and shameless insistence, transforms herself into a dream of Eros; and then, suddenly flinging back all her shivering flounces, her robes of severed lips, inverts and exposes herself, laid furiously open.[5]

This extension of Valéry's thought seems to invert it, exposing its sexual secret much as the medusa exposes hers. The dance, which had earlier been emptied of mimetic reference, now urgently summons the aroused spectator to fulfill the ballerina's "besoin de prostitution." The medusa has been transformed by the fervently fantasizing writer from a floating signifier, analogous to the male poet's creative freedom, into a very specific organic signified, a gaping female sexual organ that threatens the poet's artistic control.[6] It is as if the fascinated spectator-writer were now confronted with the symbolic meaning Freud associated with the mythological Medusa's petrifying gaze: the fear of castration. Under the skirts provocatively lifted and lowered, under the dress made up of severed lips, is the furious openness that poisons every dream of Eros.

Who is the subject of this erotic fantasm? Evidently Valéry himself, the captivated viewer of the film of giant medusas, but also, by extension, Mallarmé, the truth of whose dictum about ballerinas not being women and not dancing Valéry is documenting. Still another implied subject is Degas, known as "le peintre des Danseuses," whom Valéry mentions at the outset of this meditation drawn from *Degas Danse Dessin*, a text of 1936. Yet Valéry notes that Degas's dancers are only superficially idealized images: their bodies bear the marks of their subjugation to the male artist's corporeal writing. Degas's passionate commitment in creating the danseuses, he argues, involved the display of female slavery rather than the elision of the body's travail in the glory of its aestheticization. "Degas was passionately determined," writes Valéry, "to reconstruct the specialized female animal as the slave of the dance, the laundry, or the streets; and the more or less distorted bodies whose articulated structure he always arranges in very precarious attitudes (tying a ballet shoe, or pressing the iron down on linen with both fists) make the whole mechanical system of a living being seem to *grimace* like a face."[7] This grimace is the physiognomic manifestation of the sexualized inversion of the medusa. The grimace is a kind of furious openness displayed as bodily distortion and disarticulation.

In the social and historical context that Valéry does not evoke, this openness is quite specifically that of "the mimic summons of the urge to prostitution," for the dancers, like all the other female professionals Degas painted, be they laundresses, milliners, or café-concert singers, were known to be involved in clandestine prostitution.[8] Indeed, Degas often portrays top-hatted messieurs, probably members of the notorious Jockey Club who had privileged access behind the scenes at the Opéra, negotiating in the *coulisses* with dancers from the corps de ballet.[9] Thus he illustrates a double slavery of the danseuse, to the specialized artistic vocabulary of male corporeal scripture and to a capitalist economy of desire, which defines lower-class women as objects of sexual consumption for middle- and upper-class men. The grimacing body—distorted, disarticulated, unstable, even inverted—this "reconstructed" body of "the female animal" is, according to Valéry, the victim of Degas's misogyny.

Is this an accurate reading of Degas's images? What is the meaning of the identification of the sexualized female body with the distorted and "precarious" female body? In reference to what norms can distortion be measured? Does this argument make the distorted body fundamentally the same as the castrated body? If so, what is the relation between a psychoanalytic interpretation of misogyny that would trace its origins to castration fears and an economic one that would ascribe female deformation and disfigurement to patriarchal practices of domination and control?

No images in Degas's oeuvre generate these difficult questions more imperatively than his brothel monotypes. In these pictures of naked prostitutes blatantly offering their bodies for sale, the erotic subtext of the dancer paintings becomes the explicit subject of representation. This brutal explicitness, however, does not make the text of female sexuality any more legible than it was when disguised under the masks of more acceptable social identities. My readings of the brothel monotypes will suggest ways in which Degas's images destabilize the male viewer's gaze and confront him with the ideological assumptions underlying his voyeuristic position. This argument, however, will itself prove to be unstable, as Degas's representational practice is seen to involve us in a reading experience that vacillates uncomfortably between psychological and social determinants, constructing its viewing subject in terms of male bourgeois hegemony while simultaneously revealing the suspect ideological artifice of that construction.

For an interpretation of Degas's portrayals of prostitutes in brothels, the medium is most certainly a good part of the message, but one whose visual language is peculiarly ambiguous and difficult. The works are all monotypes, images created through a technique that lies halfway between drawing and painting. A monotype can be made in two ways: one can either cover a metal or celluloid plate with thick, greasy printer's ink and then wipe and scrape some away to make a design (the so-called "dark-field" manner) or one can apply printer's ink directly to a clean plate with a brush, rag, or other instrument (the "light-field" manner). Once the composition is finished, it is transferred by laying a piece of dampened paper on the plate and running both through a rolling press. Most of the ink is used up in this process, though a second, lighter impression can sometimes be pulled. The technique is imprecise and unpredictable by its very nature, since one cannot control exactly how the ink will respond in the printing operation. The primary advantage the method offers over direct drawing is the time available (up to an hour) to manipulate the ink on the plate before it loses pliability and must be fixed in the paper. This manipulation is a physically immediate, sensuously tactile process: Degas used rags, brush handles, hard bristles, sponges, pins, and even thumb and finger applications to produce desired effects. There is no tradition of monotypemaking. Through the centuries, various artists discovered it but never took it seriously enough for their discovery to be significant to subsequent generations.[10] Degas used the medium not only for itself but also as a chiaroscuro base, a tonal map, for further elaboration in pastel and gouache.[11]

Scholars have recorded approximately fifty extant monotypes by Degas of brothel scenes, most done in the light-field manner, with dimensions varying from about 4 × 6 inches to 8 × 11, the majority being 6 × 8. Degas's friend, the art dealer Ambroise Vollard, declared that as many as seventy more monotypes were destroyed by the painter's brother at the time of his death, probably because they were considered obscene. Most were made in 1879 and 1880, a time when literary versions of the prostitute's life were arriving on the cultural scene in rapid succession (Huysmans's *Marthe* was published in 1876; Edmond de Goncourt's *La Fille Elisa* appeared in 1877; Zola's *Nana* created a sensation in 1880, also the year of Maupassant's "Boule de suif," followed in 1881 by his "La Maison Tellier."). Of these, we can be sure that Degas read *La Fille Elisa* since he made a number of sketches illustrating scenes in that novel, and it is very likely that he knew the others as well.[12] We do not know to whom precisely he showed the brothel monotypes, which were never exhibited in his lifetime. Françoise Cachin believes that he showed them only to his closest friends (under what circumstances? to wives as well as husbands?) and perhaps to a few artists he liked and respected.[13] But there are no accounts of the monotypes written by any of those who may have seen them during Degas's lifetime. The public first got a chance to view them when Vollard used a selection to illustrate his 1934 edition of Maupassant's *La Maison Tellier* and his 1935 edition of *Mimes de courtisanes* by Pierre Louÿs.

Art historians have had relatively little to say about the subject of the monotypes, choosing instead to treat them as formal and technical experiments. Their usefulness, so the story goes, was to help liberate Degas from the excessively linear graphic mode he had inherited from Ingres and to enable him to explore the constructive potential of strong contrasts in light and shadow and to judge the relationships between broad compositional masses.[14] The images are characteristically praised for their dispassionate, documentary realism, their effects of casual immediacy, and their morally neutral perspective. Equally characteristic is that this appreciation of the impersonal, objective quality of Degas's observation goes along with a claim, such as that made by Françoise Cachin in the introduction to her 1974 edition of the monotypes, that "studying the monotypes puts one in a privileged position to understand Degas's work, giving access to his most personal and private concerns, his relations with women and with femininity."[15] However, what Cachin finds most private about Degas is an entirely traditional reading of his sexual perspective: he was, she claims, a voyeur preoccupied with woman's animal nature.

This interpretation fits into a tradition of Degas criticism, founded by Huysmans, that has had an astonishing endurance.[16] In a review of the series of pastels that Degas exhibited in 1886, featuring, among other images of women bathing and drying themselves, one entitled *The Tub* (fig. 1), Huysmans claims that Degas's point of view conveys "an attentive cruelty, a patient hatred."[17] Huysmans does not disapprove of this cruelty anymore than he accuses Degas of misogyny. On the contrary, he praises the painter for conveying a lucid and chaste "disdain for the flesh"[18] such as has not been seen in art since the Middle Ages.[19] He argues that Degas shows fat, short, graceless women in the humiliating and degrading positions of intimate hygiene, because the artist is a brilliant iconoclast attacking the false idolization of Woman in conventional artistic practice.[20] Then Huysmans goes on to construct the subjectivity of Degas's bathing women as a function of

FIGURE 1. Edgar Degas, *The Tub*, pastel on cardboard, 1886.
Musée d'Orsay, Paris. Photo courtesy of the Musées
nationaux.

their masochistic collaboration with a sadistic male gaze. The bathers convey, he
writes, "the penetrating, sure execration of a few women for the devious joys of
their sex, an execration that causes them to be overwhelmed with dreadful proofs
and to defile themselves, openly confessing the humid horror of a body that no
lotion can purify."[21]

With this evident fantasy projection, Huysmans's ideological reading of
Degas's iconoclasm becomes hostage to his horrified fascination with the inerad-
icable dirt of female sexuality and to his need to imagine punishment for female
deviance. Like Valéry, like Mallarmé, Huysmans fears his own dream of Eros, the
Medusa's "mimic summons of the urge to prostitution." In reaction, he places
himself in the position of a voyeur, sadistically fantasizing that his penetrating
look punishes and humiliates the woman it secretly observes. According to the
psychoanalytic account, the male voyeur is trying to escape anxiety by obsessively
reenacting an original trauma, his imagined perception of female castration,
from a situation of mastery and control. Huysmans's hypothesis of female self-
disgust and bodily loathing perfectly fulfills this fantasy of erotic domination.
Woman in Huysmans's interpretation of Degas's images is not simply the object
of male disdain; she has internalized that disdain to the point that she is the

degraded object of her own virulent execration. The voyeur thus displaces his own guilt for his covert misogynist gaze onto the object of that controlling surveillance. What he sees is imaginary evidence of woman's enlightened awareness of her irredeemably debased sexuality.

Huysmans's fantasy scenario locates woman in the position of Truth insofar as she openly confesses the horror of her sexual embodiment, the humid wound of her mutilated flesh. His vocabulary is uncannily Freudian as he praises Degas for creating in his paintings "la sensation de l'étrange exact, de l'invu si juste" (the sensation of exact strangeness, of the precisely right unseen).[22] I hardly need stress that castration for Freud is the unseeable whose provocative strangeness threatens the male subject's physical integrity and his power of accurate perception. It is this imagined threat that the misogynist voyeur overcomes, repeatedly, as he reassures himself of the visibility of the unseen. His misogyny is inherently narcissistic: the voyeur sees in female lack the evidence of his own phallic coherence. Woman's body is perceived as other only insofar as it can be marked with the signs of man's desire for himself.[23]

A number of recent readings of the bather pastels help explain how the construction of these images might provoke a defensive, self-reflective male response such as that of Huysmans. These readings, by Edward Snow, Eunice Lipton, and Carol Armstrong, all stress the extraordinary self-sufficiency, separateness, and sensuous privacy of the women depicted. Specifically countering Huysmans's argument, Snow writes that "these women are rendered as physical beings in their own right rather than as projected, complicit objects of masculine desire. [They are] delivered not only from the male gaze but from any introjected awareness of it."[24] Armstrong's analysis confirms this split between excluded male gaze and self-absorbed female embodiment. The woman's body in *The Tub*, she observes, folds over on itself in a reflexive movement signifying circularity and closure. This inverted movement, "turned in on the body's thicknesses and silences,"[25] deflects and excludes the male viewer, thereby negating the offer of erotic appropriation traditionally associated with the female nude. Indeed, both Armstrong and Lipton suggest that the paintings, far from expressing female self-disgust and sexual guilt, "invite empathy and the contemplation of narcissism" (Lipton)[26] "in a kind of pictorial onanism" (Armstrong).[27]

These strong contemporary readings suggest that Huysmans's reaction to these pastels, like that of the critics who subsequently have agreed with him, constitutes an aggressive defense of the phallic right to annex woman's sexuality, mounted in the face of images that emphatically assert her intrinsic, autonomous, guiltless capacity for sensual fulfillment. His reaction is, moreover, a defense of the traditional prerogatives of male spectatorship, especially of the voyeur's implied presence in a position of fantasized mastery, mounted in the face of the dislocation and problematization of that position.[28] As Armstrong points out, the dislocation of perspective in a picture such as *The Tub* is a deliberate strategy designed to radicalize the spectator's external viewpoint to the extent that it loses all corporeality and becomes "a gaze without a body."[29] Impossibly located above the right-hand ledge but not on it, in a kind of dematerialized point in space, the viewing presence loses its capacity for discursive union with its object. The voyeur's fantasy of power is subverted by the precariousness of his implied position in space. Snow interprets this subversion as "a denial of masculine will, desire, and, above all, sexual presence." "Degas's privileges as an artist," he goes on to assert, "stem from and reinforce his ontologically negative sense of himself as a man."[30]

Let us turn now from the pastels to the monotypes. In terms of subject matter, this is not much of a turn, for, as at least one critic of the 1886 impressionist show observed, Degas's bathers are quite likely prostitutes performing the frequent ablutions their profession required.[31] Like the bather pastels and the dancer pictures, the brothel monotypes constitute a series of repetitive images in which the variety of expressive gesture is minimized, individual physiognomic difference is reduced, and complexities of composition, such as costume and decor, are greatly simplified. But the brothel scenes go farther than any other of Degas's iconographic repertoires toward negating traditional aesthetic norms of legibility and corporeality. The pastels may subvert expectations about the correct formal display of the nude; they remain nevertheless luxuriantly colorful and sensuously rich. The monotypes, in contrast, present crude, scribbled, smudged, murky forms in what are frequently almost illegible juxtaposed masses of light and shadow. The images are quite baffling at first sight, almost cartoonish or caricatural in the clumsy quality of the figural delineation, strangely unfinished, abbreviated, and apparently hasty in execution. One has the impression of a rapid sketch made *sur place*, although these monotypes are actually remembered images composed *après coup*. (But just what is Degas remembering? He kept his private life so secret that we do not know if his brothel imagery derives from first-hand personal experience or from fantasies fueled by viewing previous representations of brothel life, notably those of Constantin Guys, and by reading in the extensive contemporary literature of prostitution.)[32] Degas did not arrange the monotypes in any particular order, as far as we know, so my selection of images to analyze is largely a matter of personal preference and rhetorical strategy.

The monotype entitled *The Tub* (fig. 2) provides a revealing comparison to the pastel of the same title. Here the male gaze is explicitly embodied in the image, but hardly in a way that expresses the dominating, controlling point of view of the voyeur. The man, a client in a brothel, sits hunched over in a barely articulated, murky mass. His body seems to be closed in on itself in a circular form that rhymes with the tub below and the mirror above. The sense of enclosure and separation is furthered by the perceptible echo of the man's muddled form captured from the back in the heavily framed mirror, as if pulled thereby into the dark recesses of pictorial reflection. His space is rigidly divided off from that of the woman by a sharp line that defines a black ground against which her plump, white body stands out. Although she is sitting on the floor, her upright back gives her a strong verticality, which is counterbalanced on one side by the horizontal movement of her arm and extended on the other by the upward thrust of the cheval glass. From his cringing, regressive, closed-off position, with half his face buried in his hand, the client observes his sexual purchase. The meaning of his one-eyed look is articulated by the structure of the composition: although he has economic power over this woman's sexuality, he experiences her as a dominating presence from which he is definitively exiled. His look does not debase her, it appears rather to confirm his inadequacy, his inability to emerge out of the enclosures that inhibit his sexuality. The blurred area where her head should be suggests the generalized quality of this woman's confident embodiment. Her body may have none of the bountiful luxuriance of the pastel bathers, but its power to deny appropriation by the male gaze remains undiminished.

Two monotypes that show a client emerging from outside the frame into a brothel room suggest that Degas associates hesitancy and ambivalence rather than voyeuristic power with the threshold position. In the first, entitled *The Client*

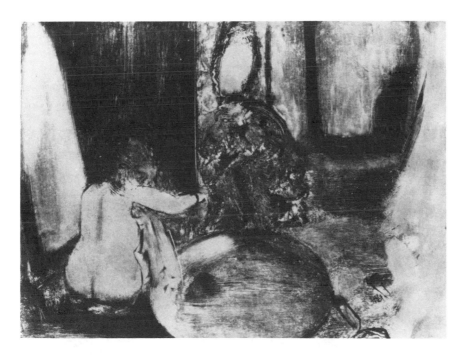

FIGURE 2. Degas, *The Tub*, monotype. Private collection. From Jean Adhémar and Françoise Cachin, *Degas: The Complete Etchings, Lithographs, and Monotypes* (London, 1974), plate 130. Photo Princeton University Library.

(fig. 3), the forward thrust of the man's only visible leg is strongly countered by the backward tilt of his entire stiff, linear body. He seems reluctant to enter the domain of the two swollen, sitting women. The primitive graphic mode of their portrayal decomposes their bodies, randomly eliding detail, smudging outlines, erasing contours, and defacing features. The physical amorphousness and disarticulation of these figures make it seem as if they had emerged organically out of their environment, whose barely legible, splotchy, dappled, muddy forms have a certain metamorphic quality about them. In contrast, the sticklike client appears alien, his dark clothing and formal hat more defensive than authoritative. He arrives armored with the semiotics of social class—top hat, dark suit—but he seems to be retreating from the exercise of his privilege. A similar defensiveness is termed "seriousness" in the title of the second monotype, *The Serious Client* (fig. 4). Here the man, again decked out in bourgeois regalia, is being actively pulled

FIGURE 3. Degas, *The Client*, monotype. Picasso donation, Musée du Louvre, Cabinet des Estampes. FIGURE 4. Degas, *The Serious Client*, monotype. Private collection, London. From Adhémar and Cachin, *Degas*, plate 96. Photo Princeton University Library.

away from his position on the margin of the pictorial space. The umbrella, fulcrum of contending pressures, may suggest the sexual issue involved, as well as demark an internal threshold of male anxiety. The fact that the angle of the umbrella exactly parallels the backward lean of the client suggests that his fearful seriousness is successfully resisting the fleshy solicitation of the four prostitutes.

Should this resistance be read psychoanalytically as due to a fear of woman's castrated sexuality? Do the clients resist the incitements to desire and possession because of an unconscious horror of the uncanny unseen? This was the interpretation given to these images by Pablo Picasso, who in 1971 made a series of forty superb etchings that constitute a remarkable reading of the eleven Degas monotypes he owned (including *The Client* and a picture that I will analyze shortly, *Waiting*).[33] Picasso frequently portrays Degas, an alter-ego figure, in a position much like that of the clients in the two monotypes we have just discussed. In figure 5, Degas, fully dressed, hands behind his back, leans against a wall as he

FIGURES 5–8. Pablo Picasso, etchings. From Georges Bloch, *Pablo Picasso*, vol. 4, *Catalogue of the Printed Graphic Work, 1970–1972* (Berne, 1979), plates 1944, 1936, 1964, 1899. Copyright ARS N.Y./ SPADEM, 1989. Photo Princeton University Library.

stares at exhibitionistic and wildly made-up prostitutes. A line descending from the witch-like madam's head defines a wedge-shaped space that safely separates him from the whirling sexual forms on display. Eyes, nipples, and anuses resemble each other and seem to multiply vertiginously. Figure 6 portrays Degas sketching an image of himself, in diminished, shadowy, but still fully dressed form, surrounded by naked women offering him their highly sexed bodies. Degas's creative inspiration, Picasso suggests, comes from imagining himself inside the female erotic space he fears to penetrate. In another etching (fig. 7),

Degas's placement inside a frame removes and distances him from an orgiastic scene of female bodies so closely intertwined that it is hard to determine what members belong to what bodies.

In all these scenes, the Degas figure, like the implied spectator of the mono-types, remains impassive, hugging the margin, cherishing the frame, refusing involvement. Yet what his fixed stare sees is worlds apart from what Degas himself records in the monotypes. Although the prostitutes in *The Serious Client* are spa-tially separate from the customer, this division is not a function of a male drive to fantasize woman. The client seems to be confronted with a weight of female embodiment that will not yield to any appropriative fantasy. In contrast, Picasso's prostitutes are the voyeuristic projections of a (perhaps impotent?) fantasist who transforms the real into a theater of private hallucinations and erotic imaginings. This is the home territory of Valéry's dancing medusas, dreams of an inverted Eros laid furiously open to the terrified male gaze (see fig. 8). That terror, however, is controlled and overcome by the very openness and exuberance of the sexual display put on to provoke and stimulate the voyeur. If these lasciviously cavorting women are objectified as the castrated other, they are still more powerfully subjectified as fetishized figures of the same. Woman's desire, seemingly in evidence throughout Picasso's bordello images, is exhibited only for the benefit of male narcissism. Her sexuality is annexed to the project of representing the male artist's ability to create the feminine as an aesthetic fiction.[34]

In nineteenth-century aesthetic practice it was above all the courtesan, rather than the prostitute, who figured as representative of male narcissistic desire. The distinction, of course, was not always easy to make, especially since many courtesans had once been prostitutes, but it was clear that courtesans did not work in brothels. Their stage was far more public, social, and outwardly glamorous. In their conduct they mimed respectable women, while maintaining an edge of difference sufficient to tip off prospective clients. The courtesan, as T. J. Clark has observed, "was the person who moved most easily between roles in the nineteenth century, trying on the seemingly fixed distinctions of class society and discarding them at will, declaring them false like the rest of her poses. And falsity is what made her modern."[35] In the male imaginary, the courtesan could be fantasized both voyeuristically, as the sexually desiring woman whose powerful independence provoked stimulating castration fears, and fetishistically, as an antidote to those fears embodying a modern aesthetic of artifice, illusion, duplicity. The myth of the courtesan made legible as social spectacle the male artist's imaginary control over the threat of female sexuality. Her falsity corresponded to that of the fetish: she veiled the real, creating in its place a fiction of male dominance.

Versions of this fiction are embodied in Picasso's prostitutes and in Valéry's medusa. Of the latter, Valéry writes that, in the film he saw, she finally rose like a balloon "to the forbidden luminous region, the domain of the sun and the mortal air."[36] This displacement upwards is the price the medusa must pay for her wanton exposure of what should have remained veiled. The darkness of the medusa's overwrought sexuality cannot survive exposure to the bright light of masculine, abstractionist control, a light that transforms woman into a metaphor for her absence. "A savoir," writes Mallarmé, "que la danseuse *n'est pas une femme qui danse*, pour ces motifs juxtaposés qu'elle *n'est pas une femme*, mais une métaphore résumant un des aspects élémentaires de notre forme, glaive, coupe, fleur, etc., et *qu'elle ne danse pas*" (So the ballerina *is not a woman who dances*, for the juxtaposed reasons that *she is not a woman*, but a metaphor summing up one of the elementary aspects of our form, sword, cup, flower, etc., and that *she does not dance*).[37] The feminine thus becomes an elementary figure of "our" rhetorical form, that is, of the poet's favorite images for the poetic, and sexual difference (suggested by "glaive" and "coupe") becomes a function of the male writer's aesthetic choice.

This rhetorization of female difference may be the most sophisticated of misogynistic strategies, conflating the contradictions of voyeurism and fetishism. The voyeur fictionalizes woman's otherness by constantly postponing his knowledge of it: what he sees never has the indelible stamp of truth; it must be seen again, and then again, each sight being no better than a representation of an original traumatic discovery. The fetishist avoids the knowledge of that discovery by adopting the fiction that a particular object can function, in Freud's terms, as "a token of triumph over the threat of castration and a safeguard against it."[38] Although the voyeur's compulsively ongoing investigation of female difference contrasts with the fetishist's equally compulsive fascination with displaced immediacy, both modes make woman available to the male gaze only insofar as her sexuality can be fantasized as something denatured, deflected, substitutive. She is seen as what she is not, as a metaphor, at best, of what she is.[39]

Now it is evident that the conception of female sexuality as in some way lacking or negative is not the peculiar province of voyeurs and fetishists alone. Or, to put it another way, one would be right to argue that the mechanisms of voyeurism and fetishism pervade the culture of late capitalism, of which we, like Degas, are a part, to such an extent that they influence every aspect of spectatorship and of gender relations. This argument, which, in the present context, can be no more than an assertion, is helpful for our purposes insofar as it suggests that the psychodynamics put into operation by viewing Degas's monotypes in 1880 would not have been significantly different from the psychodynamics generated by viewing the pictures today. This hypothesis is plausible, I believe, despite the media explosion of the past century that has disseminated countless images of women displayed as sexualized objects for male consumption. The more troublesome issue is to know what discourses, visual and verbal, would have been available in 1880 to make sense of the viewer's response, to define his horizon of expectations, a matter further complicated by our ignorance of who the intended viewer, apart from Degas himself, may have been. Might this viewer have processed his response in terms of a semiotics of caricature, an imagistic discourse with which Degas was thoroughly familiar?[40] Would such an identification of Degas's discursive vocabulary have elicited laughter and wit in response? Or might the viewer have related the monotypes to the rich tradition of popular erotic prints of women dressing, undressing, getting in and out of baths, and seen them as a typically "realist" debunking of this libertine imagery?[41] Finally, might the viewer not have associated the small monotype pictures with licentious photographs, often seen enhanced through the stereoscope or passed around among men for their private titillation?[42] Would his perception of this cultural homology have undermined the viewer's ability to distinguish between Degas's images and intentionally pornographic representations? These questions need to be raised, even though I know of no satisfactory way of answering them. The specific historical context of the works' reception is nearly impossible to interpret. However, from our present point of view, the images themselves seem to critically encode the cultural context of their production. The focus of this critique, I propose to argue, is the commodification of gender relations.

Degas's brothel images sever the metaphorical bond between artist-viewer and the signs of his creative triumph over the prostitute's erotic threat. Degas seems to invite the viewer to adopt the position of voyeur, but then he de-psychologizes that position to such an extent that no desiring subjectivity appears to inhabit it. This is part of what makes looking at Degas's images of prostitution such an uncomfortable experience. The threshold position is familiar to the male viewer as one conventionally adopted to offer him the scary but alluring secrets of female undress. The small dimensions of the monotype, allowing it to be easily held in the hand, further suggest that these are fetishistic images made for a connoisseur's private enjoyment. But it is precisely the fantasy potential of these images of available female sexuality that Degas suppresses. He simultaneously grants the spectator a wish-fulfilling viewpoint and confronts the spectator so positioned with images that, by denying his desire, empty his position of its subjective privilege.

This de-privileging operates through a generalization of the process of substitution that replaces psychological determinants with economic ones. Degas's brothel images offer the client-viewer an economic transaction that entails *his* substitutability, given that any other monied male could just as well assume his position. Any male can take advantage of the system of exchange that allows female sexual products to be purchased on the marketplace. Whereas both voyeur and fetishist assert their phallic domination by treating any individual woman as a mere provisional substitute, an inferior proxy for the real thing, the phallus itself appears to be substitutable when it comes to serve a purely instrumental function dependent on a prior financial transaction. Unlike Picasso's prostitutes, who promiscuously offer themselves to the voyeur as a vehicle for his own signifying practice, and whose polymorphous sexuality is a metaphor for the artist's own creative desire, Degas's prostitutes exist materially, phenomenally, as alienated products of a consumer culture. Unlike the courtesans in nineteenth-century art and literature whose sexualized bodies are camouflaged to serve the ostentatious male enterprise of dominating (female) nature, Degas's prostitutes cover nothing up. There is no masochistic self-debasement here, only the flesh made available to the other, the body waiting to fulfill its role as capital. "Commodities, women, are a mirror of value of and for man," writes Luce Irigaray. "In order to serve as such, they give up their bodies to men as the supporting material of specularization, of

FIGURE 9. Degas,
Waiting, monotype.
Picasso donation,
Musée du Louvre,
Cabinet des Estampes.

speculation. They yield to him their natural and social value as a locus of imprints, marks, and mirage of his activity."[43]

This is the locus and the activity that Degas illustrates. The would-be voyeur at the brothel threshold contemplates women who have been denaturalized and marked in an economy of exchange that offers little stimulus for his narcissistic fantasy.[44] In the place of castration, the perverse goal of his private voyeurism, he sees commodification, the sign of woman's exchangeability in a system of value established to maintain the hegemony of his sex.[45] The four prostitutes in *Waiting* (fig. 9) are sprawled naked, or nearly so, on a couch in a brothel salon. Their faces have next to no particularity; their heavy, bloated bodies are crudely outlined; the strongly emphasized sexual triangle repeats itself in an insistent pattern that focuses the viewer's attention. There is no interaction among the women, nor any narrative content apart from their passive waiting for a client to appear. The negative space of the carpet is echoed in small by that of the pubic areas, setting up an analogy between the common usage values of the living and the fabricated, the sexual and the material. The abstract formalism of the four pubic triangles suggests woman's generic subjugation to an ideology that transforms her body into the sign of social relations among male consumers. Despite their frontality and uninhibited exhibition, these brothel inmates are not posing seductively for the benefit of the male viewer. They do not invite the fetishizing male gaze any more than the sensuously self-absorbed bathers do. They reflect back to the viewer not so much the power of his private privilege as the discomforting impersonality of his ideological position. The dislocation and disembodiment of the observer's viewpoint that Armstrong analyzed in *The Tub* is also in evidence in *Waiting*, where its function as a reflection of the depersonalizing impact of ideology makes itself forcefully felt. We look down and across at the four prostitutes from a kind of floating, dematerialized, spatial perspective that suggests the way ideology abstracts the individual and asserts power through invisibility and absence.

This analysis helps explain why Degas's brothel images, despite their sexual

FIGURE 10. Degas, *Siesta in the Salon*, monotype. Private collection. From Adhémar and Cachin, *Degas*, plate 111. Photo Princeton University Library.

explicitness, are not pornographic.[46] Pornographic imagery is constructed to suggest woman's desire to submit pleasurably to phallic power. She is seen as complicitous in the display of her sexuality, which is offered to the male viewer as a fantasized extension of his own erotic body, as a narcissistic gift. Thus if a woman is shown masturbating in a pornographic picture, she is not only the object of sadistic voyeurism but also of narcissistic identification, her orgasm becoming, in fantasy, a function of male self-enjoyment. In contrast, when Degas portrays women masturbating, as he does in a number of the monotypes (see fig. 10), he short-circuits the process of identification, cancels any illusion of female subjectivity, and makes the sexual gesture seem entirely banal, a casual pastime. Whereas pornographic representation always assumes woman's dependence on the phallus as access to pleasure, Degas shows women whose sexuality is an autonomous behavioral function they perform among themselves. There is no invitation to mastery here: these prostitutes have found a means to survive objectification by the other by becoming the agents of their own *jouissance*. The material space appears to absorb the female bodies into its splotchy, amorphous texture rather than to articulate their privileged position as figures of erotic fantasy.

This absorption does not denigrate or degrade the women. They actually seem to gain in strength through their assimilation into an unthreatening, comfortable world of things, as if their reification involved a kind of detached enjoyment, on the artist's part, of the ideological pressures conveyed in their representation. This enjoyment may derive from a perspective similar to that Walter Benjamin attributes to the petty bourgeoisie of Baudelaire's day. It sought pleasure, Benjamin claims, in a displaced or deferred awareness of the commodity nature of its own labor power. "If it wanted to achieve virtuosity in this kind of enjoyment, it could not spurn empathizing with commodities. It had to enjoy this identification with all the pleasure and the uneasiness which derived from a presentiment of its own destiny as a class. Finally, it had to approach this destiny with a sensitivity that perceives charm even in damaged and decaying goods." Degas's class position, which I will discuss briefly in a moment, was not so firmly established at the upper echelons for him not to feel the ambivalence about commodification that Benjamin, in this passage, judges characteristic of Baudelaire. Significantly, it is in his treatment of prostitution that Benjamin finds Baudelaire most sensitive to the equivocal charms of commodity culture. "Baudelaire," continued Benjamin, "who in a poem to a courtesan called her heart 'bruised like a peach, ripe like her body, for the lore of love,' possessed this sensitivity. To it he owed his enjoyment of this society as someone who had already half withdrawn from it."[47] The pleasure Degas derived from portraying bruised and ripe brothel inmates may well have had an analogous source.

To summarize my argument so far: Degas's brothel monotypes appear to address the male viewer's social privilege, to construe him as a voyeur, and to cater to his misogyny. They appear, in other words, to construct the spectator as a bourgeois psychological subject who desires his (phallic) self through the (castrated) other. But they undertake this construction duplicitously, the better to dismantle the voyeur's privileged position, depersonalize it, and reveal its primarily social determination. The viewer's imaginary domination is short-circuited by the confrontation of a psychologically constructed subject position with ideologically constructed objects of desire. Misogyny, cruelty, disdain—attitudes often attributed to Degas as if his art were a space of self-representation—can more accurately be interpreted as functions of the capitalist ideology that defines and confines woman's value in representational practice. That confining definition is the materialist counterpart to the Mallarmé-Valéry idealist conception of the ballerina who is not a woman. On the one hand is a female body made useless in daily life so that it can become the instrument of the male poet's "corporeal writing"; on the other hand is a female body whose value is produced and consumed in its daily exchange among men and whose matter is inscribed by the marks of that commerce. Valéry is complicitous in the repression of the female sexual threat: he kills the medusa by lifting her out of the water into the mortal air of metaphor. Degas exposes the material effects of this repression. As against the misogynist identification of woman with her inherent mutilation, the horror that must be dis-regarded, he sets a sympathetic identification of woman with her social and historical commodification. Degas suggests that the Medusa's look is no more than the reflection back to the male viewer of his own initial gaze, which paralyzes, objectifies, and commodifies woman. This gaze is the vehicle not of Degas's private obsession but of his uneasy awareness of his participation in a hegemonic ideology based on sexual counterphobia. He displays the construction of his own spectatorship as historically engendered in misogynist social practices.

The continuing power of these practices accounts for the appeal of the critical tradition identifying Degas with misogyny. Unwilling to acknowledge the discomforting ways through which Degas's images of prostitutes expose the Medusa gaze of patriarchal ideology, critics have preferred to imagine Degas implicated in the very aggression he unmasks. Biographical anecdotes—Berthe Morisot's 1869 report to her sister about how Degas sat down beside her and, instead of courting her as she expected, began a long commentary on Solomon's proverb "Woman is the desolation of the righteous";[48] Manet's comment to Morisot that Degas "lacks spontaneity; he isn't capable of loving a woman, even less of telling her that he does or of doing anything about it";[49] Degas's remark to George Moore, possibly in regard to the pastel entitled *The Tub*, that this image shows "the human animal taking care of herself, a cat licking herself"[50]—this kind of contemporary testimony has been cited to prove Degas's disdain for women. But what it proves is only that such statements were once interpreted as evidence of misogyny and that they still can be read as part of an historically identifiable misogynistic discourse. Placed in a different context of reception, these statements may take on quite different meanings. Thus Norma Broude has convincingly demonstrated that

Degas's insensitivity to the traditional manifestations of female charm may have been a deliberate iconoclastic gesture that, far from expressing his desire to debase women, reflected his conviction that strong women never conform to conventional ideals.[51]

The biographical evidence thus cuts both ways, and Degas's supposed misogyny, as Carol Armstrong has acutely observed, becomes a part of the "myth" of Degas, deliberately constructed by the artist himself and then elaborated by his biographers.[52] The essence of the myth is enigma, opacity, isolation, withdrawal, repression. Degas's life was lived self-consciously on the margins of life and hence of the narrative forms created to make it accessible and legible.[53] Even the artist's class background is contradictory: his family was proud of an aristocratic lineage that was actually an invention,[54] while his father and brothers were bourgeois bankers and wine merchants, whose adoption of a genteel *ancien régime* lifestyle was a major cause of the collapse of their family banking enterprise. Acquaintances often found Degas excessively dry and orderly, "a notary, a bourgeois of the time of Louis-Philippe," said Gauguin.[55] He was elitist and refined in his tastes, nationalistic and conservative in his anticapitalist politics. Yet he enjoyed the social mixtures and ambiguities of popular life in cafés and on the boulevards, was enthusiastic about new technologies (photography, for instance) and, inevitably, participated in the commercial market for art.[56] In brief, an analysis of Degas's class offers no more coherent an explanation of his subjectivity than do the biographical anecdotes adduced to construct the story of his life. We are left with fragments and glimpses, often contradictory and enigmatic, with deliberate mystifications and staged self-effacements.[57] In this context of dissolving figurations, my critical reading of Degas's alleged misogyny as his critical reading of a misogynistic ideology seems far too stable a hermeneutic construction.

What if the male viewer I have supposed to be made uncomfortably self-conscious about his complicity in the exploitation of women actually felt quite at ease with the marks he sees of her subjugation?[58] Could not the flattening of the prostitute's body into a common-place of male sexual privilege serve to reinforce, rather than subvert, the viewer's satisfaction with patriarchal gender arrangements? Even if Degas's images frustrate a specifically voyeuristic desire, they still might be felt to offer the misogynist the sadistic pleasure of inscribing the signs of patriarchal economic hegemony on the female body. Perhaps the viewer's castration fears need not be overcome by the metaphorizing displacements of psychic defense precisely because capitalist exploitation offers a still more alluring, since more objectively verifiable, means to triumph over them. Considerations such as these appear to bring us full circle, the distinction between voyeuristic modes of domination and economic ones being impossible to maintain, given that woman's commodification may be appropriated in fantasy to gratify reactionary psychic impulses. Exacerbating this hermeneutic quandary is our ignorance of the circumstances in which Degas showed the monotypes to a select

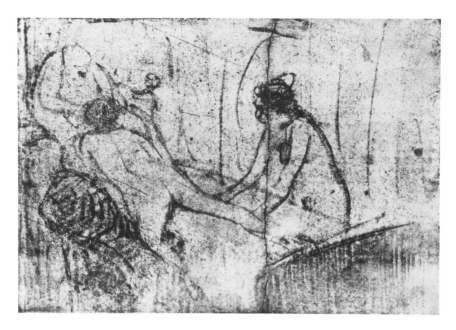

FIGURE 11. Degas, untitled, zinc plate used to print a monotype now destroyed or lost. Bibliothèque Nationale, Paris, Cabinet des Estampes.

few friends. Is it not possible, as I suggested earlier, that he shared with them the pleasures of viewing female objects available for purchase and of building up a rich pictorial collection of these sexual commodities? And just what might have been the role of these pictures in Degas's private sexual rituals (assuming he had any)? How can we account for those monotypes reportedly destroyed by Degas's brother that may well have portrayed explicit scenes of sexual activity? One of these that survived after being torn in two (fig. 11) shows, in the crudest outline, a woman in bed apparently performing fellatio on a man, while a second standing woman caresses the first woman's leg. Could such an image conceivably be integrated into our analysis of Degas's empathetic portrayal of female commodification in the brothel? The picture, in the primitive coarseness of its graphic mode, seems to have more of a documentary than a pornographic quality about it. But would it not then be appropriate to argue that to undertake such documentation is itself a sexist project?

There seems to be no way to reconcile these considerations with our earlier interpretation of the monotypes. Two perspectives appear to be constructed simultaneously by Degas's images. In the first, the viewer is made to feel guilt about the ideological impact of his gaze; in the second, the viewer finds his patriarchal prejudice reinforced. In the first, the misogynist recognizes himself as desiring psychological subject in the mirror of his capitalist activity; in the second, the misogynist recognizes only the reward of that activity, the other denied her subjectivity and desire. The first perspective is reflexive and entails moral reflection about the viewer's participation in a prostitutional economy. The second identifies the viewer unproblematically with that economy and endorses his controlling power within its system of exchange. The first suggests a materialist critique of the psychic mechanisms sustaining patriarchal ideology, the second embraces that ideology in its purely material effects.

The discomforting oscillation between these perspectives no doubt contributes significantly to the interpretative difficulty of Degas's brothel monotypes. However, this reading in terms of a final undecidability leaves an important element of the representation out of account. This is the de-eroticized power these female figures gain by their assimilation into a material world whose intransigent physicality is reflexively constituted at the level of facture. In figure 10, for example, the dark ink that spreads over the upper body of the right-hand figure and extends over her left shoulder onto the wall not only blends her body with the ground of the couch and associates her with the similarly textured carpet but also reflexively evokes the materiality of her production, a production whose effects even the artist himself cannot fully control. The prostitute's body seems virtually obliterated by the pressures of her facture. It is as if her presence were being absorbed into absence and her body, mutilated by the brute physical means of its depiction, were curiously privileged by its involvement in this mimetic negation. The monotype clients never participate in this reflexive process in quite the same way: their embodiment is a function of, and a response to, their gaze. We have seen that this response tends to erase the corporeality of the observing male presence as it retreats outside the frame and floats in space. The women, in contrast, barely emerge from their material surroundings. Their smudged, obscured forms reflect the crude technical means of their production. This reflexivity associates them with a nonhumanistic, modernist aesthetic practice that attempts to subvert the whole ideological structure of subjectivity within which our oscillating response to the pictures is generated. The dismembered, disheveled, "grimacing" prostitutes are the sacrificial victims of this subversion. They figure the modern precisely insofar as their subjective privilege is denied and their bodies are reified as facture. Far from expressing Degas's misogyny, the thumb prints, smudges, blots, and other traces of his gestural life that efface and disfigure the prostitutes' bodies constitute a history of his identification with these mutilated forms. The marks that we have read as signs of the prostitute's commodification are also material residues of Degas's creative desire to attack the norms of representational practice. The loss of full artistic control that he deliberately solicited by his choice to work in the monotype medium now appears as a move toward an aesthetic of randomness, whereby effects due to production technology displace the artist from the immediacy of his creative relation. The loss of immediacy thematized in the gender dynamics of the pictures might consequently be seen to reflect the artist's experimental distanciation and detachment from his medium. For the viewer, no longer morally implicated, the difficulties of formal apprehension then come to displace the dilemmas of ethical judgment.

But this displacement remains problematic. The reflexive emphasis seems deviously perverse, granting Degas's brothel inmates strength by insisting on the aesthetic value of their objectification. The strategy could be viewed as a materialist version of Valéry's sublimation of the medusa into a high-flying balloon: here woman's threat is neutralized by her absorption into ink. And so the interpreter's oscillation continues, now between at least three perspectives. Degas is reported to have said that "a picture is a thing that requires as much craftiness, malice, and vice as the perpetration of a crime."[59] My detective work has followed a few of the twisting trails of Degas's transgression. The crime, if there has been one, remains provocatively obscure.

Notes

It gives me great pleasure to acknowledge the help I received from friends and colleagues at various stages of writing this article. Michael Fried first alerted me to the existence of the monotypes. Steve Nichols invited me to present my Degas work at an MLA divisional session. As mentioned below, Susan Suleiman's acute reading made clear the necessity for further interpretive work. Bill Warner wrote a careful, sophisticated, and challenging critique of an early draft, which helped me sharpen and extend my argument. Eunice Lipton and Carol Armstrong reassured me that specialists in the field did not find my readings aberrant. (Unfortunately, Eunice Lipton's book, *Looking into Degas: Uneasy Images of Women and Modern Life* [Berkeley, 1986], was published too late for me to be able to take its findings into account.) Susanna Barrows offered useful suggestions from the historian's point of view. Audiences at Louisiana State University, the University of Pennsylvania, the State University of New York at Buffalo, Boston University, and New York University forced me to confront the bewildering diversity of viewers' responses to the monotypes.

1. Paul Valéry, *Degas Danse Dessin* in *Oeuvres*, ed. J. Hytier, 2 vols. (Paris, 1960), 2:1173. All translations in this essay are my own.
2. Ibid.
3. Paul Valéry, "Philosophie de la danse," in ibid., 1:1403.
4. Stéphane Mallarmé, "Crayonné au théâtre," in *Oeuvres complètes*, ed. H. Mondor and G. Jean-Aubry (Paris, 1945), 304.
5. Valéry, *Degas Danse Dessin*, 1173.
6. This metamorphosis follows the story told by Ovid of the beautiful Gorgon, raped in the temple of Athena by Poseidon, god of the sea, and then punished by Athena by having her lovely hair turned into snakes.
7. Valéry, *Degas Danse Dessin*, 1202. Theodore Reff echoes Valéry's remark in "Edgar Degas and Dance": "Like the laundress pressing down hard on her iron or yawning, overheated and exhausted, like the street-walker waiting on the café terrace in a

torpor, the dancer in Degas' work is often not an embodiment of feminine charm but of the lower-class woman's struggle for survival, burdened and deformed by her labors"; *Arts Magazine* 53, no. 3 (November 1978): 147.

8. "Marchandes à la toilette" and "danseuses" are already associated with prostitution by Alexandre Parent-Duchâtelet in his pioneering study *De la Prostitution dans la ville de Paris*, 2 vols. (Paris, 1836), 1:183–84. Subsequent studies mention "blanchisseuses," "repasseuses," and "modistes" as likely to be sexually available. See for example C. J. Lecour, *La Prostitution à Paris et à Londres 1789–1877*, 3rd ed. (Paris, 1882), 197–200; or Octave Uzanne, *Parisiennes de ce temps* (Paris, 1910), 421–22. Both are cited by Carol Armstrong in her brilliant doctoral dissertation, *Odd Man Out: Readings of the Work and Reputation of Edgar Degas* (Princeton University, 1986), 74–75. Susan Hollis Clayson attributes the appeal of the "modiste" as a motif for the impressionist painters (Renoir, Degas, Manet) to her combining an ambiguous sexuality (was she or was she not for sale like the hats in her store?) with a "commodified" social condition. See her stimulating dissertation, *Representations of Prostitution in Early Third-Republic France* (University of California, Los Angeles, 1984). The social and cultural conditions for the prevalent association of laundresses with a debased working-class sexuality are read from an illuminating ideological perspective by Eunice Lipton, "The Laundress in Late Nineteenth-Century French Culture: Imagery, Ideology, and Edgar Degas," *Art History* 3, no. 3 (September 1980): 295–313. For an analysis of the role of the café-concert as a prostitutional arena, see T. J. Clark's superb chapter "A Bar at the Folies-Bergère," in *The Painting of Modern Life* (New York, 1985).

9. As Carol Armstrong points out, Degas's *Famille Cardinal* monotype series, made to illustrate Ludovic Halévy's stories about two sisters, both dancers at the Paris Opéra, is his most explicit rendering of the social and sexual meanings of the *coulisses*; *Odd Man Out*, 84–99. For reproductions of these images, see Jean Adhémar and Françoise Cachin, *Degas: The Complete Etchings, Lithographs, and Monotypes* (London, 1974), monotypes nos. 56–82. For a discussion of the Jockey Club's special role in these venal transactions, see Joseph-Antoine Roy, *Histoire du Jockey Club de Paris* (Paris, 1958).

10. The monotype technique was apparently invented by the Genovese artist Giovanni Benedetto Castiglione (1600–1665). William Blake made a series of twelve beautiful monotypes in 1795 on themes from the Bible, Milton, and Shakespeare. For other artists who have used the medium, see the catalogue of the Metropolitan Museum exhibition, *The Painterly Print: Monotypes from the Seventeenth to the Twentieth Century* (New York, 1980).

11. Carol Armstrong, *Odd Man Out*, 215–16, has persuasively shown that Degas's use of the monotype base is remarkably original in that it actually *reverses* the traditional role of chiaroscuro. Instead of reinforcing the bond between surface and ground, the monotype foundation, she argues, produces a kind of negative effect, as of an emptiness that tends toward the obliteration of surface gesture and detail.

12. The sketches illustrating *La Fille Elisa* have been published by Theodore Reff in *The Notebooks of Edgar Degas*, 2 vols. (New York, 1985), notebook 28, nos. 26–27, 29, 31, 33, 35, 45, and 65 (described by Reff in 1:130).

13. Adhémar and Cachin, *Degas*, 75. Among Degas's friends, Cachin mentions the Halévys and Rouarts. Artists she considers likely to have seen the monotypes (no evidence is cited) are Paul-Albert Bartholomé and Camille Pissaro and, perhaps, Toulouse-Lautrec and Gauguin. A number of monotypes in the dark-field manner of scenes not explicitly related to brothel life carry scratched-in dedications to friends of Degas; see ibid., monotypes nos. 160, 161, 163, and 165.

14. See Eugenia Janis, "The Role of the Monotype in the Working Method of Degas," *Burlington Magazine* 109 (January-February 1967). Janis drew up the first comprehensive catalogue of the monotypes for an exhibition at the Fogg Art Museum in 1968; *Degas Monotypes: Essay, Catalogue, and Checklist* (Cambridge, Mass., 1968).

15. Adhémar and Cachin, *Degas*, 80.

16. Typically, Valéry refers to Huysmans's writing on Degas precisely at the moment when he wants to buttress his assertion of the artist's misogyny; *Degas Danse Dessin*, 1204.

17. J.-K. Huysmans, *Certains* (Paris, 1975), 294.

18. Ibid., 296.

19. Auguste Renoir also found something peculiarly chaste about Degas's bordello images. Ambroise Vollard quotes him as saying: "When one paints a bordello, it's often pornographic, but always hopelessly sad. Only Degas could give an air of rejoicing to such a subject along with the look of an Egyptian bas-relief. This quasi-religious and chaste aspect of his work, which makes it so great, becomes still more pronounced when he treats the prostitute"; *Degas* (Paris, 1924), 59–60.

20. Here Huysmans, who did not publish his comments on Degas's pastels until 1889, is echoing the praise Octave Mirbeau proclaimed three years earlier for Degas's rigorously unsentimental and antiromantic depictions of women. They do not "inspire passion or sensual desire," Mirbeau writes. "On the contrary, there is a ferocity that speaks clearly of a disdain for women and a horror of love. It is the same bitter philosophy, the same arrogant vision, that one finds in his studies of dancers"; *La France*, 21 May 1886; quoted in *The New Painting: Impressionism 1874–1886*, The Fine Arts Museums of San Francisco catalogue (San Francisco, 1986), 453. Huysmans, it seems, codified in its most extreme terms an interpretation of Degas's attitude toward women that had already gained a certain acceptance among professional critics. See Martha Ward's excellent review of the criticism of the 1886 exhibition, as focused on the question of Degas's misogyny, "The Rhetoric of Independence and Innovation," in *The New Painting*, 430–34.

21. Huysmans, *Certains*, 297.

22. Ibid.

23. Freud remarks of the scopophilic instinct that it begins as a narcissistic formation. Its first stage, which is never left behind, is autoerotic: "It has indeed an object, but that object is part of the subject's own body"; "Instincts and Their Vicissitudes," *Standard Edition of the Complete Psychological Works*, ed. James Strachey, 24 vols. (London, 1964), 14:130.

24. Edward Snow, *A Study of Vermeer* (Berkeley, 1979), 28.

25. Carol Armstrong, "Edgar Degas and the Representation of the Female Body," in *The Female Body in Western Culture: Contemporary Perspectives*, ed. Susan Rubin Suleiman (Cambridge, Mass., 1985), 239.

26. Eunice Lipton, "Degas' Bathers: The Case for Realism," *Arts Magazine* 54 (May 1980): 96.

27. Armstrong, "Degas and the Female Body," 238.

28. A number of the reviewers of Degas's contribution to the 1886 exhibition specifically define the observer's perspective as that of a voyeur: Degas, writes Gustave Geffroy, "wanted to paint a woman *who did not know she was being watched*, as one would see her hidden by a curtain or through a keyhole"; *La Justice*, 26 May 1886; quoted in *The New Painting*, 453. Geffroy notes the obliqueness of Degas's points of view but apparently considers them to be realistically determined by the voyeur's adoption of concealed places for clandestine observation. As Martha Ward, "Rhetoric of Independence and

Innovation," 432, remarks, the voyeuristic perspective was felt by the critics to reveal woman as instinctual animal. Only one critic, Octave Maus, in *L'Art moderne* (Brussels), 27 June 1886, was able to see anything positive about the exposure of woman's un-self-conscious physicality. He imagined the bathers as domestic cats cleaning themselves, whereas the majority of the critics chose to compare their gestures to the wild movements of monkeys or frogs; see *The New Painting*, 432–33.

29. Armstrong, "Degas and the Female Body," 239.

30. Snow, *Study of Vermeer*, 30. In a letter of 1884, Degas describes what seems to be precisely such an ontologically negative self-assessment: "If you were a bachelor and fifty years old (which I became a month ago), you would have moments such as I have when you would close yourself up like a door, and not only to friends. You suppress everything around you, and, once alone, you annihilate yourself, you kill yourself finally, out of disgust"; *Lettres de Degas*, ed. Marcel Guérin (Paris, 1931), 64–65.

31. In *La Revue de demain* for May-June 1886, Henri Fèvre remarked: "Degas lays bare for us the streetwalker's modern, swollen, pasty flesh. In the ambiguous bedrooms of registered houses, where certain ladies fill the social and utilitarian role of great collectors of love, fat women wash themselves, brush themselves, soak themselves, and wipe themselves off in basins as big as troughs"; quoted in *The New Painting*, 453. Another reviewer, J. M. Michel, associated Degas's bathing women with Zola's notorious heroine Nana: "Nana bathing, washing herself with a sponge, taking care of herself, arming herself for battle—that is the Impressionist ideal," he remarks sarcastically; *La Petite Gazette*, 18 May 1886; quoted in *The New Painting*, 453. In her article on the bathers, Eunice Lipton argues that the only women they could conceivably represent are prostitutes because depiction of middle-class women bathing would have constituted an ideologically unthinkable breach of decorum. Moreover, the postures of the women washing themselves and the decor of their surroundings are reproduced quite clearly in a number of the brothel scenes, whose only difference from the bather pastels is that in the former a client is looking on. Although this resemblance is indubitable, it is strange that more reviewers did not see the bathing women as whores and that Huysmans, attuned as he was to this subject matter, did not spell out the identification. One can only conclude that the signs of the figures' social identity must have been ambiguous enough that they failed to add up into a single readily acceptable meaning.

32. The derivation from personal experience is put into question not only by Degas's notorious personal shyness and sexual reticence but also by his having represented prostitutes naked in the brothel salon when they usually appeared partially clothed in shifts and corsets. This is how they are dressed, as they wait for clients and gossip among themselves, in the brothel scenes painted by Constantin Guys, some of which were owned by Degas's friend Manet. Susan Hollis Clayson argues that the props of Degas's brothel scenes, upholstered furniture, large mirrors, and fancy chandeliers are sufficient to identify the category of brothel portrayed as a deluxe *grande tolérance*, where specialized erotic services were available to a wealthy clientele of connoisseurs; "Avant-Garde and Pompier Images of Nineteenth-Century Prostitution: The Matter of Modernism, Modernity, and Social Ideology," in *Modernism and Modernity: The Vancouver Conference Papers*, ed. Benjamin H. D. Buchloh (Halifax, N.S., 1983), 56–58. The prostitutes' nudity may have been a feature of such luxurious establishments. This argument, though plausible, is not totally convincing because the props of Degas's scenes are so repetitive that they seem to belong to a typically Degasian repertoire of motifs, which could well have a literary origin, rather than to any specifically realistic inten-

tion. First among the literary descriptions of prostitutes that Degas would surely have known and admired are those of Baudelaire in his essay on Guys, "Le Peintre de la vie moderne." Baudelaire's marvelous evocation of life in a bordello could almost serve as a description of Degas's images:

> Without trying, sometimes they assume poses so daring and noble that the most fastidious sculptor would be enchanted, were the sculptors of today sufficiently bold and imaginative to seize on nobility wherever it was to be found, even in the mire. At other times, they show themselves prostrated in attitudes of desperate boredom, in the apathetic poses of public house patrons, masculine in their cynicism, smoking cigarettes to kill time, with the resignation of oriental fatalism. They sprawl on sofas, with their skirts rounded in back, spread out like a double fan in front, or they balance on the edge of stools and chairs. They are heavy, dull, stupid, extravagant, with eyes varnished by alcohol and foreheads swollen by stubbornness.

Oeuvres complètes (Paris, 1961), 1189.

33. All these etchings are included in Georges Bloch, *Pablo Picasso*, vol. 4: *Catalogue of the Printed Graphic Work, 1970–1972* (Berne, 1979).

34. The degree to which this project is free to treat the real as material for private fantasy is strikingly illustrated by two etchings in the Degas series (Bloch, nos. 1968 and 1969), where suddenly the whorehouse appears as an ideal Hellas and a prostitute becomes an Arcadian deity dallying with a faun.

35. T. J. Clark, *Painting of Modern Life*, 111. Clark's brilliant and challenging chapter on *Olympia* demonstrates how Manet's painting subverts both the conventions of the nude and the social category of the *courtisane* and inscribes the signs of class, albeit ambivalently, in the prostitute's nakedness.

36. Valéry, *Degas Danse Dessin*, 1173.

37. Mallarmé, *Oeuvres complètes*, 304.

38. Sigmund Freud, "Fetishism," in *Sexuality and the Psychology of Love*, ed. Philip Rieff (New York, 1963), 216.

39. Here my argument joins up with that developed by R. Howard Bloch in his stimulating contribution to this issue of *Representations*. Bloch shows that the early misogynistic tradition of biblical exegesis interpreted woman as "a tropological turning away" from the proper and literal, which is synonymous with male being.

40. For an excellent discussion of the relation of Degas's imagery to the graphic language of caricature, see Carol Armstrong's chapter "Reading the Oeuvre of Degas" in *Odd Man Out*.

41. Beatrice Farwell has written interestingly about the relation of "realist" treatments of the nude to the popular tradition of erotic imagery. See "Courbet's 'Baigneuses' and the Rhetorical Feminine Image," in *Woman as Sex Object: Studies in Erotic Art, 1730–1970*, ed. Thomas Hart and Linda Nochlin (New York, 1972), 65–79.

42. The influence of pornographic photographs on the iconography of Manet's *Olympia* has been studied by Gerald Needham, "Manet, 'Olympia,' and Pornographic Photography," in ibid., 81–89. The stereoscopic photograph that Needham reproduces of a bare-breasted woman ironing shows a motif used by Degas treated from a purely voyeuristic point of view.

43. Luce Irigaray, *This Sex Which Is Not One* (Ithaca, N.Y., 1985), 177.

44. Many of the monotype images, especially those done in the dark-field manner, convey an almost tactile sense of this marking, insofar as Degas often modeled the women's bodies by pressing on the ink with his fingers, leaving visible imprints.

45. I first encountered this interpretation of the monotypes in Clayson, *Representations of*

Prostitution in Early Third-Republic France, to which I am greatly indebted. Although Clayson remarks that "it is a hopeless task to gauge the misogynistic content of an image" (105), her illuminating analysis of the monotypes constitutes an implicit defense of Degas's representational practice. "The point of [the prostitutes'] particular, tenacious physicality," she writes, "seems to embed them in a world of the sheerly material, where the subjective 'self' has been suspended, cancelled, or long since overridden. Degas' prostitutes lead an existence in which the 'self' and the body have become the same, and the women's sexuality has been lost entirely to the world of exchange" (115).

46. My thinking about pornography is indebted to two articles, John Ellis, "Photography/ Pornography/Art/Pornography," *Screen* 21, no. 1 (Spring 1980); and Graham Knight and Berkeley Kaite, "Fetishism and Pornography: Some Thoughts on the Pornographic Eye/I," *Canadian Journal of Political and Social Theory* 9, no. 3 (Fall 1985). I would like to thank Constance Penley for recommending these articles.

47. Walter Benjamin, *Charles Baudelaire: A Lyric Poet in the Era of High Capitalism* (London, 1973), 59. In *Das Passagen-Werk*, 2 vols. (Frankfurt, 1982), 1:637, Benjamin declares pithily that "love of prostitutes is the apotheosis of intuitive feeling for the commodity [*Einfühlung in die Ware*]."

48. Berthe Morisot, *Correspondance*, ed. Denis Rouart (Paris, 1950), 23.

49. Ibid., 31.

50. Quoted in Adhémar and Cachin, *Degas*, 86.

51. Norma Broude, "Degas' 'Misogyny,'" *The Art Bulletin* 59 (March 1977): 95–107. Broude combines a biographical approach with thematic and visual analysis to conclude that Degas valued intellectual independence, creative accomplishments, and individual character in women. Broude's argument, based on her readings of Degas's portraits of women of his own social class, has trouble accounting for his pictures of lower-class women, whom she finds to be "reduced to types" (101).

52. Carol Armstrong, "The Myth of Degas," chap. 5 of *Odd Man Out*, esp. 352–58. The components of the myth that I enumerate below are those identified by Armstrong.

53. At the outset of a monumental four-volume monograph on Degas, P. A. Lemoisne suggests that the peculiarity of his subject makes the endeavor he is undertaking almost impossible. Since Degas's works are "so full of reticences, so willfully effaced," he remarks, to understand the artist's evolution one should get to know the man.

> But if there was ever a man difficult to know, walled up as he was in an impregnable discretion, a kind of timidity that made him caustic and often severe when he felt menaced, that man was Degas. . . . When you try to get closer to the man, you soon find yourself turning in a vicious circle, Degas having been truly himself, audacious despite an insurmountable modesty, ardent despite a fierce reserve, decisive despite eternal scruples, brilliant despite an innate sobriety of expression, only in his works.

Degas et son oeuvre, 4 vols. (Paris, 1942), 1:1–2. One aspect of the Degas myth that biographers have built up from the meagerest of evidence into an indisputable cause of the artist's misogyny is his impotence. For example, Roy McMullen declares that "there can be little doubt that [the] reason for [Degas's] celibacy . . . was impotence— either psychic or physical impotence, and perhaps, as is often the case, a combination of the two"; *Degas: His Life, Times, and Work* (London, 1985), 268. In an article entitled "Degas as a Human Being," the thesis of which is that the artist barely qualified, Benedict Nicholson speculates that "there may be something in the theory that he was a repressed homosexual"; *Burlington Magazine* 105 (June 1963): 239.

54. See Roy McMullen, *Degas*, 7–8. In the 1830s the family paid to have a bogus genealogy drawn up to confirm their noble heritage and their claim to the aristocratic name *de Gas*. According to his niece's report, Degas said that he changed the spelling of the family name because "the nobility is not in the habit of working. Since I want to work, I will assume the name of a commoner"; Jeanne Fevre, *Mon oncle Degas* (Geneva, 1949), 23.

55. Paul Gauguin, *Paul Gauguin's Intimate Journals* (Bloomington, Ind., 1958), 131.

56. Noting this and other conflicts in Degas's class position, Eunice Lipton concludes that it was because "Degas had little at stake in the prejudices of a particular social group" and was located "outside conventional social and emotional structures" that he was able to develop "a unique and subversive vision of society"; "The Laundress in French Culture," 310. Although the implied causality here is somewhat reductive, Lipton's analysis is helpful insofar as it locates Degas on the margins of the dominant ideology. According to her interpretation, Degas is aware of his implication in the ideological structures of patriarchy, especially in its voyeuristic debasement of women, but is determined to distance himself from those structures so as to frame their operation in art.

57. In the brilliant conclusion to her thesis, Carol Armstrong discusses Degas's photographic self-portraits as exercises in viewing a self that cannot be represented as a subject seeing and discusses the portrait of Mallarmé and Renoir, in which Degas is an effaced presence reflected and negated in a play of mirror images. She reads these photographs as emblematic of Degas's life-long preoccupation with "the act of vision as a fact of self-negation"; *Odd Man Out*, 411.

58. The possibility of such a reading was suggested in Susan Suleiman's discussion of an earlier version of this paper presented at the third annual Conference on Twentieth-Century Literature in French at Baton Rouge. I am grateful to Professor Suleiman for her perceptive and stimulating critique, to which I hope the present version of my paper is at least a partially adequate response.

59. Lemoisne, *Degas et son oeuvre*, 1:119.

CAROL J. CLOVER

Her Body, Himself:
Gender in the Slasher Film

The Cinefantastic and Varieties of Horror

ON THE HIGH SIDE OF HORROR lie the classics: F. W. Murnau's *Nosferatu*, *King Kong*, *Dracula*, *Frankenstein*, and various works by Alfred Hitchcock, Carl Theodor Dreyer, and a few others—films that by virtue of age, literary ancestry, or fame of director have achieved reputability within the context of disreputability.[1] Further down the scale fall the productions of Brian De Palma, some of the glossier satanic films (*Rosemary's Baby*, *The Omen*, *The Exorcist*), certain sci-fi hybrids (*Alien/Aliens*, *Blade Runner*), some vampire and werewolf films (*Wolfen*, *An American Werewolf in London*), and an assortment of other highly produced films, often with stars (*Whatever Happened to Baby Jane*, *The Shining*). At the very bottom, down in the cinematic underbrush, lies—horror of horrors—the slasher (or spatter or shocker) film: the immensely generative story of a psycho-killer who slashes to death a string of mostly female victims, one by one, until he is himself subdued or killed, usually by the one girl who has survived.

Drenched in taboo and encroaching vigorously on the pornographic, the slasher film lies by and large beyond the purview of the respectable (middle-aged, middle-class) audience. It has also lain by and large beyond the purview of respectable criticism. Staples of drive-ins and exploitation houses, where they "rub shoulders with sex pictures and macho action flicks," these are films that are "never even written up."[2] Books on horror film mostly concentrate on the classics, touch on the middle categories in passing, and either pass over the slasher in silence or bemoan it as a degenerate aberration.[3] The one full book on the category, William Schoell's *Stay Out of the Shower*, is immaculately unintelligent.[4] Film magazine articles on the genre rarely get past technique, special effects, and profits. The Sunday *San Francisco Examiner* relegates reviews of slashers to the syndicated "Joe Bob Briggs, Drive-In Movie Critic of Grapevine, Texas," whose low-brow, campy tone ("We're talking two breasts, four quarts of blood, five dead bodies. . . . Joe Bob says check it out") establishes what the paper and others like it deem the necessary distance between their readership and that sort of film.[5] There are of course the exceptional cases: critics or social observers who have seen at least some of these films and tried to come to grips with their ethics or aesthetics or both. Just how troubled is their task can be seen from its divergent results. For one critic, *The Texas Chain Saw Massacre* is "the *Gone With the Wind* of meat movies."[6] For another it is a "vile little piece of sick crap . . . nothing but a hysterically paced, slapdash, imbecile concoction of cannibalism, voodoo, astrology, sundry hippie-esque cults, and unrelenting sadistic violence as extreme and hideous as a complete lack of imagination can possibly make it."[7] Writes a third: "[Director Tobe] Hooper's cinematic intelligence becomes more apparent in every viewing, as one gets over the initial traumatizing impact and learns to respect the pervasive felicities of camera placement and movement."[8] The Museum of Modern Art bought the film in the same year that at least one country, Sweden, banned it.

Robin Wood's tack is less aesthetic than anthropological. "However one may shrink from systematic exposure to them [slasher films], however one may deplore the social phenomena and ideological mutations they reflect, their popularity . . . suggests that even if they were uniformly execrable they shouldn't be ignored."[9] We may go a step further and suggest that the qualities that locate the slasher film outside the usual aesthetic system—that indeed render it, along with pornography and low horror in general, the film category "most likely to be betrayed by artistic treatment and lavish production values"[10]—are the very qualities that make it such a transparent source for (sub)cultural attitudes toward sex and gender in particular. Unmediated by otherworldly fantasy, cover plot, bestial transformations, or civilized routine, slasher films present us in startlingly direct terms with a world in which male and female are at desperate odds but in which, at the same time, masculinity and femininity are more states of mind than body. The premise of this essay, then, is that the slasher film, not despite but exactly because of its crudity and compulsive repetitiveness, gives us a clearer picture of current sexual attitudes, at least among the segment of the population that forms its erstwhile audience, than do the legitimate products of the better studios.

Before we turn to the generic particulars, however, let us review some of the critical and cinematic issues that attend the study of the sensation genres in general and horror in particular. We take as our point of departure not a slasher film but Brian De Palma's art-horror film *Body Double* (1984). The plot—a man witnesses and after much struggle solves the mysterious murder of a woman with whom he has become voyeuristically involved—concerns us less than the three career levels through which the hero, an actor named Jake, first ascends and then descends. He aspires initially to legitimate roles (Shakespeare), but it becomes clear during the course of a method-acting class that his range of emotional expression is impaired by an unresolved childhood fear. For the moment he has taken a job as vampire in a "low-budget, independent horror film," but even that job is threatened when, during a scene in which he is to be closed in a coffin and buried, he suffers an attack of claustrophobia and must leave the set. A plot twist leads him to the underworld of pornography, where he takes on yet another role, this time in a skin flick. Here, in the realm of the flesh with a queen of porn, the sexual roots of Jake's paralysis—fear of the (female) cavern—are exposed and finally resolved. A new man, he returns to "A Vampire's Kiss" to master the burial scene, and we are to understand that Shakespeare is the next stop.

The three cinematic categories are thus ranked by degree of sublimation. On the civilized side of the continuum lie the legitimate genres; at the other end, hard on the unconscious, lie the sensation or "body" genres, horror and pornography, in that order. For De Palma, the violence of horror reduces to and enacts archaic sexual feelings. Beneath Jake's emotional paralysis (which emerges in the "high" genre) lies a death anxiety (which is exposed in the burying-alive of horror), and beneath *that* anxiety lies a primitive sexual response (which emerges, and is resolved, in pornography). The layers of Jake's experience accord strikingly, and perhaps not coincidentally, with Freud's archaeology of "uncanny" feelings. "To some people," Freud wrote, "the idea of being buried alive by mistake is the most uncanny thing of all. And yet psycho-analysis has taught us that this terrifying phantasy is only a transformation of another phantasy which originally had nothing terrifying about it at all, but was qualified by a certain lasciviousness—the phantasy, I mean, of intra-uterine existence [*der Phantasie vom Leben im Mutterleib*]."[11] Pornography thus engages directly (in pleasurable terms) what horror explores at one remove (in painful terms) and legitimate film at two or more. Beneath the "legitimate" plot of *The Graduate* (in which Ben must give up his relationship with a *friend*'s mother in order to marry and take his proper social place) lies the plot of *Psycho* (in which Norman's unnatural attachment to his *own* mother drives him to murder women to whom he is attracted); and beneath *that* plot lies the plot of the porn film *Taboo*, in which the son simply has sex with his mother ("Mom, am I better than Dad?"). Pornography, in short, has to do with sex (the act) and horror with gender.

It is a rare Hollywood film that does not devote a passage or two—a car chase, a sex scene—to the emotional/physical excitement of the audience. But horror and pornography are the only two genres specifically devoted to the arousal of bodily sensation. They exist solely to horrify and stimulate, not always respectively, and their ability to do so is the sole measure of their success: they "prove themselves upon our pulses."[12] Thus in horror-film circles, "good" means scary, specifically in a bodily way (ads promise shivers, chills, shudders, tingling of the spine; Lloyds of London insured audiences of *Macabre* against death by fright);[13] and *Hustler's Erotic Film Guide* ranks pornographic films according to the degree of erection they produce (one film is ranked a "pecker popper," another "limp"). The target is in both cases the body, our witnessing body. But *what* we witness is also the body, another's body, in experience: the body in sex and the body in threat. The terms "flesh film" ("skin flicks") and "meat movies" are remarkably apt.

Cinema, it is claimed, owes its particular success in the sensation genres (witness the early and swift rise of vampire films) to its unprecedented ability to manipulate point of view. What written narrative must announce, film can accomplish silently and instantaneously through cutting. Within the space of seconds, the vampire's first-person perspective is displaced by third-person or documentary observation. To these simple shifts can be added the variables of distance (from the panorama of the battlefield to the closeup of an eyeball), angle, frame tilt, lighting effects, unsteadiness of image, and so on—again, all subject to sudden and unannounced manipulation.[14] A current horror-film favorite locates the I-camera with the killer in pursuit of a victim; the camera is hand-held, producing a jerky image, and the frame includes in-and-out-of-focus foreground objects (trees, bushes, window frames) behind which the killer (I-camera) is lurking—all accompanied by the sound of heartbeat and heavy breathing. "The camera moves in on the screaming, pleading victim, 'looks down' at the knife, and then plunges it into the chest, ear, or eyeball. Now that's sick."[15]

Lagging behind practice is a theoretical understanding of effect. The processes by which a certain image (but not another) filmed in a certain way (but not another) causes one person's (but not another's) pulse to race finally remains a mystery—not only to critics and theorists but even, to judge from interviews and the trial-and-error (and baldly imitative) quality of the films themselves, by the people who make the product. The process of suture is sensed to be centrally important in effecting audience identification, though just how and why is unclear.[16] Nor is identification the straightforward notion some critics take it to be.[17] Where commentators by and large agree is in the importance of the "play of pronoun function."[18] If the fantastic depends for its effect on an uncertainty of vision, a profusion of perspectives and a confusion of subjective and objective, then cinema is preeminently suited to the fantastic. Indeed, to the extent that film can present "unreal" combinations of objects and events as "real" through the camera eye, the "cinematic process itself might be called fantastic."[19] The "cine-fantastic" in any case succeeds, far more efficiently and effectively and on a far greater scale than its ancestral media, in the production of sensation.

The fact that the cinematic conventions of horror are so easily and so often parodied would seem to suggest that, individual variation notwithstanding, its basic structures of apperception are fixed and fundamental. The same is true of the stories they tell. Students of folklore or early literature recognize in the slasher film the hallmarks of oral story: the free exchange of themes and motifs, the archetypal characters and situations, the accumulation of sequels, remakes, imitations. This is a field in which there is in some sense no original, no real or right text, but only variants; a world in which, therefore, the meaning of the individual example lies outside itself. The "art" of the horror film, like the "art" of pornography, is to a very large extent the art of rendition, and it is understood as such by the competent audience.[20] A particular example may have original features, but its quality as a horror film lies in the ways it delivers the cliché. James B. Twitchell rightly recommends an ethnological approach, in which the various stories are analyzed as if no one individual telling really mattered. . . . You search for what is stable and repeated; you neglect what is "artistic" and "original." This is why, for me, auteur criticism is quite beside the point in explaining horror. . . . The critic's first job in explaining the fascination of horror is not to fix the images at their every appearance but, instead, to trace their migrations to the audience and, only then, try to understand why they have been crucial enough to pass along.[21]

That auteur criticism is at least partly beside the point is clear from interviews with such figures as John Carpenter (*Halloween*, *The Fog*)—interviews that would seem to suggest that, like the purveyors of folklore, the makers of film operate more on instinct and formula than conscious understanding. So bewildered was Hitchcock by the unprecedented success of *Psycho* that he approached the Stanford Research Institute about doing a study of the phenomenon.[22]

What makes horror "crucial enough to pass along" is, for critics since Freud, what has made ghost stories and fairy tales crucial enough to pass along: its engagement of repressed fears and desires and its reenactment of the residual conflict surrounding those feelings. Horror films thus respond to interpretation, as Robin Wood puts it, as "at once the personal dreams of their makers and the collective dreams of their audiences—the fusion made possible by the shared structures of a common ideology."[23] And just as attacker and attacked are expressions of the same self in nightmares, so they are expressions of the same viewer in horror film. Our primary and acknowledged identification may be with the victim, the adumbration of our infantile fears and desires, our memory sense of ourselves as tiny and vulnerable in the face of the enormous Other; but the Other is also finally another part of ourself, the projection of our repressed infantile rage and desire (our blind drive to annihilate those toward whom we feel anger, to force satisfaction from those who stimulate us, to wrench food for ourselves if only by actually devouring those who feed us) that we have had in the name of civilization to repudiate. We are both Red Riding Hood *and* the Wolf; the force of the experience, the horror, comes from "knowing" both sides of the story—from giving ourselves over to the cinematic play of pronoun functions. It is no surprise that the first film to which viewers were not admitted once the theater darkened was *Psycho*. Whether Hitchcock actually meant with this measure to intensify the "sleep" experience is unclear, but the effect both in the short run, in establishing *Psycho* as the ultimate thriller, and in the long run, in altering the cinema-going habits of the nation, is indisputable. In the current understanding, horror is the least interruptable of all film genres. That uninterruptability itself bears witness to the compulsive nature of the stories it tells.

Whatever else it may be, the slasher film is clearly "crucial enough to pass along." Profits and sequels tell much of the story. *Halloween* cost $320,000 to make and within six years had grossed over $75,000,000; even a highly produced film like *The Shining* has repaid itself tenfold.[24] *The Hills Have Eyes*, *The Texas Chain Saw*

Massacre, and *Alien* (a sci-fi/slasher hybrid) are currently at Part Two. *Psycho* and *A Nightmare on Elm Street* are at Part Three. *Halloween* is at Part Four, and *Friday the Thirteenth* is at Part Six. These are better taken as remakes than sequels; although the later part purports to take up where the earlier part left off, it in most cases simply duplicates with only slight variation the plot and circumstances—the formula—of its predecessor. Nor do different titles indicate different plots; *Friday the Thirteenth* is set at summer camp and *Halloween* in town, but the story is much the same, compulsively repeated in those ten films and in dozens like them under different names. The audience for that story is by all accounts largely young and largely male—most conspicuously groups of boys who cheer the killer on as he assaults his victims, then reverse their sympathies to cheer the survivor on as she assaults the killer.[25] Our question, then, has to do with that particular audience's stake in that particular nightmare; with what in the story is "crucial" enough to warrant the price of admission, and what the implications are for the current discussion of women and film.

The Slasher Film

The immediate ancestor of the slasher film is Hitchcock's *Psycho* (1960). Its elements are familiar: the killer is the psychotic product of a sick family, but still recognizably human; the victim is a beautiful, sexually active woman; the location is not-home, at a Terrible Place; the weapon is something other than a gun; the attack is registered from the victim's point of view and comes with shocking suddenness. None of these features is original, but the unprecedented success of Hitchcock's particular formulation, above all the sexualization of both motive and action, prompted a flood of imitations and variations. In 1974, a film emerged that revised the *Psycho* template to a degree and in such a way as to mark a new phase: *The Texas Chain Saw Massacre* (Tobe Hooper). Together with *Halloween* (John Carpenter, 1978), it engendered a new spate of variations and imitations.

The plot of *Texas Chain Saw* is simple enough: five young people are driving through Texas in a van; they stop off at an abandoned house and are murdered one by one by the psychotic sons of a degenerate local family; the sole survivor is a woman. The horror, of course, lies in the elaboration. Early in the film the group picks up a hitchhiker, but when he starts a fire and slashes Franklin's arm (having already slit open his own hand), they kick him out. The abandoned house they subsequently visit, once the home of Sally's and Franklin's grandparents, turns out to be right next door to the house of the hitchhiker and his family: his brother Leatherface; their father; an aged and only marginally alive grandfather; and their dead grandmother and her dog, whose mummified corpses are ceremonially included in the family gatherings. Three generations of slaughterhouse workers, once proud of their craft but now displaced by machines, have taken up killing and cannibalism as a way of life. Their house is grotesquely decorated with human and animal remains—bones, feathers, hair, skins. The young people drift apart in their exploration of the abandoned house and grounds and are picked off one by one by Leatherface and Hitchhiker. Last is Sally. The others are attacked and killed with dispatch, but Sally must fight for her life, enduring all manner of horrors through the night. At dawn she manages to escape to the highway, where she is picked up by a passing trucker.

Likewise the nutshell plot of *Halloween*: a psychotic killer (Michael) stalks a small town on Halloween and kills a string of teenage friends, one by one; only Laurie survives. The twist here is that Michael has escaped from the asylum in which he has been incarcerated since the age of six, when he killed his sister minutes after she and her boyfriend parted following an illicit interlude in her parents' bed. That murder, in flashback, opens the film. It is related entirely in the killer's first person (I-camera) and only after the fact is the identity of the perpetrator revealed. Fifteen years later, Michael escapes his prison and returns to kill Laurie, whom he construes as another version of his sister (a sequel clarifies that she is in fact his *younger* sister, adopted by another family at the time of the earlier tragedy). But before Michael gets to Laurie, he picks off her high school friends: Annie, in a car on her way to her boyfriend's; Bob, going to the kitchen for a beer after sex with Lynda; Lynda, talking on the phone with Laurie and waiting for Bob to come back with the beer. At last only Laurie remains. When she hears Lynda squeal and then go silent on the phone, she leaves her own baby-sitting house to go to Lynda's. Here she discovers the three bodies and flees, the killer in pursuit. The remainder of the film is devoted to the back-and-forth struggle between Laurie and Michael. Again and again he bears down on her, and again and again she either eludes him (by running, hiding, breaking through windows to escape, locking herself in) or strikes back (once with a knitting needle, once with a hanger). In the end, Doctor Loomis (Michael's psychiatrist in the asylum) rushes in and shoots the killer (though not so fatally as to prevent his return in the sequels).

Before we turn to an inventory of generic components, let us add a third, more recent example: *The Texas Chain Saw Massacre II*, from 1986. The slaughter-house family (now named the Sawyers) is the same, though older and, owing to their unprecedented success in the sausage business, richer.[26] When Mr. Sawyer begins to suspect from her broadcasts that a disk jockey named Stretch knows more than she should about one of their recent crimes, he dispatches his sons Leatherface and Chop Top (Hitchhiker in Part One) to the radio station late at night. There they seize the technician and corner Stretch. At the crucial moment, however, power fails Leatherface's chainsaw. As Stretch cowers before him, he presses the now still blade up along her thigh and against her crotch, where he holds it unsteadily as he jerks and shudders in what we understand to be orgasm.

After that the sons leave. The intrepid Stretch, later joined by a Texas Ranger (Dennis Hopper), tracks them to their underground lair outside of town. Tumbling down the Texas equivalent of a rabbit hole, Stretch finds herself in the subterranean chambers of the Sawyer operation. Here, amidst all the slaughterhouse paraphernalia, the Sawyers live and work. The walls drip with blood. Like the decrepit mansion of Part One, the residential parts of the establishment are quaintly decorated with human and animal remains. After a long ordeal at the hands of the Sawyers, Stretch manages to scramble up through a culvert and beyond that up onto a nearby pinnacle, where she finds a chainsaw and wards off her final assailant. The Texas Ranger evidently perishes in a grenade explosion underground, leaving Stretch the sole survivor.

The spiritual debt of all the post-1974 slasher films to *Psycho* is clear, and it is a rare example that does not pay a visual tribute, however brief, to the ancestor—if not in a shower stabbing, then in a purling drain or the shadow of a knife-wielding hand. No less clear, however, is the fact that the post-1974 examples have, in the usual way of folklore, contemporized not only Hitchcock's terms but also, over time, their own. We have, in short, a cinematic formula with a twenty-six-year history, of which the first phase, from 1960 to 1974, is dominated by a film clearly rooted in the sensibility of the 1950s, while the second phase, bracketed by the two *Texas Chain Saw* films from 1974 and 1986, responds to the values of the late sixties and early seventies. That the formula in its most recent guise may be in decline is suggested by the campy, self-parodying quality of *Texas Chain Saw II*, as well as the emergence, in legitimate theater, of the slasher satire *Buckets of Blood*. Between 1974 and 1986, however, the formula evolved and flourished in ways of some interest to observers of popular culture, above all those concerned with the representation of women in film. To apprehend in specific terms the nature of that mutation, let us, with *Psycho* as the benchmark, survey the genre by component category: killer, locale, weapons, victims, and shock effects.

Killer. The psychiatrist at the end of *Psycho* explains what we had already guessed from the action: that Norman Bates had introjected his mother, in life a "clinging, demanding woman," so completely that she constituted his other, controlling self. Not Norman but "the mother half of his mind" killed Marion—had to kill Marion—when he (the Norman half) found himself aroused by her. The notion of a killer propelled by psychosexual fury, more particularly a male in gender distress, has proved a durable one, and the progeny of Norman Bates stalk the genre up to the present day. Just as Norman wears his mother's clothes during his acts of violence and is thought, by the screen characters and also, for a while, by the film's spectators, to *be* his mother, so the murderer in the *Psycho*-imitation *Dressed to Kill* (Brian De Palma, 1980), a transvestite psychiatrist, seems until his unveiling to be a woman; like Norman, he must kill women who arouse him sexually. Likewise, in muted form, Hitchhiker/Chop Top and Leatherface in the *Texas Chain Saw* films: neither brother shows overt signs of gender confusion, but their cathexis to the sick family—in which the mother is conspicuously absent but the preserved corpse of the grandmother (answering the treated body of Mrs. Bates in *Psycho*) is conspicuously present—has palpably arrested their development. Both are in their twenties (thirties, in Part Two), but Hitchhiker/Chop Top seems a gangly kid and Leatherface jiggles in baby fat behind his butcher's apron. Like Norman Bates, whose bedroom still displays his childhood toys, Hitchhiker/Chop Top and Leatherface are permanently locked in childhood. Only when Leatherface "discovers" sex in Part Two does he lose his appetite for murder. In *Motel Hell*, a sendup of modern horror with special reference to *Psycho* and *Texas Chain Saw I*, we are repeatedly confronted with a portrait of the dead mother, silently presiding over all manner of cannibalistic and incestuous doings on the part of her adult children.

No less in the grip of boyhood is the killer in *The Eyes of Laura Mars* (1978). The son of a hooker, a hysterical woman gone for days at a time, the killer has up to now put his boyish anger to good use in police work—the film makes much of the irony—but the sight of Laura's violent photographs causes it to be unleashed in full force. The killer in *Hell Night* is the sole member of his family to survive, as a child, a murderous rampage on the part of his father; the experience condemned him to an afterlife as a murderer himself. In *Halloween* the killer *is* a child, at least in the first instance: Michael, who at the age of six is so enraged at his sister (evidently for her sexual relations with her boyfriend) that he stabs her to death with a kitchen knife. The remainder of the film details his return rampage at the age of twenty-one, and Dr. Loomis, who has overseen the case in the interim, explains that although Michael's body has attained maturity, his mind remains frozen in infantile fury. In *It's Alive*, the killer is literally an infant, evidently made monstrous through intrauterine apprehension of its parents' ambivalence (early in the pregnancy they considered an abortion).

Even killers whose childhood is not immediately at issue and who display no overt gender confusion are often sexually disturbed. The murderer in *Nightmare on Elm Street* is an undead child molester. The killer in *Slumber Party Massacre* says to a young woman he is about to assault with a power drill: "Pretty. All of you are very pretty. I love you. Takes a lot of love for a person to do this. You know you want it. You want it. Yes." When she grasps the psychodynamics of the situation in the infamous crotch episode of *Texas Chain Saw II*, Stretch tries a desperate gambit: "You're really good, you really are good," she repeats; and indeed, immediately after ejaculation Leatherface becomes palpably less interested in his saw. The parodic *Motel Hell* spells it out. "His pecker don't work; you'll see when he takes off his overalls—it's like a shrivelled prune," Bruce says of his killer-brother Vincent when he learns of Terry's plans to marry him. Terry never does see, for on her wedding night he attempts (needless to say) not sex but murder. Actual rape is practically nonexistent in the slasher film, evidently on the premise—as the crotch episode suggests—that violence and sex are not concomitants but alternatives, the one as much a substitute for and a prelude to the other as the teenage horror film is a substitute for and a prelude to the "adult" film (or the meat movie a substitute for and prelude to the skin flick).[27] When Sally under torture (*Texas Chain Saw I*) cries out "I'll do anything you want," clearly with sexual intention, her assailants respond only by mimicking her in gross terms; she has profoundly misunderstood the psychology.

Female killers are few and their reasons for killing significantly different from men's. With the possible exception of the murderous mother in *Friday the Thirteenth I*, they show no gender confusion. Nor is their motive overtly psychosexual; their anger derives in most cases not from childhood experience but from specific moments in their adult lives in which they have been abandoned or cheated on by men (*Strait Jacket, Play Misty for Me, Attack of the 50-Foot Woman*). (Films like *Mother's Day, Ms. 45*, and *I Spit On Your Grave* belong to the rape-revenge category.) *Friday the Thirteenth I* is something of an anomaly. The killer is revealed as a middle-aged woman whose son, Jason, drowned years earlier as a consequence of negligence on the part of the camp counselors. The anomaly is not sustained in the sequels (Parts Two to Six), however. Here the killer is Jason himself, not dead after all but living in a forest hut. The pattern is a familiar one; his motive is vengeance for the death of his mother, his excessive attachment toward whom is manifested in his enshrining of her severed head. Like Stretch in the crotch episode of *Texas Chain Saw II*, the girl who does final combat with Jason in Part Two sees the shrine, grasps its significance (she's a psych major), and saves herself by repeating in a commanding tone, "I am your mother, Jason; put down the knife." Jason, for his part, begins to see his mother in the girl (I-camera) and obeys her.

In films of the *Psycho* type (*Dressed to Kill, Eyes of Laura Mars*), the killer is an insider, a man who functions normally in the action until, at the end, his other self is revealed. *Texas Chain Saw* and *Halloween* introduced another sort of killer: one whose only role is that of killer and one whose identity as such is clear from the outset. Norman may have a normal half, but these killers have none. They are emphatic misfits and emphatic outsiders. Michael is an escapee from a distant asylum; Jason subsists in the forest; the Sawyer sons live a bloody subterranean existence outside of town. Nor are they clearly seen. We catch sight of them only in glimpses—few and far between in the beginning, more frequent toward the end. They are usually large, sometimes overweight, and often masked. In short, they may be recognizably human, but only marginally so, just as they are only marginally visible—to their victims and to us, the spectators. In one key aspect, however, the killers are superhuman: their virtual indestructibility. Just as Michael (in *Halloween*) repeatedly rises from blows that would stop a lesser man, so Jason (in the *Friday the Thirteenth* films) survives assault after assault to return in sequel after sequel. Chop Top in *Texas Chain Saw II* is so called because of a metal plate implanted in his skull in repair of a head wound sustained in the truck accident in Part One. It is worth noting that the killers are normally the fixed elements and the victims the changeable ones in any given series.

Terrible Place. The Terrible Place, most often a house or tunnel, in which the victims sooner or later find themselves is a venerable element of horror. The Bates mansion is just one in a long list of such places—a list that continues, in the modern slasher, with the decaying mansion of *Texas Chain Saw I*, the abandoned and haunted mansion of *Hell Night*, the house for sale but unsellable in *Halloween* (also a point of departure for such films as *Rosemary's Baby* and *Amityville Horror*), and so on. What makes these houses terrible is not just their Victorian decrepitude but the terrible families—murderous, incestuous, cannibalistic—that occupy them. So the Bates mansion enfolds the history of a mother and son locked in a sick attachment, and so the *Texas Chain Saw* mansion/labyrinth shelters a lawless brood presided over by the decaying corpse of the grandmother. Jason's forest hut (in the *Friday the Thirteenth* sequels) is no mansion, but it houses another mummified mother (or at least her head), with all the usual candles and dreadful paraphernalia. The terrors of the *Hell Night* mansion stem, we learn, from an early owner's massacre of his children. Into such houses unwitting victims wander in film after film, and it is the conventional task of the genre to register in close detail those victims' dawning understanding, as they survey the visible evidence, of the human crimes and perversions that have transpired there. That perception leads directly to the perception of their own immediate peril.

In *Texas Chain Saw Massacre II*, house and tunnel elide in a residential labyrinth underground, connected to the world above by channels and culverts. The family is intact, indeed thrives, but for reasons evidently having to do with the nature of their sausage business has moved residence and slaughterhouse underground. For Stretch, trying desperately to find a way out, it is a ghastly place: dark, full of blind alleys, walls wet with blood. Likewise the second basement of the haunted mansion in *Hell Night*: strewn with decaying bodies and skeletons, lighted with masses of candles. Other tunnels are less familial: the one in *Body Double* that prompts Jake's claustrophobic faint, and the horror-house tunnel in *He Knows You're Alone* in which the killer lurks. The morgue episode in the latter film, certain of the hospital scenes in *Halloween II*, and the bottom-cellar scenes from various films may be counted as Terrible Tunnels: dark, labyrinthine, exitless, usually underground and palpably damp, and laced with heating ducts and plumbing pipes. In *Hell Night*, as in *Texas Chain Saw II*, Terrible House (the abandoned mansion) and Terrible Tunnel (the second basement) elide.

The house or tunnel may at first seem a safe haven, but the same walls that promise to keep the killer out quickly become, once the killer penetrates them, the walls that hold the victim in. A phenomenally popular moment in post-1974 slashers is the scene in which the victim locks herself in (a house, room, closet, car) and waits with pounding heart as the killer slashes, hacks, or drills his way in. The action is inevitably seen from the victim's point of view; we stare at the door (wall, car roof) and watch the surface break with first the tip and then the shaft of the weapon. In Hitchcock's *The Birds*, it is the birds' beaks we see penetrating the door. The penetration scene is commonly the film's pivotal moment; if the victim has up to now simply fled, she has at this point no choice but to fight back.

Weapons. In the hands of the killer, at least, guns have no place in slasher films. Victims sometimes avail themselves of firearms, but like telephones, fire alarms, elevators, doorbells, and car engines, guns fail in the squeeze. In some basic sense, the emotional terrain of the slasher film is pretechnological. The preferred weapons of the killer are knives, hammers, axes, icepicks, hypodermic needles, red hot pokers, pitchforks, and the like. Such implements serve well a plot predicated on stealth, the unawareness of later victims that the bodies of their friends are accumulating just yards away. But the use of noisy chainsaws and power drills and the nonuse of such relatively silent means as bow and arrow, spear, catapult, and even swords,[28] would seem to suggest that closeness and tactility are also at issue. The sense is clearer if we include marginal examples like *Jaws* and *The Birds*, as well as related werewolf and vampire genres. Knives and needles, like teeth, beaks, fangs, and claws, are personal, extensions of the body that bring attacker and attacked into primitive, animalistic embrace.[29] In *I Spit On Your Grave*, the heroine forces her rapist at gunpoint to drop his pants, evidently meaning to shoot him in his genitals. But she changes her mind, invites him home for what he all too readily supposes will be a voluntary follow-up of the earlier gang rape. Then, as they sit together in a bubble bath, she castrates him with a knife. If we wondered why she threw away the pistol, now we know: all phallic symbols are not equal, and a hands-on knifing answers a hands-on rape in a way that a shooting, even a shooting preceded by a humiliation, does not.[30]

Beyond that, the slasher evinces a fascination with flesh or meat itself as that which is hidden from view. When the hitchhiker in *Texas Chain Saw I* slits open his hand for the thrill, the onlookers recoil in horror—all but Franklin, who seems fascinated by the realization that all that lies between the visible, knowable outside of the body and its secret insides is one thin membrane, protected only by a collective taboo against its violation. It is no surprise that the rise of the slasher film is concomitant with the development of special effects that let us see with our own eyes the "opened" body.

Victims. Where once there was one victim, Marion Crane, there are now many: five in *Texas Chain Saw I*, four in *Halloween*, fourteen in *Friday the Thirteenth III*, and so on. (As Schoell puts it, "Other filmmakers figured that the only thing better than one beautiful woman being gruesomely murdered was a whole series of beautiful women being gruesomely murdered.")[31] Where once the victim was an adult, now she is typically in her teens (hence the term "teenie-kill pic"). Where once she was female, now she is both girl and boy, though most often and most conspicuously girl. For all this, her essential quality remains the same. Marion is first and foremost a sexual transgressor. The first scenes show her in a hotel room dressing at the end of a lunch hour, asking her lover to marry her. It is, of course, her wish to be made an honest woman of that leads her to abscond with $40,000, an act that leads her to the Bates motel in Fairvale. Here, just as we watched her dress in the opening sequences, we now watch her undress. Moments later, nude in the shower, she dies. A classic publicity poster for *Psycho* shows Janet Leigh with a slightly uncomprehending look on her face sitting on the bed, dressed in a bra and half-slip, looking backward in such a way as to outline her breasts. If it is the task of promotional materials to state in one image the essence of a film, those breasts are what *Psycho* is all about.

In the slasher film, sexual transgressors of both sexes are scheduled for early destruction. The genre is studded with couples trying to find a place beyond purview of parents and employers where they can have sex, and immediately afterwards (or during) being killed. The theme enters the tradition with the Lynda-Bob subplot of *Halloween*. Finding themselves alone in a neighborhood house, Lynda and Bob make hasty use of the master bedroom. Afterwards, Bob goes downstairs for a beer. In the kitchen he is silently dispatched by the killer, Michael, who then covers himself with a sheet (it's Halloween), dons Bob's glasses, and goes upstairs. Supposing the bespectacled ghost in the doorway to be Bob, Lynda jokes, bares her breasts provocatively, and finally, in irritation at "Bob's" stony silence, dials Laurie on the phone. Now the killer advances, strangling her with the telephone cord, so that what Laurie hears on the other end are squeals she takes to be orgasmic. *Halloween II* takes the scene a step further. Here the victims are a nurse and orderly who have sneaked off for sex in the hospital therapy pool. The watching killer, Michael again, turns up the thermostat and, when the orderly goes to check it, kills him. Michael then approaches the nurse from behind (she thinks it's the orderly) and strokes her neck. Only when he moves his hand towards her bare breast and she turns around and sees him does he kill her.

Other directors are less fond than John Carpenter of the mistaken-identity twist. Denise, the English vamp in *Hell Night*, is simply stabbed to death in bed during Seth's postcoital trip to the bathroom. In *He Knows You're Alone*, the student having the affair with her professor is stabbed to death in bed while the professor is downstairs changing a fuse; the professor himself is stabbed when he returns and discovers the body. The postcoital death scene is a staple of the *Friday the Thirteenth* series. Part Three offers a particularly horrible variant. Invigorated by sex, the boy is struck by a gymnastic impulse and begins walking on his hands; the killer slices down on his crotch with a machete. Unaware of the fate of her boyfriend, the girl crawls into a hammock after her shower; the killer impales her from below.[32] Brian De Palma's *Dressed to Kill* presents the infamous example of the sexually desperate wife, first seen masturbating in her morning shower during the credit sequence, who lets herself be picked up later that day in a museum by a man with whom she has sex first in a taxi and later in his apartment. On leaving his place in the evening, she is suddenly attacked and killed in the elevator. The cause-and-effect relationship between (illicit) sex and death could hardly be more clearly drawn. *All* of the killings in *Cruising* occur during (homo)sexual encounters; the difference here is that the killer is one of the participants, not a third party.

Killing those who seek or engage in unauthorized sex amounts to a generic imperative of the slasher film. It is an imperative that crosses gender lines, affecting males as well as females. The numbers are not equal, and the scenes not equally charged; but the fact remains that in most slasher films after 1978 (following *Halloween*), men and boys who go after "wrong" sex also die. This is not the only way males die; they also die incidentally, as girls do, when they get in the killer's way or try to stop him, or when they stray into proscribed territory. The victims of *Hell Night*, *Texas Chain Saw*, and the *Friday the Thirteenth* films are, respectively, those who trespass in Garth Manor, those who stumble into the environs of the slaughterhouse family, and those who become counselors at a cursed camp, all without regard to sex. Boys die, in short, not because they are boys but because they make mistakes.

Some girls die for the same mistakes. Others, however, and always the main one, die—plot after plot develops the motive—because they are female. Just as Norman Bates's oedipal psychosis is such that only female victims will do, so Michael's sexual anger toward his sister (in the *Halloween* series) drives him to kill her—and after her a string of sister surrogates. In much the same way, the transsexual psychiatrist in *Dressed to Kill* is driven to murder only those women who arouse him and remind him of his hated maleness. In *The Eyes of Laura Mars*, the killer's hatred of his mother drives him to prey on women specifically—and, significantly, one gay male. *He Knows You're Alone* features a killer who in consequence of an earlier jilting preys exclusively on brides-to-be.

But even in films in which males and females are killed in roughly even numbers, the lingering images are inevitably female. The death of a male is always swift; even if the victim grasps what is happening to him, he has no time to react or register terror. He is dispatched and the camera moves on. The death of a male is moreover more likely than the death of a female to be viewed from a distance, or viewed only dimly (because of darkness or fog, for example), or indeed to happen offscreen and not be viewed at all. The murders of women, on the other hand, are filmed at closer range, in more graphic detail, and at greater length. The pair of murders at the therapy pool in *Halloween II* illustrates the standard iconography. We see the orderly killed in two shots: the first at close range in the control room, just before the stabbing, and the second as he is being stabbed, through the vapors in a medium long shot; the orderly never even sees his assailant. The nurse's death, on the other hand, is shot entirely in medium closeup. The camera studies her face as it registers first her unwitting complicity (as the killer strokes her neck and shoulders from behind), then apprehension, and then, as she faces him, terror; we see the knife plunge into her repeatedly, hear her cries, and watch her blood fill the therapy pool. This cinematic standard has a venerable history, and it remains intact in the slasher film. Indeed, "tits and a scream" are all that is required of actresses auditioning for the role of victim in "Co-Ed Frenzy," the fictive slasher film whose making constitutes the frame story of *Blow-Out*. It is worth noting that none of the auditioners has both in the desired amount, and that the director must resort to the use of doubles: one for the tits, one for the screams.

Final Girl. The image of the distressed female most likely to linger in memory is the image of the one who did not die: the survivor, or Final Girl. She is the one who encounters the mutilated bodies of her friends and perceives the full extent of the preceding horror and of her own peril; who is chased, cornered, wounded; whom we see scream, stagger, fall, rise, and scream again. She is abject terror personified. If her friends knew they were about to die only seconds before the event, the Final Girl lives with the knowledge for long minutes or hours. She alone looks death in the face; but she alone also finds the strength either to stay the killer long enough to be rescued (ending A) or to kill him herself (ending B). She is inevitably female. In Schoell's words: "The vast majority of contemporary shockers, whether in the sexist mold or not, feature climaxes in which the women fight back against their attackers—the wandering, humorless psychos who populate these films. They often show more courage and levelheadedness than their cringing male counterparts."[33] Her scene occupies the last ten to twenty minutes (thirty in the case of *Texas Chain Saw I*) and constitutes the film's emphatic climax.

The sequence first appears in full-blown form (ending A) in *Texas Chain Saw I* with Sally's spirited self-defense and eventual rescue. Her brother and companions were dispatched suddenly and uncomprehendingly, one by one, but Sally survives the ninth round: long enough to see what has become of her fellows and is in store for her, long enough to meet and even dine with the whole slaughterhouse family, long enough to undergo all manner of torture (including the ancient grandfather's effort to strike a fatal hammer blow on the temple as they bend her over a washtub), and long enough to bolt and rebolt, be caught and recaught, plead and replead for her life, and eventually escape to the highway. For nearly thirty minutes of screen time—a third of the film—we watch her shriek, run, flinch, jump through windows, sustain injury and mutilation. Her will to survive is astonishing; in the end, bloody and staggering, she finds the highway, Leatherface and Hitchhiker in pursuit. Just as they bear down on her, a truck comes by and crushes Hitchhiker. Minutes later a pickup driver plucks Sally up and saves her from Leatherface. The final shots show us Leatherface from her point of view (the bed of the pickup): standing on the highway, wounded (having gashed open his abdomen during the truck episode) but upright, waving the chainsaw crazily over his head.

Halloween's Final Girl is Laurie. Her desperate defense is shorter in duration than Sally's but no less fraught with horror. Limping from a knife wound in the leg, she flees to a garden room and breaks in through the window with a rake. Neighbors hear her screams for help but suspect a Halloween prank and shut the blinds. She gets into her own babysitting house—by throwing a potted plant at a second-story window to rouse the children—just as the killer descends. Minutes later he comes through the window and they grapple; she manages to fell him with a knitting needle and grabs his butcher knife—but drops it when he seems dead. As she goes upstairs to the children, the killer rises, takes the knife, and goes after her. She takes refuge in a closet, lashing the two doorknobs together from the inside. As the killer slashes and stabs at the closet door—we see this from her inside perspective—she bends a hanger into a weapon and, when he breaks the door down, stabs him in the eye. Again thinking him vanquished, she sends the children to the police and sinks down in pain and exhaustion. The killer rises again, but just as he is about to stab her, Doctor Loomis, alerted by the children, rushes in and shoots the killer.

Given the drift in just the four years between *Texas Chain Saw* and *Halloween*—from passive to active defense—it is no surprise that the films following *Halloween* present Final Girls who not only fight back but do so with ferocity and even kill the killer on their own, without help from the outside.[34] Valerie in *Slumber Party Massacre* (a film directed by Amy Jones and scripted by Rita Mae Brown) takes a machete-like weapon to the killer, striking off the bit from his drill, severing his hand, and finally impaling him. Alice assaults and decapitates the killer of *Friday the Thirteenth*. Pursued by the killer in *Hell Night*, Marti pries the gate key from the stiff fingers of a corpse to let herself out of the mansion grounds to safety; when the car won't start, she repairs it on the spot; when the car gets stuck in the roadway, she inside and the killer on top, she releases it in such a way as to cast the killer on the gate's upper spikes. The grittiest of the Final Girls is Nancy of *Nightmare on Elm Street I*. Aware in advance that the killer will be paying her a visit, she plans an elaborate defense. When he enters the house, she dares him to come at her, then runs at him in direct attack. As they struggle, he springs the contraptions she has prepared; he is stunned by a swinging sledge hammer, jolted and half incinerated by an electrical charge, and so on. When he rises yet again, she chases him around the house, bashing him with a chair.[35] In *Texas Chain Saw II*, from 1986, the Final Girl sequence takes mythic measure. Trapped in the underground slaughterhouse, Stretch repeatedly flees, hides, is caught, tortured (at one point forced to don the flayed face of her murdered technician companion), and nearly killed. She escapes with her life chiefly because Leatherface, having developed an affection for her after the crotch episode, is reluctant to ply his chainsaw as the tyrannical Mr. Sawyer commands. Finally Stretch finds her way out, leaving the Texas Ranger to face certain death below, and clambers up a nearby pinnacle, Chop Top in pursuit. At the summit she finds the mummified grandmother, ceremoniously enthroned in an open-air chamber, and next to her a functional chainsaw. She turns the saw on Chop Top, gashing open his abdomen and tossing him off the precipice. The final scene shows her in extreme long shot, in brilliant sunshine, waving the buzzing chainsaw triumphantly overhead. (It is a scene we are invited to compare to the final scene of *Texas Chain Saw I*, in which the wounded Leatherface is shown in long shot at dawn, staggering after the pickup on the highway waving his chainsaw crazily over *his* head.) In Part One the Final Girl, for all her survivor pluck, is, like Red Riding Hood, saved through male agency. In Part Two, however, there is no male agency; the figure so designated, the Texas Ranger, proves so utterly ineffectual that he cannot save himself, much less the girl. The comic ineptitude and failure of would-be "woodsmen" is a repeated theme in the later slasher films. In *Slumber Party Massacre*, the role is played by a woman—though a butch one (the girls' basketball coach). She comes to the slumber party's rescue only to fall victim to the drill herself. But to focus on just who brings the killer down, the Final Girl or a male rescuer, is—as the easy alternation between the two patterns would seem to suggest—to miss the point. The last moment of the Final Girl sequence is finally a footnote to what went before—to the quality of the Final Girl's fight, and more generally to the qualities of character that enable her, of all the characters, to survive what has come to seem unsurvivable.

The Final Girl sequence too is prefigured, if only rudimentarily, in *Psycho*'s final scenes, in which Lila (Marion's sister) is caught reconnoitering in the Bates mansion and nearly killed. Sam (Marion's boyfriend) detains Norman at the motel while Lila snoops about (taking note of Norman's toys). When she perceives Norman's approach, she flees to the basement. Here she encounters the treated corpse of Mrs. Bates and begins screaming in horror. Norman bursts in and is about to strike when Sam enters and grabs him from behind. Like her generic sisters, then, Lila is the spunky inquirer into the Terrible Place: the one who first grasps, however dimly, the past and present danger, the one who looks death in the face, and the one who survives the murderer's last stab.

There the correspondences end, however. The *Psycho* scene turns, after all, on the revelation of Norman's psychotic identity, not on Lila as a character—she enters the film midway and is sketchily drawn—and still less on her self-defense. The Final Girl of the slasher film is presented from the outset as the main character. The practiced viewer distinguishes her from her friends minutes into the film. She is the girl scout, the bookworm, the mechanic. Unlike her girlfriends (and Marion Crane) she is not sexually active. Laurie (*Halloween*) is teased because of her fears about dating, and Marti (*Hell Night*) explains to the boy with whom she finds herself sharing a room that they will have separate beds. Although Stretch (*Texas Chain Saw II*) is hardly virginal, she is not available, either; early in the film she pointedly turns down a date, and we are given to understand that she is, for the present, unattached and even lonely. So too Stevie of Carpenter's *The Fog*, like Stretch a disk jockey; divorced mother and a newcomer in town, she is unattached and lonely but declines male attention. The Final Girl is also watchful to the point of paranoia; small signs of danger that her friends ignore she takes in and turns over. Above all she is intelligent and resourceful in extreme situations. Thus Laurie even at her most desperate, cornered in a closet, has the wit to grab a hanger from the rack and bend it into a weapon; Marti can hot-wire her getaway car, the killer in pursuit; and the psych major of *Friday the Thirteenth II*, on seeing the enshrined head of Mrs. Voorhees, can stop Jason in his tracks by assuming a stridently maternal voice. Finally, although she is always smaller and weaker than the killer, she grapples with him energetically and convincingly.

The Final Girl is boyish, in a word. Just as the killer is not fully masculine, she is not fully feminine—not, in any case, feminine in the ways of her friends. Her smartness, gravity, competence in mechanical and other practical matters, and sexual reluctance set her apart from the other girls and ally her, ironically, with the very boys she fears or rejects, not to speak of the killer himself. Lest we miss the point, it is spelled out in her name: Stevie, Marti, Terry, Laurie, Stretch, Will. Not only the conception of the hero in *Alien* and *Aliens* but also her name, Ripley, owes a clear debt to slasher tradition.

With the introduction of the Final Girl, then, the *Psycho* formula is radically altered. It is not merely a question of enlarging the figure of Lila but of absorbing into her role, in varying degrees, the functions of Arbogast (investigator) and Sam (rescuer) and restructuring the narrative action from beginning to end around her progress in relation to the killer. In other words, *Psycho*'s detective plot, revolving around a revelation, yields in the modern slasher film to a hero plot, revolving around the main character's struggle with and eventual triumph over evil. But for the femaleness, however qualified, of that main character, the story is a standard one of tale and epic.

Shock. One reason that the shower sequence in *Psycho* has "evoked more study, elicited more comment, and generated more shot-for-shot analysis from a technical viewpoint than any other in the history of cinema" is that it suggests so much but shows so little.[36] Of the forty-odd shots in as many seconds that figure the murder, only a single fleeting one actually shows the body being stabbed. The others present us with a rapid-fire concatenation of images of the knife-wielding hand, parts of Marion, parts of the shower, and finally the bloody water as it swirls down the drain. The horror resides less in the actual images than in their summary implication.

Although Hitchcock is hardly the first director to prefer the oblique rendition of physical violence, he may, to judge from current examples, be one of the last. For better or worse, the perfection of special effects has made it possible to show maiming and dismemberment in extraordinarily credible detail. The horror genres are the natural repositories of such effects; what can be done is done, and slashers, at the bottom of the category, do it most and worst. Thus we see a head being stepped on so that the eyes pop out, a face being flayed, a decapitation, a hypodermic needle penetrating an eyeball in closeup, and so on.

With this new explicitness also comes a new tone. If the horror of *Psycho* was taken seriously, the "horror" of the slasher films is of a rather more complicated sort. Audiences express uproarious disgust ("gross!") as often as they express fear, and it is clear that the makers of slasher films pursue the combination. More particularly: spectators fall silent while the victim is being stalked, scream out at the first stab, and make loud noises of revulsion at the sight of the bloody stump. The rapid alternation between registers—between something like "real" horror on one hand and a camp, self-parodying Horror on the other—is by now one of the most conspicuous characteristics of the tradition. In its cultivation of intentionally outrageous excess, the slasher film intersects with the cult film, a genre devoted to such effects. Just what this self-ironizing relation to taboo signifies, beyond a remarkably competent audience, is unclear—it is yet another aspect of the phenomenon that has lain beyond criticism—but for the time being it stands as a defining characteristic of the lower genres of popular culture.

The Body

On the face of it, the relation between the sexes in slasher films could hardly be clearer. The killer is with few exceptions recognizably human and distinctly male; his fury is unmistakeably sexual in both roots and expression; his victims are mostly women, often sexually free and always young and beautiful ones. Just how essential this victim is to horror is suggested by her historical durability. If the killer has over time been variously figured as shark, fog, gorilla, birds, and slime, the victim is eternally and prototypically the damsel. Cinema hardly invented the pattern. It has simply given visual expression to the abiding proposition that, in Poe's famous formulation, the death of a beautiful woman is the "most poetical topic in the world."[37] As slasher director Dario Argento puts it, "I like women, especially beautiful ones. If they have a good face and figure, I would much prefer to watch them being murdered than an ugly girl or a man."[38] Brian De Palma elaborates: "Women in peril work better in the suspense genre. It all goes back to the *Perils of Pauline*. . . . If you have a haunted house and you have a woman walking around with a candelabrum, you fear more for her than you would for a husky man."[39] Or Hitchcock, during the filming of *The Birds*: "I always believe in following the advice of the playwright Sardou. He said 'Torture the women!' The trouble today is that we don't torture women enough."[40] What the directors do not say, but show, is that "Pauline" is at her very most effective in a state of undress, borne down upon by a blatantly phallic murderer, even gurgling orgasmically as she dies. The case could be made that the slasher films available at a given neighborhood video rental outlet recommend themselves to censorship under the Dworkin-MacKinnon guidelines at least as readily as the hard-core films the next section over, at which that legislation is aimed; for if some victims are men, the argument goes, most are women, and the women are brutalized in ways that come too close to real life for comfort. But what this line of reasoning does not take into account is the figure of the Final Girl. Because slashers lie for all practical purposes beyond the purview of legitimate criticism, and to the extent that they have been reviewed at all have been reviewed on an individual basis, the phenomenon of the female victim-hero has scarcely been acknowledged.

It is, of course, "on the face of it" that most of the public discussion of film takes place—from the Dworkin-MacKinnon legislation to Siskel's and Ebert's reviews to our own talks with friends on leaving the movie house. Underlying that discussion is the assumption that the sexes are what they seem; that screen males represent the Male and screen females the Female; that this identification along gender lines authorizes impulses toward sexual violence in males and encourages impulses toward victimization in females. In part because of the massive authority cinema by nature accords the image, even academic film criticism has been slow—slower than literary criticism—to get beyond appearances. Film may not appropriate the mind's eye, but it certainly encroaches on it; the gender characteristics of a screen figure are a visible and audible given for the duration of the film. To the extent that the possibility of cross-gender identification has been entertained, it has been in the direction female-with-male. Thus some critics have wondered whether the female viewer, faced with the screen image of a masochistic/narcissistic female, might not rather elect to "betray her sex and identify with the masculine point of view."[41] The reverse question—whether men might not also, on occasion, elect to betray their sex and identify with screen females—has scarcely been asked, presumably on the assumption that men's interests are well served by the traditional patterns of cinematic representation. Then too there is the matter of the "male gaze." As E. Ann Kaplan sums it up: "Within the film text itself, men gaze at women, who become objects of the gaze; the spectator, in turn, is made to identify with this male gaze, and to objectify the women on the screen; and the camera's original 'gaze' comes into play in the very act of filming."[42] But if it is so that all of us, male and female alike, are by these processes "made to" identify with men and "against" women, how are we then to explain the appeal to a largely male audience of a film genre that features a female victim-hero? The slasher film brings us squarely up against a fundamental question of film analysis: where does the literal end and the figurative begin; how do the two levels interact and what is the significance of the particular interaction; and to which, in arriving at a political judgment (as we are inclined to do in the case of low horror and pornography), do we assign priority?

A figurative or functional analysis of the slasher begins with the processes of point of view and identification. The male viewer seeking a male character, even a vicious one, with whom to identify in a sustained way has little to hang on to in the standard example. On the good side, the only viable candidates are the schoolmates or friends of the girls. They are for the most part marginal, undeveloped characters; more to the point, they tend to die early in the film. If the traditional horror film gave the male spectator a last-minute hero with whom to identify, thereby "indulging his vanity as protector of the helpless female,"[43] the slasher eliminates or attenuates that role beyond any such function; indeed, would-be rescuers are not infrequently blown away for their efforts, leaving the girl to fight her own fight. Policemen, fathers, and sheriffs appear only long enough to demonstrate risible incomprehension and incompetence. On the bad side, there is the killer. The killer is often unseen, or barely glimpsed, during the first part of the film, and what we do see, when we finally get a good look, hardly invites immediate or conscious empathy. He is commonly masked, fat, deformed, or dressed as a woman. Or "he" *is* a woman: woe to the viewer of *Friday the Thirteenth I* who identifies with the male killer only to discover, in the film's final sequences, that he was not a man at all but a middle-aged woman. In either case, the killer is himself eventually killed or otherwise evacuated from the narrative. No male character of any stature lives to tell the tale.

The one character of stature who does live to tell the tale is of course female. The Final Girl is introduced at the beginning and is the only character to be developed in any psychological detail. We understand immediately from the attention paid it that hers is the main story line. She is intelligent, watchful, level-headed; the first character to sense something amiss and the only one to deduce from the accumulating evidence the patterns and extent of the threat; the only one, in other words, whose perspective approaches our own privileged understanding of the situation. We register her horror as she stumbles on the corpses of her friends; her paralysis in the face of death duplicates those moments of the universal nightmare experience on which horror frankly trades. When she downs the killer, we are triumphant. She is by any measure the slasher film's hero. This is not to say that our attachment to her is exclusive and unremitting, only that it adds up, and that in the closing sequence it is very close to absolute.

An analysis of the camerawork bears this out. Much is made of the use of the I-camera to represent the killer's point of view. In these passages—they are usually few and brief, but powerful—we see through his eyes and (on the sound track) hear his breathing and heartbeat. His and our vision is partly obscured by bushes or windowblinds in the foreground. By such means we are forced, the argument goes, to identify with the killer. In fact, however, the relation between camera point of view and the processes of viewer identification are poorly understood; the fact that Steven Spielberg can stage an attack in *Jaws* from the shark's point of view (underwater, rushing upward toward the swimmer's flailing legs) or Hitchcock an attack in *The Birds* from the birds-eye perspective (from the sky, as they gather to swoop down on the streets of Bodega Bay) would seem to suggest either that the viewer's identificatory powers are unbelievably elastic or that point-of-view shots can sometimes be pro forma.[44] But let us for the moment accept the equation point of view = identification. We are linked, in this way, with the killer in the early part of the film, usually before we have seen him directly and before we have come to know the Final Girl in any detail. Our closeness to him wanes as our closeness to the Final Girl waxes—a shift underwritten by story line as well as camera position. By the end, point of view is hers: we are in the closet with her, watching with her eyes the knife blade stab through the door; in the room with her as the killer breaks through the window and grabs at her; in the car with her as the killer stabs through the convertible top, and so on. With her, we become if not the killer of the killer then the agent of his expulsion from the narrative vision. If, during the film's course, we shifted our sympathies back and forth, and dealt them out to other characters along the way, we belong in the end to the Final Girl; there is no alternative. When Stretch eviscerates Chop Top at the end of *Texas Chain Saw II*, she is literally the only character left alive, on either side.

Audience response ratifies this design. Observers unanimously stress the readiness of the "live" audience to switch sympathies in midstream, siding now with the killer and now, and finally, with the Final Girl. As Schoell, whose book on shocker films wrestles with its own monster, "the feminists," puts it:

Social critics make much of the fact that male audience members cheer on the misogynous misfits in these movies as they rape, plunder, and murder their screaming, writhing female victims. Since these same critics walk out of the moviehouse in disgust long before the movie is over, they don't realize that these same men cheer on (with renewed enthusiasm, in fact) the heroines, who are often as strong, sexy, and independent as the [earlier] victims, as they blow away the killer with a shotgun or get him between the eyes with a machete. All of these men are said to be identifying with the maniac, but they enjoy *his* death throes the most of all, and applaud the heroine with admiration.[45]

What filmmakers seem to know better than film critics is that gender is less a wall than a permeable membrane.[46]

No one who has read "Red Riding Hood" to a small boy or participated in a viewing of, say, *Deliverance* (an all-male story that women find as gripping as men) or, more recently, *Alien* and *Aliens*, with whose space-age female Rambo, herself a Final Girl, male viewers seem to engage with ease, can doubt the phenomenon of cross-gender identification.[47] This fluidity of engaged perspective is in keeping with the universal claims of the psychoanalytic model: the threat function and the victim function coexist in the same unconscious, regardless of anatomical sex. But why, if viewers can identify across gender lines and if the root experience of horror is sex blind, are the screen sexes not interchangeable? Why not more and better female killers, and why (in light of the maleness of the majority audience) not Pauls as well as Paulines? The fact that horror film so stubbornly genders the killer male and the principal victim female would seem to suggest that representation itself is at issue—that the sensation of bodily fright derives not exclusively from repressed content, as Freud insisted, but also from the bodily manifestations of that content.

Nor is the gender of the principals as straightforward as it first seems. The killer's phallic purpose, as he thrusts his drill or knife into the trembling bodies of young women, is unmistakeable. At the same time, however, his masculinity is severely qualified: he ranges from the virginal or sexually inert to the transvestite or transsexual, is spiritually divided ("the mother half of his mind") or even equipped with vulva and vagina. Although the killer of *God Told Me To* is represented and taken as a male in the film text, he is revealed, by the doctor who delivered him, to have been sexually ambiguous from birth: "I truly could not tell whether that child was male or female; it was as if the sexual gender had not been determined . . . as if it were being developed."[48] In this respect, slasher killers have much in common with the monsters of classic horror—monsters who, in Linda Williams's formulation, represent not just "an eruption of the normally repressed animal sexual energy of the civilized male" but also the "power and potency of a *non-phallic* sexuality." To the extent that the monster is constructed as feminine, the horror film thus expresses female desire only to show how monstrous it is.[49] The intention is manifest in *Aliens*, in which the Final Girl, Ripley, is pitted in the climactic scene against the most terrifying "alien" of all: an egg-laying Mother.

Nor can we help noticing the "intrauterine" quality of the Terrible Place, dark and often damp, in which the killer lives or lurks and whence he stages his most terrifying attacks. "It often happens," Freud wrote, "that neurotic men declare that they feel there is something uncanny about the female genital organs. This *unheimlich* place, however, is an entrance to the former *Heim* [home] of all human beings, to the place where each one of us lived once upon a time and in the beginning. . . . In this case too then, the *unheimlich* is what once was *heimisch*, familiar; the prefix '*un*' ['un-'] is the token of repression."[50] It is the exceptional film that does not mark as significant the moment that the killer leaps out of the dark recesses of a corridor or cavern at the trespassing victim, usually the Final Girl. Long after the other particulars have faded, the viewer will remember the images of Amy assaulted from the dark halls of a morgue (*He Knows You're Alone*), Sally or Stretch facing dismemberment in the ghastly dining room or underground labyrinth of the slaughterhouse family (*Texas Chain Saw I–II*), or Melanie trapped in the attic as the savage birds close in (*The Birds*). In such scenes of convergence the Other is at its bisexual mightiest, the victim at her tiniest, and the component of sadomasochism at its most blatant.

The gender of the Final Girl is likewise compromised from the outset by her masculine interests, her inevitable sexual reluctance (penetration, it seems, constructs the female), her apartness from other girls, sometimes her name. At the level of the cinematic apparatus, her unfemininity is signaled clearly by her exercise of the "active investigating gaze" normally reserved for males and hideously punished in females when they assume it themselves; tentatively at first and then aggressively, the Final Girl looks *for* the killer, even tracking him to his forest hut or his underground labyrinth, and then *at* him, therewith bringing him, often for the first time, into our vision as well.[51] When, in the final scene, she stops screaming, looks at the killer, and reaches for the knife (sledge hammer, scalpel, gun, machete, hanger, knitting needle, chainsaw), she addresses the killer on his own terms. To the critics' objection that *Halloween* in effect punished female sexuality, director John Carpenter responded:

They [the critics] completely missed the boat there, I think. Because if you turn it around, the one girl who is the most sexually uptight just keeps stabbing this guy with a long knife. She's the most sexually frustrated. She's the one that killed him. Not because she's a virgin, but because all that repressed energy starts coming out. She uses all those phallic symbols on the guy. . . . She and the killer have a certain link: sexual repression.[52]

For all its perversity, Carpenter's remark does underscore the sense of affinity, even recognition, that attends the final encounter. But the "certain link" that puts killer and Final Girl on terms, at least briefly, is more than "sexual repression." It is also a shared masculinity, materialized in "all those phallic symbols"—and it is also a shared femininity, materialized in what comes next (and what Carpenter, perhaps significantly, fails to mention): the castration, literal or symbolic, of the killer at her hands. His eyes may be put out, his hand severed, his body impaled or shot, his belly gashed, or his genitals sliced away or bitten off. The Final Girl has not just manned herself; she specifically unmans an oppressor whose masculinity was in question to begin with. By the time the drama has played itself out, darkness yields to light (often as day breaks) and the close quarters of the barn (closet, elevator, attic, basement) give way to the open expanse of the yard (field, road, lakescape, cliff). With the Final Girl's appropriation of "all those phallic symbols" comes the quelling, the dispelling, of the "uterine" threat as well. Consider again the paradigmatic ending of *Texas Chain Saw II*. From the underground labyrinth, murky and bloody, in which she faced saw, knife, and hammer, Stretch escapes through a culvert into the open air. She clambers up the jutting rock and with a chainsaw takes her stand. When her last assailant comes at her, she slashes open his lower abdomen—the sexual symbolism is all too clear—and flings him off the cliff. Again, the final scene shows her in extreme long shot, standing on the pinnacle, drenched in sunlight, buzzing chainsaw held overhead.

The tale would indeed seem to be one of sex and parents. The patently erotic threat is easily seen as the materialized projection of the dreamer's (viewer's) own incestuous fears and desires. It is this disabling cathexis to one's parents that must be killed and rekilled in the service of sexual autonomy. When the Final Girl stands at last in the light of day with the knife in her hand, she has delivered herself into the adult world. Carpenter's equation of the Final Girl with the killer has more than a grain of truth. The killers of *Psycho*, *The Eyes of Laura Mars*, *Friday the Thirteenth II–VI*, and *Cruising*, among others, are explicitly figured as sons in the psychosexual grip of their mothers (or fathers, in the case of *Cruising*). The difference is between past and present and between failure and success. The Final Girl enacts in the present, and successfully, the parenticidal struggle that the killer himself enacted unsuccessfully in his own past—a past that constitutes the film's backstory. She is what the killer once was; he is what she could become should she fail in her battle for sexual selfhood. "You got a choice, boy," says the tyrannical father of Leatherface in *Texas Chain Saw II*, "sex or the saw; you never know about sex, but the saw—the saw is the family."

But the tale is no less one of maleness. If the early experience of the oedipal drama can be —is perhaps ideally—enacted in female form, the achievement of full adulthood requires the assumption and, apparently, brutal employment of the phallus. The helpless child is gendered feminine; the autonomous adult or subject is gendered masculine; the passage from childhood to adulthood entails a shift from feminine to masculine. It is the male killer's tragedy that his incipient femininity is not reversed but completed (castration) and the Final Girl's victory that her incipient masculinity is not thwarted but realized (phallicization). When De Palma says that female frailty is a predicate of the suspense genre, he proposes, in effect, that the lack of the phallus, for Lacan the privileged signifier of the symbolic order of culture, is itself simply horrifying, at least in the mind of the male observer. Where pornography (the argument goes) resolves that lack through a process of fetishization that allows a breast or leg or whole body to stand in for the missing member, the slasher film resolves it either through eliminating the woman (earlier victims) or reconstituting her as masculine (Final Girl). The moment at which the Final Girl is effectively phallicized is the moment that the plot halts and horror ceases. Day breaks, and the community returns to its normal order.

Casting psychoanalytic verities in female form has a venerable cinematic history. Ingmar Bergman has made a career of it, and Woody Allen shows signs of following his lead. One immediate and practical advantage, by now presumably unconscious on the part of makers as well as viewers, has to do with a preestablished cinematic "language" for capturing the moves and moods of the female body and face. The cinematic gaze, we are told, is male, and just as that gaze "knows" how to fetishize the female form in pornography (in a way that it does not "know" how to fetishize the male form),[53] so it "knows," in horror, how to track a woman ascending a staircase in a scary house and how to study her face from an angle above as she first hears the killer's footfall. A set of conventions we now take for granted simply "sees" males and females differently.

To this cinematic habit may be added the broader range of emotional expression traditionally allowed women. Angry displays of force may belong to the male, but crying, cowering, screaming, fainting, trembling, begging for mercy belong to the female. Abject terror, in short, is gendered feminine, and the more concerned a given film with that condition—and it is the essence of modern horror—the more likely the femaleness of the victim. It is no accident that male victims in slasher films are killed swiftly or offscreen, and that prolonged struggles, in which the victim has time to contemplate her imminent destruction, inevitably figure females. Only when one encounters the rare expression of abject terror on the part of a male (as in *I Spit on Your Grave*) does one apprehend the full extent of the cinematic double standard in such matters.[54]

It is also the case that gender displacement can provide a kind of identificatory buffer, an emotional remove, that permits the majority audience to explore taboo subjects in the relative safety of vicariousness. Just as Bergman came to realize that he could explore castration anxiety more freely via depictions of hurt female bodies (witness the genital mutilation of Karin in *Cries and Whispers*), so the makers of slasher films seem to know that sadomasochistic incest fantasies sit more easily with the male viewer when the visible player is female. It is one thing for that viewer to hear the psychiatrist intone at the end of *Psycho* that Norman as a boy (in the backstory) was abnormally attached to his mother; it would be quite another to see that attachment dramatized in the present, to experience in nightmare form the elaboration of Norman's (the viewer's own) fears and desires. If the former is playable in male form, the latter, it seems, is not.

The Final Girl is, on reflection, a congenial double for the adolescent male. She is feminine enough to act out in a gratifying way, a way unapproved for adult males, the terrors and masochistic pleasures of the underlying fantasy, but not so feminine as to disturb the structures of male competence and sexuality. Her sexual inactivity, in this reading, becomes all but inevitable; the male viewer may be willing to enter into the vicarious experience of defending himself from the possibility of symbolic penetration on the part of the killer, but real vaginal penetration on the diegetic level is evidently more femaleness than he can bear. The question then arises whether the Final Girls of slasher films—Stretch, Stevie, Marti, Will, Terry, Laurie, and Ripley—are not boyish for the same reason that the female "victims" in Victorian flagellation literature—"Georgy," "Willy"—are boyish: because they are transformed males. The transformation, Steven Marcus writes, "is itself both a defense against and a disavowal of the fantasy it is simultaneously expressing—namely, that a *boy* is being beaten—that is, loved—by another man."[55] What is represented as male-on-female violence, in short, is figuratively speaking male-on-male sex. For Marcus, the literary picture of flagellation, in which *girls* are beaten, is utterly belied by the descriptions (in *My Secret Life*) of real-life episodes in which the persons being beaten are not girls at all but "gentlemen" dressed in women's clothes ("He had a woman's dress on tucked up to his waist, showing his naked rump and thighs. . . . On his head was a woman's cap tied carefully round his face to hide whiskers") and whipped by prostitutes. Reality, Marcus writes, "puts the literature of flagellation out of the running . . . by showing how that literature is a completely distorted and idealized version of what actually happens."[56] Applied to the slasher film, this logic reads the femaleness of the Final Girl (at least up to the point of her transformation) and indeed of the women victims in general as only apparent, the artifact of heterosexual deflection. It may be through the female body that the body of the audience is sensationalized, but the sensation is an entirely male affair.

At least one director, Hitchcock, explicitly located thrill in the equation victim = audience. So we judge from his marginal jottings in the shooting instructions for the shower scene in *Psycho*: "The slashing. An impression of a knife slashing, as if tearing at the very screen, ripping the film."[57] Not just the body of Marion is to be ruptured, but also the body on the other side of the film and screen: our witnessing body. As Marion is to Norman, the audience of *Psycho* is to Hitchcock; as the audiences of horror film in general are to the directors of those films, female is to male. Hitchcock's "torture the women" then means, simply, torture the audience. De Palma's remarks about female frailty likewise contemplate a male-on-"female" relationship between director and viewer. Cinefantastic horror, in short, succeeds in the production of sensation to more or less the degree that it succeeds in incorporating its spectators as "feminine" and then violating that body—which recoils, shudders, cries out collectively—in ways otherwise imaginable, for males, only in nightmare. The equation is nowhere more plainly put than in David Cronenberg's *Videodrome*. Here the threat is a mind-destroying video signal and the victims television viewers. Despite the (male) hero's efforts to defend his mental (and physical) integrity, a deep, vagina-like gash appears on his lower abdomen. Says the media conspirator as he thrusts a videocassette into the victim's gaping wound, "You must open yourself completely to this."

If the slasher film is "on the face of it" a genre with at least a strong female presence, it is in these figurative readings a thoroughly strong male exercise, one that finally has very little to do with femaleness and very much to do with phallocentrism. Figuratively seen, the Final Girl is a male surrogate in things oedipal, a homoerotic stand-in, the audience incorporate; to the extent she "means" girl at all, it is only for purposes of signifying phallic lack, and even that meaning is nullified in the final scenes. Our initial question—how to square a female victim-hero with a largely male audience—is not so much answered as it is obviated in these readings. The Final Girl is (apparently) female not despite the maleness of the audience, but precisely because of it. The discourse is wholly masculine, and females figure in it only insofar as they "read" some aspect of male experience. To applaud the Final Girl as a feminist development, as some reviews of *Aliens* have done with Ripley, is, in light of her figurative meaning, a particularly grotesque expression of wishful thinking.[58] She is simply an agreed-upon fiction, and the male viewer's use of her as a vehicle for his own sadomasochistic fantasies an act of perhaps timeless dishonesty.

For all their immediate appeal, these figurative readings loosen as many ends as they tie together. The audience, we have said, is predominantly male; but what about the women in it? Do we dismiss them as male-identified and account for their experience as an "immasculated" act of collusion with the oppressor?[59] This is a strong judgment to apply to large numbers of women; for while it may be that the audience for slasher films is mainly male, that does not mean that there are not also many female viewers who actively like such films, and of course there are also women, however few, who script, direct, and produce them. These facts alone oblige us at least to consider the possibility that female fans find a meaning in the text and image of these films that is less inimical to their own interests than the figurative analysis would have us believe. Or should we conclude that males and females read these films differently in some fundamental sense? Do females respond to the text (the literal) and males the subtext (the figurative)?[60]

Some such notion of differential understanding underlies the homoerotic reading. The silent presupposition of that reading is that male identification with the female as female cannot be, and that the male viewer/reader who adjoins feminine experience does so only by homosexual conversion. But does female identification with male experience then similarly indicate a lesbian conversion? Or are the processes of patriarchy so one-way that the female can identify with the male directly, but the male can identify with the female only by transsexualizing her? Does the Final Girl mean "girl" to her female viewers and "boy" to her male viewers? If her masculine features qualify her as a transformed boy, do not the feminine features of the killer qualify him as a transformed woman (in which case the homoerotic reading can be maintained only by defining that "woman" as phallic and retransforming her into a male)? Striking though it is, the analogy between the Victorian flagellation story's Georgy and the slasher film's Stretch falters at the moment that Stretch turns on her assailant and unmans him. Are we to suppose that a homoerotic beating fantasy suddenly yields to what folklorists call a "lack-liquidated" fantasy? Further: is it simple coincidence that this combination tale—trials, then triumph—bears such a striking resemblance to the classic (male) hero story? Does the standard hero story featuring an anatomical female "mean" differently from one featuring an anatomical male?

As Marcus perceived, the relationship between the Georgy stories of flagellation literature and the real-life anecdote of the Victorian gentleman is a marvelously telling one. In his view, the maleness of the latter must prove the essential or functional maleness of the former. What his analysis does not come to full grips with, however, is the clothing the gentleman wears—not that of a child, as Marcus's "childish" reading of the scene contemplates, but explicitly that of a woman.[61] These women's clothes can of course be understood, within the terms of the homoerotic interpretation, as a last-ditch effort on the part of the gentleman to dissociate himself from the (incestuous) homosexuality implicit in his favored sexual practice. But can they not just as well, and far more economically, be explained as part and parcel of a fantasy of literal femaleness? By the same token, cannot the femaleness of the gentleman's literary representatives—the girls of the flagellation stories—be understood as the obvious, even necessary, extension of that man's dress and cap? The same dress and cap, I suggest, haunt the margins of the slasher film. This is not to deny the deflective convenience, for the male spectator (and filmmaker), of a female victim-hero in a context so fraught with taboo; it is only to suggest that the femaleness of that character is also conditioned by a kind of imaginative curiosity about the feminine in and of itself.

So too the psychoanalytic case. These films do indeed seem to pit the child in a struggle, at once terrifying and attractive, with the parental Other, and it is a rare example that does not directly thematize parent-child relations. But if Freud stressed the maternal source of the *unheimlich*, the Other of our films is decidedly androgynous: female/feminine in aspects of character and place (the "intra-uterine" locale) but male in anatomy. Conventional logic may interpret the killer as the phallic mother of the transformed boy (the Final Girl), but the text itself does not compel such a reading. On the contrary, the text at every level presents us with hermaphroditic constructions—constructions that draw attention to themselves and demand to be taken on their own terms.

For if we define the Final Girl as nothing more than a figurative male, what do we then make of the context of the spectacular gender play in which she is emphatically situated? In his essay on the uncanny, Freud rejected out of hand Jentsch's theory that the experience of horror proceeds from intellectual uncertainty (curiosity?)—feelings of confusion, induced by an author or a coincidence, about who, what, and where one is.[62] One wonders, however, whether Freud would have been quite so dismissive if, instead of the mixed materials he used as evidence, he were presented with a coherent story corpus—forty slashers, say—in which the themes of incest and separation were relentlessly played out by a female character, and further in which gender identity was repeatedly thematized as an issue in and of itself. For although the factors we have considered thus far—the conventions of the male gaze, the feminine constitution of abject terror, the value for the male viewer of emotional distance from the taboos in question, the special horror that may inhere, for the male audience, in phallic lack, the homoerotic deflection—go a long way in explaining why it is we have Pauline rather than Paul as our victim-hero, they do not finally account for our strong sense that gender is simply being played with, and that part of the thrill lies precisely in the resulting "intellectual uncertainty" of sexual identity.

The "play of pronoun function" that underlies and defines the cinefantastic is nowhere more richly manifested than in the slasher; if the genre has an aesthetic base, it is exactly that of a visual identity game. Consider, for example, the by now standard habit of letting us view the action in the first person long before revealing who or what the first person *is*. In the opening sequence of *Halloween I*, "we" are belatedly revealed to ourselves, after committing a murder in the cinematic first person, as a six-year-old boy. The surprise is often within gender, but it is also, in a striking number of cases, across gender. Again, *Friday the Thirteenth I*, in which "we" stalk and kill a number of teenagers over the course of an hour of screen time without even knowing who "we" are; we are invited, by conventional expectation and by glimpses of "our" own bodily parts—a heavily booted foot, a roughly gloved hand—to suppose that "we" are male, but "we" are revealed, at film's end, as a woman. If this is the most dramatic case of pulling out the gender rug, it is by no means the only one. In *Dressed to Kill*, we are led to believe, again by means of glimpses, that "we" are female—only to discover, in the denouement, that "we" are a male in drag. In *Psycho*, the dame we glimpse holding the knife with a "visible virility quite obscene in an old lady" is later revealed, after additional gender teasing, to be Norman in his mother's clothes.[63] *Psycho II* plays much the same game. *Cruising* (in which, not accidentally, transvestites play a prominent role) adjusts the terms along heterosexual/homosexual lines. The tease here is whether the originally straight detective assigned to the string of murders in a gay community does or does not succumb to his assumed homosexual identity; the camerawork leaves us increasingly uncertain as to his (our) sexual inclinations, not to speak of his (our) complicity in the crimes. Even at film's end we are not sure who "we" were during several of the first-person sequences.[64]

The gender-identity game, in short, is too patterned and too pervasive in the slasher film to be dismissed as supervenient. It would seem instead to be an integral element of the particular brand of bodily sensation in which the genre trades. Nor is it exclusive to horror. It is directly thematized in comic terms in the recent "gender benders" *Tootsie* (in which a man passes himself off as a woman) and *All of Me* (in which a woman is literally introjected into a man and affects his speech, movement, and thought). It is also directly thematized, in the form of bisexual and androgynous figures and relations, in such cult films as *Pink Flamingos* and *The Rocky Horror Picture Show*. (Some version of it is indeed enacted every few minutes on MTV.) It is further thematized (predictably enough, given their bodily concerns) in such pornographic films as *Every Woman Has a Fantasy*, in which a man, in order to gain access to a women's group in which sexual fantasies are discussed, dresses and presents himself as a woman. (The degree to which "male" pornography in general relies for its effect on cross-gender identification remains an open question; the proposition makes a certain sense of the obligatory lesbian sequences and the phenomenal success of *Behind the Green Door*, to pick just two examples.[65]) All of these films, and others like them, seem to be asking some version of the question: what would it be like to be, or to seem to be, if only temporarily, a woman? Taking exception to the reception of *Tootsie* as a feminist film, Elaine Showalter argues that the success of "Dorothy Michaels" (the Dustin Hoffman character), as far as both plot and audience are concerned, lies in the veiling of masculine power in feminine costume. *Tootsie*'s cross-dressing, she writes,

is a way of promoting the notion of masculine power while masking it. In psychoanalytic theory, the male transvestite is not a powerless man; according to the psychiatrist Robert Stoller, in *Sex and Gender*, he is a "phallic woman" who can tell himself that "he is, or with practice will become, a better woman than a biological female if he chooses to do so." When it is safe or necessary, the transvestite "gets great pleasure in revealing that he is a male-woman. . . . The pleasure in tricking the unsuspecting into thinking he is a woman, and then revealing his maleness (e.g., by suddenly dropping his voice) is not so much erotic as it is proof that there is such a thing as a woman with a penis." Dorothy's effectiveness is the literal equivalent of speaking softly and carrying a big stick.[66]

By the same literalistic token, then, Stretch's success must lie in the fact that in the end, at least, she "speaks loudly" *even though* she carries *no* "stick." Just as "Dorothy's" voice slips serve to remind us that her character really is male, so the Final Girl's "tits and scream" serve more or less continuously to remind us that she really is female—even as, and despite the fact that, she in the end acquits herself "like a man."[67] Her chainsaw is thus what "Dorothy Michaels's" skirt is: a figuration of what she *does* and what she *seems*, as opposed to—and the films turn on the opposition—what she *is*. The idea that appearance and behavior do not necessarily indicate sex—indeed, can misindicate sex—is predicated on the understanding that sex is one thing and gender another; in practice, that sex is life, a less-than-interesting given, but that gender is theater. Whatever else it may be, Stretch's waving of the chainsaw is a moment of high drag. Its purpose is not to make us forget that she is a girl but to thrust that fact on us. The moment, it is probably fair to say, is also one that openly mocks the literary/cinematic conventions of symbolic representation.

It may be just this theatricalization of gender that makes possible the willingness of the male viewer to submit himself to a brand of spectator experience that

Hitchcock designated as "feminine" in 1960 and that has become only more so since then. In classic horror, the "feminization" of the audience is intermittent and ceases early. Our relationship with Marion's body in *Psycho* halts abruptly at the moment of its greatest intensity (slashing, ripping, tearing). The considerable remainder of the film distributes our bruised sympathies among several lesser figures, male and female, in such a way and at such length as to ameliorate the Marion experience and leave us, in the end, more or less recuperated in our (presumed) masculinity. Like Marion, the Final Girl is the designated victim, the incorporation of the audience, the slashing, ripping, and tearing of whose body will cause us to flinch and scream out in our seats. But unlike Marion, she does not die. If *Psycho*, like other classic horror films, solves the femininity problem by obliterating the female and replacing her with representatives of the masculine order (mostly but not inevitably males), the modern slasher solves it by regendering the woman. We are, as an audience, in the end "masculinized" by and through the very figure by and through whom we were earlier "feminized." The same body does for both, and that body is female.

The last point is the crucial one: the same *female* body does for both. The Final Girl 1) undergoes agonizing trials, and 2) virtually or actually destroys the antagonist and saves herself. By the lights of folk tradition, she is not a heroine, for whom phase 1 consists in being saved by someone else, but a hero, who rises to the occasion and defeats the adversary with his own wit and hands. Part 1 of the story sits well on the female; it is the heart of heroine stories in general (Red Riding Hood, Pauline), and in some figurative sense, in ways we have elaborated in some detail, it is gendered feminine even when played by a male. Odysseus's position, trapped in the cave of the Cyclops, is after all not so different from Pauline's position tied to the tracks or Sally's trapped in the dining room of the slaughterhouse family. The decisive moment, as far as the fixing of gender is concerned, lies in what happens next: those who save themselves are male, and those who are saved by others are female. No matter how "feminine" his experience in phase 1, the traditional hero, if he rises against his adversary and saves himself in phase 2, will be male.

What is remarkable about the slasher film is that it comes close to reversing the priorities. Presumably for the various functional or figurative reasons we have considered in this essay, phase 1 wants a female: on that point all slashers from *Psycho* on are agreed. Abject fear is still gendered feminine, and the taboo anxieties in which slashers trade are still explored more easily via Pauline than Paul. The slippage comes in phase 2. As if in mute deference to a cultural imperative, slasher films from the seventies bring in a last-minute male, even when he is rendered supernumerary by the Final Girl's sturdy defense. By 1980, however, the male rescuer is either dismissably marginal or dispensed with altogether; not a few films have him rush to the rescue only to be hacked to bits, leaving the Final Girl to save herself after all. At the moment that the Final Girl becomes her own savior, she becomes a hero; and the moment that she becomes a hero is the moment that the male viewer gives up the last pretense of male identification. Abject terror may still be gendered feminine, but the willingness of one immensely popular current genre to re-represent the hero as an anatomical female would seem to suggest that at least one of the traditional marks of heroism, triumphant self-rescue, is no longer strictly gendered masculine.

So too the cinematic apparatus. The classic split between "spectacle and narrative," which "supposes the man's role as the active one of forwarding the story, making things happen," is at least unsettled in the slasher film.[68] When the Final Girl (in films like *Hell Night*, *Texas Chain Saw II*, and even *Splatter University*) assumes the "active investigating gaze," she exactly reverses the look, making a spectacle of the killer and a spectator of herself. Again, it is through the killer's eyes (I-camera) that we saw the Final Girl at the beginning of the film, and through the Final Girl's eyes that we see the killer, often for the first time with any clarity, toward the end. The gaze becomes, at least for a while, female. More to the point, the female exercise of scopic control results not in her annihilation, in the manner of classic cinema, but in her triumph; indeed, her triumph *depends* on her assumption of the gaze. It is no surprise, in light of these developments, that the Final Girl should show signs of boyishness. Her symbolic phallicization, in the last scenes, may or may not proceed at root from the horror of lack on the part of audience and maker. But it certainly proceeds from the need to bring her in line with the epic laws of Western narrative tradition—the very unanimity of which bears witness to the historical importance, in popular culture, of the literal representation of heroism in male form—and it proceeds no less from the need to render the reallocated gaze intelligible to an audience conditioned by the dominant cinematic apparatus.

It is worth noting that the higher genres of horror have for the most part resisted such developments. The idea of a female who outsmarts, much less outfights—or outgazes—her assailant is unthinkable in the films of De Palma and Hitchcock. Although the slasher film's victims may be sexual teases, they are not in addition simple-minded, scheming, physically incompetent, and morally deficient in the manner of these filmmakers' female victims. And however revolting their special effects and sexualized their violence, few slasher murders approach the level of voluptuous sadism that attends the destruction of women in De Palma's films. For reasons on which we can only speculate, femininity is more conventionally elaborated and inexorably punished, and in an emphatically masculine environment, in the higher forms—the forms that *are* written up, and not by Joe Bob Briggs.

That the slasher film speaks deeply and obsessively to male anxieties and desires seems clear—if nothing else from the maleness of the majority audience.

And yet these are texts in which the categories masculine and feminine, traditionally embodied in male and female, are collapsed into one and the same character—a character who is anatomically female and one whose point of view the spectator is unambiguously invited, by the usual set of literary-structural and cinematic conventions, to share. The willingness and even eagerness (so we judge from these films' enormous popularity) of the male viewer to throw in his emotional lot, if only temporarily, with not only a woman but a woman in fear and pain, at least in the first instance, would seem to suggest that he has a vicarious stake in that fear and pain. If it is also the case that the act of horror spectatorship is itself registered as a "feminine" experience—that the shock effects induce bodily sensations in the viewer answering the fear and pain of the screen victim— the charge of masochism is underlined. This is not to say that the male viewer does not also have a stake in the sadistic side; narrative structure, cinematic procedures, and audience response all indicate that he shifts back and forth with ease. It is only to suggest that in the Final Girl sequence his empathy with what the films define as the female posture is fully engaged, and further, because this sequence is inevitably the central one in any given film, that the viewing experience hinges on the emotional assumption of the feminine posture. Kaja Silverman takes it a step further: "I will hazard the generalization that it is always the victim—the figure who occupies the passive position—who is really the focus of attention, and whose subjugation the subject (whether male or female) experiences as a pleasurable repetition from his/her own story," she writes. "Indeed, I would go so far as to say that the fascination of the sadistic point of view is merely that it provides the best vantage point from which to watch the masochistic story unfold."[69]

The slasher is hardly the first genre in the literary and visual arts to invite identification with the female; one cannot help wondering more generally whether the historical maintenance of images of women in fear and pain does not have more to do with male vicarism that is commonly acknowledged. What distinguishes the slasher, however, is the absence or untenability of alternative perspectives and hence the exposed quality of the invitation. As a survey of the tradition shows, this has not always been the case. The stages of the Final Girl's evolution—her piecemeal absorption of functions previously represented in males—can be located in the years following 1978. The fact that the typical patrons of these films are the sons of marriages contracted in the 1960s or even early seventies leads us to speculate that the dire claims of that era—that the women's movement, the entry of women into the workplace, and the rise of divorce and woman-headed families would yield massive gender confusion in the next generation—were not entirely wrong. We may prefer, in the eighties, to speak of the cult of androgyny, but the point is roughly the same. The fact that we have in the killer a feminine male and in the main character a masculine female—parent and Everyteen, respectively—would seem, especially in the latter case, to suggest a loosening of the categories, or at least of the equation sex = gender. It is not that these films show us gender and sex in free variation; it is that they fix on the irregular combinations, of which the combination masculine female repeatedly prevails over the combination feminine male. The fact that masculine males (boyfriends, fathers, would-be rescuers) are regularly dismissed through ridicule or death or both would seem to suggest that it is not masculinity per se that is being privileged, but masculinity in conjunction with a female body—indeed, as the term victim-hero contemplates, masculinity in conjunction with femininity. For if "masculine" describes the Final Girl some of the time, and in some of her more theatrical moments, it does not do justice to the sense of her character as a whole. She alternates between registers from the outset; before her final struggle she endures the deepest throes of "femininity"; and even during that final struggle she is now weak and now strong, now flees the killer and now charges him, now stabs and is stabbed, now cries out in fear and now shouts in anger. She is a physical female and a characterological androgyne: like her name, not masculine but either/or, both, ambiguous.[70]

Robin Wood speaks of the sense that horror, for him the by-product of cultural crisis and disintegration, is "currently the most important of all American [film] genres and perhaps the most progressive, even in its overt nihilism."[71] Likewise Vale and Juno say of the "incredibly strange films," mostly low-budget horror, that their volume surveys: "They often present unpopular—even radical—views addressing the social, political, racial, or sexual inequities, hypocrisy in religion or government."[72] And Tania Modleski rests her case against the standard critique of mass culture (stemming from the Frankfurt School) squarely on the evidence of the slasher, which does *not* propose a spurious harmony; does *not* promote the "specious good" (but indeed often exposes and attacks it); does *not* ply the mechanisms of identification, narrative continuity, and closure to provide the sort of narrative pleasure constitutive of the dominant ideology.[73] One is deeply reluctant to make progressive claims for a body of cinema as spectacularly nasty toward women as the slasher film is, but the fact is that the slasher does, in its own perverse way and for better or worse, constitute a visible adjustment in the terms of gender representation. That it is an adjustment largely on the male side, appearing at the furthest possible remove from the quarters of theory and showing signs of trickling upwards, is of no small interest.

Notes

I owe a special debt of gratitude to James Cunniff and Lynn Hunt for criticism and encouragement. Particular thanks to James (not Lynn) for sitting with me through not a few of these movies.
1. Films referred to in this essay are: *Alien* (Ridley Scott, 1979), *Aliens* (James Cameron,

1986), *All of Me* (Carl Reiner, 1984), *An American Werewolf in London* (John Landis, 1981), *The Amityville Horror* (Stuart Rosenberg, 1979), *Behind the Green Door* (Mitchell Brothers, 1972), *The Birds* (Alfred Hitchcock, 1963), *Blade Runner* (Ridley Scott, 1982), *Blood Feast* (Herschell Gordon Lewis, 1963), *Blow-Out* (Brian De Palma, 1981), *Body Double* (Brian De Palma, 1984), *Cries and Whispers* (Ingmar Bergman, 1972), *Cruising* (William Friedkin, 1980), *Deliverance* (John Boorman, 1972), *Dracula* (Tod Browning, 1931), *Dressed to Kill* (Brian De Palma, 1980), *Every Woman Has a Fantasy* (Edwin Brown, 1984), *The Exorcist* (William Friedkin, 1973), *The Eyes of Laura Mars* (Irvin Kershner, 1978), *The Fog* (John Carpenter, 1980), *Frankenstein* (James Whale, 1931), *Frenzy* (Alfred Hitchcock, 1972), *Friday the Thirteenth* (Sean S. Cunningham, 1980), *Friday the Thirteenth, Part II* (Steve Miner, 1981), *Friday the Thirteenth, Part III* (Steve Miner, 1982), *Friday the Thirteenth: The Final Chapter* (Joseph Zito, 1984), *Friday the Thirteenth, Part V: A New Beginning* (Danny Steinmann, 1985), *Friday the Thirteenth, Part VI: Jason Lives* (Tom McLoughlin, 1986), *Halloween* (John Carpenter, 1978), *Halloween 2* (Rick Rosenthal, 1981), *Halloween III: The Witch* (Tommy Lee Wallace, 1983), *He Knows You're Alone* (Armand Mastroianni, 1981), *Hell Night* (Tom DeSimone, 1981), *I Spit on Your Grave* (Meir Zarchi, 1981), *It's Alive* (Larry Cohen, 1974), *Jaws* (Steven Spielberg, 1975), *King Kong* (Merian B. Cooper, Ernest B. Schoedsack, 1933), *Last House on the Left* (Wes Craven, 1972), *Macabre* (William Castle, 1958), *Motel Hell* (Kevin Connor, 1980), *Mother's Day* (Charles Kauffman, 1980), *Ms. 45* (Abel Ferrara, 1981), *A Nightmare on Elm Street* (Wes Craven, 1985), *A Nightmare on Elm Street, Part 2: Freddy's Revenge* (Jack Sholder, 1985), *Nosferatu* (F. W. Murnau, 1922), *The Omen* (Richard Donner, 1976), *Pink Flamingos* (John Waters, 1973), *Play Misty for Me* (Clint Eastwood, 1971), *Psycho* (Alfred Hitchcock, 1960), *Psycho II* (Richard Franklin, 1983), *The Rocky Horror Picture Show* (Jim Sharman, 1975), *Rosemary's Baby* (Roman Polanski, 1968), *The Shining* (Stanley Kubrick, 1980), *Slumber Party Massacre* (Amy Jones; screenplay by Rita Mae Brown, 1983), *Splatter University* (Richard W. Haris, 1985), *Strait-Jacket* (William Castle, 1964), *Taboo* (Kirdy Stevens, 1980), *The Texas Chain Saw Massacre* (Tobe Hooper, 1974), *The Texas Chain Saw Massacre II* (Tobe Hooper, 1986), *Tootsie* (Sydney Pollack, 1982), *Videodrome* (David Cronenberg, 1983), *The Virgin Spring* (Ingmar Bergman, 1959), *What Ever Happened to Baby Jane?* (Robert Aldrich, 1962), *Wolfen* (Michael Wadleigh, 1981).

2. Morris Dickstein, "The Aesthetics of Fright," *American Film* 5 (1980): 34.

3. "Will Rogers said he never met a man he didn't like, and I can truly say the same about the cinema," Harvey R. Greenberg says in his paean to horror, *The Movies on Your Mind* (New York, 1975); yet his claim does not extend to the "plethora of execrable imitations [of *Psycho*] that debased cinema" (137).

4. William Schoell, *Stay Out of the Shower* (New York, 1985).

5. "Job Bob Briggs" was evidently invented as a solution to the *Dallas Times Herald*'s problem of "how to cover trashy movies." See Calvin Trillin's "American Chronicles: The Life and Times of Joe Bob Briggs, So Far," *The New Yorker*, 22 December 1986, 73–88.

6. Lew Brighton, "Saturn in Retrograde; or, The Texas Jump Cut," *The Film Journal* 7 (1975): 25.

7. Stephen Koch, "Fashions in Pornography: Murder as Cinematic Chic," *Harper's*, November 1976, 108–9.

8. Robin Wood, "Return of the Repressed," *Film Comment* 14 (1978): 30.

9. Robin Wood, "Beauty Bests the Beast," *American Film* 8 (1983): 63.

10. Dickstein, "The Aesthetics of Fright," 34.

11. "The 'Uncanny,'" in *The Standard Edition of the Complete Psychological Works of Sigmund*

Freud, ed. and trans. James Strachey, 24 vols. (London, 1953–74), 17:244. Originally published in *Imago* 5/6 (1919): 317.

12. Steven Marcus, *The Other Victorians: A Study of Sexuality and Pornography in Mid-Nineteenth-Century England* (New York, 1964), 278.

13. William Castle, *Step Right Up! I'm Gonna Scare the Pants Off America* (New York, 1978).

14. Given the number of permutations, it is no surprise that new strategies keep emerging. Only a few years ago, a director hit upon the idea of rendering the point of view of an infant through use of an I-camera at floor level with a double-vision image (Larry Cohen, *It's Alive*). Nearly a century after technology provided a radically different means of telling a story, filmmakers are still uncovering the possibilities.

15. Mick Martin and Marsha Porter, in reference to *Friday the Thirteenth I*, in *Video Movie Guide: 1987* (New York, 1987), 690. Robin Wood, "Beauty Bests the Beast," 65, notes that the first-person camera also serves to preserve the secret of the killer's identity for a final surprise—crucial to many films—but adds: "The sense of indeterminate, unidentified, possibly supernatural or superhuman Menace feeds the spectator's fantasy of power, facilitating a direct spectator-camera identification by keeping the intermediary character, while signified to be present, as vaguely defined as possible." Brian De Palma's *Blow-Out* opens with a parody of just this cinematic habit.

16. On this widely discussed topic, see especially Kaja Silverman, *The Subject of Semiotics* (New York, 1983), 194–236; and Lesley Stern, "Point of View: The Blind Spot," *Film Reader* 4 (1979): 214–36.

17. In this essay I have used the term *identification* vaguely and generally to refer both to primary and secondary processes. See especially Mary Ann Doane, "Misrecognition and Identity," *Cine-Tracts* 11 (1980): 25–32; also Christian Metz, "The Imaginary Signifier," in his *The Imaginary Signifier: Psychoanalysis and the Cinema* (Bloomington, Ind., n.d.).

18. Mark Nash, "*Vampyr* and the Fantastic," *Screen* 17 (1976): 37. Nash coins the term *cinefantastic* to refer to this play.

19. Rosemary Jackson, *Fantasy: The Literature of Subversion* (London, 1981), 31.

20. As Dickstein puts it, "The 'art' of horror film is a ludicrous notion since horror, even at its most commercially exploitative, is genuinely subcultural like the wild child that can never be tamed, or the half-human mutant who appeals to our secret fascination with deformity and the grotesque"; "The Aesthetics of Fright," 34.

21. James B. Twitchell, *Dreadful Pleasures: An Anatomy of Modern Horror* (New York, 1985), 84.

22. Donald Spoto, *The Dark Side of Genius: The Life of Alfred Hitchcock* (New York, 1983).

23. Wood, "Return of the Repressed," 26. In Wes Craven's *Nightmare on Elm Street*, it is the nightmare itself, shared by the teenagers who live on Elm Street, that is fatal. One by one they are killed by the murderer of their collective dream. The one girl who survives does so by first refusing to sleep and then, at the same time that she acknowledges her parents' inadequacies, by conquering the feelings that prompt the deadly nightmare. See, as an example of the topic dream/horror, Dennis L. White, "The Poetics of Horror," *Cinema Journal* 10 (1971): 1–18.

24. It is not just the profit margin that fuels the production of low horror. It is also the fact that, thanks to the irrelevance of production values, the initial stake is within the means of a small group of investors. Low horror is thus for all practical purposes the only way an independent filmmaker can break into the market. Add to this the filmmaker's unusual degree of control over the product and one begins to understand why it is that low horror engages the talents of such people as Stephanie Rothman,

George Romero, Wes Craven, and Larry Cohen. As V. Vale and Andrea Juno put it, "The value of low-budget films is: they can be transcendent expressions of a single person's individual vision and quirky originality. When a corporation decides to invest $20 million in a film, a chain of command regulates each step, and no person is allowed free rein. Meetings with lawyers, accountants, and corporate boards are what films in Hollywood are all about"; *Incredibly Strange Films*, ed. V. Vale and Andrea Juno, *Re/Search* 10 (San Francisco, 1986), 5.

25. Despite the film industry's interest in demographics, there is no in-depth study of the composition of the slasher-film audience. Twitchell, *Dreadful Pleasures*, 69–72 and 306–7, relies on personal observation and the reports of critics, which are remarkably consistent over time and from place to place; my own observations concur. The audience is mostly between the ages of twelve and twenty, disproportionately male. Some critics remark on a contingent of older men who sit separately and who, in Twitchell's view, are there "not to be frightened, but to participate" specifically in the "stab-at-female" episodes. Roger Ebert and Gene Siskel corroborate the observation.

26. The development of the human-sausage theme is typical of the back-and-forth borrowing in low horror. *Texas Chain Saw Massacre I* hints at it; *Motel Hell* turns it into an industry ("Farmer Vincent's Smoked Meats: This is It!" proclaims a local billboard); and *Texas Chain Saw Massacre II* expands it to a statewide chili-tasting contest.

27. "The release of sexuality in the horror film is always presented as perverted, monstrous, and excessive, both the perversion and the excess being the logical outcome of repressing. Nowhere is this carried further than in *Texas [Chain Saw] Massacre [I]*. Here sexuality is totally perverted from its functions, into sadism, violence, and cannibalism. It is striking that there is no suggestion anywhere that Sally is the object of an overtly sexual threat; she is to be tormented, killed, dismembered, and eaten, but not raped"; Wood, "Return of the Repressed," 31.

28. With some exceptions: for example, the spear gun used in the sixth killing in *Friday the Thirteenth III*.

29. Stuart Kaminsky, *American Film Genres: Approaches to a Critical Theory of Popular Film* (New York, 1977), 107.

30. The shower sequence in *Psycho* is probably the most echoed scene in all of film history. The bathtub scene in *I Spit on Your Grave* (not properly speaking a slasher, though with a number of generic affinities) is to my knowledge the only effort to reverse the terms.

31. Schoell, *Stay Out of the Shower*, 35. It may be argued that *Blood Feast* (1963), in which a lame Egyptian caterer slaughters one woman after another for their bodily parts (all in the service of Ishtar), provides the serial-murder model.

32. This theme too is spoofed in *Motel Hell*. Farmer Vincent's victims are two hookers, a kinky couple looking for same (he puts them in room #1 of the motel), and Terry and her boyfriend Bo, out for kicks on a motorcycle. When Terry (allowed to survive) wonders aloud why someone would try to kill them, Farmer Vincent answers her by asking pointedly whether they were married. "No," she says, in a tone of resignation, as if accepting the logic.

33. Further: "Scenes in which women whimper helplessly and do nothing to defend themselves are ridiculed by the audience, who find it hard to believe that anyone—male or female—would simply allow someone to kill them with nary a protest," Schoell, *Stay Out of the Shower*, 55–56.

34. *Splatter University* (1984) is a disturbing exception. Professor Julie Parker is clearly established as a Final Girl from the outset and then killed just after the beginning of

what we are led to believe will be the Final Girl sequence (she kicks the killer, a psychotic priest-scholar who keeps his knife sheathed in a crucifix, in the groin, runs for the elevator—and then is trapped and stabbed to death). So meticulously are the conventions observed, and then so grossly violated, that we can only assume sadistic intentionality. This is a film in which (with the exception of an asylum orderly in the preface) only females are killed, and in highly sexual circumstances.

35. This film is complicated by the fact that the action is envisaged as a living dream. Nancy finally kills the killer by killing her part of the collective nightmare. See note 23 above.

36. Spoto, *Dark Side of Genius*, 454. See also William Rothman, *Hitchcock: The Murderous Gaze* (Cambridge, Mass., 1982), 246–341.

37. "The Philosophy of Composition," in *Great Short Works of Edgar Allan Poe*, ed. G. R. Thompson (New York, 1970), 55.

38. As quoted in Schoell, *Stay Out of the Shower*, 56.

39. As quoted in ibid., 41.

40. Spoto, *Dark Side of Genius*, 483.

41. Silvia Bovenschen, "Is There a Feminine Aesthetic?" *New German Critique* 10 (1977): 114. See also Doane, "Misrecognition and Identity."

42. E. Ann Kaplan, *Women and Film: Both Sides of the Camera* (London, 1983), 15. The discussion of the gendered "gaze" is lively and extensive. See above all Laura Mulvey, "Visual Pleasure and Narrative Cinema," *Screen* 16 (1975): 6–18; reprinted in *Film Theory and Criticism: Introductory Readings*, ed. Gerald Mast and Marshall Cohen, 3rd ed. (New York, 1985), 803–16; also Christine Gledhill, "Recent Developments in Feminist Criticism," *Quarterly Review of Film Studies* (1978); reprinted in Mast and Cohen, *Film Theory and Criticism*, 817–45.

43. Wood, "Beauty Bests the Beast," 64.

44. The locus classicus in this connection is the view-from-the-coffin shot in Carl Dreyer's *Vampyr*, in which the I-camera sees through the eyes of a dead man. See Nash, "*Vampyr* and the Fantastic," esp. 32–33. The 1987 remake of *The Little Shop of Horrors* (itself originally a low-budget horror film, made the same year as *Psycho* in two days) lets us see the dentist from the proximate point of view of the patient's tonsils.

45. Two points in this paragraph deserve emending. One is the suggestion that rape is common in these films; it is in fact virtually absent, by definition (see note 27 above). The other is the characterization of the Final Girl as "sexy." She may be attractive (though typically less so than her friends), but she is with few exceptions sexually inactive. For a detailed analysis of point-of-view manipulation, together with a psychoanalytic interpretation of the dynamic, see Steve Neale, "*Halloween*: Suspense, Aggression, and the Look," *Framework* 14 (1981).

46. Wood is struck by the willingness of the teenaged audience to identify "against" itself, with the forces of the enemy of youth. "Watching it [*Texas Chain Saw Massacre I*] recently with a large, half-stoned youth audience, who cheered and applauded every one of Leatherface's outrages against their representatives on the screen, was a terrifying experience"; "Return of the Repressed," 32.

47. "I really appreciate the way audiences respond," Gail Anne Hurd, producer of *Aliens*, is reported to have said. "They buy it. We don't get people, even rednecks, leaving the theater saying, 'That was stupid. No woman would do that.' You don't have to be a liberal ERA supporter to root for Ripley"; as reported in the *San Francisco Examiner Datebook*, 10 August 1986, 19. *Time*, 28 July 1986, 56, suggests that Ripley's maternal

impulses (she squares off against the worst aliens of all in her quest to save a little girl) give the audience "a much stronger rooting interest in Ripley, and that gives the picture resonances unusual in a popcorn epic."

48. Further: "When she [the mother] referred to the infant as a male, I just went along with it. Wonder how that child turned out—male, female, or something else entirely?" The birth is understood to be parthenogenetic, and the bisexual child, literally equipped with both sets of genitals, is figured as the reborn Christ.

49. Linda Williams, "When the Woman Looks," in *Re-Vision: Essays in Feminist Film Criticism*, ed. Mary Ann Doane, Patricia Mellencamp, and Linda Williams, American Film Institute monograph series (Los Angeles, 1984), 90. Williams's emphasis on the phallic leads her to dismiss slasher killers as a "non-specific male killing force" and hence a degeneration in the tradition. "In these films the recognition and affinity between woman and monster of classic horror film gives way to pure identity: she *is* the monster, her mutilated body is the only visible horror" (96). This analysis does not do justice to the obvious bisexuality of slasher killers, nor does it take into account the new strength of the female victim. The slasher film may not, in balance, be more subversive than traditional horror, but it is certainly not less so.

50. Freud, "The 'Uncanny,'" 245. See also Neale, "*Halloween*," esp. 28–29.

51. "The woman's exercise of an active investigating gaze can only be simultaneous with her own victimization. The place of her specularization is transformed into the locus of a process of seeing designed to unveil an aggression against itself"; Mary Ann Doane, "The 'Woman's Film,'" in *Re-Vision*, 72.

52. John Carpenter interviewed by Todd McCarthy, "Trick and Treat," *Film Comment* 16 (1980): 23–24.

53. This is not so in traditional film, nor in heterosexual pornography, in any case. Gay male pornography, however, films some male bodies in much the same way that heterosexual pornography films female bodies.

54. Compare the visual treatment of the (male) rape in *Deliverance* with the (female) rapes in Hitchcock's *Frenzy* or Wes Craven's *Last House on the Left* or Ingmar Bergman's *The Virgin Spring*. The latter films study the victims' faces at length and in closeup during the act; the first looks at the act intermittently and in long shot, focusing less on the actual victim than on the victim's friend who must look on.

55. Marcus, *The Other Victorians*, 260–61. Marcus distinguishes two phases in the development of flagellation literature: one in which the figure being beaten is a boy, and the second, in which the figure is a girl. The very shift indicates, at some level, the irrelevance of apparent sex. "The sexual identity of the figure being beaten is remarkably labile. Sometimes he is represented as a boy, sometimes as a girl, sometimes as a combination of the two—a boy dressed as a girl, or the reverse." The girls often have sexually ambiguous names, as well. The beater is a female, but in Marcus's reading a phallic one—muscular, possessed of body hair—representing the father.

56. Ibid., 125–27.

57. Further: "Suspense is like a woman. The more left to the imagination, the more the excitement. . . . The perfect 'woman of mystery' is one who is blonde, subtle, and Nordic. . . . Movie titles, like women, should be easy to remember without being familiar, intriguing but never obvious, warm yet refreshing, suggest action, not impassiveness, and finally give a clue without revealing the plot. Although I do not profess to be an authority on women, I fear that the perfect title, like the perfect woman, is difficult to find"; as quoted by Spoto, *Dark Side of Genius*, 431.

58. This would seem to be the point of the final sequence of Brian De Palma's *Blow-Out*,

in which we see the boyfriend of the victim-hero stab the killer to death but later hear the television announce that the woman herself vanquished the killer. The frame plot of the film has to do with the making of a slasher film ("Co-Ed Frenzy"), and it seems clear that De Palma means his ending to stand as a comment on the Final Girl formula of the genre. De Palma's (and indirectly Hitchcock's) insistence that only men can kill men, or protect women from men, deserves a separate essay.

59. The term is Judith Fetterly's. See her *The Resisting Reader: A Feminist Approach to American Fiction* (Bloomington, Ind., 1978).

60. On the possible variety of responses to a single film, see Norman N. Holland, "I-ing Film," *Critical Inquiry* 12 (1986): 654–71.

61. Marcus, *The Other Victorians*, 127. Marcus contents himself with noting that the scene demonstrates a "confusion of sexual identity." In the literature of flagellation, he adds, "this confused identity is also present, but it is concealed and unacknowledged." But it is precisely the femaleness of the beaten figures that does acknowledge it.

62. Freud, "The 'Uncanny,'" esp. 219–21 and 226–27.

63. Raymond Durgnat, *Films and Feelings* (Cambridge, Mass., 1967), 216.

64. Not a few critics have argued that the ambiguity is the unintentional result of bad filmmaking.

65. So argues Susan Barrowclough: The "male spectator takes the part not of the male, but of the female. Contrary to the assumption that the male uses pornography to confirm and celebrate his gender's sexual activity and dominance, is the possibility of his pleasure in identifying with a 'feminine' passivity or subordination." See her review of *Not a Love Story* in *Screen* 23 (1982): 35–36. Alan Soble seconds the proposal in his *Pornography: Marxism, Feminism, and the Future of Sexuality* (New Haven, 1986), 93. Porn/sexploitation filmmaker Joe Sarno: "My point of view is more or less always from the woman's point of view; the fairy tales that my films are based on are from the woman's point of view; I stress the efficacy of women for themselves. In general, I focus on the female orgasm as much as I can"; as quoted in Vale and Juno, *Incredibly Strange Films*, 94. "Male identification with women," Kaja Silverman writes, "has not received the same amount of critical attention [as sublimation into professional 'showing off' and reversal into scopophilia], although it would seem the most potentially destabilizing, at least as far as gender is concerned." See her discussion of the "Great Male Renunciation" in "Fragments of a Fashionable Discourse," in *Studies in Entertainment: Critical Approaches to Mass Culture*, ed. Tania Modleski (Bloomington, Ind., 1986), 141.

66. Elaine Showalter, "Critical Cross Dressing: Male Feminists and the Woman of the Year," *Raritan* 3 (1983): 138.

67. Whatever its other functions, the scene that reveals the Final Girl in a degree of undress serves to underscore her femaleness. One reviewer of *Aliens* remarks that she couldn't help wondering why in the last scene, just as in *Alien*, "we have Ripley wandering around clad only in her underwear. A little reminder of her gender, lest we lose sight of it behind all that firepower?"; Christine Schoefer, *East Bay Express*, 5 September 1986, 37.

68. Mulvey, "Visual Pleasure and Narrative Cinema," 12.

69. Kaja Silverman, "Masochism and Subjectivity," *Framework* 12 (1979): 5. Needless to say, this is not the explanation for the girl-hero offered by the industry. *Time* magazine on *Aliens*: "As Director Cameron says, the endless 'remulching' of the masculine hero by the 'male-dominated industry' is, if nothing else, commercially shortsighted. 'They choose to ignore that 50% of the audience is female. And I've been told that it has been proved demographically that 80% of the time it's women who decide which film

to see'"; 28 July 1986. It is of course not Cameron who established the female hero of the series but Ridley Scott (in *Alien*), and it is fair to assume, from his careful manipulation of the formula, that Scott got her from the slasher film, where she has flourished for some time with audiences that are heavily male. Cameron's analysis is thus both self-serving and beside the point.

70. If this analysis is correct, we may expect horror films of the future to feature Final Boys as well as Final Girls. Two recent figures may be incipient examples: Jesse, the pretty boy in *A Nightmare on Elm Street II*, and Ashley, the character who dies last in *The Evil Dead* (1983). Neither quite plays the role, but their names, and in the case of Jesse the characterization, seem to play on the tradition.

71. For the opposite view (based on classic horror in both literary and cinematic manifestations), see Franco Moretti, "The Dialectic of Fear," *New Left Review* 136 (1982): 67–85.

72. Vale and Juno, *Incredibly Strange Films*, 5.

73. Tania Modleski, "The Terror of Pleasure: The Contemporary Horror Film and Postmodern Theory," in *Studies in Entertainment*, 155–66. (Like Modleski, I stress that my comments are based on many slashers, not all of them.) This important essay (and volume) appeared too late for me to take it into full account in the text.

CONTRIBUTORS

CHARLES BERNHEIMER is the author of *Flaubert and Kafka: Studies in Psychopoetic Structure* (New Haven, 1982) and co-editor of *In Dora's Case: Freud-Hysteria-Feminism* (New York, 1985). The essay in the present volume is part of his *Figures of Ill Repute: Representing Prostitution in Nineteenth-Century France*, forthcoming from Harvard University Press. He is Professor of French and Comparative Literature at the University of Pennsylvania.

R. HOWARD BLOCH is chair of the French Department, University of California, Berkeley. His recent *Scandal of the Fabliaux*, a study of medieval humor (Chicago, 1986), inspired a comic novel, *Moses in the Promised Land* (Layton, Utah, 1988). He is currently completing a book entitled *Medieval Misogyny and the Invention of Western Romantic Love*.

GILLIAN BROWN is Assistant Professor of English at Rutgers University. Her book *Domestic Individualism: Nineteenth-Century American Fictions of Self* will be published by the University of California Press in 1990. She is also working on a study of feminist theory and "women's diseases."

CAROL J. CLOVER is Professor of Scandinavian and Comparative Literature at University of California, Berkeley. Her publications include books and articles in the field of medieval literature and culture as well as film reviews and reviews of books on film. She is also working on a book on popular film, *The Horror of Gender*.

FRANCES FERGUSON is Professor of English at Johns Hopkins University. She is the author of *Solitude and the Sublime: The Aesthetics of Individualism*, forthcoming from Routledge in 1989.

JOEL FINEMAN's *Shakespeare's Perjured Eye* was published by University of California Press in 1986. Until his death in March 1989, he was Associate Professor of English, University of California, Berkeley.

JACQUELINE LICHTENSTEIN recently finished a book on rhetoric and painting, *La Couleur éloquente*, forthcoming from Flammarion (Paris). She is Assistant Professor of French, University of California, Berkeley.

NAOMI SCHOR is Professor of French at Duke University. Her books include *Breaking the Chain: Women, Theory, and French Realist Fiction* (New York, 1985) and *Reading in Detail: Aesthetics and the Feminine* (New York, 1987). She is currently working on a book on George Sand.

INDEX OF NAMES

Trillin, Calvin, 222n.5
Trotter, W. F., 87n.13
Twitchell, James B., 190–91, 223n.21,
    224n.24

Valadon, Suzanne, 113
Vale, V., 221, 224n.24
Valéry, Paul, xi, 158–59, 162, 170, 176,
    180nn.1, 3 and 7, 182n.16, 184n.36
Van Laun, Henry, 86n.1
Veblen, Thorstein, 154n.26
Viner, Charles, 111n.11
Vollard, Ambroise, 161, 182n.19

Walker, Alice, 131n.6
Wallis, Brian, 132n.27
Ward, Martha, 182nn.20 and 28

Warner, William Beatty, 101, 107,
    111nn.26, 32, and 180
Watkins, Mel, 131n.6
Watt, Ian, 99, 111n.22
Wellbury, David, 72n.17
Westphal, D. C., 153n.5
White, Dennis L., 223n.23
Williams, Linda, 209, 226n.49
Wilt, Judith, 111n.25
Wood, Robin, 188, 191, 221, 222nn.8
    and 9, 223nn.15 and 23, 224n.27,
    225nn.40 and 46
Woolf, Virginia, 116, 131n.5

Zola, Emile, 161, 183n.31
Zumthor, Paul, 1

Compositor: Wilsted & Taylor
Text: 10/13 Baskerville
Display: Baskerville Bold
Printer: Malloy Lithographing, Inc.
Binder: John H. Dekker & Sons